W. Frederic Morrison

The Aldine History of Queensland

Embracing sketches and portraits of her noted people; the rise and progress of her varied enterprises; and illustrations of her boundless wealth, together with maps of latest survey. Vol. 1

W. Frederic Morrison

The Aldine History of Queensland
Embracing sketches and portraits of her noted people; the rise and progress of her varied enterprises; and illustrations of her boundless wealth, together with maps of latest survey.
Vol. 1

ISBN/EAN: 9783337324889

Printed in Europe, USA, Canada, Australia, Japan

Cover: Foto ©ninafisch / pixelio.de

More available books at **www.hansebooks.com**

PREFACE.

The author of this history acknowledges his indebtedness to the many excellent books on Australian life and habits by persons of fame and scholarship. The facts and statistics of each succeeding generation can only be preserved for the people following by putting them upon the printed page—while, therefore, we are glad to pay due court to others who have gone before us, we realise the need of a history for popular use, fully illlustrated, to meet the wants, and be a fitting memorial of this Centennial Year.

This work presents to the people of Australia a brief history of its discovery and early settlement, and fully sets forth its rise and progress for the past one hundred years. No nation can, with greater pride, point to her splendid achievements in so short a time, and can celebrate her first Centennial with such a splendid record. The marvellous and rapid development of her mines and soil, the push and enterprise of her statesmen, merchants, and professional men, and the magnitude of her industries and commerce, are subjects of wonder and congratulation. Hence we give in succinct form a sketch of many of her noted people, both of the past and now living, who have won the honors of the nation, or who have in their several branches of industry distinguished themselves by their business successes, professional emoluments, or national services. We acknowledge the inadequacy of any book like the present one to portray fully every fact of historic value and interest of Australian life. The glowing pages of the artist and the pen of the historian will fail to reveal a tithe of her luxuriance, wealth, and greatness. Her treasures of flora, fauna, mines, lands, flocks, herds, and commerce—dazzling as they are in eyes of the world, who witness her Centennial products—are but the first fruits of a grander future.

No country in the world has been more extensively written about than Australia, and yet it is a difficult matter to find upon our bookshelves any work that will give the inquirer of this or other lands an adequate idea of the history, resources, enterprises, and development of the country— partly because most that has been published is now out of print, and partly for the reason that writers have confined themselves to only one phase of colonial life.

The ALDINE HISTORY, as the title indicates, is intended to be artistic, and to represent in its mechanism the perfection of Australian art. The work will speak for itself. The paper is of the best quality and finish. The letter-press is executed in a style worthy of the well-known house of Messrs. George Murray and Co., the printers thereof, who have taken special pains to execute the work in a style equal to that done in any other country in the world. The type used has been made in Sydney, having been cast in the Australian Type Foundry, 91A Clarence-street. The artists who have illustrated the work are colonial—viz., Messrs. Carver, Sedgefield, Tarrant, Fullwood, Baron, Mahony, and the Phillip-Stephan Co. The work is purely Australian in all its mechanical and artistic excellencies. We are therefore sure that our many patrons will feel pride in giving us their hearty endorsement. We have aimed at giving our patrons the best in ever particular, and we flatter ourselves that in this respect we have fulfilled every promise made, and much more. That errors have crept in is quite possible, having had to rely upon conflicting statements and views, we have had to elect what appeared to have strongest support. We trust that the perusal of this work will call forth all necessary corrections, and put us in possession of additional historic facts that may be of value in a future volume.

THE AUTHOR.

CONTENTS.

VOL I.

	PAGE.
CHAPTER I.—EARLY EXPLORATIONS: *Terra Incognita*—Alexander the Great—Batholomew Diaz—Spaniards—Mandaña—Quiros—Torres—Zaachen—Dirk Hertog—Edels—Nuyts—General Carpenter—Pelsart—Tasman	1—9
CHAPTER II.—ENGLISH EXPLORERS: Dampier—Cook—Banks—Solander	10—17
CHAPTER III.—AUSTRALIAN CONTINENT: Geographical Description—Area—Boundaries—Coast Northward—Coast Westward—Southward and Eastward—Chief Rivers—Mountains	18—27
CHAPTER IV.—THE ABORIGINES: Native Condition—Habits—Weapons—Corrobboree—Combats—Notions Respecting a Supreme Being—Laws—Rum—Their Decrease	28—36
CHAPTER V.—QUEENSLAND: Geography—Physical Description—Coastal Belt—Tablelands—Great Plains—The Great Mountain Range—Climate—Rivers—Area—Valleys and Mountains	37—43
CHAPTER VI.—FAUNA: Animals—The Kangaroo—Walleroo—Wallaby—Kangaroo Dance—Opossums—Native Bears—Flying Squirrels—Native Cat—Australian Hedgehog—Platypus—Birds—Reptiles—Fish—Insects	44—56
CHAPTER VII.—FLORA: Eucalyptus—Acacia—Yellow Wood—Rosewood—Cedar—Figtree—Pine—Palm—Apple—Mangrove—Australian Oak—Honeysuckle—Tea Tree—Food Plants—Medicinal Plants—Flowers—Waratah—Gigantic Lily, etc.	57—66

CONTENTS.

CHAPTER VIII.—GOVERNOR PHILLIP: England's Penal Policy—First Fleet —Botany Bay—Port Jackson—Sydney Cove—First Landing—Perouse— Semi-Starvation—Second Fleet—New South Wales Corps—Interregnum— Major Grose and Captain Patterson ... ... 67—74

CHAPTER IX.—GOVERNOR HUNTER: "Sirius" Wrecked at Norfolk Island— New South Wales Corps—Scarcity of Clothing—Coastal Explorations—Bass and Flinders ... ... 75—80

CHAPTER X.—GOVERNOR KING: Norfolk Island—New South Wales Corps —Rum, Medium of Exchange—Flinders—Coastal Explorations—*Syndey Gazette* Founded—Pastoral Interests Begun ... ... 81—83

CHAPTER XI.—GOVERNOR BLIGH: Need of Rigid Discipline—Drunkenness Prevalent—Bligh Tries to Break up the Power of Rum—Troubles with McArthur—Rebellion—Seizure of Government by Major Johnson—Arrest of Bligh—McArthur and Johnson Summoned to England—Tried and Condemned—Governor Bligh Ordered to be Restored ... ... 84—88

CHAPTER XII.—GOVERNOR MACQUARIE: Proclamation—New South Wales Corps Ordered Home, and the 73rd Regiment take their place—Opening of Roads—Wentworth, Blaxland, and Lawson Cross Blue Mountains—Bathurst Plains Discovered—Farming Extended—Colony Prosperous ... ... 89—94

CHAPTER XIII.—GOVERNOR BRISBANE: Favored Free Settlers—Large Tracts of Land Given Away—Espoinage—Free Immigration—Two Classes, "Exclusionists" and "Emancipists"—Conflict—Legislative Council Established—Freedom of Press Proclaimed—The *Australian* and *Monitor* Started —Moreton Bay Explored by Oxley ... ... 95—100

CHAPTER XIV.—GOVERNOR DARLING: A Scholar Method was Enjoined on all Departments—Board of Inquiry—Unrest of Emancipists—Road Construction—The Australian Agricultural Company Formed—Growth of Wool Business—Drought—Newspaper War—Sudd's and Thompson's Petty Crime and Cruel Death—Captain Sturt's Explorations... ... ... 101—106

CHAPTER XV.—GOVERNOR BOURKE: Depression—The Land Question— Rental for Sheep Runs—The *Sydney Gazette* Ceases to be a Government Organ—Reforms—Statue of Bourke—Exploration by Mitchell, and Settlement of Port Phillip ... ... 107—109

CHAPTER XVI.—GOVERNOR GIPPS: Brought into Notice by Canadian Rebellion—Land Speculation—Land Price—Three Land Districts—Low Price of Sheep—Tallow—Transportation—Annexation of New Zealand— Islands of New Zealand a Colony by Itself—Storm of Opposition—Constitution Act—Mrs. Chisholm ... ... 110—118

CONTENTS. VII.

PAGE.

CHAPTER XVII.—GOVERNOR FITZROY: Question of Reviving Transportation Ship "Hashemy"—the Coalfields Resumed by the Government—Death of Lady Fitzroy—An Act for Better Government of the Colonies—Constitutional Changes—Separation of Port Phillip, Tasmania, etc., etc.—Sydney University—Statistics of Growth ... ... 119—127

CHAPTER XVIII.—GOVERNOR DENISON: Steam Service—Postal Service—Resolutions re "Crimean War"—Opening Railway to Parramatta—Constitution Granted to New South Wales—First Ministry, Donaldson's—Second Ministry, Cowper's—Third Ministry, Parker-Cowper Ministry—Moreton Bay District Apply for Separation—Separation Granted, and the District named Queensland ... ... 128—138

CHAPTER XIX.—PENAL EXPANSION—Penal Establishment—A tHumpy-Bung—At Brisbane—Torren's Title Act—The Governor's Retirement ... ... 139—144

CHAPTER XX.—GENESIS—Early Occupancy—Brisbane Started—Ipswich or Limestone in its Penal Days—Captain Logan Murdered—The Several Captains who Governed the Settlement—First White Settlers, Leslies, Wickham, Simpson, Rolleston, Petries, &c. ... ... 145—160

CHAPTER XXI.—THE GOVERNORS: Bowen, O'Connell, Blackall, Marquis of Normanby, Cairns, Kennedy, Bell, Palmer, Musgrave, Norman ... 161—173

CHAPTER XXII.—THE MINISTRIES: Responsible Ministries—1. Herbert Ministry—2. MacAlister Ministry—3. Herbert Ministry—4. MacAlister Ministry—5. Mackenzie Ministry—6. Lilley Ministry—7. Palmer Ministry—8. McAllister Ministry—9. Thorne Ministry—10. Douglas Ministry—11. McIlwraith Ministry—12. Griffith Ministry—13. McIlwraith Ministry 174—192

CHAPTER XXIII.—CELEBRATIONS: Exhibition of 1877—Exhibition of 1879—Soudan Contingent—Jubilee Rejoicings—Queen Victoria's Life—Centennial Celebrations, 1888—Press Banquet—Several Colonies United—Colonial Celebrations, 1888 — Centennial Banquet — Sir Henry Parkes' Centennial Oration ... ... 193—226

CHAPTER XXIV.—THE CONSTITUTION: Its History—The Act Conferring a Constitution ... ... 227—242

CHAPTER XXV.—INTERIOR EXPLORATIONS: Lawson, Blaxland, and Wentworth—Oxley—Evans—Cunningham—Stewart—King—Hume and Hovell—Sturt—Mitchell—Grey—Lushington—Strzelecki—Eyre—Stuart—Leichhardt—Kennedy—Burke and Wills—Giles—Warburton—Forrest, John and Alexander—Gregory ... ... 243—267

CHAPTER XXVI. — AUSTRALIAN RESOURCES: Pastoral — Sheep — Cattle—Horses—Pigs—Agriculture—Wheat—Maize—Barley—Oats—Rye—Millet

—Hay—Pasture—Dairy—Farming—Tobacco—Peas—Beans and Vetches—Roots—Vine Culture—Minor Products—Sugar—Honey—Garden Products—Oranges—Fruit—Minerals—Coal—Gold—Silver—Copper—Tin—Iron, etc. ... ... 268—295

CHAPTER XXVII.—SECONDARY RESOURCES: Commerce—Manufactures ... 296—300

CHAPTER XXVIII.—COLONIAL GOVERNMENTS: Federal Council—New South Wales—Victoria—Queensland—South Australia—Western Australia—Tasmania—New Zealand—Fiji—New Guinea ... ... 301—317

CHAPTER XXIX.—EDUCATION: History of Common School Act—Ten Classes of Schools—High Schools—Colleges, etc. ... ... 318—345

CHAPTER XXX.—RELIGIOUS WORK: Church of England—Wesleyan—Presbyterian—Congregational—Catholic, etc.—Statistics, etc. ... ... 346—367

CHAPTER XXXI.—RECREATIONS: Cricket—Football—Lawn Tennis—Running—Rowing—Beach and Hanlan—Bowling—Theatres—Music—Out-door Pleasures—Picnics—Fishing, Hunting, etc. ... ... 368—378

CHAPTER XXXII.—THE ACTING MINISTRY: Sir S. W. Griffith, ex-Premier and Opposition Leader—Sir T. McIlwraith—Hon. J. H. Macrossan—Hon. Mr. Nelson—Hon. Mr. Morehead—Hon. Mr. Black—Hon. Mr. Donaldson—Hon. Mr. Thyne—Hon. Mr. Pattison—Hon. Mr. Norton ... 379—384

THE
ALDINE HISTORY
OF
QUEENSLAND.

VOLUME I.

SYDNEY:
GEORGE MURRAY AND Co., PAPER MILLS PRINTING WORKS,
91 CLARENCE STREET.

CHAPTER I.

EARLY EXPLORATIONS.

ONE hundred years ago Australia was "terra incognita"—a land unknown, for up to that time the foot of the white man had scarcely more than touched her shores. For ages prior it had been the unmolested abode of the native black, whose dominion extended from ocean to ocean, and whose right to roam over her vast territory and reap the benefit of her wealth of unrivalled climate and soil none cared to dispute.

Her quiet slumber for centuries, during which kingdoms rose to greatness and fell back again, and civilisation in her varied forms of splendour and achievement won continents and fashioned them after her higher modes of life, was undisturbed by any foreign power or ambitious adventurer.

A century has just past and wrought a wondrous transformation in her social, moral, and commercial condition. What marvellous changes have here been witnessed in that comparatively short period, changes which awaken in the breast of every true Englishman feelings of national pride and gratification. A century ago the world scarcely ever turned its thoughts in the direction of this land, and, if at all, thought only of it as a vast unknown region, affording few attractions for the warrior, merchant, or missionary.

What was then known as "terra incognita" has now come to be recognised in history as the "Land of the Golden Fleece." When the historian uttered for the first time this golden designation and made it descriptive of Australia's historic wealth, he must have had in mind its enormous resources of mines, agriculture, and commerce, not of the past merely, but of the grander future, and fastened upon her historic page a phrase that would in all time be the pride and glory of every true citizen.

Its first discovery, or, more properly speaking, its first accidental contact with civilisation, may be justly accorded to some of the many explorers who claim the honor of priority. It is a very difficult matter to decide, among the myriads of claimants, as to which should be credited with the honor.

There are those who credit its discovery to the time of Alexander the Great, 327 B.C., and although there is no definite knowledge of this as a fact, yet there are to be found allusions to a great Southern land by geographers and historians of that time. There was, without doubt, great activity and enterprise among the islands of the Indian Seas. Commerce was carried on extensively among them at a very early period, and it is quite possible and probable that the spirit of enterprise may have led those of Alexander's day into the far distant Southern Seas in quest of new fields of trade.

The pages of ancient history have gleams of light upon this subject, which make them read like the fairy tales of some romance. And yet in the light of our day and with the experience of one hundred years of actual colonisation and industry, we can turn to these same pages of ancient record and learn how great was the activity of former ages, and how extensive the observation and learning of other people, whose share in the development of knowledge and the extension of civilisation was by no means limited or insignificant, and their utterances we are by no means justified in regarding as the fancy of dreamers or the speculations merely of such enthusiasts as would make the wish of discovery the fountain and source of all the facts of their histories. There can be little doubt that when Strabo wrote fifty years before Christ, and Pliny in the latter part of the first Christian century, and Ptolemy in the second, "of a land of beauty and bounty stretching far to the south of India and beyond the equator, to an unknown distance," they did not write of what they imagined might be; they doubtless told the story of some early explorers, who, venturing out into the vast unknown expanse of the Southern

Seas, beheld this land, and returning recounted to their friends and countrymen their trials and conquests, and left the record in the legends and tales which were passed from age to age and from sire to son down along the revolving years, until caught by the historian's pen and told again and again by geographers, literati and others whose office it was to keep alive the treasures of the past for the benefit of the ages to come.

There is scarcely a century to be found in which some mention has not been made of this great Southern land, which, in the language of Agathemerus, of the third century, "was the greatest island in the world."

It seems very evident, therefore, that the great island or continent of Australia was known to the Greeks and Romans at a very early time, although it does not appear that they knew much either concerning its extent, resources, or people. In fact, from the very brief mention made of this south land and the very small interest that it seemed to awaken, we are justified in believing that to them all it appeared to be a region of barrenness and desolation, hardly worth the toil and hardships endured by the few who dared the dangers and privations of the sea in the work of exploration.

When the ancient civilisation began to wane and the literature and commerce of the west suffered, the Persians then controlled the trade of the Indian Ocean, and did much towards developing commerce among the islands of the south.

The Arabian race came next in order. Their navigators in the ninth century, if not earlier, had penetrated beyond the golden Chersonesus, through the Straits of the Archipelago, and as far as China. In the course of time their language and religion became general in the Indian Islands. It is said that traces of the Arabic tongue can be found in the language of all of the inhabitants of the islands of the South Seas, and also in that of the Australian blacks. There are also to be found distinct traces of the Greek tongue as well, which would seem to indicate the origin of this people to be from many sources, and it is more than probable that they were floated hither from numerous lands, and at different periods, in the rude barks of the sons of Ham from the coast of Africa; from the numerous islands of the Indian Seas, which were originally peopled by the Arabians; also from the tribes of Japanese and Malayan races that peopled the islands of the north; and doubtless, too, from other parts of the world.

EARLY EXPLORATIONS.

The words of different races found in their language, and the rites that obtain among them and that are not common to every tribe, conclusively point to the fact that the several tribes had a distinct origin, and that some of them descended from races, at least in part, that were advanced in civilisation.

In 1486 the route to India by the Cape of Good Hope was discovered by a Portuguese, Bartholomew Diaz, and in less than fifty years his nation possessed itself of the principal island of the Indian Archipelago. The time had now arrived when more reliable information could be obtained. The Portuguese were soon followed by the Spanish, Dutch, and English, all of whom were ambitious to become interested in the rich trade of the east.

Just at this time (1492) America was discovered by Columbus, which diverted the attention of all for a time, but soon other navigators were ambitious to discover that other great continent that the centuries had a vague sense existed in the south of the Indian Ocean.

The Spaniards for the most part seemed to have led the way. Their explorations were made from settlements on the western coast of South America. Although France has claimed the honor of being the first of modern discoverers who obtained a knowledge of this land by actual visitation, she rests her claim on the mere accident of Paulovier de Gonneville, who was driven upon the coast of Australia as early as the year 1504, but it does not appear that this Frenchman ever regarded the incident as one worthy of record beyond a paragraph in his daily journal, or as being other than a very small island whose barren shores rendered the only service of which it was capable when it saved him from an untimely grave.

In 1568, Alonzo Mandaña de Neyva was seized with a spirit of adventure, and fitting out an expedition from Peru in South America, he sailed in a westerly course and came upon the Solomon Islands, thence around San Christoval and other islands contiguous thereto. This group is in the latitude of Torres Strait, not far beyond its most easterly part, and within a few days' sail of the Australian Continent. Mandaña returned and gave most glowing reports of his expedition and its results, and urged the Spanish Court to allow him to make another. His request was neglected, but he continued to press it for thirty long weary years, when his patient appeal was at last heard, and he set sail on his second

EARLY EXPLORATIONS.   5

expedition in 1595. In this trip he fell in with the Marquesas
Islands, but failed to find those he discovered years before. After
suffering great hardships, he returned and soon died from disappointment
and anxiety. His pilot, a Portuguese, named Fernandes de Quiros,
succeeded to the control of the expedition, and evinced even greater
enthusiasm than his chief. He pleaded the cause earnestly before the
Spanish Court, and with such arguments that Phillip the Third supplied
funds to build three ships for another expedition, of which the chief
command was entrusted to Quiros, and the second place was given to Luis
Vaez de Torres, a Spanish navigator of great ability.

Quiros and his fleet sailed from Lima on the 20th December, 1605.
He steered westward for fifty days, and on the 10th of February, 1606,
discovered Tahiti. He continued his course in a westerly direction, and
on the 26th of April sighted land which he believed to be part of the
new continent he was in search of, and named it Terra Austral del Espiritu
Santo (the South Land of the Holy Spirit). It is generally believed now
that the land was not Australia, but New Hebrides.

Quiros and Torres agreed to separate in their course, that their
search might embrace a wider range. Soon after the separation of the two
captains a dispute arose between Quiros and his officers which threatened a
mutiny, and which prevented him from prosecuting a further search. He
hastily decided to return. Two of the ships of the expedition, under
command of Torres, and in entire ignorance of Quiros' determination,
continued their course to the westward, and in a few days passed safely
through the straits dividing New Guinea from the continent of Australia,
and which bears the name of Torres Strait. He sighted land in the distance,
but passed it by, believing it to be only one of the many small islands that
they were likely to meet in their course.

Quiros finally returned to Acapulco.

Nine months after his departure he presented a report to the King
of Spain, in which he mentions the discovery of twenty-three islands
besides the Australian continent, which he erroneously imagined he had
discovered. He used every endeavour to induce the successor of Phillip
the Third, his former patron, to furnish funds for another expedition, but
failed utterly, and soon died like his old master, Mandaña, a victim of
disappointment and grief. Though by birth a Portuguese, he was most of

his life in the service of Spain, and is regarded generally as the last of those old Spanish navigators who belonged to a class of men never surpassed in daring, energy, and seamanship.

While these efforts were being made by the Spanish, the Dutch were by no means idle. They made repeated efforts to discover the great south land towards the end of the sixteenth century and the beginning of the seventeenth. So successful were they that the Dutch can produce unimpeachable testimony of having landed on the shores of Australia in March, 1606.

A few days before Quiros discovered his Austral de Spiritu Santo, which most people believe to be the New Hebrides, the Dutch Government at Bantam despatched in the latter part of 1605 a small vessel named "Duyfhen" (the dove) to explore the coasts of New Guinea. This vessel continued south, and sailed along the eastern shore of the Gulf of Carpentaria. She proceeded as far as Cape Turnagain, in latitude $13\frac{3}{4}°$ South, so named from the dangers to which they were exposed from the savage attacks of the natives, which induced them to turn back again, and which resulted in the death of at least two of their crew.

In 1618 Captain Zaachen sailed along the northern coast, and he named it Arnheim, after his vessel.

The Dutch were earnest and most successful in their explorations during the first part of the seventeenth century. The records of explorations made at this period are comparatively full, and clearly accord to the Dutch the honor of making frequent and satisfactory efforts to investigate especially the western portion of the south continent.

In 1616 Theodore Hertoge, commonly known as Dirk Hertog, sailed along the north-west coast in the ship "Eutracht," of Amsterdam.

In 1619 Captain Jean Edels sailed along the western coast and gave his own name to a large portion of the south part of Western Australia.

In 1622 the ship "Leeuwin" (the lioness), made a voyage along the the south-west corner of Western Australia, and attached its name to the most prominent cape, which still bears this honor.

In 1623 the Dutch Governor-General of the island of Amboyna fitted out a vessel to follow up the good work of the "Duyfhen." This resulted in the discovery of Staten River in 17° South.

In 1627 Captain Nuyts, in command of the ship "Gulde Zeepart," sailed along the south-western portion of the coast of Australia, in that part that constitutes now the southern coast of Western Australia, and gave to it his own name, which it bore for many years. Nuytsland is a name recognised by many of the old settlers of Australia to this day. The tree known as the *Nuytsia Florabunda*, commonly named "Cabbage" and "Christmas" tree, was given its technical name by Robert Brown, the naturalist, in honor of Captain Nuyts, and because its magnificent floral bloom is itself honored by a name so worthy of perpetuation.

In 1628 the coast between Shark's Bay, inland from Hartog's Island, and Champion Bay, latitude 29° was discovered, and named Dewittland, after its discoverer.

In the same year General Carpenter explored the entire gulf in the northern part of the continent and called it the Gulf of Carpentaria. Though not the first of Dutch discoverers who visited this gulf, yet he seems to have been the first to have entertained the idea of utilising his discovery for purposes of colonisation, and hence his report to the Dutch authorities was most glowing and promising. He was impressed with the richness of the soil, the salubrity of the climate, and the many advantages to be derived from early occupation of this continent by a class of industrious poor who would obtain a comfortable livelihood on the easiest of conditions, and that would develope resources of wealth that would ere long afford trade for their merchant ships. Upon these representations a large fleet of eleven ships was fitted out for the expedition, well supplied with stores of food, clothing, and ammunition sufficient to meet their wants for years. The fleet was placed under command of Captain Pelsart, who had charge of the war-ship "Batavia." They set sail from their homes in Holland on the 28th of October, 1628, and reached the Cape of Good Hope in fine condition. Shortly after having left the Cape a violent storm scattered their fleet, and most of the ships were lost and very little known of their destiny. Captain Pelsart, with his war-ship "Batavia," after battling with the storm, was at last driven eastward and wrecked on the group of rocks about thirty miles west of Australia's western coast, called Houtman's Abrolhos. Her crew and list of intending colonists numbered about two hundred souls. They endeavoured to reach the islands seen in the distance, but many perished. In the effort starvation seemed to confront them on every side. In their extremity Captain Pelsart rigged a small boat, and, with a few men, undertook as a last resort the perilous journey across two thousand miles of ocean to the nearest Dutch settlement, in the hope that he might secure provisions and speedily return to rescue his comrades from their peril. While absent a portion of the sailors concocted a scheme to rob those of their fellows of all they possessed, seize the vessel and its supply on the return of Captain Pelsart, and use their ill-acquired possessions in the further businsss of a base piracy. Their plans met with considerable opposition from some of their companions. These they put to death, but in their designs of mutiny they failed. The captain and his men conquered the mutineers and executed them on the spot, as the only means of safety possible under such conditions. The balance of the crew constructed from the wreck a craft, crude, but sufficient to enable them to reach in safety the island of Java, two thousand miles distant.

This was the only attempt at colonisation the Dutch ever made. The reports of disaster and suffering experienced by these first colonists to New Holland deterred their countrymen from repeating the experiment.

It was nigh fourteen years afterwards before the Dutch made another attempt in this direction. In the year 1642 Antony van Dieman, the Governor of the East India Company, fitted out two ships, and placed them under the command of his esteemed friend, Abel Jansen Tasman, with the object of again exploring the southern seas. He sailed south and then eastward, and discovered the island of Tasmania, but supposed it to be a part of the Australian continent. He did not land his entire crew, but merely sent on shore a few in a small boat. These reported the inhabitants to be giants, stalwart and strong; the trees also to be of gigantic growth. They soon set sail south and eastward, having given the name of Van Dieman to the land he was leaving behind, which name it bore until 1856, when it received its present constitution and deemed it prudent to change its name in honor of its first acknowledged discoverer, Tasman.

In pushing his course eastward he discovered the islands of New Zealand. These he found to be peopled by savages. A few of the crew having been murdered by the natives, he deemed it not prudent to land, but made a brief survey of the coast, and then returned speedily to Batavia to report the success of his expedition.

In 1644, two years later, he was sent the second time to the great southern continent. On this occasion he explored the west and north-western portions of the Australian continent, but of its results little is known, and beyond the fact that he is the first to have viewed Tasmania and to have placed it in the maps of the scientific world as a part of the New Holland of the South, there is little other service of worth rendered to posterity by this worthy young navigator. It does not very clearly appear that either of the above explorers attached much importance to the fact that such a land existed, or that they regarded it in any other light than a landing place of safety, affording a providential deliverance from a watery grave.

It is quite possible, and more than probable, that among the myriads of explorers that ventured out among the islands of the Pacific, Indian Ocean, or South Seas, there have been many, even in earlier times, who have found this continent to be a "terra firma" where they have been only too glad to find a resting place upon which they were content to dwell after being tossed by the seas and starved into quiet submission to their new conditions of life that were here forced upon them, and have mingled with, or themselves have been the progenitors of the savage race that Captain Cook found a century ago in possession of this continent.

CHAPTER II.

ENGLISH EXPLORERS.

THE English were slow to push their explorations out into the vast unknown South Seas, but not so slow to seize every advantage which the new territory offered. "She came" in time, "and saw and conquered" the new Asia of the South. The land whose inhabitants were wild, and whose soil was arid and desolate, she claimed and clothed with the verdure of Spring, and crowned with every evidence of civilisation. William Dampier was the first Englishman who set his foot upon her shores. He was young, brave, and daring. His youthful spirit of travel first led him to leave Old England and go to Jamaica to manage a large estate, but tiring soon of the drudgery of slave life, he crossed over to Campeachy. Here he became acquainted with the buccaneers, whose wild, reckless daring life of plunder and gain fired his young mind with ardor and ambition. He soon joined one of these bands, and started on a cruise around the world. In about a year they reached the East Indies. They continued in their quest for plunder, and succeeded in enriching themselves by the capture of trading vessels and their booty, and finally sought seclusion and retirement in the unknown Southland, chiefly because it was remote from civilisation, and by its obscurity they were safe from the observation of civilised people. It was not in the interest of discovery they sought out this Continent, but rather that their ill-gotten gain might be preserved from attack, and that they might enjoy unmolested the results of a successful cruise of piracy and fraud. Dampier and his party landed on the north-west coast of Australia, but only continued a very short time on its inhospitable and barren shores. He saw nothing to invite a prolonged stay among a people that were so repulsive in their habits and conditions of life, and the country itself did not enchant him by its visions of splendor or magnificence. He resolved upon a more peaceful kind of life, and returned to his motherland, and settled for a period on an estate that would afford most men all the happiness their life was capable of. This was too tame for him after a career of adventure in which were joined both danger and excitement, and having become accustomed to change and hardships, his ardent nature did not take kindly to the spirit of peaceful society that everywhere reigned around him. He resolved therefore to quit again the home of his youth and the luxury with which wealth had surrounded him, this time not to plunder, or through any greed of further gain, but rather from an earnest desire to discover more fully the extent and possibilities of the land it was his good fortune in former years to have sought as a refuge. He applied to the British Government for permission to guide an expedition to the Australian Continent. It was granted, the "Roebuck," a small ship, was placed at his disposal. He forthwith set sail and made his second visit to this land in 1699. He reached the western coast and set about making a thorough examination of its bays and harbours for a space of nigh one thousand miles from Shark Bay to Roebuck Bay. His examination of every part and point he visited was most complete and satisfactory, and after a lapse of two hundred years subsequent visits to the same localities by many, who were equally well qualified to judge, have never changed the character of the report made by Mr. Dampier touching that region. His observations were full and just, and his report to the English Government was honest, and yet remains a true description of what can be witnessed in the same regions even at the present day. Hence, in this our Centennial year, we in fact celebrate the second Centennial of England's discovery, although it is the first Centennial of England's colonisation of this continent of the south.

An extract from his journal will doubtless be of great interest to the reader who is curious to know what the first Englishman who came to Australia thought of this land. "We anchored (Jan. 5th, 1688) two miles from the shore, in twenty-nine fathoms, good hard sand, and clean ground. New Holland is a very large tract of land. It is not yet determined whether it is an island or a main continent, but I am certain that it joins neither to Asia, Africa, nor America. This part of it that we saw, is all low, even land, with sandy banks against the sea, only the points are rocky, and so are some of the islands in this bay. The land is of a dry sandy soil, destitute of water, except you make wells, yet producing divers sorts of trees, but the woods are not thick, nor the trees very big. Most of the trees that we saw are dragon-trees as we supposed, and these too are the largest trees of any there. They are about the bigness of our large apple-trees, and about the same height, and the rind is blackish, and somewhat rough, the leaves are of a dark color, the gum distills out of the knots or cracks that are in the bodies of the trees. We compared it with some gum dragon, or dragon's blood that was aboard, and it was of the same colour and taste. The other sort of trees were not known by any of us. There was pretty long grass growing under the trees, but it was very thin, we saw no trees that bore fruit or berries. We saw no sort of animal nor any track of beast but once, and that seemed to be the tread of a beast as big as a great mastiff dog.

"Here are a few small land birds, but none bigger than a blackbird, and but few sea fowls, neither is the sea very plentifully stored with fish, unless you reckon the manatee and turtle as such, of these creatures there is plenty, but they are extraordinary shy, though the inhabitants cannot trouble them much, having neither boats nor iron.

"The inhabitants of this country are the miserablest people in the world. The Hodmadods of Monomatapa, though a nasty people, yet for wealth, are gentlemen to these, who have no houses, and skin garments, sheep, poultry, and the fruit of the earth, ostrich eggs, etc., as the Hodmadods have, and setting aside their human shape, they differ but little from brutes. They are tall, straight-bodied, and thin, with small long limbs. They have great heads, round foreheads, and great brows. Their eyelids are always half closed to keep the flies out of their eyes, they being so troublesome here, that no fanning will keep them from coming to one's face, and without the assistance of both hands to keep them off they will creep into one's nostrils and mouth too if the lips are not shut very close, so that from their infancy being thus annoyed with these insects, they do never open their eyes as other people, and therefore they cannot see far, unless they hold up their heads as if they were looking at somewhat over them. They have great bottle noses, full lips, and wide mouths, the two fore-teeth of their upper jaw are wanting in all of them, men and women, old and young, whether they draw them out I know not, neither have they any beards. They are long-visaged, and of a very unpleasant aspect, having no one graceful feature in their faces. Their hair is black, short, and curly, like that of the negroes, and not long and lank like that of the common Indians. The color of their faces and the rest of their body is coal black, like that of the negroes of Guinea. They have no sort of clothes, but a piece of the rind of a tree tied like a girdle about their waists, and a handful of long grass or three or four small green boughs full of leaves thrust under their girdle to cover their nakedness. They have no houses, but lie in the open air without any covering, the earth being their bed, and the heavens their canopy.

"Whether they cohabit one man to one woman or promiscuously I know not, but they do live in companies of twenty or thirty, men, women, and children together. Their only food is a small sort of fish. They have no instrument to catch great fish, nor could we catch any fish with our hooks and lines all the while we lay there. In other places at low water they seek for cockles, mussels, and periwinkles, of these shell-fish there are fewer still, so that their chiefest dependence is upon what the sea leaves in their waves, which be it much or little they gather up, and march to the places of their abode.

"There the old people that are not able to stir abroad by reason of their age, and the tender infants wait their return, and what Providence has bestowed upon them, they presently broil on the coals and eat it in common. Sometimes they get as many fish as makes them a plentiful banquet, and at other times they scarce get every one a taste, but be it little or much that they get, every one has his part, as well the young and tender, the old and feeble, who are not able to go abroad, as the strong and lusty. When they have eaten, they lie down till the next low water, and then all that are able march out, be it night or day, rain or shine, it is all one, they must attend the waves, or else they must fast, for the earth affords them no food at all. There is neither herb, root, pulse, nor any sort of grain for them to eat that we saw, nor any sort of bird or beast that they can catch, having no instruments wherewithall to do so. I did not perceive that they did worship anything.

"These poor creatures have a sort of weapon to defend their ware, or fight with their enemies if they have any that will interfere with their poor fishing. They did at first endeavour with their weapons to frighten us, who lying ashore, deterred them from one of their fishing places. Some of them had wooden swords, others had a sort of lance. The sword is a piece of wood, shaped somewhat like a cutlass, the lance is a long straight pole, sharp at one end, and hardened afterwards by heat. I saw no iron, nor any other sort of metal, therefore it is probable they use stone hatches as some Indians in America do."

Such is the account given by the first Englishman who visited these shores. How far his observations harmonise with what has been subsequently noted by travellers and colonists who have had a more intimate knowledge of the natives will appear in another chapter. This account did not put the English Government in possession of a full report concerning this land.

For over sixty years there was very little additional knowledge obtained by the subsequent navigators sent thither by the Dutch, French, or English, until in the year 1768, when it was resolved by the British Admiralty who took the matter in hand and despatched Capt. Jas. Cook on a voyage, partly to observe the transit of Venus, but chiefly to solve the problem that had for a considerable time perplexed the different nations of Europe as to whether Australia or New Holland was a continent, island, or peninsula.

On the 26th August, he set sail in the "Endeavour," a small ship of 370 tons burden. Having successfully made his astronomical observations at Tahiti, Cook entered upon his enterprise of explorations, spent some months on the coast of New Zealand, thence westward. On the 19th April, 1770, he sighted land near the southern extremity of Australia. To this Cook gave the name of Point Hicks, as Mr. Hicks, first lieutenant of the ship, had first sighted it. The "Endeavour" coasted along the shore, and Ram Head, Cape Howe, Point Dromedary, Point Upright, Cape George were named, and finally Botany Bay was reached. Cook's own narrative of the cruise runs thus :—" At daybreak (of the 28th) we discovered a bay (Botany Bay) which seemed to be well sheltered from all winds, and into which, therefore, I determined to go with the ship, the pinnace being repaired, I sent her, with the master, to sound the entrance, while I kept turning up, having the wind right out. At noon, seeing a smoke on the shore, we directed our glasses to the spot, distant about a mile, and we soon discovered ten people, who upon our nearer approach left their fires and retired to a little eminence, whence they could observe our motions. Soon after, two canoes, each having two men on board, came to the shore just under the eminence, and the men joined the rest on the top of it. The pinnace which had been sent ahead to sound now approached the place, upon which all the Indians retired further up the hill, except one, who hid himself among some rocks near the landing place." Captain Cook further adds:—"The Indians seeing the ship approach, used many threatening gestures, and brandished their weapons, particularly two, who made a very singular appearance, for their faces seemed to have been dusted with a white powder, and their bodies painted with broad streaks of the same color, which passing obliquely over their breasts and backs, looked not unlike cross-belts worn by our soldiers; the same kind of streaks were also drawn round their legs and thighs, like broad garters. Each of these men held in his hand the weapon that had been described to us as like a cimeter, which appeared to be about two feet and a-half long, and they seemed to talk to each other with great earnestness. Early in the afternoon we anchored under the south shore, about two miles within the entrance, in six fathoms of water. The place where the ship anchored was abreast of a small village, consisting of about six or eight huts, and while we were preparing to hoist out the boat, we saw an old woman, followed by three children, come out of the wood. She was loaded with firewood, and each of the children had also its little burden. When she came to the huts, three more children, younger than the others, came out to meet her. She often looked at the ship, but expressed neither fear nor surprise. In a short time she kindled a fire, and the four canoes came in from fishing. The men landed, and having hauled up their boats, began to dress their dinner, to all appearance wholly unconcerned about us, though we were within half-a-mile of them. We thought it remarkable that of all the people we had yet seen, not one had the least appearance of clothing, the old woman herself being destitute even of a fig-leaf." Captain Cook relates in a lengthy and minute report, how he made repeated efforts to approach these people, and by gifts, and signs to win their confidence, but the many trinkets, curios, and ribbons, he had left in their huts and in their most frequented haunts were untouched, and by menaces, excited talk, and the free display of their native weapons they showed their detestation of Captain Cook and his party. It was only after several spears, boomerangs, and other missiles had been thrown by the natives, and answered by the ship's crew, in a few light volleys from the musketry, that the natives were sufficiently intimidated, and made to feel the necessity of leaving the place, and removing to more remote quarters. A thorough examination having been made of their huts, of the whole region round about, there was discovered, as relics, barbed spears, shields, bark canoes, broiling fish, all left in the confusion incident upon their hurry to retire from the presence of their daring foe. Cook says, "All the inhabitants that we saw were stark naked; they did not appear to be numerous, nor to live in societies, but like animals, were scattered about along the coast and in the woods. Of their manner of life, however, we could know but little, as we were never able to form the least connection with them. After the first contest at our landing they would never come near enough to parley, nor did they touch a single article of all that we left in their huts on purpose for them to take away."

Mr. Banks and Dr. Solander, the naturalists, discovered and collected a great variety of strange plants and flowers that grew in profusion around this bay, and which suggested to Captain Cook the name of Botany, and which still remains in history to attest the purpose of its early discoverers, and the success of their enterprise.

The "Endeavour" sailed from Botany Bay on the 6th of May, and at noon, says Cook, "we were abreast the entrance of a bay or harbour in which there appeared to be good anchorage, and which I called Port Jackson." No doubt this name was applied in recognition of the friendship that existed between himself and his zealous patron, Sir George Jackson, who was for many years Joint Secretary to the Admiralty, and afterwards Judge-Advocate of the Fleet. In coasting along northwards Cook gave to various bays, rivers, and promontories names which they still bear. When off the north-eastern coast, at a place where shoals and rocks abound, the "Endeavour" suddenly struck a coral reef, and was with difficulty kept from foundering. The vessel was run into a suitable place for repairs, which was named afterwards Endeavour River, and here Cook first saw the kangaroo.

Captain Cook not only made a careful exploration of the entire eastern coast of New Holland, but at every point he hoisted the British flag and took possession of the country in the name of his king, George the Third, and baptised it New South Wales.

Captain Cook was sent on a second voyage in 1772, this time being furnished with two ships, namely, the "Resolution" and his old ship, the "Endeavour," commanded by Captain Furneaux. Cook did not visit any part of Australia on this voyage, but Captain Furneaux, who had separated from his consort, proceeded to Tasmania and explored the eastern coast.

On his third voyage, in 1777, Cook anchored at Adventure Bay, on the south-eastern coast of Tasmania, and, remaining there several days, had excellent opportunities of becoming acquainted with the people and the natural resources of the country.

The next recorded expedition to the shores of Australia inaugurated the era of its colonisation, and marks a period in its history full of interest to every intelligent reader.

CHAPTER III.

THE AUSTRALIAN CONTINENT.

TO appreciate the importance of any one of the colonies that comprise the Australian Continent we must make a brief survey of its extent and geographical boundaries.

Although it is the smallest of the continents, it is by no means insignificant in area. From east to west, across its greatest length, is 2,400 miles, and from its most northern to its most southern point it is 2,000 miles. It contains more than 3,000,000 square miles, and 1,909,366,720 acres. Adding the island of Tasmania, which lies to the south, and the islands of New Zealand, to the south-east, we have a grand aggregate of nearly 2,000,000,000 acres, making an area as large as the United States of America, and almost as large as the continent of Europe. It is situated between the latitudes 10° 39′ and 39° 11′ South and the meridians 113° 5′ and 154° East longitude.

It is bounded on the north by Torres Strait, Gulf of Carpentaria, and the Indian Ocean; on the west by the Indian Ocean; on the south by the Southern Ocean and Bass' Strait; and on the east by the Pacific Ocean. To sail around the continent would necessitate a trip of over ten thousand miles. It would take a full month in one of our fastest ocean steamers, at the rate of three-hundred-and-fifty miles per day, to accomplish the journey. The reader will therefore perceive that the continent is by no means a small one. It is divided into five colonies at present. West Australia takes a little more than a third of the continent. South Australia,

THE AUSTRALIAN CONTINENT.   19

with the Northern Territory attached, embraces about a third more, and stretches from north to south, a belt of land two thousand miles in length and three hundred miles in breadth. And Queensland, New South Wales, and Victoria, in the order named, from north to south, occupy the eastern portion of Australia. If we start from Sydney, the capital of New South Wales, on the eastern side, and direct our course northward, with a view of following the coast line to mark its character and make a circuit around the continent, we will observe many capes, promontories, bays, rivers, and islands in our course, and will best learn the general appearance of the coast in this way. It is proper that we should make our starting point from Port Jackson, as that was the starting point of colonisation and much of the explorations of early times.

Going north we first come to Broken Bay, about twenty miles distant from Sydney, so named by Captain Cook because of its wild and broken appearance as seen from the ocean. It is a very large sheet of water, into which the Hawkesbury River empties. The scenery surrounding this bay is rugged and grand. As we proceed northward we pass Port Hunter, at the mouth of the Hunter River. Thence northward we pass many small bays, capes, and broken coast, until we come to Cape Byron, which extends out into the sea a distance of two miles; and beyond it Point Danger, named by Captain Cook because of the reefs that lie around this point in the sea, and which make it exceedingly dangerous to ships in passing.

Cape Byron is the most easterly point on the continent, and lies in 154° East longitude.

We now pass the dividing line which separates the colony of New South Wales from Queensland, and we soon come in sight of Moreton Island, which lies in front of Moreton Bay or at the mouth of the Brisbane River. Still further north we round Sandy Cape, so called from the sandy character of the island of which it is a part. Our course now will be in a north-westerly direction, and for over one thousand miles runs along the coast the Great Barrier Reef, which consists of a chain of islands formed by the coral insect that in the ages of the past have built these island homes. We pass Hervey Bay, in latitude 25°, Halifax Bay, in latitude 19°, Cape Melville and Princess Charlotte Bay, in 14° 20′ South latitude, and finally reach the extreme northern point, called Cape York.

Turning westward in our course we pass through Torres Strait, leaving Banks Island to our right and Prince of Wales Island to our left. We now sail almost due south into the Gulf of Carpentaria, that stretches inland for more than three hundred miles. Thence, turning westward and northward, we make the circuit of the largest Australian gulf. In this circuit we pass Wellesley Island and Groote Eylandt. Thence westward we pass around the great northern territory at present forming part of South Australia. In our passage we have left Cape Arnheim to our left, and sailing westward through several islands we round Coburg Peninsula, and turning south enter through the Dundas Straits into Van Dieman's Gulf, with the islands of Melville and Bathurst to our right. In this trip so far we have observed the variety of vegetation characteristic of the different latitudes. As we approached the tropics the palm and the mangrove began to appear in the foliage of the islands and vegetable growths that fringe the shore. The coast north of Sydney seems to be well-wooded, except on the rocky cliffs that form a considerable part of the shore. Even here there is to be seen sufficient verdure to tone their barrenness into a landscape of beauty. One is constantly refreshed with the changes in color that everywhere stamp an Australian landscape. The variety of even her ubiquitous gum-tree, in color and shade, gives it a charm that the artist cannot rival, but she is not dependent upon the foliage of the Eucalyptus for her loveliness. She can boast a plentiful supply of tropic growth, and hence, as we have sailed along her coast, we have observed the palm in its grace and beauty, and the mangrove in its luxuriance and verdure clothe the myriads of little islands we have passed on our way, and give the mainland in its long stretches of low sandy levels or its many hilly elevations that go out into the sea, or in its fruitful valleys that here and there mark the presence of rivulets and streams, a loveliness that relieves it of all gloom and augurs well for a future like that foretold by the prophet's pen: "When the wilderness shall blossom as the rose."

We continue our sail through the Clarence Strait and southward, and we come into Cambridge Bay. Turning westward, we round Cape Londonderry, and directing our course west-by-south we pass a rocky coast broken by small bays and valleys, some of which are covered with verdure. We pass King's Sound and then round Cape Leveque, and continue our course south-westerly. For more than eight hundred miles the coast here is low and sandy. Here and there it is relieved by a slight elevation. Desolation seems to reign supreme in this portion of Western Australia. We pass Exmouth Gulf, and, taking a westward course, we round North-west Cape, noted for nothing except its enormous stretches of sandy soil that extend inland for hundreds of miles. We proceed due south for about one hundred miles, and we pass Cape Cuvier, a rocky coast. Thence south we reach Shark Bay. Leaving this bay we round Steep Point, the most westerly part of the continent, and thence proceeding south-by-east about five hundred miles we come to Perth, the capital of Western Australia. Thence south and west for about one hundred miles we pass through Geographe Bay and round Cape Naturaliste, named after Baudin's two ships. A short distance further south we pass around Cape Leeuwin. Thence, eastward by south, we reach King George's Sound, where is situated Albany, the most southern point in Western Australia.

Taking a course almost directly east we cross the Great Australian Bight, as it is called. It is a sort of gulf that sweeps in on the southern coast of the continent and gives it the shape of a crescent. We sail along on a straight line on latitude 35° South for nearly one thousand miles, and we come to Cape Catastrophe, so called by Captain Flinders, who sent a few of his men in a small boat in search of fresh water, but was capsized, his men drowned, and the boat afterwards found wrecked.

Turning northward from this point we enter Spencer Gulf. This is beautifully skirted with a goodly growth of timber. We turn south and round Cape Spencer and enter the Gulf of St. Vincent. All around this gulf are to be seen verdure and loveliness. On its eastern side is situated the city of Adelaide, the capital of South Australia, a city universally admired for its parks, lawns, gardens, artistic buildings and general beauty. Sailing south we meet Kangaroo Island, but turning eastward before we reach it we round Cape Jervis and pass through what is known as the Backstairs Passage, which is regarded as the eastern portion of Investigator Strait, called after the vessel in which Captain Flinders made his investigations. We now sail through Encounter Bay, where Captain Flinders encountered the Frenchman, Captain Baudin, who was engaged in a similar task, but making his explorations from another direction. Proceeding south-west we come to Cape Northumberland and Cape Nelson, the extreme southernmost point of the colony of South Australia, in latitude

38° South. Thence onward in the same direction we pass Portland Bay and reach Cape Otway. We pass Port Phillip by for the present, on which is situated Melbourne, the capital of Victoria, and sailing eastward we come to Wilson's Promontory and pass through Bass' Strait, which separates the Australian continent from the island of Tasmania, (formerly known as Van Dieman's Land). We now direct our course north of east, and in the space of twelve hours we round Cape Howe, near the first point discovered by Captain Cook in 1770. Thence east of northward we sail past Twofold Bay and Jervis Bay, and reach Port Jackson, the point from which we started.

In this journey around the continent we have gained an approximate idea of its size and physical appearance. When viewed from its coast one can scarcely conceive how magnificent are its proportions until he has completed the circuit. His observations of its extent gives him a wider view of its capabilities. He can easily comprehend the practicability of making it the home of countless millions of the human race.

When some of the early explorers of Australia returned to their fatherlands, they reported it "barren and desolate," but a brief one hundred years of colonisation and occupancy has demonstrated the fact that it is eminently fitted to become the abode of millions of the human race. That its soil is capable of sustaining and developing life may be seen in the enormous increase in the flocks and herds of inconceivable proportions that now roam on its extended plains. They can scarcely be accurately numbered, but, at the very least calculation, are not less than from seventy to one hundred millions of sheep and cattle, not including the other live stock of all kinds and the "rabbit pest," that has multiplied with a rapidity so great as to alarm all classes of farmers and squatters who see in their increase the destruction of a vast quantity of vegetable substance that ought to go towards the development of their flocks and herds.

Australia furnishes about one-third of the wool product of the earth, and what it will yet accomplish in this one particular none can dare prophesy.

In general appearance she is low and flat. There is an absence, as a rule, of those grand mountains and hills characteristic of other continents. Nevertheless, these features are not wholly wanting. They are confined to the coast regions and chiefly to the eastern half.

There are but few elevations in the interior worthy of the name of mountains; they are mostly insignificant in height and ruggedness, and would be considered hills in other parts of the world. They lack grandeur and beauty, but are usually found to be the most attractive places on account of their rich mineral deposits.

The chief range of mountains is on the eastern coast, inland from the Pacific Ocean about fifty to eighty miles. They rise in the north of Queensland, and, running parallel with the coast through New South Wales, extend to the most southern part of the colony of Victoria. This range is known by different names. In the Queensland colony it is called the Cooyar and Burnett Ranges. In New South Wales it is known as the Liverpool Range and Blue Mountains, and in Victoria it is called the Australian Alps, whose summit is covered almost the year round with snow. The highest peak in this chain is Mount Townsend, in Victoria, just a short distance south of Mount Kosciusko. It is 7,256 feet in height. On the western coast is to be found a range of mountains, but they are not continuous as on the east. It is broken up into the Sterling Range in the south-west; the Darling Range, Herschal Range, and Victoria Range.

In the north-east is the Lockyer Range, one of whose peaks is called Mt. Augustus, 3,580 feet in height. There are also the Kennedy, Barlee, and Hammersley Ranges, of inconsiderable elevation. In the Kimberley district, in the north-west, is the King Leopold Range. On the south coast, within a few miles of the city of Adelaide, is Mount Lofty Range, only about 2,300 feet, and Gawler Range stretching to the west of Spencer Gulf. On the north coast are the Gwooling and Hart Mountains, and the Ellesmere Range south of Palmerston.

We have enumerated only some of the more prominent mountains that lie along the coast. In the interior are to be found comparatively few, and mostly of an elevation that entitles them to rank merely as good-sized hills; and when we consider the vast extent of the plains and desert stretches that meet the explorer in his wanderings over its surface, the elevations or mountains, comparatively, are but small cones, here and there relieving it of its utter monotony and desolation. Among the more important are the Stanley or Barrier Range, noted at the present time for its silver mines, and the Grey Range, in New South Wales, for its gold; the Grampian Mountains, in Victoria; the Stuart, Hanson, Macdonnell and

Reynold Ranges, in South Australia; the Hugh and Mackinlay Range in Queensland; and Marie Range in Western Australia.

The tablelands are limited in area, and nearly all confined to the mountain ranges of the eastern portion of the continent, and to some extent in the north near the Gulf of Carpentaria. They have a variable elevation of from five hundred to two thousand feet above the sea, and have a climate unsurpassed in the world for healthfulness and comfort.

The plains are vast and constitute the chief feature of the continent; they vary in character and fertility; some are of the richest, and others the most sterile; some of them are covered with a low-spreading gum tree, that does not grow very closely together, but at somewhat regular intervals, as if planted by design, sufficiently far apart to admit of a team and coach being driven with ease in any direction. It reminds one of the parks of old England, where the sportsman finds his chief delight in the exciting chase. Other portions of the plain are covered with small shrub that seems to be well adapted to the sustenance of the immense flocks of sheep which fatten on this diet, and which is claimed to be of the best kind of food.

A more extended description will be given in another chapter.

The rivers of Australia as a rule are small. They are sufficiently numerous, if you embrace within the term all streams which in other lands are designated rivulets and creeks. The rivers proper are comparatively few and short. There are, however, a few of considerable extent and deserving of special notice. Those on the eastern coast are larger and more numerous than those on the western, and flow more rapidly, for the reason they have greater waterfall. They are all liable to overflow their banks. The rains and the snows from the mountains, which soon melt, fill the creeks and streams that empty into them and swell the volume of water to an enormous extent in a remarkably short time, which rushes down with tremendous velocity and force, oftentimes carrying away bridges, dams, and other improvements that may be in its track. This overflow, though dreaded and guarded against is not an unmitigated calamity, as it always leaves its rich alluvial deposits behind on the soil that extends far on either sides of their banks, and invariably insures an abundant harvest immediately afterwards, as a kindly compensation for the destruction it may have accomplished, like the Nile that in its flow of death takes life, health and beauty, and gives back tenfold in return.

The largest river is the Murray, which has its origin in Mount Kosciusko, in the south of the continent, and flows north of westward, forming the boundary line between the colonies of New South Wales and Victoria. It continues in the same general direction, although its course is very tortuous. It receives on its way from the Victorian side the Mitta Mitta and Ovens rivers, Broken Creek, Goulburn and Campaspe rivers and many smaller streams; and from the New South Wales side it receives the Murrumbidgee, almost as large as itself, with its many tributaries, and further on the River Darling joins it near the eastern boundary of South Australia, and flowing westward to 140° meridian within that colony, suddenly turns south and empties into Lake Alexandrina, which opens to the sea. There are the Burdekin, Fitzroy and Brisbane rivers in Queensland; the Clarence, Hunter, Hawkesbury and Shoalhaven, in New South Wales; the Snowy, Tambo, Mitchell, Yarra and Glenelg rivers in Victoria; the Swan, Murchison, Gascoyne and Ashburton Rivers of Western Australia, together with very many others that flow into the Indian Ocean and the Gulf of Carpentaria.

The Lakes are few, or at least those of any size. There are many scattered throughout the continent that are no larger than good sized ponds. In dry seasons they entirely disappear. These inland lakes are nearly all of a brackish character, and hence are not well adapted to the use of man or flocks.

One of its chief attractions is its boundless mineral wealth. There is, perhaps, no country in the world that possesses such a variety. As yet, there is comparative ignorance concerning their extent, even among her own people, and very great ignorance in other parts of the world. In conversation, the other day, with Mr. Knapp, a gentleman from America, who has spent most of his life in mining, as assayer and mining engineer, he said, "That in America there were no such mines. That while there was more gold and silver taken out in America, there were no mines that would assay such a high grade of ore as those found in most parts of the Australian continent. That the country only needed capital and the more modern machinery in use in the United States to make it the chief gold and silver producing country of the world."

The very best quality of coal is to be found in abundance in several parts of the country, and apparently without limit. It was discovered in 1796, shortly after the first colonists arrived, but was not utilised for many years afterwards, partly on account of the abundance of wood, and partly because of the great expense of operating the mines, and carrying on commerce in the article with distant countries, that were able to obtain all needed supplies of coal at a much lower rate than it could be produced here under these disadvantages. Since that date the demand has been created, and the mines have yielded to commerce an incredibly large output, which has brought enormous wealth to the continent, and is now reckoned among her richest enterprises. The extent of this trade may be judged from the fact that in 1886 she produced nearly 3,000,000 tons. We will have occasion, in another chapter, in connection with local industries to dwell more particularly on the nature, developement and extent of this special article of trade, at present only in its infancy.

No country in the world could possibly possess a better supply of stone for building purposes. The abundance of sandstone found everywhere makes the building of bridges, public improvements, and private dwellings comparatively easy and cheap. Her building material is not confined to sandstone, though this is the most widely distributed. Her limestone and granite, gypsum and marble, are scattered in every part with a plentifulness as boundless as her acres. One bed, in Queensland alone, of coral formation is 7,000 feet in thickness. In every part of the continent there is no lack of the best building stone, besides basalt, slate, shale, asbestos, gypsum, porcelain and brick clay. Hence the traveller through the continent is not surprised to find public buildings, school-houses, churches, business warehouses, private dwellings even of the middle classes constructed of stone, brick and granite, which give them the appearance of permanency and solidity never seen elsewhere in a country so young.

Her soil is variable in character and quality. In this regard, extremes meet. The most sterile deserts to be found in any part of the world are the desert plains of certain portions of the western half of Australia; also in the central and northern parts, but as to their extent we are in ignorance, as they have as yet been unexplored. Sandy plains without a vestige of verdure, or with only here and yonder a tuft of grass or some lonely shrub, meet one's gaze as he looks out upon the scene; but we are not to be misled into the idea that the continent is, to any great degree, of such a type. Doubtless, when the foot of man shall have trod this vast unknown desert, and more thoroughly explored its various parts, there will be found oases of vast extent, rivers and lakes awaiting the advent of the pioneer, who shall make their banks and shores sing with gladness. The weary traveller will yet seek rest under her " Palms of Elim," where the orange and banana, the vine and the cane will grow in such profusion and luxuriance as to draw from the streets and lanes, and slums of the old world the poor and the wretched who, driven out of their wretchedness by the sheer necessity of hunger and want, will find an elysium, where plenty reigns and tyranny grinds not, where the kingly crown rests upon the honest toilers' brow, and manhood is the quality most justly prized.

The reader must not regard this as a fancy picture. Every word of it is true in regard to other portions of this continent. If sterility marks some parts of the western and central plains, fertility is equally the characteristic of the great balance of the country. The great bulk of the soil cannot anywhere be surpassed in its ability to produce; and not the products of one climate only, but of nearly all climates. The cereals of the north, the fruit of the tropics, and the luxuries and variety of products of the temperate zone all find a soil here congenial to their growth and development. The orange cannot be surpassed in quality or prolificness; the grape has won the encomiums of the best judges of the old world through her wines, which lack only age to give them first rank. Her sugar-cane, banana, pine-apple, wheat, maize, barley, oats, potatoes, and all root crops are grown in abundance, and can be produced *ad libitum,* when the laborer shall be so disposed.

Wool is the great staple article and product of this land. In every part of it flocks of immense extent and number may be seen. These multiply with amazing rapidity in favourable seasons; and a favourable season is one when it rains sufficiently to fill the streams and keep them in a good supply of water. Occasionally, perhaps once every five years, from lack of rain and scarcity of water the flocks perish in large numbers, though experience has taught most of the shepherds to conserve the supply, or where this is impossible, to drive them to new regions where there is no lack.

Its metals are most numerous and valuable, gold, silver, copper, tin, iron, lead, antimony, zinc, bismuth, arsenic, cobalt, manganese and mercury; and of precious stones—rubies, diamonds, sapphires, and topaz. These and many others make it one of the most attractive portions of the globe.

CHAPTER IV.

THE ABORIGINES.

THERE has been a great deal written about the "blacks" of this fair land, some of which has been extravagant in its laudation, and, on the other hand, much has been said adverse to them equally wide of the mark. Between these two classes of writers we may expect to find the truth somewhere. It has been asserted by many that it is utterly impossible to civilise the native Australian, that is, to induce him by any system of instruction to settle down to the cultivation of the soil, build and occupy houses, much less to adopt a life akin to the modes adopted by his white brethren. On the other hand, with equal earnestness, writers have asserted the possibility of the blacks being raised to a high rank or status in education, religious enlightenment, and other habits of industry, sobriety, and general conduct, found associated with all ranks of civilised people.

There can be no question at all that in some instances there have been satisfactory evidences of a good degree of culture, earnest religious zeal, and praiseworthy deeds of morality and prudence—not a few cases of genuine conversion to the Christian religion and practices have been reported by the early missionaries. Notwithstanding all this, we believe we but express the sentiment of nearly everyone who has been brought into contact with them, that they are, above all other races of savages yet discovered, the lowest in the scale of humanity. They build no houses, perform no labour except such little as is required by the absolute necessity of hunger. They respect no moral code save that of brute force.

THE ABORIGINES.

Their condition at the time of the discovery by Captain Cook, and for many years afterwards, was as low as that of the beasts of the field. In fact, in no sense were they superior, except in the low sagacity and cunning they evinced in capturing the birds of the air, the animals of the forests and plains, and the fish of their rivers and sea, and in making them tributary to their sustenance and support on the very easiest conditions. "They toil not neither do they spin," neither are they clad in the "glory of a Solomon or in the beauty of the flowers of the field."

The "Voice of God" moved our first parents, Adam and Eve, to seek in very shame a covering to their nakedness, and, as a rule, among all barbarous tribes there is recognised the same "voice" that bids man to make, from palm leaves or other woody fibres of branch or grass, aprons to cover himself; but in the black tribes of Australia we find a race that lives in utter disregard of all rules and requirements of dress, in fact, whose manner of life antedates even Adamic times.

May we not be pardoned for suggesting that one of the first evidences of an intelligence which raises man above the brute and makes him susceptible to civilising influences, is the fact that he is able to appreciate and value the great worth of a garment. The place in civilisation that dress occupies is perhaps not sufficiently understood by any of us. How far its influence for good extends is yet an unsolved problem. It is one of those incidental circumstances that is taken in this life like the air we breathe and the water we drink and the sunshine we hail, as a matter of course. It is so abundantly bestowed, and hence so common in its plentitude, that we fail to see its worth and absolute value in developing that æsthetic nature that fits man to walk with God in the gardens of earth and transforms it into a Paradise, in which is heard the "voice" divine.

It is not our purpose to wander off into the æsthetic field of science and philosophy, except to merely impress the reader with the great contrast between these savage people and the conquering hosts that came from English shores one hundred years ago, hastening in the track of Captain Cook, and from whose toil and brain has sprung up throughout this glorious land a civilisation whose chief glory consists in the benefits it imparts to all its people with a free and liberal hand, upon equal terms and upon conditions so favorable that all her sons and daughters may share in the general good.

THE ABORIGINES.

There is a slight difference in the habits of the several tribes. Those along the coast are more settled than those in the interior. The former live in huts formed of bark, grasses and mud, and maintain a sort of stability. The abundance of fish in the streams and on the coast favors the habit of contentment and permanancy. Those in the interior wander from place to place yet beyond in search of game or plunder, it matters little to them which. The women, who are called "gins" in black parlance, and the children have the hardest lot. They do nearly all the work, while the men in lordly fashion take their comfort, smoke their pipes, and literally "take no thought for the morrow." When one comes to think of the climate they enjoy and the natural bounty with which nature has scattered her gifts in this land, we scarcely wonder at the universal absence of anxiety in regard to the future. The women, as a rule, are lank and lean and hard of feature; the men of much larger and rounder physical development, the difference in their condition being, no doubt, the result of hardships endured by the one and ease and comfort enjoyed by the other sex. That they are capable of labour and industry is quite apparent to those who have had the best opportunities of studying their habits and nature. The squatter, miner, and explorer, have each in their way been compelled to press them into service in a variety of ways, and by numerous devices of kindness and severity have arrived at the same conclusions respecting them. They are capable but not willing; they are strong but lazy; they could with little exertion earn a comfortable livelihood, but they would rather steal; they could have settled homes, but would rather wander. They have intelligence, are quick-witted, and possessed of good oratorical ability, but lack conscience or any sense of gratitude. The kindest treatment by the white squatter or humane miner may be repaid by the stealing of his sheep or gold, and possibly by the murder of his wife or child. An injury, or a supposed one, is never forgotten by the native black or any of his tribe, and the avenging of it on the offender's household or possessions seems to be regarded as a sacred duty, and is sure, sooner or later, to come. Their intelligence is well illustrated in their weapons of warfare and the rules by which all their battles are fought. A singular intelligence also characterises their methods of obtaining their game. The instruments they use both in warfare and in gaming are numerous and well suited to their purpose. In their hands they are pliant and effective,

THE ABORIGINES.

and by their use they can render service on the battle-field and on the plain.

Among their weapons we may mention a few: the boomerang, spear, nullah-nullah, waddy, hatchet, knife, boombermart, and shield, all of which imply a large amount of intelligence to make and much more to handle. There are many other weapons in common use among the various tribes, many of them modifications of the above, as the spear, for instance. The hunting spear is comparatively light, and is made from the long stem of the ti-tree, and on the point is dexterously bound a smooth sharpened bone. With this the skilled gamester can spear eel, fish, or birds, with almost unerring certainty. For larger game a heavier kind of spear is used, of much the same manufacture. Sharp flints are sometimes set in each side near the point of the spear, presenting a serrated appearance like the edge of a large saw. This spear can be thrown to a great distance and with tremendous force when the wommera is used.

The wommera is a piece of wood about two feet in length, a hook at one end to receive the spear, and by its aid the strong arm of the thrower can impart such force to the weapon that nothing in its way can resist its momentum. With this instrument the blackfellow can gather the fowls of the air and the fish of the sea, and in times of warfare strike terror into the heart of a foeman. The war spear proper is a more formidable instrument. Its point is barbed for a space of two feet up, either by notches cut in the wood, or the fangs of the crocodile are arranged along its edges so as to serve the same purpose. It is frequently dipped in the putrid blood or decaying flesh of a dead body, that it may carry in its deathly flight the rankling germs of a certain death.

The boomerang is a weapon above all others the most wonderful. It is simple enough in its construction, for it consists of a thin piece of hard wood about half-an-inch in thickness, nearly three inches in width, about two feet in length, and in shape like a crescent or quarter of a new moon. In the hands of a black man it is hurled in such a manner as to take a sort of spiral or serpentine course in the direction of the enemy, but failing to strike its object, it makes a few wonderful gyrations and falls perchance at the feet of the thrower. It requires skill and practice of no ordinary kind to so manipulate its motions, as to be of service in time of warfare or in successfully bringing down the birds and beasts of the field. The native is trained from infancy in the art of throwing this weapon, and by constant use can direct its motions so as to deceive the bird in its flight, and quickly bring it to the ground; on the other hand, cause the brave warrior to yield to its superior cunning. Its course, when dexterously thrown, is never direct, but always tortuous, and it is this fact that makes it impossible for even the watchful and well-trained enemy to be on his guard against its subtle attacks. The warrior or huntsman, by his keen well-practiced eye, measures distance with such accuracy and cunning that he can give the boomerang just the twist and force necessary, and make it exceedingly uncomfortable to both man and bird who may chance to be for the time the object of his aim. The reader might live, as the writer has done, for a considerable time in the immediate neighbourhood of these people, and never be able to witness a good exhibition of this kind of sport. The time has gone by for the stranger who makes but a passing visit to these Colonies to find these customs. Nevertheless, the frequency with which one meets the boomerang, and the reliability of the many who claim to have seen it used both in warfare and in the chase, precludes the possibility of any error in our description of its nature and use.

Mr. Ernest L. Fattorina, who has spent most of his life on the Corrella Downs, near the Gulf of Carpentaria, in the northern territory, where the natives are to be found in greatest numbers, and who has had much to do with them, has assured us that he himself has frequently witnessed them in their conflicts throw the boomerang with such skill as to wound an enemy and make him halt where it has not been deemed desirable to kill, but merely to conquer; and on one occasion he saw a blackfellow scalp a gin, his own wife, at a distance of thirty yards, because of her falseness to him, and thus avenging the wrong.

The boombermart is a device they frequently use to catch birds. It is a sort of a screen made of grass and branches, which the native holds in one hand, and, walking behind it, he cautiously approaches his prey, and then, with a loop of grass held in his other hand, manages to steal a quiet march on the unsuspecting bird, and thus entrap it in the meshes of the grass-loop or net. The wild turkey is most easily caught by these means, as its natural curiosity leads it to investigate every brush or shrub or the appearance of one, on all occasions when danger does not appear imminent. Though very timid naturally, yet its curiosity and great desire to examine things that are strange makes it an easy prey to the huntsman. The shield is a weapon of defence, and is very important in warfare. It is made of either wood or bark, about three feet in length, or more, and ten to twelve inches in width, with a handle cut in on the back surface. It is elaborately painted in fantastic designs, and serves them well when assailed by the enemy. It is a marvel to see one in the hands of a black-fellow. Being trained from an early period in its use they show great skill in warding off missiles that are thrown with deadly aim. An expert can safely defend himself against a dozen antagonists. It is said that when one of their prisoners, who is condemned to death by being shot, is surrounded by several of their best marksmen, the prisoner is given a shield, and if by its dexterous use he can save himself from being wounded by their deathly spears for a certain number of attacks, he thereby wins a commutation of sentence, and this consideration, among others, makes it a very important part of the young native's education always to become well skilled in its use.

The waddy is an ordinary club, about twenty inches in length, a knob at one end and a roughened handle at the other. By practice the huntsman can throw this with wonderful directness, and bring down a bird on wing or kill small game. This instrument is seldom used in fighting, although in milder conflicts it is sometimes employed.

The Leeangle is a longer and heavier club, chiefly useful for its service in deadly combats. This weapon is a savage-looking instrument of destruction. It is made of the hardest kind of wood. When dry, it is heavy and tough. The knob end is cut into small cone-like processes, which give it a roughened prickly aspect. Sometimes it is shaped after the manner of a hatchet. Altogether it is a repulsive ugly weapon one scarcely wishes to meet in the hands of an enemy. Armed with this club and a shield, one can imagine but cannot realise how terrible is a native combat.

The Corrobboree is the native dance. In its nature it partakes of the theatrical and the ordinary dance. With this they celebrate all important events of warfare, matrimony, or other occasions of rejoicing. It is difficult for any white man to understand fully all its significance. By it they perpetuate great historic events, such as their mythical origin and their numerous victories over other tribes. When game is abundant and the season is favorable, and there is an absence of want, they join in the dance to attest their joy, and express their gladness at the success that attends them. The war dance is perhaps the most exciting of them all. All their people join in this. The multitude assemble in the woods, which have been chosen for their suitableness. The place is usually one where hills rise on many sides and ravines or valleys stretch between. The time chosen is after nightfall. A fire is kindled, and the flames lighten up the weird ghostly forest as with phantoms from the nether regions. The warriors assemble in their war-paint, and in a condition of absolute nudity, save a few leaves or grasses dangling from their knees, as decorations; the women are at a respectful distance, drumming on tightened skins and singing their songs of encouragement to their timely beating. The dance moves on with measured step. The attitude assumed by each is uniform; their movements and motions are in concert. The time quickens and the excitement rises higher and higher still, until, exhausted by the wearied joy, they seek repose on the hill-sides. This is repeated and continues sometimes for weeks. In connection with this dance or war corrobboree the ceremony of conferring their weapons of warfare on their boys or young men takes place. They are thus made men, or, to use the expression of the civilised white race when their daughters are first introduced to the social circle, "they are brought out." All the boys join with their elders in the closing part of the corrobboree dance, while the women are permitted to witness the scene from the hill-side and utter their approval by song and drum.

In their real combats they invariably use all their weapons before they fight with knives, and when fighting with this last, one rigid rule governing the contest is that an attack shall only be made in the fleshy parts of the body. When one death occurs, no matter how many are engaged in the fight, they all retire. The battle is then declared over.

They believe in a hereafter and that there is a Supreme Being; that "blackfellow when he dies shall jump up whitefellow." They believe also in a wicked spirit.

They are law abiding. The rules of government among their respective tribes are rigid, and enforced with severity and strictness.

Rum is their ruin, and seems to be so intimately associated with Christian civilisation that they are not always able to separate the two. The missionary has not always been an abstainer, and very frequently we find the Christian as great a lover of the bottle as he is of a native's soul. We

THE ABORIGINES.

must not, therefore, be surprised to find the poor blackfellow following hastily in the footsteps of his moral guide, and even to excel him in the high estimate he puts on a glass of wine. It is but natural for him to think that drunkenness is one of the virtues of Christianity, when both the missionary and first traders that come into contact with them are so eager to teach him its use.

The first white man killed by the natives was in May, 1788. This provoked a spirit of revenge, not on the murderer, but on the race. It is not on record, nevertheless it is generally believed, that the first murder committed by the blacks was brought on by the wrong purposed or accomplished by the victim or his associates. It is well known that for many years after the first landing of the whites the practice of kidnapping young native women for base purposes was not unfrequent. The natives were by no means favorably impressed with this incident of Christian civilisation, and other kinds of abuse, which made the early attempts of the settlers to occupy and till the soil dangerous. Had they pursued a course of kindness towards them, and sought to conciliate them by gifts and other considerations, and, on the other hand, refrained from teaching them the habit of drunkenness, no doubt as a race they would have attained a higher rank in civilisation and the nation would have won them as co-workers in the development of the country. As it is, the Churches have largely failed in giving them spiritual life. The expenditure of large sums of money by the Government and benevolent associations have proved a comparative failure, and little remains to show a harvest worthy of a seed-time in which multitudes were eager to sow.

Few institutions of learning are to be found among them, and few Churches are actively engaged in Christianising them. At the same time they are fast disappearing in numbers, and doubtless soon will be reckoned among the extinct races of the earth.

In the colder latitudes their decrease has been more rapid than in the more tropical regions of the north. In Tasmania they have disappeared entirely. In Victoria there are but few natives, and they speedily decreasing. Towards the north, in Queensland, the aboriginal tribes are to be found in the greater numbers, but even here are evidences of a rapid decay. The work of extermination by the whites still goes silently on, not as a purpose or by concerted plan, nevertheless, steadily and surely. The occupancy by the whites of their land and civilisation in her triumphant march carries along with her a hundred concomitants against which the blackfellow cannot successfully stand. A generation or two will in all probability wipe them out, and the second centennial will record their existence as a thing of the past.

Theirs has been a sad history thus far in the Australian Colonies. We can scarcely charge Christian civilisation with their ruin, yet possibly the Church has been somewhat at fault. The great English nation thought to do them good, and did make liberal provision for their temporal and spiritual benefit. She has largely failed in realising her expectations. The British heart has been full of compassion for this people and her benevolence has been frequently strained in their behalf, and how far she can justify herself in her treatment of the natives, whose lands and game and homes she has taken, and how far she can rejoice in the wealth she has acquired from them in exchange for her rum and Christianity, is a question that only a higher and wiser power than man can correctly answer.

CHAPTER V.

QUEENSLAND.

QUEENSLAND was originally embraced in the colony of New South Wales, which, up to the formation of South Australia, in 1836, included all the eastern half of the Australian continent. It extended to the meridian 135° East longitude. A line, if drawn from north to south on this meridian would cut the continent in halves. That lying eastward was once designated New South Wales. It extended from latitude 10° 37′, to 43° 20′ South, and from 135° to 154° East longitude. It therefore embraced an area of about a million and a half square miles—half the size of Europe or the United States of America. In this original territory are at present situated the eastern portion of South Australia, which was constituted a colony in 1836; Victoria, which separated in 1851; and Queensland, which became an independent colony in 1859, previous to which date the latter was known as the Moreton Bay District, its history being incorporated with that of New South Wales.

Queensland Colony contains about half the territory, which for sixty years bore the name of New South Wales. It occupies the north-eastern portion of the Continent, and lies between the latitudes 10° 40′ and 28°, and the meridan 138° and 154° East longtitude. Its area is 668,224 square miles. Forty millions of people can find homes on its soil, and live in comfort on its bounty; and forty millions more would not crowd it to repletion. It is the wealthiest of the Australian colonies, in proportion to its inhabitants.

The Colony is naturally divided into three parts. The coast district lies between the great coast range and the Pacific Ocean; in extent about fifty miles in width, and 1500 miles in length. The Tablelands are great plateaux formed by the mountains, and well suited, by their elevation and rich soil, to produce wheat, maize, barley, oats, and hay.

The great plains lie beyond, and are chiefly valuable for grazing purposes. They are covered over by a class called squatters, who are mostly in possession of large runs, and engaged in the lucrative business of sheep-raising. Of these three divisions, the coast district is the most desirable portion. Though it is but a narrow strip of land, the greater portion of it is of the richest character. It is somewhat undulating and broken by streams, bays, mangrove marshes, and moderate hills and spurs which have their origin in the great mountain range, and jut out towards the ocean. This portion of the colony is occupied by a prosperous class of farmers, who have settled along the many rivers and streams that have their rise in the mountain region and run into the ocean. These, for the most part, are small, except when swollen by the rains of the Great Range that, increasing their volume and overflowing their banks, contribute greatly to the fertility of the alluvial lands in the valleys of this district. Here nature smiles and blossoms in plenty the year round. The frequent showers keep the lands in everlasting fruitfulness and perpetual verdure. Its valleys and hills are decked with flowers of varied hue. Nature has been lavish of her gifts all along this region. If she has torn from their rocky beds mountains of sandstone to fringe its coast with cliffs and promontories, she has done so with a wild loveliness rarely seen elsewhere. The dashing wave and sportive spray for ever sing their anthems of delight at the munificence with which nature has here joined together the beautiful and the good.

The Tablelands are formed by the mountains. They are broken up in several divisions, some of which are of considerable size. Those of the south are the largest. They are hedged in by loftier ranges, themselves being at a height averaging from 500 to 2,100 feet above the sea. These Tablelands are relieved of their monotony by the lofty peaks and rugged crags that rise around them in awful grandeur to join the clouds, and make a picture of sublimity and majesty calculated to fill the soul with awe and reverence. One can scarce conceive of any sight more inspiring than a rising or setting sun as seen from these Tablelands. In front some jutting rock of rugged form, moss-grown and seamed by time, or dotted here and there with shrub or creeping vine, lifts high its hoary head to drink the dewdrop from the clouds and gain the freshening vigour of young manhood's morning life; and, catching from the eastern sun its primal gleams of golden light, he paints his visage with the borrowed splendour, and flings its reflect like a friendly smile to the lonely gazer, and makes him thankful that he lives.

The fertility of these high lands has been tested for years, and is found to be well adapted to the production of cereals and fruits; the climate is salubrious, and is not surpassed in any other part of the world.

Further west we have the western slope and plains, much of which is undulating and broken up by mineral mountains and considerable hills. A part of this territory is covered with an abundance of grass and other vegetation; much of it overgrown with timber of excellent quality for roads, fencing, and building; while the greater part is covered with low shrub, on which large flocks of sheep find pasture. When these lands become cultivated, they will be utilised in the production of cotton, tobacco, sugar, or other produce of a tropical character, for which they are best suited.

It is sometimes said that almost every climate under the sun is to be had in Australia. This is only partly true. In some portions of the interior it does become intensely hot during the summer months; and also, on a few of the highest mountains, occasionally, it becomes intensely cold. These are extremes that can very easily be avoided, inasmuch as there is no necessity for anyone living under either of these conditions. The temperature, as a rule, varies from 50° to 90° Fahr., and is generally conceded to be one of the most healthful and salubrious. It is seldom that fires need be made in winter for warmth, or that the heat of summer interferes with the vigorous performance of the ordinary duties of life. There are days in summer that are oppressive towards mid-day, when both man and beast are disposed to seek rest from labour, but such are comparatively few. The almost constant breezes, or moderate winds that prevail during the hottest season modify very much the temperature, and offset its high range. The seasons come at opposite periods to those of the northern latitudes. At Christmas we are in midsummer, and winter's coldest days are in the month of July; the longest days are in December, and the shortest are in July. The mornings and evenings are agreeably cool and pleasant, even in the hottest months, and the nights refreshing. Away, in the interior, on the plains inconvenience is sometimes felt for days and weeks together from the burning rays of the summer sun, but usually the farmers prepare themselves for such an experience by arranging their work so as to avoid active exercise in the heat of the sun. They rest at noon, and do their work in the cooler portions of the day. In the winter season frost or snow is very seldom known near the coast. In the interior, to a very limited extent, does it freeze sufficient to form ice or snow, except in the mountain regions, where, as a matter of course, they have both according to the degree of elevation. A summer blast, called the "hot wind," is the most to be dreaded. This comes from the direction of the central plains, and heated occasionally to a temperature of 100° to 110° in the shade. When these winds occur, which happily is seldom, they scorch and wither vegetation, they burn like a heated furnace; but what is remarkable is the fact that they do not depress either man or animal as the ordinary heat of even 10° less. The coast regions on the east are comparatively free from their visitation, for the reason that the winds become much modified in their passage over the mountains. They nearly always terminate by a south wind, called a "buster," which seems to come as a sort of an antagonist to correct the influence of the former. The temperature changes in a few minutes, and the air becomes cool and fresh. The rainfall in this colony is large when compared with that of most other lands. The exceeding great amount of heat makes it necessary to have a large quantity of rainfall to give the moisture and fruitfulness other regions more remote from the equator possess. Even in an exceedingly dry season the rainfall is greater than that of Europe, or the northern parts of North America. In England an average depth of rain is twenty-four inches; in America, about twenty-eight; but such a fall in Australia would certainly mean drought and destruction of vegetation. The average yearly fall is over fifty inches in this colony.

When we take into account the vastness of its territory, and general heat of its climate, we become cognisant of the limited number of its streams, and yet it possesses a goodly supply. There are a few of them of considerable size, and they pass through a very great part of its area by virtue of their tortuous course. Most of them we have described in another chapter. On the eastern coast are many rivers of importance, all of which have their origin in the mountain range. The most noted of these are the Logan, Brisbane, Mary, Burnett, Calliope, Fitzroy, Pioneer, Burdekin, Endeavour, Kennedy, and Stewart.

In the interior there are numerous rivers and rivulets, which in a wet season afford an abundance of water for all purposes of agriculture and pasturage. They have for the most part their origin in the dividing range, from the confluence of many small streams, and flow westward in a very tortuous manner, thus making a great portion of the interior plains valuable for sheep and cattle farming. The Victoria, with its many tributaries, passes through the largest area, and finally joins the Barcoo, or Cooper's Creek, which empties into Lake Eyre. The Condamine, Maranoa, and the Warrego are the most noted. A hundred rivulets join these in their course, and make a network of water supply. These last-named rivers all flow into and really form the Darling River in its upper portion. It is joined by others along its way, some from Queensland and others from west and east, and drains the enormous area of nigh 200,000 square miles. The vast plains through which it runs, and the scorching heat of the sun in those parts absorb so much of its waters, that during the greater portion of the summer months its bed becomes dry, or at most is a chain of little lakes or ponds that seem by nature to have been well designed to conserve its waters for this vast territory, that otherwise would be doomed to utter desolation and death. It is navigable during the rainy season, and affords ample facilities to merchants and traders of every sort to ship their goods, and to squatters and miners to send their products to market at a comparatively small cost. This river, with its many tributaries, is the chief means by which the large territory of the West is enabled to carry on its increasing trade. The above are the principal rivers that are distributed over the interior, all having their source, more or less, in the dividing range of mountains, and flowing down the western slope spread out in every direction, making a network of water supply for the benefit and well-being of the great plains through which they flow, and finally, all blending their waters in the Darling, become one magnificent stream that flows on through New South Wales and South Australia to the sea.

On the north of the colony, flowing into the Gulf of Carpentaria, are the Mitchel, Gilbert, Norman, Flinders, Leichhardt, Albert, and Nicholson rivers. This portion of Queensland was almost wholly unknown until within the last thirty years. The rapidness of its development of late years is due to its wonderful adaptation to the wants of the pastoralist and its mineral resources. Its timber, too, of excellent quality, affords encouragement to settlers and lumbermen, who have found its manufacture to be an enterprise of profit.

The most of the rivers of this region have their origin in the high tablelands of the interior south of the Gulf. For the most part they are shallow, except in the rainy season, and drying up in summer time. As they approach the Gulf coast they spread out through a marshy region, and are frequently lost, or at least have their banks badly defined, except where the mangrove, covered with a dense mass of creepers, indicates their course. Nature has given this region a wild charm to the huntsman, for in all the many marshes that give character to the Gulf of Carpentaria there is an abundance of game, such as duck, snipe, geese, and cockatoo. There are hundreds of streams in the interior that have their origin in the more elevated portions, and after having flowed on in their tortuous courses, through burning plains for hundreds of miles, are lost in the sands by absorption, or dried up by evaporation.

The grand characteristics of the great north-western portion of Queensland are, first, the marshy belt around the Gulf of Carpentaria, extending inland fifty to one hundred miles, occasionally broken by a ridge of high land reaching to the sea, all of which belt is green and luxurious in its tropical growth: beautiful to the eye, but not desirable as a healthful home for the European, at present, but doubtless will be reclaimed and made subservient to the wants of future generations, when all the waste places of earth shall be needed for man's sustenance. Beyond this belt are high lands, for the most part rocky, sandy, and barren, with a plentiful distribution of oases, where the boxwood grows in wearisome profusion, and the palm spreads its shady leaf to the sky.

Such is the brief picture of the physical features of the colony.

We have deemed it proper to give this general outline, that the reader may be the better prepared to follow the various steps taken in its development. A more minute account will appear in future chapters, when we come to trace the local history of its towns and cities, and mark the rapid transition from a wilderness state to one of comparative cultivation and prosperity. A hundred years is a very brief period in the cycles of time, but it is an exceedingly short space in which to witness the accomplishment of so grand a change as has been here effected. Pioneers of sturdy strength and hopeful heart came, under Imperial command, not to waste time and defeat the purposes of life, but to build a civilisation that would reflect honour upon king and workman. It was no easy task to lay the foundations of a future nation. It needed a master mind to guide, and willing hearts and strong to bear the brunt of honest toil; both were found. The sunny land that stretched her valleys to the mountain's base and decked her hills and lofty knolls with floral tints of beauty, invited man from other lands to come and rest content beneath the "vine and figtree" he could call his own. Here they came, obedient to the loving call, oppressed, yet hopeful, in the flush of noon; they dug, and toiled, and won.

CHAPTER VI.

THE FAUNA.

Animals.

THE animal kingdom in Australia differs from that of all other parts of the world. The reason of this must remain a secret so far as the conditions of animal life indicate. The soil, climate, and necessities of man all prove the adaptation of the continent to the development and improvement of those useful species in the animal kingdom that man has for ages been able to control and use for his comfort and benefit.

In the *Mammalia* class there is to be found a very poor representation. It is only in a few orders they are numerous. The *Quadrumana*, *Pachydermata* and *Ruminantia* of the old and new worlds are entirely absent: that is, none of the monkey tribe, nor any of the thick-skinned animals, such as the elephant, rhinoceros, or horse, and none of the ruminants, such as the deer, cattle and sheep, are found native of Australia; and yet, when brought to this country, they flourish and thrive well under the conditions here imposed—as witness, the unparalleled growth and development of the sheep and cattle enterprise.

The land animals that are most numerous on this continent are of the marsupial order, so named from the females having a pouch *(marsupium)* in which they carry their young. In fact, this is preëminently the land of marsupials.' A few are to be found in some of the Pacific islands and in America, but in other parts of the world they are unknown.

THE FAUNA.

The chief quadrupeds found in Australia are the kangaroos, embracing almost one hundred species. This animal was first seen by Captain Cook on the Endeavour River, on the occasion of his first visit to this continent, and then not until he was on his way back to England, in the year 1770. Under favorable conditions they multiply rapidly and their increase would become a universal pest were it not for the ravages of the dingo or native dog. The kangaroo lives upon vegetables, grass, roots and fruit. They go very rapidly, by a sort of a jump. They have very small heads compared with the size of the body. Their chief muscular and physical development is in the hinder parts. In size, some are as large as a man, weighing 200 lbs., and others not greater than a rat. They are of a timid, inoffensive nature, but show great vigour and strength in resisting an attack. When closely pursued in the chase they will turn and use their formidable claws with terrific force. They are valued by the natives for food, and hunted by the white man for sport. As civilisation advances the kangaroo disappears, being hunted down by both black and white, and must soon be an order of the past.

The Great Kangaroo (*Macropus major*) is to be found on the eastern coast, and is never seen in the western portions of the continent. Its tail is as thick as a man's arm, and is solid, and by its aid it not only balances its body but is able to accelerate all movements by its assistance.

The Western Kangaroo (*Macropus ocydromus*) is similar to the great kangaroo in appearance, with the exception that it is only about one-half the size. Its fur is finer and of a darker shade, and it confines itself to the western portion of Australia.

The Red Kangaroo (*Macropus rufus*) is of a bright orange color. It is found in the eastern part of the continent. Its habits are similar to the above.

The Red Wallaroo (*Macropus antilopus*) is a species that grows about four feet high, has short fur, brown color, with a lighter shade on the belly.

The Black Wallaroo inhabits the mountainous regions of New South Wales. It has shorter legs, but much more powerful than the red species, and is of a slate-grey color. Its skin makes a very beautiful fur rug.

Wallabies, or Brush Kangaroos (genus *Halmaturus*), are very numerous in nearly all portions of the Continent. They are very much smaller and shorter proportionately than the kangaroo, nocturnal in their habits, and committing their depredations at night. They are very destructive to roots and vegetables, when they are allowed to multiply in a community, which they do very rapidly when undisturbed by the dingo or huntsman.

Parry's Wallaby *(Halmaturus Parryi)* is the fleetest of all the species. It can outspeed the swiftest race-horse, is of a silver grey, and is valued highly for its excellent fur.

There is also the Black Wallaby, the Red-necked Wallaby, and the Rock Wallaby, differing from one another only in some slight manner, as their names would indicate.

There are other varieties, as the Silky Haired, or Nail-tailed Kangaroo; the Hare Kangaroo, very much like the common Hare; the Bettong, or Jerboah (genus *Bettongia*); and the Kangaroo Rats, some of these last-named species not weighing more than three pounds.

A Kangaroo hunt is said to be a sport of great interest and excitement. A party of two or four is organised, with a team of fast horses and open carriage, and a sufficient supply of food for men, horses, and dogs for a day or two's chase. A pack of greyhounds is put upon the hunt. The whole party dash in pursuit through the wooded plains after the kangaroo, which sometimes go in crowds of a hundred or more. Being more fleet than the dogs and horses, they outrun them, and leave them in the rear, but not for any great length of time, for the keen scent of the dogs enables the party to continue the chase until they are at last run down. It not unfrequently happens that the kangaroo will make for any water that may be near (and it is seldom they venture far from the streams), that they may have the means of protection, and hold the hounds at bay. They are thus able at times to seize the dogs with their fore feet, and drown them by keeping them under the water. When this means of protection is not at hand, they frequently back up against a tree, and fight with terrible desperation, and occasionally succeed in ripping or otherwise injuring the dogs with their hind claws. The huntsman, with his superior weapons, usually succeeds in the hunt, and the kangaroo, with all his fleetness, succumbs in the unequal chase.

A Native hunt is conducted on a plan peculiar to themselves. Without dogs or carriages, horses or guns, the black man might appear to be at a great disadvantage; but he is quite the equal of the white, being more cunning, and having greater powers of endurance, he starts on the track of the kangaroo, and follows it with indomitable perseverance until he overtakes the animal. Its flight is swift, but the huntsman, accustomed to his task, pursues it, regardless of hunger, thirst, or weariness, and is in no special hurry. At the close of the first day he sits down, builds his fire, and sleeps in quietness during the night. In the morning he renews the chase, resting as each night comes on, and knows full well that it is only a question of time when the object of his pursuit will fall exhausted, an easy prey to his greater endurance.

Among the Aborigines there is what is called the "Kangaroo Dance." It consists of a sort of imitation of the kangaroo in companies of one hundred or more; some in the act of grazing, some looking about them, others jumping in imitation of their spring, while others in the characters of dogs or huntsmen in close pursuit surround them in a noisy dance, and make the woods and hills ring with the barking and general jingle of their mimic clatter.

Phalangers *(Phalangistidæ)*, including Opossums, Native Bears, and Flying Squirrels are very numerous in many parts of the continent.

The Common Opossum *(Phalangista vulpina)* is an animal much valued for its fine long fur, of a woolly texture, and of an ash-grey color. It has large brown eyes, of a mild character. Its habits are nocturnal. It sleeps in the day, and, wide awake, goes forth at night to commit its depredations upon maize, roots and vegetables. There is the Ringtailed Opossum *(Phalangista Cookii)*, and other specimens differing therefrom in some minor characteristic, but all pretty much alike in their general appearance and habits. They live in hollow trees.

The Kaola, or Native Bear *(Phascolaretos cinereus)*, differs somewhat from the order of the Opossum. It is about two feet long, has fine short fur, white spots near its haunches, a tail so short that many have reported it from sight as having none. It is not a bear, but is nearer the type of an opossum, and, like the opossum, it sleeps in the day time, and wanders out at night in search of food. It cries like a baby, is inoffensive, and readily becomes domesticated. We have seen children carrying it in their arms, and fondling it as they would a pet dog or cat.

Flying Squirrels *(Pelaurista)* are very numerous, but being so nearly like those of other lands we deem it unnecessary to do more than mention the fact.

The Native Cat *(Dasyuridæ)* is of many species, and is ferocious. Some are very large, and do not hesitate to attack sheep, kangaroos, and opossums; and more especially is this the fact in the case of the Native Cat, classed *Dasyures viverrinus*, which is the most ferocious known, and has black fur and white spots, which distinguish it from all others.

The Native Tiger, or Hyæna *(Thylacinus cynocephalus)*, and the Devil of Tasmania *(Sarcophilus ursinus)* are of the cat order, and more ferocious still than any of the others named.

The Bandicoot *(Peramelidæ)* is very much like the kangaroo rat. Its food is grass, roots, and insects. There are three known varieties: (1) The Rabbit-eared Peragalia *(Peragalia legatis)*; (2) the Pig-foot Bandicoot; and (3) the Short-eared Bandicoot. They are all burrowing animals, and make their homes in the ground. And of the same nature is the Wombat *(Phascolomyidæ)*, a class not numerous at present; nocturnal, and very much resembling the opossum. There are many varieties, among which are the Black Wombat, the Broadfaced Wombat, the Sandy-furred, and the Black varieties.

Of the *Monotremata* order, which is the lowest form of mammalian life, are two specimens:

The Australian Hedge-hog, or Spring Ant-eater (*Echidna hystriæ*) is an animal of repulsive appearance, but useful. Its back is covered with sharp, spiny ridges. It has no teeth, but its tongue is furnished with thorny skin, which aids in mastication. It is said to be a delicacy as food, which the natives very much relish.

The Duck-billed Platypus, or Water Mole (*Ornithorhynchus anatinus*) is the most peculiar animal of Australia. It is said when it was presented to the scientists of Europe for examination and classification, they were suspicious that some imposture was attempted to be practised on them by persons whose aim was to play a practical joke. It has the bill and webbed feet of the duck, and in body very much resembles the otter. It is at home either in the water or burrowing in the ground, hence it is to be found in the creeks, lagoons and marshy places. The fur is short, soft, and of a brownish hue. They are exceedingly shy, and are usually seen in companies of many scores. On hearing the slightest noise they duck under water or burrow in the ground. It is the most marvellous of all the beasts of the animal kingdom. It partakes of the nature of quadruped, bird and reptile.

Of the *Placentalia* order there are to be found three species:

The Dingo, or Native Dog (*Canis dingo*), is the most prominent of the mammal genera. It is of a sandy colour, although there is a great variety of shades. It is sly, cunning, and harmless as a rule, but will attack man and beast when pressed by hunger. They collect in large numbers, and, like the wolves, destroy sheep, fowls, etc., if not watched and scattered. It is not larger than a foxhound, has a long nose, bushy tail, and resembles a cross between a dog and a wolf. It is easily tamed, but cannot be trusted. It is a silent, tenacious fighter. It does not cry when in pain, but howls dismally in the dead silence of midnight. It no doubt has served a good purpose in keeping in check the increase of many of the marsupial race, which otherwise would become an unbearable pest.

The Flying Fox (*Pteropus poleocephalus*) is a remarkable member of the bat tribe, of which there are no less than twenty-five species. It sleeps in daytime suspended from a tall branch. At night they visit orchards and fruit trees, and are very destructive on account of their numbers.

Birds.

In variety, beauty of plumage, and gorgeousness in colouring, the birds of Australia surpass those of all other parts of the world. It is said by most writers that they are "without song." This last stricture must be taken with some abatement. It is true that there are birds of lovlier song, whose notes charm by their variety and exquisite tones, but music is not wanting in the birds of Australia by any means. I think we put it fairly when we assume that what they lack in music they make up in their unequalled beauty of plumage; and to the extent that birds of other lands possess beauty in comparison, so those of this land possess song. The woods here ring with notes sweet enough to charm the listener.

The Cassowary (*Casuarius Johnsonii*) is the largest bird found in the country. It stands about six or seven feet in height, and is in appearance like the ostrich in color, shape and habits, but having hairy down instead of long feathers, and small wings, blue neck, and horny helmet. It is more fleet than the horse, has keen sight, and hence takes to the plains, where it can observe at a distance any foe and take to flight. It is a powerful bird, and in combat is a dangerous enemy, its kick having been known to break a horse's leg. They are rapidly disappearing from the country.

THE FAUNA.

The Parrot tribe, in which every color in the rainbow is found in combination, is the most numerously represented bird of the Continent, there being over eighty species, of which we mention only some of the more prominent.

The Sulphur-crested Cockatoo is a large white bird, with a yellow crest. It is a stately specimen of this family, and gives one the impression of its superiority. They are generally found in great numbers, and destroy crops of maize and other grains, showing cunning in selecting two of their number to watch as sentinels and give an alarm if approached by an enemy.

The Rose-breasted Cockatoo is a very common variety, and is seen generally on the plains in large flocks. When in flight overhead the rose color gives a most beautiful view.

The Black Cockatoo is a suspicious bird, and keeps at a distance from the haunts of men. It delights to dwell on the branches of the Banksiæ, Casuarinæ, and Eucalypti, these trees having a special charm for it. They generally go in pairs, and feed on seeds and fruits.

The Gang-Gang resembles the black Cockatoo.

The King Parrot is so called from its being the most showy member of the family. The male bird is more gorgeously decked in brilliant colors than the female, and seems to be aware of his own superior splendor, if one may judge from the ostentatious manner in which he behaves himself when strutting in the presence of his mate. They abound in the jungle growths of the river lands, and feed upon maize when opportunity presents.

The Lory is one of the most beautiful species—one of the most domestic birds of this class. It is crimson, with all the other colors blended harmoniously and in every manner of combination.

The Parrakeets number over forty varieties. They are as a rule much smaller than the above-named, yet possess nearly the same other characteristics. They seek high branches, and out-of-the-way spots in which to congregate and carry on their ceaseless chatter. They are remarkable for their brilliant colors.

The *Laniidæ*, or Shrikes, include the various Magpies, Butcher Birds, and the Caruck of the aborigines. They are found in all parts of the Continent. They resemble the crow (*Corvidæ*) family, and, like that bird, are capable of doing great damage to the orchards, being very fond of fruit.

THE FAUNA. 51

The Fly Catcher family (*Musciapidæ*) are also found in all parts of Australia. The species peculiar to the country is the Fan-tailed. Its coloring is varied and beautiful.

Robins are numerous, and are of the scarlet-breasted sort, much the same as found in America, except being more brilliant in color.

The Lyre Bird (*Menura superba*), called sometimes the Australian Pheasant, is not of that family, but is said to belong to the thrush genera. It is about as large as a domestic fowl, with a tail two feet long in the male, the chief feathers of which are arranged in the form of a lyre. It is one of the most beautiful of the bird creation, very shy and timid, and seeks the most sequestered spots. It is never seen near the abodes of civilisation, except when captured. In the seclusion of some ravine, overgrown with masses of tangled creepers, whose solitude is broken only by the rushing of the mountain stream, the loud and liquid notes of this bird is heard sometimes for days together, resembling the sound of "bleu-bleu," with the emphasis on the letter "u." It is said that this bird can make a perpendicular spring of ten feet from the ground to a branch, and, repeating the feat, rise from branch to branch in a remarkably short time, and reach the highest point almost as if in a continuous ascent. It is a mimic of great power, and can imitate the howl of the dingo, the scream of the cockatoo, or the bleating of the lamb.

The Wren of Australia is a bird of many species. The one most interesting is known under the name of the Blue Wren—remarkable for the great change in color it undergoes. In the winter season it is plain and unassuming, but as spring comes on it becomes transformed into one of the most gorgeous of the feathered tribe. Its beauty—chiefly in the male—rivals the most brilliant coloring found in any species. A corresponding change takes place in its life and song.

The Australian Lark is not a bird of very great interest, either in regard to plumage or music, and needs but a passing notice.

The Reed Warbler and the Long-billed Reed Warbler are varieties, found in all parts of the continent, of the *Silviadæ* family. They are singers of passable note, but cannot compare with their class in other parts of the world, whose chief glory is their power to warble forth music of exquisite sweetness.

The Finch is numerous, and remarkable for its vivacity and its ability to relieve the plains and valleys of their monotony.

The *Corcidæ* has but one species worthy of special mention, and that bears the not very euphonious name of White-eyed Crow, very much in appearance like the raven of the British Isles, and whose distinctive character is sufficiently expressed in its name.

The Honey Eater (*Melephagidæ*) is represented in more than fifty species, and is among the most numerous of the birds of this land. Their chief delight seems to be an increasing devotion to the flowers of the field. Their low songs of gladness speedily announce their presence with the coming of spring time. Where the flowers bloom they congregate. These birds are not remarkable for the sweetness of their music, yet their notes are sufficiently clear to win for them names which they have fairly won— as the Bell Bird, whose notes are clear as the ringing of a bell; Friar Bird, whose voice, low and solemn, chants forth a strain as doleful as the tomb; and Knife Grinder, as sharp as the grindstone's wail till its work is done. They prefer the *Banksiæ*, or Honeysuckle.

Among the Kingfisher family (*Alcedinidæ*) there are some remarkable birds, of most beautiful plumage, among which we mention Leach's Kingfisher, peculiar to the north of the continent; the Fawn-breasted Kingfisher, confined to Western Australia, the Sacred Kingfisher, found on the rivers, chiefly where the mangrove abounds; the Red-backed Kingfisher, of the interior; the Sordid, the Macleay, Yellow-billed, White-tailed, Azure, and little Kingfisher. But the most wonderful specimen of this tribe is the Laughing Jackass (*Dacelo gigas*), or the Gogobera of the natives. It is a marvellous bird. Why it is called by such a repulsive name is not difficult to understand when one becomes better acquainted with its nature and habits. It is one of the oddest of the winged tribe in the Australian Continent. It is a kingfisher of great size, almost as large as a crow. It is of a brownish hue, and has a remarkably large head and long heavy beak. Its chief delight is to pounce down upon the snake, or other reptile, and carry it by the neck to the branch of some neighbouring tree, where he is joined by his mate, sometimes by a great number of others. They delight in biting their prey, or amusing themselves by dropping it on the ground and picking it up again, and repeating the amusement amid the clatter of a general din. As the traveller passes near them, they seem to take great delight in joining in a most hideous exhibition of their vocal organs, that reminds one very much of the braying of an ass. When many of them are together they provoke laughter by the ridiculous tones they make in concert, ludicrous in the extreme, and contagious in effect. It is very easily tamed, and seems very much pleased with the advance of civilisation, for he has a jollier time of it under the new conditions of life that are thus thrust upon him.

Among *Raptores*, or birds of prey, there are but few species compared with those of other countries.

The Wedge-tailed Eagle is found in all parts of Australia—a noble-looking bird, and, like the golden eagle of the North, it is king; and among the feathered tribes none is more feared. It feeds upon small wallabies, kangaroos, and other animals of various kinds.

The White-bellied Sea Eagle is found only in the southern portion of the continent, and in the island of Tasmania. It is not so courageous as the above, but selects the fish of the sea for its prey.

The Whistling Eagle, or White Hawk, is plentiful in the brush lands, and is the terror of farmers' fowls, lizards, fish and lambs.

The White-headed Osprey is a fishing bird, not numerous, but frequently seen along the coast. It soars most gracefully.

The Hawk family is well represented in the Brown Hawk, Nankeen, White Goshawk, Radiated, Australian, and the Collared Sparrow Hawk varieties.

Among the genus *Falco* are the Grey Falcon, Black Cheeked, and Black and White breasted varieties.

Kites are numerous in all parts, among which are the Allied, Square-tailed, Black-shouldered, and Letter-winged species, some of which are interesting on account of their peculiarity.

There are also of Harriers the Allied and Jardine species, noted only for their beauty of plumage.

The family *Strigidæ* includes the true Night Owl, of which there are to be found in Australia the following species: The Masked Owl, the Sooty, the Delicate, the Rufus, the Winking, the Boobook, the Spotted Owls, and the Great Owl of the brush country. There is neither beauty nor loveliness in this bird to claim our attention.

The Rifle Bird, next to the Lyre Bird, is one worthy of honorable record, more on account of its beauty than for its music.

Of the genus *Podargus* there are twenty species in Australia and Tasmania. The tawny-shouldered species frequents the brush lands, sleeps on the high branches of a tree in daytime, and wanders out at night to search for insects.

More-pork, so called for its cry, is common in Tasmania, and loves to make his home in the branches of the *Casuarinæ*. Other varieties are the Moth-plumaged, Short-winged, Papuan Plumed, Marbled Podargi, and Goat Sucker.

The Swift (*Cypselidæ*) is a bird of migration. It appears in Australia in the summer season, and comes in clouds.

The Swallow (*Hirundinidæ*) arrives in the spring season, and is very similar to the sparrow of other lands. There is a great number of species, among which the Fairy Martin, Welcome Swallow, the Tree Swallow, and White-breasted Swallow are the most beautiful. Many other fine specimens exist.

The Australian Bee Eater (*Merops ornatus*) is an elegant bird, universally admired for the lovely blending of color in its plumage. It is migratory, and its presence is always hailed as the evidence of the approach of spring.

The Diamond Bird has six varieties in Australia and Tasmania.

Rasores, or Scratchers, are not largely represented. There are no Grouse, Partridges, Pheasants, or Ostriches.

The Pigeon (*Columbæ*) is the most conspicuous of the *Rasores* tribe. There are over twenty species, and all interesting to the ornithologist in point of color, form, and habits. The Wonga-Wonga and the Bronzewing are the most sought after for the delicateness of their flesh.

The Top-knot Pigeon is chiefly found on the eastern coast, but is speedily disappearing, on account of the resistance he meets with from civilisation. His habits lead him in immense numbers to visit the cornfields of the farmer in preference to the wild fig and cabbage palm of the forest; and hence he is deemed an enemy, and as such has fallen under the ban of the white settler. His flesh is coarse, and is not valued highly either by black or white.

THE FAUNA.

Among the smaller members of this family are many species of Doves, being very beautiful in plumage and valuable for the table.

The *Megapodidæ*, or Mound Builders, have three distinct genera: The Brush Turkey (*Talegalla*) is a bird about half the size of the domestic turkey, the same in color and general appearance, except in the tail, which more nearly resembles that of the barn fowl. It is remarkable for its mound-building. It scratches together an immense pyramid of leaves, brush, and dirt, until a mound about eight feet wide and six feet high has been formed, and then it proceeds to place its eggs, a few inches apart, as one would plant potatoes, and covers them up a foot deep, and allows the heated mass to do the work of incubation.

The Native Pheasant (*Leepoa ocellata*) is a genus of a single species. It is not properly a pheasant. It resembles the common fowl, but its habits are much more nearly like that of the Brush Turkey. It builds mounds of grass, sand, and sticks.

The Jungle Fowl is another mound builder. It builds of sand, shells, sticks and grass, frequently twenty feet in circumference, and five feet in height.

The Quail of this country is more like the Plover. There are two species, the Stubble and the Brown Quail.

Cursores, or Runners, are found in all parts of the continent.

The Emu (*Dromaius*) is the king of this family. We simply mention it in this classification, having more fully described it in a previous page. There is also the Spotted Emu of Western Australia; and, lastly, the Australian Bustard, known as the wild turkey of the plains.

Of the *Grallatores*, or Waders, there are many species, a few of which are worthy of special notice.

The Native Companion is a tall, stately bird, of most graceful bearing. This member of the *Gruidæ* family is found in the swamps and shallow lagoons.

The Straw-necked Ibis is a beautiful specimen of this class, and the White Ibis, of the same family, is large, shy, and seeks the seclusion of some lonely creek or shallow marsh.

Among the remaining members of this order are the Oyster Catcher, Water Hen, Crane, Plover, Sand Piper, Snipe and Spoonbill (all of which

THE FAUNA.

are birds of interest), together with the Bittern, Curlew, Crake and Rail, and Heron tribe.

The order of *Natatores* (Swimmers) are represented largely everywhere, among which is the Black Swan. This bird is peculiar to Australia. It is harmless, easily tamed, and is found in large flocks in lagoons and shallow rivers. They are chiefly hunted for their feathers and down, which are of a very superior quality.

The Cape Barren Goose is tame and scarce. The Wild Duck, or Black Duck, is sought for by the huntsman on account of its delicate flesh.

The Freckled and Pink-eyed Duck is common in Western Australia. There are several other species, less appreciated, called Shovel-nosed, Bluebill, Wood, and Musk Duck. The last-named is easily recognised by its smell.

On the sea coast there are several species, among which are the Seagull, Tern, Albatross, Petrel, Booby, Penguin, and Cormorant.

The Australian Pelican is found on the rivers, lagoons and swamps of all parts of the continent. They live on fish and molluscs.

Reptiles.

Reptiles are abundant, but few of them are of a venomous nature. The Black Snake, Brown, Brown-backs, Broad Scaled, Orange-bellied, and the Death Adder are the most venomous, but they are few in number. The non-venomous are the Diamond, Carpet (various), Pythons, Blind, Tree Snake, Sea and Fresh Water Snake.

Crocodiles, Lizards and Frogs, in several varieties, are met with in different parts.

Fish.

The Fish tribe is well represented in the following varieties, which are chiefly valued, and in many others of little importance: The Schnapper, Bream, Whiting, Pike, Groper, Sole, Flounder, Flathead, Sea Mullet, Gurnard, Dory, Taylor, Yellowtail, Jewfish, Rock Cod, Tarwhine, Black Fish, and Salmon, Perch, Garfish and Eel are abundant and delicious.

Molluscs, Common Oysters, Cockles, Mussels, Crayfish, Crabs, etc., are plentiful and cheap.

Insects.

Among Insects are Mosquitoes, Sandflies, Butterflies, Fireflies, and the Native Bee. Mosquitoes in marshy places and sandflies on the plains are the most annoying.

CHAPTER VII.

THE FLORA.

THE forms of vegetation in Australia are very distinct from those of all other countries, even in the same latitudes. The trees, grasses, ferns, flowers and mosses are of an exceedingly different type; and this fact cannot be traced to any peculiarity of soil, for the plants and vegetation of all other lands seem to flourish when introduced to this climate, with some few exceptions. One sees in the Botanical Gardens of Australia the Pine, Birch, and Maple of North America, the Oak of England, the Grape and Figtree of Southern Europe, and nearly every plant and shrub of other climes, taking kindly to its soil and flourishing to perfection. Notwithstanding its wonderful adaptation to all forms of vegetable life, the character of its trees and plants is unique, and without a parallel anywhere. The same trees meet you north and south, east and west. The Gum and Wattle (or, to use more classical terms, the *Eucalypti* and the *Acaciæ*) are the predominant genera. A peculiarity of these and many other species found here is the fact their leaves are vertical, and not horizontal, as is the case in North America and Europe. This arrangement must be regarded as a wise adaptation of the foliage to the unique conditions and imperative needs of the country. The leaves do not shed off the rain or sunshine from their roots; they admit both, on which account there springs up an undergrowth of grass and verdure that afford ample grazing for sheep and cattle.

The forests here are never dense and dark, but light and airy. They afford sufficient protection from the scorching rays of the sun, and answer all the requirements of the climate in being best adapted to modify its warmth, to equalise its temperature, and to afford timber of such quality as to be of greatest utility to the farming classes, who chiefly need its benefits.

Trees.

In appearance the Eucalyptus, as an ornamental part of Nature's handiwork, has been extensively criticised. Artists have with ridiculous unanimity pronounced it unpicturesque, and have decried its glory. They assume to say it is positively "ugly," but this the writer most emphatically denies. Without claiming artistic qualities that would entitle him to first place among authorities on such a subject, he begs at least the right in a free land to be his own judge of beauty. As in choosing a wife, or a horse, a man clings to his own judgment in regard to the beauty of the one and the value of the other, in preference to the arbitrary dictum of the expert, whose keener sense of what is beautiful is oftentimes warped by his blind submission to the rules of his art. The Gum Tree, in our judgment, possesses much of beauty. Its variety in form and color is an element that gives it a foremost place in the æsthetic realm. Every shade of green is apparent to the observer in its ceaseless change of tint from the brightest to the dullest hues. The eye can never tire as it rests upon the foliage and the form, for both assume an aspect new with every changing day. We have sometimes thought that the difficulties that confront the artist when he undertakes to paint it is the latent and unexpressed reason for his condemnation of the tree. The artist cannot paint it—it is above his art, and remains a subtle beauty that eludes his grasp and laughs to scorn his futile efforts to produce its form; and hence the eternal war. There are said to be over one hundred species of the eucalyptus, or gum tree.

The young tree is exceedingly beautiful. They are of a lighter and fresher-looking green. The eucalyptus sometimes grows to an enormous size, occasionally reaching four hundred and eighty feet in height and forty feet in circumference. It is not uncommon to see one rise a hundred feet before it sends out a branch. They boast a few specimens larger than the mammoth trees of California, both in height and girth. They are of every size, from the giant as above to the scrubs of the plains.

The Acacia, or Wattle Tree as it is generally called, is both useful and ornamental. It is distinguished by a vast number of yellow flowers, which bloom in tufts, and give it the appearance of a golden halo to the emerald landscape. It is useful for fencing and building purposes, and is much esteemed in this respect because of the ease with which it can be used. Its chief value is, however, its bark, which is largely used in tanning.

The Yellow Wood (*Flindersia Oxleyana*), Rose Wood (*Dysonylon Fraserianum*), and Cedar (*Cedrela Australis*) varieties are very much esteemed for ornamental work, household furniture and finishings. The Cedar grows abundantly along the rivers, and is of a quality superior to that of other lands; in fact it equals both in appearance, firmness, and polish the mahogany of Central America, which it very much resembles. Public buildings and private residences of the wealthier classes are usually finished in the natural grain of these woods, and present a very elegant appearance.

The Fig Tree is widely distributed. It grows in the very best soil, and attains a remarkable size. It is peculiar in its formation. At its base spring out great columns, that give one the impression of buttresses, or supports to the trunk from the roots, somewhat like a banyan tree, with the difference that the supports form part of the trunk. There are a great many species, such as the Rough-leaved Fig Tree (*Ficus aspera*), the Native Fig Tree (*Ficus eugenioides*), Moreton Bay Fig (*Ficus macrophyllus*), and the Small-leaved Fig (*Ficus rubiginosa*). All of these varieties are used for ornamentation in parks and roadways. They have large spreading branches, and thick foliage.

The Moreton Bay Fig has a leaf ten inches in length by four in width. It grows to an enormous size in some parts. It is of no value except as firewood, and food for birds and natives.

Of Pines (*Coniferæ*) there are several species, and here, as in other countries, they are most valuable for building purposes.

The Norfolk Island Pine is the finest member of this family. In New South Wales it has been known to grow to the height of two hundred and fifty feet, and twelve feet in diameter. It makes the very best weatherboards, flooring and farming timber, and hence is valued very highly.

The Moreton Bay Pine is another variety that grows chiefly in Queensland, near the coast; tall and slender, and is also valued for building purposes.

Another pine is known as the Bunya-Bunya. A remarkable tree. First, in appearance it is very much like an umbrella when viewed at a distance. Frequently it rises one hundred feet straight, and without the slightest decrease in its diameter, when suddenly the branches spring out regularly for a short distance, giving the impression of an open umbrella. It is also a fruit-bearing tree, resembling in that respect, though not at all in form, the nut pine of the Sierra-Nevadas in America. Every third year its crop of seeds or nuts is large, and is regarded by the natives on this account with much interest, for they gather the nuts and feast upon them in a banquet of general enjoyment, to which all the surrounding tribes are invited.

The Palm has only a very few specimens indigenous to the continent. The Cabbage Tree (*Livistona Australis*) grows in the coast district to a height of one hundred and twenty feet. It is used for fences and rough rural building. The leaves are on the top, and spread out like open fans. The natives use the young leaves as food, and it is averred that they equal in taste the cabbage. When more matured they make them into hats and fans.

The Bangalow is a palm of the same order. It grows about sixty feet in height, and is chiefly valued for its ornamentation.

The Apple is a spreading tree, very much in appearance like the apple tree of other lands. Its wood is hard and tough, and serves for naves of wheels. It is very little used, except as an ornamental tree for parks, gardens and roads.

The Mangrove is a low branching tree, found on the salt water estuaries on the coast. It is very abundant in the north and northern portions of the continent. Its wood is hard, and of very little commercial value beyond the small demand for stonemasons' mallets, made of this material.

The Australian Oak (*Casuarina*) grows abundantly on the coast, and is used for timber in house building, and in furniture of a special design.

The Honeysuckle varieties (*Banksia coccinea, integrifolia,* and *serrata*) are close grained, and are valuable for gun stocks, ribs and knees of boats. They grow on poor soil.

The Tea Tree is valuable for fencing, as it is imperishable, and lasts a lifetime.

THE FLORA.

The Tree Fern (*Alsophila* and *Dicksonia*) is one of the most beautiful to be found on the continent. It grows most abundantly in the mountain gorges through which some stream rushes on to the plains below. It forms a dense mass of foliage on either side of a river flowing through rocks and crevices, hiding from view the watercourse, except as it may be indicated by the rich verdure that invariably accompanies these rivulets. There are two varieties of special importance—*Dicksonia antarctica* and *Youngiæ*.

The Gigantic Nettle (*Laportea gigas*) is a most singular and dangerous tree. It grows sometimes sixty feet high and three feet in diameter. Its leaf is large and in shape of a heart, mulberry, or geranium, and, covering its surface, has a very fine nettle, which stings one upon the slightest touch, and which is most dangerous, as it has the power to excite cutaneous inflammations, which soon give the parts affected the appearance of numerous blisters, or many small ones blended in one, and not infrequently resulting in constitutional disturbances of a threatening character. Horses, cattle, and other animals are in danger as much as man in coming into contact with this tree.

The Grass Tree (*Xanthorrhæa arborea*) is one of the peculiar trees met extensively in rocky regions. Its presence always indicates barren, poor soil. It springs first in the form of long, tapering leaves directly from the roots, which continue to fall, and from which is formed a rough stem of about eight to ten feet high and a foot in diameter. From the top depends a cluster of grass-like foliage, and from the centre of this springs up a long stalk, which the natives use for the manufacture of spears, together with a gum that exudes from the tree. Some portion of the pith of the tree is used for food.

Food Plants.

The Food Plants are exceedingly scarce, at the same time sufficiently numerous to afford interest to the botanist and lover of natural history.

The Davidsonia Plum (*Davidsonia pruriens*) is one of the best fruit-growing trees of the continent. The fruit is small, but juicy and acid, with a pleasant flavour.

The Herbert River Cherry (*Antidesma Dallachyanum*) grows in the northern part of the continent, and is much relished for its acidity.

The Native Kumquat (*Atalantia glauca*) is found chiefly in the Maranoa. The flowers of this tree are sweet-scented, and like the orange blossom, are steeped in water and the essence used in the manufacture of jam.

The Native Lime (*Citrus Australis*) grows in the northern portions of the continent. It is said to rival the cultivated fruit, and is much sought after both by the natives and white settlers.

The Quandong (*Fusanus acuminatus*) is a small tree—grows to the height of twenty or thirty feet. The fruit is somewhat like a small plum, of a crimson color. It grows on the banks of rivers and streams. Its wood is fine grained, and is used for engraving.

The Native Plum (*Achras Australis*) is a very beautiful tree. It grows one hundred feet high. Its fruit, in appearance, is like the cultivated plum, but is of no account as an article of diet.

The Native Pear (*Xylomelum pyriforme*). This fruit only resembles a pear in appearance. It is about two and a-half by one inch in size, but is of no use.

The Native Cherry (*Exocarpus cupressiformis*) is remarkable for having the stone outside. The pulp is palatable, and much esteemed.

Jerry-Jerry is an annual plant, found among the grass. It is gathered by the natives, dried, and ground between stones. The woody fibre is separated, and the flour is made into a coarse bread, much relished by the aborigines.

The Native Pomegranate (*Capparis Mitchelli*) has dark green leaves. It bears a small fruit that is eaten raw.

A Melon grows in the northern part of the continent called by the natives Bingy-Bingy. It is very plentiful after a wet season. It is eaten raw, and is said to be palatable.

There is a small Cucumber (*Cucumis pubescens*) grows in swampy places. The fruit is hairy, and is eaten by Europeans.

The Karroo (*Dioscorea sativa*) is a robust annual vine that clings to trees and dwellings, and flourishes in wet seasons. Its tuberous roots are crushed in water, washed, and then mixed into a porridge, and regarded as a choice dish.

There is a small root like a potato that grows in the southern portions of the continent the natives cook in ashes, and deem it a luxury.

Wild Rice (*Oryza sativa*), called Kincyah, grows in the north in a wet season in the swampy regions around the Gulf of Carpentaria. The seeds are ground between stones, roasted, and eaten.

THE FLORA. 63

Tindil is another grass that grows in the same region whose seeds are gathered, made into a paste, baked, and eaten as a coarse bread.

The Boab Tree is one of the most important of food trees. It grows in the region of the Gulf of Carpentaria. It has flowers of sweetest scent, and its fruit grows to the size of an emu's egg. It has a woody shell. When broken the seeds inside are like large beans, and when baked in the ashes are eaten.

The Mimosæ are most beautiful in appearance. Bright yellow festoons hang from the branches of trees and from the rocks, from which an aroma comes that fills the air with perfume the most delightful. The wild bees suck honey from its blossoms.

Medicinal Plants.

The Medicinal Plants discovered in this land are neither few nor unimportant, though the methods adopted by the natives in securing their virtue were crude and unsatisfactory. But science and art have succeeded in finding many of great value in the treatment of diseases peculiar to this climate.

The Coolibar, or Flooded Gum, is a species of the Eucalyptus. It is found in low places, and is abundant in the vicinity of Carpentaria. Its leaves are used to capture fish. By placing a branch in the water the fish become stupefied, and are easily caught.

Messmate, a species of the Eucalyptus, grows all over the Australian continent. Its leaves, when young, are valuable as an anti-fever remedy.

Mooda, or Bulla-Bulla (*Ocimum sanctum*) is a small shrub about two feet high. It grows in Queensland and the northern part of New South Wales. An extract made from its leaves, called by the natives and first settlers bush tea, is found to be of great value in the treatment of fevers.

Flowers.

There is nothing that astonishes the stranger who visits this country for the first time so much as the variety and beauty of her flowers. If one has opportunities of making a thorough examination of the various parts of the continent he is overwhelmed with the magnitude and grandeur of the floral kingdom. The landscape everywhere is a shifting panorama of loveliness. The undulations that mark even the plains, and the wild grandeur of the rougher regions of the coast district, lend enchantment to the view;

but one is especially struck with the profusion of beauty that tints the landscape from one end of the continent to the other. There is a plethora of color in the flowers that everywhere meet you. They are not placed here and there only, to give one the impression of limit; they cover mountains and valleys in all kinds of form and shades of beauty. Climbers, rich in crimson and interspersed with every other color, are multiplied by millions, and scattered with a lavish hand that knows no stint or bound, save that of infinitude itself, until every shrub, and plant, and bush, robed in splendor, makes the wide continent gay with blue and gold and many-colored dyes.

When Dr. Solander and Mr. Banks, the first English botanists who visited this continent, looked out upon the hills and plains surrounding the bay where Captain Cook's party first entered, they were delighted with the view. While they were prepared for the discovery of new plants and species unknown to science, they were astonished to find in this strange land a gorgeous display of beauty that rivalled all other parts of the world in variety, extent, and the tints that their great numbers gave to the landscape.

No more appropriate name could have been bestowed upon the place than the term Botany—a name, it is true, that has been associated in the minds of many in this and other parts of the world with the degradation incident to the enslaved servitude characteristic of its first years, yet one that can never be tarnished by any historic accident—as it is at once suggestive of all that is lovely and truly characteristic. The hills and valleys of this country are rarely seen without a beautiful covering of the most variegated colors, that seem to paint the scene with all the changes of the rainbow. It is so mild in winter that Nature seems to continue in her accustomed task of clothing herself most gorgeously. When the Creator of the Universe conceived a plan by which He should carry on His work, He thought it good to stamp every part with beauty. He never failed to fix this feature on all the works of His hands—the heavens that are stretched out like a garment, studded with a countless host of twinkling stars; the mountains, that toss their craggy heads to the sky; valleys, hills, and plains; rivers, brooks, and lakes; clouds and snow, and all forms of life are clothed in beauty that comes from a mind full of the best thoughts towards man. Beauty follows in His footsteps, whether in sky or land, in continent or island. In noting this fact, we are only attempting to read a language none of us can fully understand, and which the ages alone can reveal.

This continent can boast of most gorgeous coloring in its floral kingdom, and of a greater variety than is to be found elsewhere. It would be hardly expected in a work of this kind to enumerate every species and characteristic. We will confine ourselves to the task of examining what we find most peculiar and attractive.

Mimosæ have small yellow flowers that grow in the mountainous regions, and cover the slopes with their bright golden tints.

The Waratah (*Telopea speciosissimæ*), or native tulip, is one of the most brilliant in color. It grows about four or five feet high, has a slender stem, surmounted by a most vivid crimson. It blooms in November.

The *Doryanthes excelsa*, or Gigantic Lily, is one of the most beautiful clusters anywhere to be found, of a gorgeous crimson. There first springs up a cluster of bending leaves that curve gracefully towards the ground From the centre a stalk grows some ten or fifteen feet high, on the top of which is formed a cluster of about a dozen buds, which expand into bloom like a well-arranged table bouquet, about a foot in diameter. While its prevailing color is that of crimson, it is shaded often into pink and brown. It flowers in October and November.

The *Magnolia grandiflora* is a tree of dark, glossy foliage and large white flowers, from which an exquisite perfume is derived, and which makes it a welcome habitant in the gardens of all. You will meet it in the walks of culture as an ornamentation, and in the wilds of the mountains.

The Rock Lily is an attractive flower, that grows in the rocky mountainous regions.

The Native Rose is a small flower that is found all over the continent. Of all the beauty that blooms the rose stands pre-eminent. This Australian species is modest, small, and enduring, and sought by all for its value in decoration.

The Christmas Tree (*Ceratopetalum gummiferum*) is one of the most valued of all that grows; even the ground where it is found is held sacred. It is used as a Christmas decoration; red in color, with tints of pink. In November it is covered with small white blossoms, which gradually change to red in December, caused by the falling of the white.

THE FLORA.

The Rice Paper Plant is cultivated for its beauty. It is delicate in form and color.

The Ferns are in great variety and beauty of design.

The Trumpet Jasmine (*Tecoma jasminoides* and *Tecoma Australis*) are flowers of a deep red.

Sterculia acerifolia (Flame Tree) is a large timber tree; leaves eight to ten inches in diameter; oblong lanceolate; flowers of a rich red. One of the most gorgeously colored. Cultivated as a flower plant.

Castanospermum Australe, or Bean Tree. Leaves large, unequally pinnate. Flower is large, yellow, in loose axillary or lateral racemes. Seed like a chestnut, eaten roasted; and is much valued as an ornamental tree.

Styphelia trifolia, a tall shrub, quite glabrous; branches very minutely pubescent; leaves obovate-oblong one inch; flowers, pale pink and yellow. Grows in vicinity of Blue Mountains and Port Jackson.

Grevillea robusta, a tree sometimes small and slender. Sometimes eighty to one hundred feet high. Leaves pinnate, six to eight inches long, and nearly as broad.

Callistemon lanceolatus. Tall shrub; leaves lanceolate, one to three inches in length; flowers pink; spikes two to four inches long; stamens red, and beautiful.

There are also the *Hebiscus splendens*, a magnificent flower; the *Actinotus helianthe*, exquisite and lovely; and *Clianthus Dampiere*; and a few others that present sufficient variety and beauty to make nature lovely in its coloring.

What is most astonishing is the utter indifference of most Australians to this widespread wealth of flora nature seems to have poured from her lap in such munificence and beauty; that, reared among its grandeur and sublimity, and long accustomed to its variety, the multitudes are content to remain in total ignorance of their worth and the honorable place they have assigned them by the learned scientists of the world.

CHAPTER VIII.

GOVERNOR PHILLIP.

1788-1792.

THE loss of the American colonies in 1776, when they declared themselves independent of English rule, put an end to the practice of sending over to America their felons, as was the custom of the mother country. The spirit of self-government had won in the new world, and, emboldened by the victory, many in Ireland and England sought to resist the authorities in the hope that the masses at home might be induced to assert the same freedom; but they were adjudged political agitators worthy of bonds. The jails of England soon became filled to repletion, not alone by the ordinary criminal, but by a large number of political offenders, who were deemed an unsafe element to be at large in the body politic of that day.

What to do with a large and increasing number of people who were restless under the restraints imposed by the law had been for a long time a "problem most difficult to solve." To crowd the jails and prisons with such would only arouse the latent spirit of brotherhood that would too surely awaken sympathy and assistance, and throw upon the State the care and burden of an element dangerous to its peace and stability, and expensive to maintain; and, to adopt the principle of making her convicts defray the expense of their own maintenance by employing them in the manufacture of useful articles, would bring their labor into competition with the working masses, and demoralise the working man, lessen his chances of honest toil, and tend to increase crime by making it profitable to the manufacturer who trades in convict labor for his own financial benefit. England solved this problem in a broader and grander sense than had ever been attempted by the nations. She was wont to send this class of her subjects to America and the West Indies, with the hope and purpose that they should have an opportunity of working out their own redemption by a career of well-doing.

England's policy was not intended to punish as much as to save the transgressor. She was the first to recognise the value of mercy as well as justice in the administration of the government. This last theory is not a new one. It is as old as Christianity itself; but even Christian governments were slow to admit the principle of mercy and forgiveness into their methods of procedure. They were always eager to visit with speedy vengeance those who were trangressors against their notions and dogmas, and hence the most cruel types the world has ever witnessed are so-called Christian governments, who, in the name of Justice, have pronounced all who differ from themselves in politics, religion, or learning, criminals; and their universal practice was to punish them with terrible severity, even unto death.

The wisdom of England in colonising new regions with such an element has frequently been called in question; nevertheless, history records but one answer, and that is favorable to English policy. In every well-tried instance it has proved successful, not only to the colony, but to the mother-country as well. England could ill afford to retain within her penal institutions a vast multitude of people, some of whose crimes consisted in the free expression of their individual political or religious sentiments; some in desperate acts, induced by the goading sense of wrong under which they were compelled to suffer at the instance of unjust laws; some as law-breakers, simply because of the conditions under which they were forced by the higher and wealthier class to live, compelling starvation or crime; and some, as a matter of course, of the ordinary type of criminality.

It was partly to get rid of this burden, and partly to colonise the new country of the south, but chiefly to give to the bound the privilege of emancipation, that England fitted out a fleet to carry the first colonists to Australia, and sufficient supplies for their support during the period necessary to inaugurate an enterprise of such great importance.

In the first book published on Australian affairs (which was but a small pamphlet, printed in the early part of 1787, presumably just before the colony was formed) we have the following words: "The plan of forming a settlement in the environs of Botany Bay has been laid before Parliament, and unanimously approved."

And from an undated letter, written by Captain Arthur Phillip, we have the following extract: "The laws of this country (England) will, of course, be introduced into New South Wales, and there is one which I would wish to take place from the moment his Majesty's forces take possession of the country—that there can be *no slavery in a free land*, and, consequently, *no slaves*."

The above extracts are sufficient to show: First—That the whole question had been seriously discussed by the British Parliament; and, second, that English law was to govern the land. The fleet consisted of eleven vessels—the "Sirius," "Supply," three store ships, named "Barrowdale," "Fishbourne," and "Golden Grove;" and the six transports, the "Prince of Wales," "Alexander," "Scarborough," "Lady Penrhyn," "Charlotte," and "Friendship." The company consisted of six hundred male convicts, two hundred and fifty females, two hundred marines as a military guard, and forty of the officers wives, besides a number of children. This number was reduced during the voyage by sickness to about one thousand souls. They left England on the 13th May, 1787, and arrived at Botany Bay on the eighteenth, nineteenth, and twentieth days of January, 1788.

Captain Phillip, finding the harbor of Botany Bay exceedingly shallow, and the surrounding country destitute of fresh water supply, became dissatisfied with the locality as a place to begin a settlement, and immediately resolved upon making a more suitable selection. With the avowed purpose of investigating Broken Bay (about twenty miles north) he, with a few of his more trusted officers, including Captain Hunter (afterwards made Governor), and three boats, set sail northward. He, however, deemed it advisable to examine Port Jackson before going further. An extract from his own account will most fully present to the reader the steps taken towards the accomplishment of this object. He says: "I began to examine the bay as soon as we anchored, and found that, though extensive, it did not afford shelter to ships from the easterly winds. I did not see any situation to which there was not some strong objection. Seeing the possibility of the swamps rendering the most eligible situation unhealthy, I judged it advisable to examine Port Jackson. I went round with three boats, taking with me Captain Hunter and several other officers, that, by examining different parts of the port at the same time, less time might be lost. We got into Port Jackson early in the afternoon, and had the satisfaction of finding the finest harbor in the world, in which a thousand sail of the line may ride in the most perfect security. The different coves were examined with all possible expedition. I fixed on the one that had the best spring of water, and in which the ships can anchor close to the shore. This cove, which I honored with the name of Sidney, is about a quarter of a mile across at the entrance, and half a mile in length. We returned to Botany Bay on the third day."

On the 26th of January, 1788, the entire fleet was brought round and anchored in Sydney Cove; the convicts landed, or at least as many of them as were needed to clear a space for the erection of the rude structures that were to receive the first settlers of Australia. For a time the sound of the axe, saw, and hammer resounded over the hills. In the incredibly short space of ten days everything was in readiness, and on the 7th of February, 1788, Governor Phillip caused all to assemble on the western side of Sydney Cove, near Dawes' Point, and there was read to them by Captain David Collins, Judge-Advocate, the Commission of the King under which the colony was established. The first officers under the Governor were appointed, and from that date began the colonial development of New South Wales.

Governor Phillip on this occasion expressed great faith in the future of the colony, and advised all present to work in the common cause of brotherhood and English colonisation. His faith in the future greatness of the country he maintained until the end of his days.

A short time subsequent to the landing of Governor Phillip and his first colonists, M. de La Perouse, a French explorer, entered Botany Bay, and expressed great surprise and pleasure at the successful inauguration of the colony. He departed on the 10th of March, 1788, after having buried a priest, who had died but a day or two previously. A monument was erected many years afterwards to the memory of this good man, and still attests the respect the French people have for his name. M. de La Perouse was wrecked on his return passage on the Mallicola Isles, as learned many years afterwards. A monument was erected by the French to his memory, and marks the place of his landing on the north of Botany Bay.

The New South Wales colony was very fortunate in having as its first governor a man of so many noble parts as Captain Arthur Phillip proved himself to possess, and the British Government chose wisely in selecting such a man for the important post of planting a colony in this far-off part of her dominions, with the various elements entrusted to his care. He was a well-tried officer before he received this commission, and was singled out from many others of equal ability, no doubt, in statesmanship, education, and general worth; but the special qualifications needed in an enterprise of this kind were not overlooked by those in authority at home, and were worthily exemplified in the official and personal character of Governor Phillip, a man esteemed by all his officers and revered by even the convict element, whose interests and welfare he never for one moment lost sight of or ignored.

The circumstances that surrounded the establishing of a colony in a land remote from the head government, and consequently removed from all direct supervision, made it imperative to clothe the first governors with almost autocratic powers. In the hands of a good man, who possesses intelligence as well, such may be used with advantage; but, in the hands of incompetency or narrow-mindedness, it is fraught with danger, not only to the individual ruled, but to the body politic also. There was no such danger anticipated in this instance, and history is glad to record the universal verdict rendered by all who were cognisant of his daily acts, both private and public, that, as Governor, he was just and benevolent; as a man, he was unselfish and sympathetic; and, as a servant of his King, he was loyal and true.

In the early part of 1789 the Hawkesbury River was explored, and its valleys pronounced most suitable for agricultural purposes. A settlement was formed, but the inexperience of the first tillers of the soil in farming methods resulted in failure, and hence from that source little could be expected to supplement the supplies they carried with them from England. The loss of the "Guardian" transport on its way out with additional supplies filled the colonists with dismay, for their stores were fast becoming exhausted as the months passed by, and starvation threatened them; and no word had been received from England since their first landing, nearly a year previously, Despair and anxiety siezed every one. It was impossible for them to replenish their stores from the country's resources, or to expect the timely arrival of help from the mother country. Between them and England was fourteen thousand miles of sea, over which they could not readily speak their wants, and the country at their feet was unknown and unexplored. No fruit or root produced fit for man's sustenance could be found, and, besides, the country was inhabited by hostile people that made it dangerous for the colonists to venture far from their settlement in quest of game.

In their extremity they sent the ship "Sirius" to the Cape of Good Hope for supplies in January, 1789, which returned in May of the same year. When their stores became short again they found it impossible to replenish in the same manner, the ship "Sirius" having been wrecked in the meantime off the coast of Norfolk Island, to which it was sent months previously with many of the convicts, in the expectation of being able to raise fruits and other products that would supplement their stores.

Governor Phillip evinced great consideration to all classes under his care in the hour of their destitution and need, foregoing his own personal comforts and sharing with all under him half rations, or less. He caused all public work to cease, the men being too weak to engage in work. The cattle and other stock were all killed to supply their immediate wants, except a few heads that escaped to the meadows, and, in a wild condition, were found years afterwards, when they had increased to a large herd. The suspense of this young colony was ended on the 3rd of June, 1790, by the arrival of the ship "Lady Juliana," with provisions and live stock, from London, and followed shortly afterwards by "Justinian," and the transports "Surprise," "Neptune," and "Scarborough." This last-named ship brought out what was afterwards known as the 102nd Regiment, or the New South Wales Corps—an organisation of volunteers, who were intended to be the guardians of the peace, and who were expected to aid the authorities in the administration of order and good government, in consideration of which they were to receive grants of land, the free service of convicts, and other privileges. This military organisation became a fruitful source of trouble and wrong. They selfishly conceived the idea that the entire colony and country existed for their own aggrandisement. Not satisfied with the liberal intentions of the Home Government, with a few honorable exceptions, they sought to control all trade—to become the possessors of the lands, and to utilise all the labor of the convict classes for their own benefit. With this condition of things it is not a matter of surprise that the enormous cruelties practised on the early convicts in carrying out the selfish aims of these masters would result in the attempted or successful escape of some, and their organisation into bands of bushrangers; and retaliation on the part of others, ending in personal violence, making a condition of society in the early years of Australian history anything but pleasant to contemplate, and over which we will draw the veil and await the judgment of Him who alone can pronounce justly.

Governor Phillip made frequent appeals to the authorities in England, on the ground of failing health, to be permitted to resign his position. This was only granted after a period of five years. He sailed for England on the 11th December, 1792. His personal sacrifice on behalf of the colony was great. He encouraged settlement on the lands, sought to afford the prisoner every opportunity to recover his manhood and regain his lost standing. At the close of his reign in 1792, there were of live stock 102; of lands under cultivation, 1,703 acres; and 3,500 inhabitants. He was pensioned by the Government, and lived in England until his death in 1814.

Interregnum.
1792-1795.
UNDER MAJOR GROSE AND CAPTAIN PATTERSON.

The administration of affairs devolved upon Major Grose, who took command on the retirement of Governor Phillip; but his career was of short duration. Neither his moral character nor military tactics gave satisfaction. He sought to merge the civil into the military, and thus begun a system of antagonism between the New South Wales Corps and the early settlers, both bond and free, that carried with it a train of evils which took years to eradicate.

After a few months Major Grose was relieved of the position, and Captain Patterson succeeded to the administration as Lieutenant-Governor of the colony. His rule was an improvement on the former, although the evils begun under Major Grose were already so well rooted that they continued to some extent at least to grow into a question of contention between the colony as a British enterprise and the rights of the New

South Wales Corps. Lieutenant-Governor Patterson did not neglect his own private interests in the struggle.

On January the 16th, 1793, the emigrant ship "Bellona" arrived with the first company of "free settlers" on board. These were furnished by the Government with two years' provisions, agricultural implements, and free servants. The first settlement was made on Liberty Plains, but this was found to be comparatively unsuited for agricultural purposes, and hence was soon abandoned, and the Hawkesbury River selected in its stead.

Attempts were made during this year to cross the Blue Mountains by Captain Patterson, Lieutenant Dawes, and Quarter-Master Hackey, but they were unsuccessful.

In the year 1793 another period of privation occurred. This time, though widespread and serious, yet it was when they were about to reap a good crop of wheat, and were in no dread of starvation, for they could live on bread alone. In this year the first place of public worship was erected in the Sydney settlement, mainly through the exertions of the Rev. Mr. Johnson. It was during this year also the Cow-pastures were found, fifty miles from Sydney, beyond the Nepean River, and named from the fact that a large number of cattle were here grazing, and the pasturage of the richest character, the cattle being the increase from those that had strayed from the Sydney herd in 1788.

CHAPTER IX.

GOVERNOR JOHN HUNTER.

CAPTAIN HUNTER, whose ship "Sirius" was wrecked off the coast of Norfolk Island in the year 1789, returned to England in 1791, and was chosen by the Home Government to succeed Governor Phillip in the management of Australian affairs. He arrived in Sydney on the 7th September, 1795. Great changes had taken place in the few years he was absent from the colony. Many of the convicts, whose term of enforced servitude had expired by limitation or by clemency, had entered upon agricultural pursuits, and had become honorable and successful farmers, having received small portions of land in accordance with Government policy. Sufficient had been accomplished in this department of labor to prove beyond a question that the soil was well adapted to the production of cereals, and that in abundance; that there need be no fear in regard to the capabilities of the soil, and that the future food supplies for the colony depended on the encouragement granted to those who were disposed to engage in that enterprise. The prospect was a bright one so far as the farming interests were concerned. On the other hand, an element of great danger to the peace and harmony of the young colony began to exert its baneful influence.

The New South Wales Corps, which was afterwards known as the 102nd Regiment, was a military organisation selected in England for service in Australia, most of whom came to the colony in the second fleet in the year 1790. Many of its officers were of a low type. They were not chosen for their high moral character, and during the early years of the colony they did not impress the early settlers or the convicts with any marked nobleness of character. Debauchery, dishonesty, and recklessness among a part tended to degrade them all in the eyes of the people generally, and to develop a condition of things altogether at variance with English notions of morality.

The brief interregnum during which the officers of the corps administered the affairs in the colony gave them precedence over all others, and they were not slow in exacting the full measure of subserviency to their will. The superiority of their position gave them great advantage in getting possession of the best lands, the best service of the convicts, and the control of trade, all of which engendered a spirit of strife between themselves and the mass of people, both bond and free, who were equally ambitious of success, and whose rights under the Crown were supposed to be guarded by this same military corps. Private speculation by the officers in the "supplies," to which they had easy access by virtue of their position, led to a selfish policy that brought them into conflict with other traders, and with the class they were to guard. They soon found that their schemes of personal aggrandisement had to be carried out by resorting to the most arbitrary measures, enforced by all the military tactics and methods of which they were capable. It was impossible to discriminate between the convict and their rulers in regard to morals. In many instances the more elevated and honorable of the two was the convict, who frequently was dealt with most cruelly for refusing to bow in a spirit of sycophantish acquiescence; and, as on a former occasion, the baser sort of rulers cried, "He saved others, himself he cannot save;" so now, officers and leading representatives of the Government, though they themselves were steeped in all kinds and degrees of crime, tauntingly cried, "Convict, you cannot help yourself," and used their power to perpetrate, in the name of "righteous discipline," the darkest crimes that ever stained the lustre of a fair land.

The officers of the corps had practically the monopoly of trade, and used their opportunities for selfish purposes; and by engaging the services of the best looking and more attractive of the female portion of the convict class, and adopting them as clerks and assistants under the thin garb of an assumed innocency, they degraded themselves to a condition far below those whom the Home Government sent here to protect. Had they formed these alliances under the sanction of a legal marriage, they would have done honor to themselves and good to the young colony, whose infant life their public and private acts had done much to destroy.

While we deem it proper to draw the veil over this chapter of gloom, we are forced to acknowledge, in justice to historic truth, that the conduct of the officers and leading members of these gaurdians of the peace was such as to produce a condition of society out of which profligacy and impurity grew, and became the prolific sources of crime.

Governor Hunter brought with him a press, type, and other requisites needed in a printing office. He encouraged free immigration, as did Governor Phillip—that is, the immigration of free people, to whom would be granted farms and servants free of all cost. As a result of this policy we find many availing themselves of the scheme, and a large settlement was formed near the Hawkesbury, that grew in a short period into a prosperous farming section, and did the colony very great service in after years.

Provisions were exceedingly costly and difficult to procure during the first years of Governor Hunter's administration, partly because of their scarcity, but chiefly on account of the manner in which they were handled by those who had control of the avenues of trade. Clothing also became a scarce article. The Governor, writing shortly after his arrival in the colony, on December 21st, 1795, to the Duke of Portland, said: "We have now no article of slops (meaning by the term ready-made clothes). Your Grace's own private feelings will suggest what I must experience by continual petitions from a people nearly naked." The scarcity of food and clothing during many of these early years did much towards discouraging immigration, and made the experiment of colonisation in Australia one of doubtful prospects. There was a constant change from hope to fear, and from plenty to want. They were not well prepared to meet seasons of drought; and, when there was an abundance, they were not sufficiently frugal to lay by in store for future emergencies. Governor Hunter did his utmost towards the comfort and prosperity of the various and somewhat conflicting elements he had to deal with in the new colony.

He encouraged exploration. It was during the first year of his administration that Bass and Flinders explored the coast southward. George Bass, a young surgeon, and Matthew Flinders, a midshipman, came out with the Governor in the ship "Reliance." They were young men of excellent character, and enthusiastic in their desire and ambition to become explorers in this new world; and within a very few weeks after landing they purchased a small boat, only eight feet in length, and christened it "Tom Thumb." Taking with them a small boy, they set sail, and their first task was to examine thoroughly Botany Bay. After doing so to the satisfaction of the Governor, who was much pleased with the chart they made of the bay, they set out on a more extended trip, ostensibly to search for a river that was reputed to flow into the ocean farther south. They battled hostile natives and a rough sea for several days, at times requiring their closest vigilance to watch the one, and constant effort to bale out the splashing waters that in a few moments would sink their miniature craft; and finally succeeded in returning to Sydney with a chart of the coast extending south forty miles, embracing a minute description of Port Hacking. At the same time an accidental exploration was made of the coast inland, or overland, by a party led by a Mr. Clark, who, with many others, had been wrecked in a vessel called "Sydney Cove," on the Furneaux Island, and who, in small boats, attempted to reach Sydney and obtain help, but were a second time wrecked on Cape Howe, and thrown ashore by a violent storm. Finding themselves in an unknown region, with hostile natives all around them, they undertook the task of reaching Sydney by walking all the way—three hundred miles. Their food and strength soon became exhausted, and many died from hunger and fatigue, some at the hands of the natives, and but Mr. Clark and a very few others reached their destination. Only a meagre report could be given of this country by the few survivors, but, as far as given, was found in after years to be correct. The crew was rescued from their imprisonment at Furneaux Island by parties sent down from Sydney, and a more thorough knowledge obtained of the coast region.

Flinders had in the meantime to join his vessel, the "Reliance," which was sent to Norfolk Island. Bass obtained from the Governor a boat, provisions, and seamen, and set sail in December, 1796, to make an exploration of the south coast, which he did in a very thorough and satisfactory manner. He visited and made a chart of Shoalhaven River, Jarvis Bay, Twofold Bay, Cape Howe, Ninety Mile Beach, Wilson's Promontory, Bass' Straits, Western Port (into which he was driven by a storm), and Corner Inlet. Altogether on this trip he sailed six hundred miles, and made an approximately correct chart of the coast.

In 1798 he and Flinders, who had returned from Norfolk Island, were gratified by having a small vessel, the "Norfolk," placed at their disposal for a further exploration of the south. This time they visited the island of Van Dieman's Land, and discovered the river Tamar and Port Dalrymple. It was on the strength of their report that a settlement was made in 1803-4 in Tasmania (Van Dieman's Land). This was the last service rendered by Bass to the cause of exploration. He entered upon a trade speculation in South America; but his vessel, with her cargo, was seized, himself sent to the mines and never heard of since. Flinders continued his investigations from Sydney northwards, and returning to England in his ship "Norfolk," he published charts of the Australian coast as far north as Hervey Bay. The British Government sent him in the ship "Investigator" to continue his explorations of the entire coast of Australia. And this he did. Sailing first to South Australia, and having discovered Kangaroo Island and Spencer's Gulf, he entered Port Phillip but ten weeks after the discovery of that port by Lieutenant Murray.

It was during the year 1798 that Lieutenant Shortland discovered a commodious harbour for small vessels about sixty miles north of Sydney, at the mouth of two rivers. Pit coal was here found. The main river running into the harbor was called Hunter, and the other one William River, in honor of Governor Hunter and William Patterson, Lieutenant-Governor.

In 1799 it was reported that a convict by the name of Wilson found a route across the Blue Mountains. This was not credited, because, in the first place, a convict reported it; and, secondly, Bass had tried it, but failed previously, and if Bass failed in an enterprise of that kind it must be on account of the impossibility of accomplishing the feat.

It was during this year (1800) that the press and printing material brought into the colony by Governor Hunter were first utilised. A printer was found among the convicts, who was forthwith employed in founding the great institution of the Press in Australia. At first official notices only were published, but within a short time, in 1803, the *Sydney Gazette* was begun, and continued for thirty years to be the Government organ.

Several floods had already occurred, which were found to be one of the chief drawbacks to the infant settlements on the Hawkesbury. The damage done to the farming interests was considerable. The floods of January, and again in August, 1795, just previous to Governor Hunter's arrival, destroyed many valuable acres of grain; and these alternated with droughts.

He left New South Wales on September 28th, 1800, and was made commander of the "Venerable," 74 guns. In the Channel one of his sailors fell overboard. He ordered the vessel to be put about in a most dangerous position, in consequence of which she was lost. At the court-martial he was asked why he had caused the ship to be put about. He replied, "That the life of a British seaman was of more value than any ship in his Majesty's service." He was honorably acquitted. He died about 1816.

The first wars with the natives occurred early in the history of the white settlement, and generally grew out of acts of plunder on both sides. The natives could never understand what right the white man had to come into his country and plunder his game and take his lands; and the white settler thought it was wicked for the natives to come down and steal his corn and cattle, and hence the conflict in their respective notions of injury done by each other. Hunger led the black man to go in search of food, cattle or corn, wherever he could find them; and the colonist believed the only way to protect his acquired interests was to seize the game and lands of the natives, and to use his superior weapons of death in shooting down like a dog a blackfellow whenever any resistance was offered to his desires.

CHAPTER X.

GOVERNOR PHILIP GIDLEY KING.

1800-1805.

CAPTAIN KING was appointed successor to Governor Hunter in the management of affairs in New South Wales. He had been brought into prominence in connection with the settlement of Norfolk Island, for it was to him that Governor Phillip entrusted this task in the year 1788. His service in that connection, and also in other parts of the colony, won for him the confidence and esteem of the authorities at home. He was, therefore, appointed governor at a time of vital importance, and when adverse elements were working discord in the new colony. It required a man of great wisdom and vast experience among men to manipulate the affairs of the young settlement with that delicacy and firmness which the conflicting interests of the parties concerned made it imperative to possess. Governor King was a man of more than ordinary judgment—a man of good executive ability, and sincerely desired to administer the law justly, and in the interests of all portions of the community; but it was no easy task to cope with the elements of licentiousness, discord, and selfishness by which he was surrounded, and hence he failed in carrying into effect many of his most cherished schemes, on which account some writers have pronounced him a failure. He found a system of trade that had done much towards making the country a settlement of universal drunkenness, which he sought to check, but failed. The officers and many of the members of the New South Wales Corps found it profitable to buy and sell to convicts and settlers at enormous profits—one writer has said "at twelve hundred per cent.—and finding the article most cherished was rum, they soon conceived the idea of making rum the medium of exchange in all kinds of barter and trade The scarcity of coin and the ease with which rum could be made to pass current at an exhorbitant percentage above its real commercial value, made the temptation too great to adhere to any coin or fixed standard. Rum was more pliable, and being in accord with the appetites and consciences of both the ruled and those in command, it soon became the universal practice to pay for all commodities in rum: a day's wages was paid in rum, a bushel of wheat, an ox, a horse, or other product of the farm was measured by this standard; a lawyer's and doctor's fees were paid in rum; rum was king, and Governor King was only second in the respect or affections of his countrymen. He sought by every possible means to restrict the importation of the article, and to check the drunkenness of the people, but failed. The profits in the business were so large that many imported stills and began the manufacture of ardent spirits. This the Governor forbade, but still the business was carried on, in secret for a time, finally in open violation of all official authority by the very officers and soldiers appointed to carry out the Governor's policy. Under such circumstances it was utterly impossible to inaugurate any change or hope for obedience to his commands. That he should have expressed himself to be disappointed and filled with disgust, is only to be expected from such a condition of things.

It was during his reign that Flinders obtained a commission from the Home authorities to follow up his important discoveries in Australia. He was sent in H.M.S. "Investigator," and his report of this expedition, published many years afterwards, credits himself with the discovery in 1801 and 1802 of the southern coast of Australia, embracing Spencer's and St. Vincent's Gulfs, Port Lincoln, Kangaroo Island, and Cape Jarvis; and, having sailed along the north-east coast, he surveyed and examined Hervey's Bay, Bustard Bay, Port Curtis, Keppel Bay, Port Bowen and Broadsound, and subsequently the Gulf of Carpentaria.

The *Sydney Gazette* was founded during his administration, the first number being issued on the 5th March, 1803. It was under the patronage of the Governor, and owned by a Mr. Howe, an ex-convict, who continued in that relationship until his death, in May, 1821, when it was conducted by his son Robert. It was the Government organ from its foundation till 1832, when the present Government *Gazette* was first published.

It was during his administration that the sheep-growing industry was inaugurated, its origin and first successful results being due to the foresight and active ambition of Captain John McArthur, who early saw the adaptability of the climate and pasturage to the development of this enterprise; and, resigning his position in the New South Wales Corps, he applied himself to the farming interests, and with a zeal that was not always according to knowledge, he strove with all the power he possessed to become first in the accumulation of wealth.

CHAPTER XI.

GOVERNOR WILLIAM BLIGH.

1806-1808.

CAPTAIN BLIGH was honorably known to the British Government as a brave officer and a man of sterling integrity, and withal a soldier of severe discipline. His experience in connection with the "Bounty," when the crew mutinied, brought him into prominence. The reader must form his own judgment from the account as to his character.

Captain Bligh was sent by the British Government to the South Seas for a shipload of bread-fruit trees. His treatment of the sailors was said to be so rigid and cruel that they mutinied, and placing their captain and some of his officers in a small open boat, they left them to drift at the mercy of the elements. It is said that the captain's skill as a seaman was such that he sailed nearly four thousand miles, and reached the island of Timor, where he was kindly taken up by a vessel and sent back to England. While history regards his treatment of his sailors as severe, yet the British Government were disposed to accord him honor on account of what it deemed a simple act of fidelity to government authority. A difference of opinion has been extensively expressed, both in regard to his temper and judgment, and therefore the reader can only expect such an expression as will leave the whole question an open one.

He was a retired gentleman in England at the time of his appointment to the position of Governor of New South Wales. There is no doubt that the wretched condition of affairs in the colony was brought about by the want of discipline in the New South Wales Corps; and the widespread drunkenness of all classes in connection therewith, and the fearful demoralisation incident thereto, were some of the reasons that induced the Home authorities to look about for some rigid disciplinarian, who would rule with a strict adherence to the requirements of the colony.

That Governor Bligh was a worthy successor to a very worthy man admits of little doubt, though his acts did not meet with universal commendation. He first applied himself to the herculean task of breaking up the abominable monopoly the New South Wales Corps had by its military character so successfully carried on for so long a time, to their own advantage and to the dishonor and disgrace of the nation. Governor Bligh found in the young colony a condition of almost universal drunkenness growing out of the practice of making ardent spirits the medium by which the trade of the young colony was carried on. The scarcity of money favored this state of things, especially under the widespread monopoly enjoyed by the officers of the corps, so that it was a sort of necessity that compelled all classes to recognise this commodity as the only one that would be accepted in trade in lieu of coin. Officers, soldiers, merchants, doctors, lawyers and clergymen, from the Bishop down, came to trade in ardent spirits, and thus aid in establishing a system of things that resulted in a degree of drunkenness that interfered greatly with the future peace and prosperity of the young nation.

Governor Bligh was specially charged with the task of breaking up this pernicious system, and therefore we are not surprised in seeing the most strenuous endeavour made to resist the Governor's purpose by the members of the Corps, who enjoyed a monopoly of this kind of business; and were aided by the drunken classes, who had acquired an excessive fondness for the "medium," and who combined with the former in resisting to the uttermost any effort to purge them of these practices.

Governor Bligh's career was of short duration; nevertheless, during his stay he manifested great zeal in effecting reforms in all departments of the colony, and he evinced great interest in the welfare of the people in a most practical manner, when they were reduced to abject poverty and distress through long continued droughts and frequent inundations. The rich valleys of the Hawkesbury, Nepean, and branch rivers offered advantages to the early tillers of the soil that lured them from the attractions of

Port Jackson. The promise of abundance had operated favorably in winning many to forsake other branches of industry and become farmers; but the drought on the one hand and floods on the other had the effect of casting a gloom over the agricultural hopes of the people. The failure of crops in these localities from the above causes was quickly felt throughout the entire colony, and was followed by a state of semi-starvation.

Governor Bligh used his utmost endeavour to encourage the farmers amid their calamity by sharing with them the government stores, and promising them a market for all their produce at the very highest prices. In this way he not only secured the confidence, goodwill and respect of this class, but contributed very largely towards the establishment and maintenance of many of the infant enterprises in which the other colonists had chosen to embark.

The Governor received the approbation of his Majesty the King and the Home authorities, who were watching with very great interest the development of the "New England of the South," and were solicitous for the well-being of every section of the colony, and who were in no sense responsible for the adverse condition to which these struggling settlers had been subjected.

As might be expected, frequent quarrels and differences existed between the Governor and leading merchants, of the military class especially. Every day and month added to the difficulty, until in the course of a short time it culminated in an open breach between the Governor on the one side and the military corps on the other, the immediate occasion of which was the refusal of Mr. John Macarthur to pay a fine imposed by Mr. Atkins, the Judge-Advocate, for allowing the escape of a convict in one of his vessels. Macarthur was summoned before the court for contempt. He declined, however, to appear, on the ground that Mr. Atkins was his enemy. The Governor issued a warrant of arrest at the instigation of the Judge-Advocate, and Macarthur was lodged in jail. The Governor thereupon appointed a Special Court of six officers, and Mr. Atkins as president. Macarthur refused to be tried by Mr. Atkins, his enemy, but intimated his willingness to abide by the decision of the six officers. The officers endorsed this protest as just, whereupon the Governor discontinued the trial, and became angry, and assumed such an atitude of antagonism to all who sided with Mr. Macarthur, even going so far as to threaten them with incarceration, that it had the effect of uniting all the friends of Mr. Macarthur and the enemies of the Governor in one solid phalanx, who were becoming thoroughly aroused against the Governor and what they were pleased to term his unjustifiable interference with the rights and privileges of the merchant classes. A large petition was gotten up, requesting Major Johnson, the military commander, to depose Governor Bligh, and to assume control of the government himself. This seems to have had the effect of flattering him into the notion that his popularity would serve him in any emergency. A request, however, was made to the Governor that a new Advocate should be appointed in the stead of Atkins. This was refused. The Governor then sent a message to Major Johnson, with a command to appear before him. His reply was, "That he was unwell." A council was held by Major Johnson and the officers on Anniversary Day, and the decision was arrived at to place the Governor under arrest. The following letter was sent to Governor Bligh from military head-quarters :—

HEAD QUARTERS,
January 26th, 1808.

SIR,—I am called upon to execute a most painful duty. You are charged by the respectful inhabitants of crimes that render you unfit to exercise the supreme authority another month in this colony, and in that charge all the officers serving under my command have joined.

I, therefore, require you, in his Majesty's most sacred name, to resign your authority, and to submit to the arrest which I hereby place you under, by the advice of all my officers, and by the advice of every respectable inhabitant of the town of Sydney.

I am, Sir,
Your most obedient servant,
GEORGE JOHNSON,
Acting Lieutenant-Governor and Major commanding N.S.W. Corps.

To William Bligh, Esq., F.R.S., &c.

The order was given to march on the Government House, and make the arrest, in compliance with which the soldiers and officers went down with colors flying and drums beating, and were met by the Governor's daughter, who pleaded with the officers to desist; but her plea was unheeded. They entered and searched for the Governor, who was finally found secreted under a bed. He was placed under arrest, and a guard appointed to prevent his escape.

Major Johnson assumed control of the government, and issued forthwith a proclamation first changing all the important officers, especially those who were even suspicioned to have a taint of sympathy with Governor Bligh. A new court was constituted, Macarthur was put upon his trial, and speedily exonerated, and was at once created Colonial Secretary. Public meetings were prohibited, to prevent agitation or the coming together of the emancipists and free settlers, all of whom were favorable to the Governor.

Bligh was kept under restraint for twelve months, and it was only after frequent appeals were made for his release that he was permitted to resume command of the "Porpoise," on condition that he should proceed to England; but, instead, he went to Van Dieman's Land. He did not succeed in obtaining this conditional release until Colonel Paterson was in command of the administration of affairs in New South Wales, having been brought from Tasmania (Van Dieman's Land) as successor to Colonel Foveaux, who had succeeded Major Johnson a very few months after the arrest of the Governor. Bligh did not immediately proceed to England, but sought to stir up sympathy among the farmers of the Hawkesbury and elsewhere, among whom he was popular, but failed, and retired to Tasmania, where he was received kindly. He remained in command of the "Porpoise" until Major-General L. Macquarie was sent out as Governor of the colony, and soon afterwards he went to England, where, after an examination by the authorities, he was exonerated from all blame, and created admiral in the English navy. Major Johnson was summoned to England, tried by court-martial, May 11th, 1811, dismissed from the service in disgrace for his acts of rebellion; and, retiring to a farm in New South Wales, he lived in comparative obscurity, though in comfort, till the day of his death, in 1817.

Mr. John Macarthur was also tried for misdemeanour, found guilty, and prohibited from returning to the colony for the space of eight years. This was deemed to be the severest punishment that could be imposed on a man whose whole soul was interested in the development of his grazing and sheep interests in the colony. He was not the kind of a man to be easily disheartened, and therefore he occupied his time in studying the sheep interests of England and the Continent, and brought back to the colony when he returned a ripened experience in his favored enterprise that tended largely to make his future efforts successful.

CHAPTER XII.

GOVERNOR MACQUARIE.
1810-1821.

LACHLAN MACQUARIE, Lieutenant-Colonel of the 73rd Regiment, was appointed successor to Governor Bligh, arrived in Sydney on the 28th December, 1809, and entered upon his administration January 1st, 1810. The colony during the two years previous to his arrival was in a condition of unrest, the whole policy of the government having passed into the hands of such as were held by the authorities to be rebels.

Governor Macquarie made haste to remedy these evils by adopting such a course as would tend to uphold the dignity and honor of the Home Government and constitutional authorities, and make those who were usurpers feel the dishonor of their acts of rebellion.

He first issued a proclamation, in which he referred to his Majesty's deep regret and displeasure at the mutinous conduct of those who joined in the acts of violence by which his predecessor, Governor Bligh, was placed under arrest and deprived of his liberty and the occupancy of Government House. He also read the command of his Majesty to reinstate that officer in his position of Captain-General and Governor-in-Chief of the colony, and who was to receive Governor Macquarie at the end of twenty-four hours as his successor. Governor Bligh being absent, this part of the command could not be carried out, except in spirit.

His second act was to issue a proclamation, removing all persons from office who had been appointed thereto during Governor Bligh's suspension; and, further, that all grants of land should become null and void.

His third act was to render all acts of the magistracy, jailers, and constables, who were illegally appointed, valid, as being the wisest, and, in fact, the only course that could be pursued under the circumstances.

When Governor Bligh, who had been absent in Tasmania, arrived in Sydney, he was received with honors due to the rank of Commodore; and thus was sought to be rectified the great wrong done to a brave soldier, if not a wise governor.

Governor Macquarie applied himself vigorously to the task of building up the colony and encouraging all classes of citizens by every proper incentive to aim at their own individual success and the honor and prosperity of the whole colony. The larger number of the colonists had been convicts, and he readily saw that the emancipist element for a long time to come would be the chief dependence of the country as farmers, merchants, politicians, and, in fact, the teachers of the rising generations; and it was his duty not only to encourage this section to aim at the highest and most honorable positions in the land, but to regard this end as the natural and just termination of an honest career, not only as a laudable goal after which they might strive, but a just and possible reward of faithful service; and, therefore, true to his theory of governing the colony well, he linked all classes to his government as co-laborers—emancipists, free settlers, native-born and foreigners, were made his helpers, and thus he gave a stimulus to the spirit of a true democracy that resulted in great good being accomplished in every department of colonial activity.

The New South Wales Corps, or 102nd Regiment, was ordered home, and the 73rd, of which Lieutenant-Colonel Macquarie was created Major-General, took their place; and hence the Governor felt that he had ample force to back and make effective any order he might see fit to issue.

One of the first requirements of a new country was, in his judgment, the opening up of suitable roads. The previous governors had all advocated the importance of immigration and the settlement of the country by an industrious class of farmers, and many had already sought the advantages to be gained in an early settlement on her lands; but a serious drawback was the difficulty of communication with Sydney. As yet few roads existed of a passable character. This defect the Governor at an early date saw, and overcame. He had a large force of the convict element that he could utilise in this way. It is true this part of his policy did not meet with universal approval, for many of the settlers were anxious to derive all the advantage from the labor they performed; they argued that part of the inducement held out to the early settlers was free labor, and they were entitled to it all. The Governor's plan was to utilise all that clement that was not absolutely needed in private enterprises in the creation of public works; and this he did not exact from the convicts as a service of drudgery, but under promise of reward to each one who, by diligence and faithful service, should evince an earnest desire to reform, and to become possessors of farms and other material interests in a legitimate way.

He opened lines of communication between all important points. The road between Sydney and Parramatta he improved and extended to Windsor and Richmond, to meet the wants of the settlers on the Hawkesbury. He built one to Liverpool, twenty-two miles in length, and afterwards continued it to the Cowpastures, forty miles distant to the south-west of Sydney—a plain rich in pasture lands, and watered by the Cowpasture River, which uniting with the Warragamba, that issues from the Blue Mountains, forms the Nepean. This river and the pasture lands along its banks were discovered in Governor Hunter's reign, in the year 1796, the lands being designated "The Cowpastures" from the fact of finding there a large herd of cattle, the increase of two bulls and three cows that had strayed from the government enclosure in Captain Phillip's time.

His greatest achievement was the construction of a road across the Blue Mountains to Bathurst, one hundred and thirty miles distant, nearly due west from Sydney, thus opening to the richest plains communication that resulted in its early settlement and prosperity.

In 1813 the Blue Mountains were crossed by Messrs. Wentworth, Blaxland and Lawson, and Bathurst Plains were discovered. The recent losses from drought and the need of better pasturage than could be obtained around Sydney induced the above staff of earnest explorers to search beyond the mountains, and they were rewarded by the discovery of the above plains.

The Governor soon saw the importance of opening a road through to the plains, and ere many months he had a force at work; and, though a most difficult task, he succeeded in making one of the most perfect roads to be found anywhere in Australia.

He had the satisfaction of seeing the farming interests speedily increasing in those parts of the country where his roads afforded the necessary facilities. Nearly three hundred miles of road was built by him in portions of the colony that seemed best suited to farming. He went everywhere through the settlement encouraging all classes. He assisted the struggling by giving advice and loans, frequently gifts from the government supplies, and everywhere was hailed as the true friend of the oppressed. He early recognised the value of education and church work among the people, and therefore he built churches, schools, and public buildings, not only for the benefit of those who were already settled in the colony, but equally for such multitudes as might be induced to come, and here find homes. Dr. Lang, in his valuable writings, does not fully approve of Governor Macquarie's extravagance in this respect, and only accords to him partial praise, for he thinks he was only too anxious to perpetuate his own illustrious name. Be that as it may, we nevertheless remember that the impetus given to public business by the improvements everywhere begun at that special period, chiefly by the employment of convict labor, gave the colony an advantage that exceeded far the somewhat lavish expenditure of moneys used in the accomplishment of these results. The influx of labor of this kind was far greater than could be utilised by the settlers to advantage, and hence the Governor acted with great foresight in erecting public buildings and other works that would in his opinion be soon needed, and would offset the expense of boarding and taking care of a large class of men, whose future interests would be better guarded and secured by the encouraging promises held out by the State to such as proved themselves worthy, rather than in the hands of private individuals, whose chief profit would be derived from the most worthy, and whose self-interest would lead them to seek to perpetuate their serfdom. One of the great evils of assigned or sold labor is its tendency to keep in chains that which pays, and release that which is a burden, and thus defeat the one great law of true reform as adopted by the great English nation, and sought to be carried into effect by Governor Macquarie in the policy he adopted. Among the historians of this country, there are those who take exception to the public spiritedness of Governor Macquarie in erecting so many buildings of a superior character, and are not slow in attributing much of the drunkenness to those "good old days" when money was plentiful; yet we can see no good grounds for such belief. The broad policy of the Governor in erecting buildings of such proportions, as the developed conditions of the colony have long since proved to be none too large, only exalts in the esteem of all succeeding generations the wisdom and foresightedness of the man who comprehended within his plans the interests, not of his own times, but of the centuries to come.

It was the Governor's policy, and also that of Governor Phillip, to grant to worthy or deserving emancipists who had served their time or had secured Executive clemency, warrants for lands of thirty or forty acres, to be selected by themselves. These orders were sometimes sold to merchants for rum or other merchandise, and hence some people were disposed to attach blame to the Governor for making it possible for such abuses to take place. It does not, however, appear that abuses of this kind existed to any great extent. On the other hand, it does seem to have been both wise and human on the part of the Government to extend every facility to this class to earn an honest livelihood by cultivating the soil, and not so bind them by the terms of these grants as not to be able to sell their farms and invest elsewhere, if their tastes or self-respect led them to part with old associations. They were often disposed of for absolute necessities during times of drought and depression.

It is quite apparent that Governor Macquarie's aim was to carry out the purposes of the Home Government, to give every encouragement to the emancipist to do well, and to make him a respected and honored member of the commonwealth, and to make the penalty as light as would be consistent with reform. The wisdom and graciousness of this policy are apparent in the long and honorable list of descendents, who are worthy examples of every virtue, found in every department of labor and enterprise—in the professions, scientists, scholars, and instructors; in the avenues of trade, and in the homes of respected and respectable citizens.

In a letter Governor Macquarie wrote to the Earl of Bathurst on his return to England in 1822, he gives a brief summary of his Australian policy, and its results, which must be of interest to the reader:—"I found the colony barely emerging from infantile imbecility, and suffering from various privations and disabilities; the country impenetrable beyond forty miles from Sydney; agriculture in a yet languishing state; commerce in its early dawn; revenue unknown; threatened with famine; distracted by factions; the public buildings in a state of dilapidation, and mouldering to decay; the population in general depressed by poverty; no public credit nor private confidence; the morals of the great mass of the population in the lowest state of debasement, and religious worship almost totally neglected. Such was the state of New South Wales when I took charge of its administration on the 1st January, 1810. I left it in February last, reaping incalculable advantages from my extensive and important discoveries in all directions, including the supposed insurmountable barrier called the Blue Mountains, to the westward of which are situated the fertile plains of Bathurst, and in all respects enjoying a state of private comfort and public prosperity." And then he gives a comparative summary of its condition in the following figures:—

	1810.	1821.
Population	11,590	38,778
Horned cattle	12,442	102,939
Sheep	25,888	290,158
Hogs	9,544	33,906
Horses	1,134	4,564
Acres cleared and cultivated	7,615	32,267

During his administration he had caused to be built two hundred and fifty public buildings, and nearly three hundred miles of road.

He paid two visits to Tasmania—the first in 1810, and the second in 1821.

In 1817 Mr. John Oxley, Surveyor-General, explored the Lachlan River for more than four hundred miles. He crossed the Wellington Valley and reached the Macquarie; which in the following year he thoroughly explored.

CHAPTER XIII.

GOVERNOR BRISBANE.
1821-1825.

MAJOR-GENERAL SIR THOMAS BRISBANE, K.C.B., was the sixth governor of New South Wales. He entered upon his duties on December 1st, 1821. It was a difficult matter for any stranger to follow Governor Macquarie—a man who was universally respected, or at least had very few enemies. There was but one circumstance of complaint, and that was his indifference to free immigration, and his excessive interest in and favor towards the emancipists, on the ground that the colony was formed for their benefit, and that they should have the first consideration. Governor Brisbane took a somewhat different view of the question, and sought in every way to encourage the introduction of free settlers. He was of Scotch descent, a brave soldier, and an efficient officer in the army, and was a distinguished astronomist. He was enthusiastically received by the colony, but did not seem to possess that amount of energy that characterised his predecessor, and his lack in this respect became very apparent by contrast. He was disinclined to work himself; and, having entrusted all matters of business into the hands of subordinates that were frequently found to be inefficient, he was constantly failing to fulfil his promises or meet the expectations of the people. He never failed in kindness or good intention, but his success in attaching the people to his administration was very slight. His administration was marked by a class of officials drawn largely from the well-to-do young scions of broken-down nobility, who, as free settlers, came with a little money, but more generally with an insatiable hunger for government assistance, with the semblance of official duties attached; and hence the policy of Governor Brisbane was to give liberal help to such. He gave them large tracts of the best lands, and as many convicts as they chose to employ; and also gave them the remunerative offices under the Crown. The public works that were inaugurated under Macquarie's rule were largely abandoned, and the force of men employed thereon distributed among private individuals. The result, as a matter of course, was the building up of large "squatters'" interests, and handing over the resources of the colony largely to a class of people who were neither remarkable for their integrity or efficiency, but were noted for their neglect, arbitrary acts, and many instances of injustice practised in the Governor's name. It is said that there was a demand for two thousand more convicts than were at the disposal of the government. Business grew to such proportions under this last policy of Governor Brisbane and so rapidly that the nation could not create convicts fast enough to meet the demand. It is well for the nation to pause and philosophise somewhat on a policy of such a type. Why was convictism so much in demand? Was it because it was found to be profitable? The few speculators in criminal labor during Macquarie's reign cried out against that governor's policy in employing it largely in public works, and thought they had a right to it; and following closely the wishes of the few, Governor Brisbane adopted the plan of handing it all over to individual enterprise, until there came speedily the insatiable cry from those who were largely gainers by their labor, "Give us two thousand more!" Did the policy of the Governor create this demand? If so, then can earth conceive a more damning record? Whenever crime is put upon the market and sold to the highest bidder, it is purchased for the profit it brings; and, if profitable, then there must ensue rivalry among men regarding its possession, and as the rivalry increases and the bidding rises higher, it cannot fail to become a factor in the politics of the nation, and the nation sets its whole machinery in motion—the police, the detective, the informer, the blackmailer, the false witness, the government official, and the lobbyist, all finding profit in handing over the weak to satisfy the demand for profitable labor.

A system of espionage ensued upon the inauguration of a policy of such a kind. It could not be otherwise; the one is always the concomitant of the other. Free immigrants came by the hundreds. It was profitable to come: free lands, free labor, and a hundredfold increase was too much for humanity to resist, and hence we have a general rush to this country at a time most favorable to its development and utilisation.

There was great need of a class of settlers who would enter upon the task of tilling the soil and developing the agricultural resources of the colony. Under the stimulus that such inducements offered many first-class people of moderate means came—people of education, respectability, and honesty —the gentleman farmer, many who had become embarrassed in business, together with some who, in a spirit of adventure, determined to gather up all they possessed and try their fortunes under new conditions. As a further inducement, upon satisfactory proof being furnished to the government that the emigrant had five hundred pounds, he was granted a free passage, a tract of land, and supplies from the King's stores for a time. They had the privilege of selecting where they chose, but chiefly they were inclined to select in the region of the Cowpastures, in the Bathurst plains, or in the valley of the Hunter, called at that time the "new country." They were given from five hundred to two thousand acres. No more liberal policy could have been adopted for the encouragement of this special class of "free settlers;" but the inevitable result was to create a feeling of antagonism between them and the emancipists, who, as a rule, were not fondled and cared for by "the powers that be." The former came to be called the "Exclusionist Party," and the freed convicts, with their friends, the "Emancipists." The special privileges accorded to the one, and the limits and restraints placed upon the other was the occasion of a bitter feud.

The broad policy of Governor Phillip, who aimed at giving every citizen an equal standing in the commonwealth, and the hearty benevolence of General Macquarie, were in striking contrast with the narrow and invidious policy of Governor Brisbane. He early saw the trouble, and sought to allay the irritation. He dined with them, and in many ways strove to conciliate them by kindly treatment, for no governor could have been more kindly disposed towards all classes; yet he failed in satisfying either one or the other of these parties.

The squatters' interests flourished on all sides. Sheep and cattle multiplied enormously. Yet the old man failed to govern in peace the factious that were assuming proportions of threatening magnitude.

A move was inaugurated by the exclusionists, looking towards the creation of a Legislative Council, that would take from the Governor much of the autocratic power he possessed, and secure a body of councillors chosen from among a class of gentlemen of the exclusionist type. A petition was accordingly gotten up and signed extensively, and presented to the Home Government, which in a degree succeeded.

In 1824, by Royal proclamation, a Legislative Council was created for the colony. The proclamation contained the names of the five principal officers who were to have seats *pro tem* in the Council, as follows: William Stewart, Lieutenant-Governor; Francis Forbes, Chief Justice; Frederick Goulburn, Colonial Secretary; James Bowman, Principal Colonial Surgeon; and John Oxley, Surveyor-General. The oath of acceptance was administered, and they continued until 10th May, 1825, when a warrant was read by the Governor revoking all previous appointments and re-appointing the same, with the exception of Mr. Oxley, who was succeeded by Archdeacon Scott. This Council continued until November, 1825.

This was an improvement over the autocratic rule of previous years. Many important laws were made for the regulation of the sale of spirits, relief of persons imprisoned for debt, the regulation of duties, etc. Trial by jury was also granted by the Home Government.

The formal declaration was made that the Press should become free, and, as a result, two new papers were begun under the management of private individuals—the *Australian*, edited by Dr. Wardell and Mr. Wentworth; and the *Monitor*, by Mr. S. Hall. A free Press found much to complain of, and it was not slow in charging much of the evils that existed to the inefficiency and prejudices of the Governor. He was fond of horse racing, and much interested in the improvement of stock. He established for this purpose "The Brisbane Cup," to encourage the breed of horses. This enterprise, under his patronage, made much progress, and considerable enthusiasm was awakened among a certain number in the improvement of all stock.

Moreton Bay was explored thoroughly by Oxley in 1823, and the river running into the bay named after Governor Brisbane. He recommended this as a suitable locality for a convict settlement. Accordingly there was begun such under command of Lieutenant Miller, of the 40th Regiment, 12th September, 1824.

Sir Thomas Brisbane was the first governor who visited the settlement, which he did in 1825.

Interregnum.

LIEUTENANT-GOVERNOR STEWART.

DECEMBER 1ST TO 19TH, 1825.

Lieutenant-Governor Stewart administered the affairs of the colony for eighteen days.

CHAPTER XIV.

GOVERNOR DARLING.
1825-1831.

SIR RALPH DARLING, K.C.B., succeeded Governor Brisbane in the management of New South Wales. He was a soldier, of no ordinary literary ability, and withal a man of good business qualifications. Regular and methodical in his habits, he sought to introduce the most rigid methods into the administration of colonial affairs. This was not easy of accomplishment, for the reason that it was a difficult matter to obtain clerical help so disposed. Long accustomed to a somewhat loose and careless manner of transacting the affairs of State, the Civil servants were not anxious to add to their own individual inconvenience by increasing their daily task. It was only by repeated instructions from head-quarters and the utmost vigilance on the part of Governor Darling that he was enabled in this respect to secure a partial compliance with his wishes. He devoted all his time assiduously to his duties as Governor. Every single case received his personal attention. Regularity and method were strictly enjoined on all departments; and this was much needed, as grave abuses had sprung up, especially in the management of the landed interests—abuses of the grossest character. The story is told by Dr. Lang, that on one occasion, "An invalid, coming to the country for his health, and hearing of the ease with which large tracts of land could be obtained, applied for a grant, and was given two thousand acres; and, without ever having seen it, he sold it for five hundred pounds, and returned to the old country improved in both health and pocket." Such abuses were certain to exist where things were done so loosely.

To correct this state of affairs, Governor Darling instituted a Board of Inquiry. The very act of establishing this method of managing the land department made enemies of a large class who had been reaping benefit from the former system, and the Governor became unpopular among the very class of exclusionists that the policy of his predecessor and that of himself was intended to encourage. Departure had to be made from this rule in behalf of many deserving people who were granted from three to six hundred acres, even where they had no money. All of this, though prompted by the utmost good-will on the part of the Governor, only widened the breach between the exclusionists on the one hand and the emancipists on the other. The latter class were encouraged by many of the first governors, and especially by Governor Macquarie, to look to the future for their reward in the possession of the lands and wealth of this country, and were stimulated to well-doing by a system of substantial reward; but now they beheld all this taken away, and themselves subjected to dishonor and degredation.

It is a principle of human activity that good results can only be achieved under the direct stimulus of a living hope; and equally true is it that moral reform can only be reasonably expected where there is a just and fair distribution made of the lands and other benefits that are equally the right of all the people. Nothing is so pernicious in the polity of any nation as class legislation and class favoritism. The admission of even a taint of unfairness is to sow the seeds of discord, which, sooner or later, will result in the vengeance that is sure to fall on the head of such as profit by the favor.

The unrest and discomfort experienced by the emancipist and the convict, whose services were too valuable to these large landholders to admit of any speedy emancipation from their thraldom, resulted in a widespread antagonism and irritation that boded little good for the future. Indifference, idleness, stubborness, and retaliation were the natural outgrowth of such a condition of affairs and its consequent punishment by the magisterial authorities, who most frequently was the clergyman of the parish. Clergymen were not qualified, by the peculiar relationship they sustained to their wealthy parishioners, to be just judges between the master and the convict servant. A complaint lodged by the master against his servant in a court presided over by his clergyman was putting too much against the servant. A sentence of thirty to fifty lashes on the mangled back of the helpless victim was an anomaly in the "good man's" daily task that our pen refuses to stigmatise. One of the darkest pages of colonial history is that written in this period, when cruelties the most bitter were practised, and all under the authority of the governor, who, doubtless, was in ignorance of the manner in which his commands were carried out by his subordinates, who were wont to justify their acts of semi-homicide on the pretext that it was "his Excellency's pleasure."

Governor Darling was much interested in the construction of roads. In this particular he followed closely the policy of Governor Macquarie. He built a road to the Hunter River, also roads westward and southward, beyond the county of Argyle.

In 1825 the enormous wealth of the country was pretty generally known in England, and an interest in all her many resources of wool, cattle, farming, mines and general capabilities was awakened; and to concentrate this sentiment and bring about practical results in connection with the same, there was organised "The Australian Agricultural Company." It had a capital of £1,000,000. It embraced many of the higher classes in England, whose ostensible object in its formation was to develop the wool interest and agricultural branches, such as the improvement of the breed of horses, cattle, and general husbandry. To encourage this enterprising firm, his Majesty granted them a million acres of land of the very choicest selection. During the previous administration free immigration was begun, and continued through Darling's term with unabated wildness. Large tracts were given to influential people at home, in the hope that there might be fostered the spirit of speculation; and this hope was soon realised. For a period every ship that came from England was freighted with a living cargo of anxious and expectant farmers. They nearly all settled in the vicinity of the Hunter, Bathurst, and Argyle districts. All this rush raised the value of produce: the old farmers found a ready market for their stock, and the "new chum" had the brightest prospects before him.

When the Australian Agricultural Company began operations in 1826, it gave an impetus to all kinds of corporations. Men came together to unite their efforts in the one direction; prices went up, a universal mania seized all classes on the subject of land; merchants, traders, barristers, clergymen, doctors, and politicians, basing their opinions on the operations of this company, rushed madly into speculation. Dr. Lang describes this condition in the following words:—" The soldier unbuttoned his military belt to become a keeper of sheep; and the priest, reversing the ancient metamorphosis in the case of the prophet Amos, forsook his altar to become a herdman of cattle."

A drought of nearly three years duration checked the unlimited craze. Men were brought to realise that land alone did not include all that was valuable. As much depends upon the rains of heaven and upon the equable diffusion of the rays of the sun. Their crops failed them; prices went down and universal confusion followed; bills began to fall due, with nothing to pay. All the products of toil and energy failed to satisfy these maturing claims. Some were lodged in jail for debt—for those were the times that men were imprisoned for even this misfortune, farms were seized, and general ruin was the result; and the blame was sought to be fastened upon the Governor. His policy of encouraging the farming interests was said to be the chief cause of the wild speculation in lands. The *Sydney Gazette* defended the Governor, and extolled him for his liberal and wise policy; but the *Gazette* was the government organ, and was said to be under the Governor's immediate patronage. The other papers, the *Australian* and the *Monitor*, denounced the Governor, and assailed the *Gazette;* and thus began what is known as "The Newspaper War."

The *Australian* was an independent paper, established under Brisbane's administration by Mr. Wentworth and Dr. Wardell; the *Monitor* was started by a Mr. Hall. Both joined in most bitter attacks upon the Governor and his official organ. At first his land policy was the chief cause of their severe strictures, but, as time passed by, with each revolving year came new grounds of adverse criticism, until the papers filled their columns with fulsome praise on one side and reckless depreciation and detraction on the other. An occasion of more than ordinary peculiarity occurred that gave rise to much severe comment. A soldier by the name of Sudds persuaded his mate, Thompson, that they could succeed better in the *role* of criminals; and it is said that they agreed to commit some crime, that they might secure the opportunities offered to the convict of becoming rich. They accordingly stole a piece of cloth, were tried, convicted, and sentenced to Van Dieman's Land for seven years, in accordance with their expressed wish. When the Governor heard of the plan, he took the matter into his own hand, and changed the sentence to one more severe, to use the mildest term. He directed that they should be " be chained together with heavy-spiked collars " fastened about their necks, and sent to hard labor in this condition on the public roads.

Sudds, who was an invalid, soon sank beneath the cruelty, and died, and his companion, Thompson, became insane. This gave the papers who were in opposition a chance of most terrible vengeance, which they did not allow to pass. He was represented as a monster of brutality. Every issue rung with detestations. The *Gazette*, with equal warmth, praised him: the whole colony was aroused. At last the Home Government was compelled to order his return.

Whether this last act of the Governor's was deserving of such terrible execration is beyond our ability to decide. Possibly it was one of those incidents that grow out of the severe discipline and training to which his own life was subjected. He may have thought that he was doing good service to the State in striving to check a wrong; and, again, it may be that a subordinate, as is often the case, more cruelly carried out the inhuman sentence than humanity would prompt.

Captain Sturt made some most valuable discoveries during this period. In 1828 he made an exploration of the Macquarie River, and proceeding westward found the Darling, named by him in honor of the Governor. In 1829 he discovered the lower portion of the river Hume, which he called the Murray, not knowing it was the same discovered years before by Hume. He followed the course of the Murray through to the ocean.

Interregnum.

Colonel Patrick Lindsay, C.B., senior officer in command of Her Majesty's forces, was Administrator from 22nd October till 2nd December, **1831.**

Hon. W. M. PATTISON,
Minister without Portfolio.

CHAPTER XV.

GOVERNOR BOURKE, K.C.B.

1831-1837.

MAJOR GENERAL SIR RICHARD BOURKE, K.C.B., arrived in the colony on the 2nd December, 1831, as Governor. He was a man of liberal education and great energy, and commanded general respect. Like General Macquarie, he had talent and kindliness combined—a man of unbounded energy and goodwill.

Sir Richard Bourke was originally educated for the law, and evinced a remarkable intellect from his youth up. In the management of the affairs of the colony he enjoyed the confidence and esteem of all classes to the end, and retired in 1837, regretted by nearly everyone.

He came at a time of great depression in the business of the country. When the "land craze" had subsided, and the hopes of hundreds who had embarked in the farming enterprise were blasted, he stood in the general crash, and, like a wise general, marshalled his broken columns into a phalanx of strength and hopefulness.

His predecessor had become exceedingly unpopular by reason of the disappointment in realising the results promised, and the failure reacted largely on Governor Darling, who was held responsible for the excessive hopes that had worked them into a condition of frenzy; and hence, in such a state of demoralisation, it was a comparatively easy matter for Governor Bourke to secure popularity by pursuing a course of moderation and prudence. Already the colony was recovering from the effects of the long drought of three years that had contributed mainly towards the depression through which the people had passed. The circumstances, therefore, under which the Governor began his administration were very auspicious. He steadily entered upon the work of making reforms in a legitimate and sensible way.

First the land question received his most careful thought and investigation, and he effected some changes that were very much needed, the justness of which the colony has ever approved. Up to that date it had been the rule with all previous governors to grant land freely to all persons who might apply for it. Under certain regulations large grants were given to such as could produce evidence of having a certain amount of money. Grants of more limited extent were given to all, even the poor, on being able to show even a moderate degree of ability to occupy. These rules were frequently set aside by subordinates, and their trusts betrayed, to the great annoyance of the poorer class of applicants, who sometimes were made to wait for months by these self-important officials, who were exceedingly obsequious to such applicants as were supposed to be men of standing or high connection. The poor immigrant, who had not influential friends to remind these officials of their duty, would have to wait sometimes for six months or more before they would succeed. Frequently their little remaining balances would become exhausted, and, with poverty and starvation staring them in the face, they would become discouraged, and seek the protection of the convict cell, or join the growing army of malcontents, whose continual mutterings of disappointment and wrong made the atmosphere of colonial existence thick with gloom. He changed the entire system of disposing of the lands. All lands were placed upon the market for sale to the highest bidder. The minimum price was fixed at five shillings per acre, and sold only in the public market; and the buyer who paid the highest price was the accredited purchaser.

The "squatter" who had previously held his "run" on the flimsiest title, could hold now, under a certain tenure, by paying a fixed rental graduated according to the number of sheep the "run" was capable of carrying. The lands under this arrangement yielded a considerable revenue, and at the same time gave great satisfaction generally. The practice, discontinued in 1818, of granting help to deserving people who wished to emigrate from England, was now resumed, and had the effect of increasing the prosperity of the country. Three thousand free persons, and an equal number of bond, came annually for several years to join the ranks of the industrious classes, and the colony rose rapidly into a condition of comparative comfort.

During his term he cut off all connection between the Government and the *Sydney Gazette*. For thirty years that paper was the official organ, and was the source of many annoyances to the Administration, and one of the leading factors in the late newspaper war. Governor Bourke saw the evil that had in the past resulted from giving the Government patronage to any private enterprise, and resolved upon putting an end to the cause of complaint.

Popular reforms were made in the management of all departments, which are mentioned in the epitome of his acts engraved upon the statue that commemorates his name, and which was erected by private subscription among a grateful people, to commemorate their appreciation and great regard.

It stands at the Macquarie Street entrance to the Domain, and bears an appropriate inscription, which groups in historic fulness the main features of his colonial life as follows :—

"This statue of Lieutenant-General Sir Richard Bourke, K.C.B., is erected by the people of New South Wales, to record his able, honest, and benevolent administration from 1831 to 1837. Selected for the government at a period of singular difficulty, his judgment, urbanity, and firmness justified the choice. Comprehending at once the vast resources peculiar to this colony, he applied them for the first time systematically to its benefit. He voluntarily divested himself of the prodigious influence arising from the assignment of penal labour, and enacted just and salutary laws for the amelioration of penal discipline.

"He was the first Governor who published satisfactory accounts of the public receipts and expenditure. Without oppression or detriment to any interest he raised the revenue to a vast amount, and from its surplus realised extensive plans of immigration. He established religious equality on a just and firm basis, and sought to provide for all, without distinction of sect, a sound and adequate system of national education. He constructed various public works of permanent utility. He founded the flourishing settlement of Port Phillip, and threw open the wilds fo

Australia to pastoral enterprise. He established Savings Banks, and was the patron of the first Mechanics' Institute. He created an equitable tribunal for determining upon claims to grants of lands. He was the warm friend of the liberty of the Press. He extended trial by jury after its almost total suspension for many years. By these and numerous other measures for the moral, religious, and general improvement of all classes, he raised the colony to unexampled prosperity, and retired amid the reverent and affectionate regret of the people, having won their confidence by his integrity, their gratitude by his services, their admiration by his public talents, and their esteem by his private worth."

This statue that so worthily records his virtues was carved by Bailey, and the position it occupies is one of the most lovely that could have been selected. Governor Gipps, in the year 1842, declared, on the occasion of unveiling it, "that the view from the spot where he stood equalled in loveliness any scene in the known world." It commands a view of the entrance to the harbour, and is one continuous picture of beauty. In the foreground is the inner Domain, Government House and grounds, Botanical Garden, and beyond are the coves which lie between the jutting points of Lady Macquarie's Chair, Potts' Point, Darling Point, and the islands in the bay, with the hills on North Shore, in the background, dotted here and there with villas, that speak of comfort and enjoyment. In the presence of such a picture he stands—his large eye watching, as of yore, the entrance and egress of ships as they come and go freighted with life or gold. His massive brow still intelligent in its grasp of problems solved and being solved for colonial good; and repose, born of an approving conscience; a sturdy manhood and a solid pedestal all speak in hopeful words of a future grander than the past.

Exploration was extensively made in the interior of the colony during this period by Major Mitchell, who examined the Darling River and its tributaries, and was the first who thoroughly explored all that region embraced in the colony of Victoria, and which he called Australia Felix, a name which it gracefully bore for many years.

It was during the latter part of his administration that a settlement had been made in the vicinity of Port Phillip. More than 500 souls were already engaged in various enterprises in that region, but chiefly in the pastoral. The Governor obtained permission to place upon the market the rich lands of this section, and very soon it was sought by a large number of immigrants of the better classes, who were drawn thither by the glowing accounts of its fruitfulness given by their friends, who were already deriving profit therefrom.

Governor Bourke died at his seat in Limerick, Ireland, in 1855.

Lieutenant-Colonel Snodgrass administered the Government from 6th December, 1837, to 23rd February, 1838.

CHAPTER XVI.

GOVERNOR SIR GEORGE GIPPS.

1838-1846.

SIR GEORGE GIPPS was appointed successor to Governor Bourke, and entered upon his duties on the 24th February, 1838. He had been brought into special notice in connection with the rebellion of the Radicals in Canada in 1836 and 1837. Whether his services in that connection were of great value in the settlement of affairs in Canada is a subject upon which Canadians entertain different opinions; but be that as it may, no doubt he received much credit from the Imperial Government, and in recognition of his military successes the honor of this appointment.

He was a man of acknowledged ability and energy, and entered upon his duties with an earnest purpose to serve well his Queen and her subjects; yet, the times were not propitious. He followed a Governor whose popularity was sung universally, and every act of the new administration was judged by the comparison.

The Port Phillip District that had been recently opened for settlement had drawn to her fertile area vast numbers of wealthy people as well as the poor emigrant, and caused a pressing demand for lands in that locality. The Governor conceived it to be an opportune time to raise their price, and thus increase the revenue; and, by limiting the quantity of lands sold, he believed it would enhance their value.

It had the effect of increasing the demand, and causing reckless speculation in that district, both in lands and live stock. A large amount of English capital began to pour into the colony. New banks were opened, and a high percentage received; and, as in Governor Darling's time, people went mad over the rise in prices. Investments were reckless and numerous, loans were obtained from the banks, and the lands were pledged as security to their full purchase price.

Previous to this the upset price was five shillings per acre, but in the neighbouring colony of South Australia it had been raised to one pound by the Home authorities, who always regulated this matter; but as the Governor was supposed to be adviser of the Crown he was usually held responsible for any changes made. On the complaint ostensibly of South Australia that the lower price ruling in Port Phillip led emigrants to discriminate in favour of that district, an injustice was being done them by the difference fixed in the price of lands. An order from the Secretary of State was received by the Governor of New South Wales changing the entire land prices; and the people held the Governor, rightly or wrongly, responsible for the same. The order commanded that, to prevent the destruction of South Australia, the other colonies should charge a higher rate, and that New South Wales should be divided into three distinct districts:—(1) The middle district around Port Jackson, extending to the Murray River on the south and the Manning River on the north; (2) the northern district around Moreton Bay, embraced between the Manning River and the northern coast; and (3) the Port Phillip District, including all south of the Murray River. That the lands should never be sold in the middle and northern districts for less than twelve shillings, and in the Port Phillip District at less than one pound. Though this order gave almost universal dissatisfaction, it did not tend to check investment. The land craze still continued, so that the income of 1840 from that source alone was three times as great as that of the first year of his administration when land ruled at five shillings per acre. As is always the case, disaster followed this fever of speculation. When deferred payments became due the great majority had nothing wherewith to pay; and, crowded by the banks, farmers found their flocks and herds—though largely increased in numbers—were less in value, and under a pressed sale in a glutted market would bring scarcely any price. This condition of distress was not confined to the district of Port Phillip, but almost to the same extent in other parts of the colony.

Amid the wide-spread ruin, on account of the low price of sheep, many flocks selling as low as sixpence per head, the plan of boiling down the entire carcase was adopted. It was discovered by a Mr. O'Brien, a squatter living at Yass, that about six shillings worth of tallow could be produced from each sheep by the boiling process. In this way the country was enabled to realise a considerable amount from its flocks, and partially avert calamity.

Governor Gipps, in pursuance of the policy mapped out in his first address to the Council, strove most arduously to effect many reforms. The bad report made of the condition of the colony by some who were desirous of inducing the Home Government to put an end to the transportation of prisoners, and who were aided in this movement by the Right Rev. Dr. Whately, Bishop of Dublin, became a matter of legislative expression in the form of a series of resolutions in the Council, the matter having been presented to it by a numerously signed petition drawn up by the citizens of New South Wales assembled in a mass meeting. The purport of the resolutions were as follows :—" (1) That the Council concurred in the opinion expressed by the numerous and respectable body of colonists who signed the memorial to His Excellency the Governor; that the character of the colony, in so far as the moral and social condition of the inhabitants was concerned, had unjustly suffered by misrepresentation put forth by certain recent publications in the Mother Country, and especially in portions of the evidence taken before a committee of the House of Commons on the subject of transportation. (2) That in the opinion of the Council this would not only be made clearly to appear from such an investigation as the memorialists solicited, but was in itself already sufficiently evident to every impartial observer who was acquainted with the true circumstances of the colony." There were other matters embraced in the resolutions directed towards establishing the fact that there was a vast improvement made in the management of convicts, and that the system of assigning the convicts was the best calculated to encourage free immigration. He strove to remedy the impression abroad concerning the moral condition of the colony, but how well he succeeded remains for his future acts to reveal. Whatever were his intentions, there is no doubt that his acts were continually bringing him into conflict with a large section of the colony, who disapproved of nearly everything he did.

Early in his administration the Governor caused a bill to be passed in the Council annexing the islands of New Zealand. This act awakened much opposition. The people of New South Wales did not desire to be burdened with the extra expense involved in having these islands made part of her territory, to be governed by a Lieutenant-Governor, and whose officials would have to draw their support from the New South Wales revenue. A protest was made, and supported by the earnest arguments of Mr. Busby, Mr. Wentworth, Mr. a'Beckett, and Mr. Darvell, all of whom sought to oppose first, annexation, or in the event of that being accomplished, they claimed that the rights to lands acquired by purchase from the natives of New Zealand should not be disturbed.

Mr. W. C. Wentworth's land acquired in this way from the chiefs was said to amount to nearly twenty millions, that of the early missionaries many millions more, and other gentlemen large tracts, embracing in all nearly the entire territory.

The Governor defended the bill, and it became law. It provided for the possession of the lands of New Zealand as part of Her Majesty's dominion, and that title should be secured through the Crown.

Many persons had secured by purchase from the Maori chiefs in New Zealand during its independency large tracts of lands for comparatively small sums of money, and they contended that their title could not be disturbed by any subsequent Act of annexation, and that their title should not come through the Crown. The Governor, however, held that they had no title, and could not secure one from any people who could not show possession thereof, not having occupied it by cultivation or by any settled form of Government.

In 1841 the Governor was pleased to announce that Her Majesty's government had erected the islands of New Zealand into a separate government, and accordingly they ceased to be a dependency of New South Wales on the 1st June, 1841.

While Governor Gipps brought down upon his own head a storm of opposition, it certainly appears plain that he conferred a lasting benefit upon the colony by boldly and effectually opposing such a scheme.

"The governors previous to Sir Thomas Brisbane were subject to no control, but that of the Secretary of State" in England. Though recommended by a select committee of the House of Commons, no Advisory Council was created until Brisbane's administration, when one was instituted, consisting of Lieutenant-Governor or Commander of the Force, the Chief Justice, the Archdeacon, and the Attorney-General.

One can scarcely conceive in this enlightened age of a Council more unfitted, by their peculiar vocation, to be advisers of the administration —the army, the law, and the church. The peculiar discipline to which the soldier is subject all through his life makes it impossible for him to have any real knowledge of the people, much less to have awakened within him a single feeling of sympathy, and for this reason it is seldom possible to find in the army a soldier who is qualified to rule.

The same may be said of the law. The very practice gives the lawyer a warped judgment concerning life and human conduct. He deals almost continually with the darker side of human nature, and is constantly brought into contact with the baser sort. His facts are generally strained out of their natural relationship; his law is not interpreted according to what is just, but according to what is possible under the terms; his mind must soon come by natural sequence to look upon every question of law with doubtfulness, and every fact with suspicion; and for this reason has the English Constitution justly taken away from the legal profession the power of deciding a grave matter of fact, and has relegated the same to the only just judges of human conduct—man's peers. One can easily see how exceedingly befogged must become the legal mind, long accustomed to the prejudicial practice of putting strained and one-sided statements as facts, and dwelling upon the possible for the probable, in a position where the thousand and one conflicting interests of the people call not for settlement on such a basis, but demand legislation on the ground of equal rights, though subject to constitutional law. And of the clergyman, may it not be conceded universally without offence, that of all men the cleric is least qualified to speak or act in that capacity; none whose judgment is so narrow, and whose knowledge of human nature is so limited. The advancing civilisation has shut out this profession in many places, even from the Council Chambers of the nation—a course we do not approve of, as it is in contravention of the principles of a true democracy, which ever aims at according to all equal rights and privileges, and condemns class legislation; though, no doubt, abuse of privilege brought the clergymen under such a ban. The world presents no more bloody picture of cruelty and heartlessness than it does in those days when the clergyman was the chief councillor of the ruler; and simply because the very tendency of dogmatic teaching is to hedge conscience about, and circumscribe it within the smallest circle.

In the administration of Darling this Council was extended to the number of fifteen. The improvement was simply in the fact that it admitted a greater number of gentlemen to be selected from other vocations, and hence infused more of the human sentiment into the Council of the nation; but seven being selected by the Crown, and the other seven from the "respectable" inhabitants induced a large number of the people to look upon such a plan with suspicion and distrust. The people earnestly desired a government that would reflect their own feelings and wishes.

In 1842 an Act, commonly known as the Constitution Act, was passed by the Imperial Government through the influence of Lord Stanley, who was then Secretary of State for the Colonies, by which was instituted a legislature of one House, consisting of thirty-six members, six of whom were to be the Government officers, six to be nominated by the Crown, and the remaining twenty-four to be elected by the people—eighteen from the district of Port Jackson or New South Wales, and six from the district of Port Phillip. This first representative legislature was hailed universally with delight. After a contest of intensest interest and excitement there was sent to it a number of gentlemen that fairly represented the talent of the colony, or at least they were the equal of any to be found in this or any other colony; and without indulging in excessive eulogy, we only state and put on record what is now generally conceded that, as a body of honorable men, they had no superiors, and in respect to talent and ability they were worthy of the young colony that chose them, and that in the work they accomplished they have done honor to their country, and left a record that subsequent parliaments will do well to copy. We think we would scarcely do the history of the colony justice were we not to put on record the names of these first representatives of the people.

The list embraces Richard Windeyer (the Joseph Hume of the Council), W. C. Wentworth, Robert Lowe (now Lord Sherbrooke), Dr.

Bland, Dr. Nicholson, Charles Cowper, Dr. Lang, Roger Therry, A. Macleay, J. B. Durvall, D'Arcy Wentworth, H. H. Macarthur, T. A. Murray, W. Bowman, W. Lawson, W. H. Suttor, W. Dumaresq, H. Condell, E. C. Hobson, W. Forster, F. Lord, C. H. Ebden, T. Walker, W. Bradley, and A. Thompson.

The Ministry embraced E. Deas Thompson, Colonial Secretary; W. Lithgow, Auditor-General; Lieutenant-General O'Connell, Commander of Forces; J. H. Plunkett, Attorney-General; C. D. Riddell, Colonial Treasurer; J. G. N. Gibbes, Collector of Customs; and Colonel Barney, Colonial Engineer. And the non-official members were: R. Jones, J. Blaxland, E. Hamilton, G. Berry, T. Icely, and H. Elwin. The unofficial portion of this body, though recognised as "independent" gentlemen, were said to be under the control, and at the bidding, of the Governor.

The question of the separation of Port Phillip District from New South Wales began to be seriously discussed in this year. The people in that part of the colony believed that it would be for their local interest to be in a position to manage their own affairs. Their wide separation from Sydney, geographically, and their separate interest commercially, made it desirable, from their own standpoint. Yearly a large sum of money, derived from the sale of lands in excess over all local expenditure, was being drawn away from the district. The people of Sydney took another view of the question, and became very much excited over the matter; and, by a strongly-worded petition to the Queen, urged their reasons in the form of a protest against such a move. They deprecated such a result on the ground of the additional expense of maintaining two governments; also, that it would interfere with "vested rights," inasmuch as many persons having their homesteads in the one district had purchased lands in Port Phillip, and had sent their flocks thither; and other arguments of a social character. The people of the Port Phillip District also met the protest and petitions of their neighbours with counter petitions. Meetings pro and con were held all over the colony, and the intensest and most acrimonious spirit was aroused during the discussions. A favourable reply to their request was received by the people of the district of Port Phillip in the year 1846, which virtually gave them all they desired, though, from a change in the administration of the Imperial Government, the Act constituting them into a separate colony was not passed until the year 1851.

A source of much grievance among the people was the withdrawal of £81,000 of the revenue from the control of the Council, and the placing of that sum in the hands of the Home Government, £51,000 of which was to be expended on the salaries of the Government, judges, and civil list, and £30,000 in the interests of religion. This, the people contended, they had a right to disburse themselves.

It does not appear that any of the money derived from the sale of lands or other sources of revenue was ever used by the Home Government, except in the payment of the above salaries and in aiding immigration. The Governor, basing his judgment upon the large revenue derived from the sale of lands in 1840 and 1841, issued county orders for emigration far beyond the limits of the decreasing revenue of subsequent years, and involved the colony in much embarrassment on that account. Multitudes of people came from the Old Country under this arrangement, having a free passage, and obtaining free grants of land, until the colony had more emigrants than they could well care for. Most of them were poor people, and had no means of support other than what they could earn or obtain from the Government. It was impossible for them to find employment, and the inevitable result was great suffering and semi-starvation. Hundreds went about the streets in search of work, but failing to obtain it, they were compelled to beg or starve; they slept in the parks; their home was under the trees. This condition of things was more especially distressing to hundreds of girls who were induced to come to the colony under promise of employment, but found on their arrival nothing to do, and nowhere to go; friendless and destitute, their case appealed most urgently to human sympathy. It found, after a time, a response in the Christian liberality of Mrs. Chisholm, who established a home for "defenceless and friendless girls," the benefits of which became immediately apparent, and were so great that it won the commendation of all classes, and continued for many years as a lasting memorial to the unselfishness and high-minded spirit of one worthy of honorable mention in the records of the nation.

Mrs. Chisholm was the wife of Captain Archibald Chisholm, of the Madras Army, who was visiting the colony for his health at this period. The terrible distress experienced by hundreds of poor people who had been induced to emigrate to the colonies, under promise of labor and cheap lands, moved that lady's pity to such a degree that she could neither rest day or night until she had moved all the machinery of the Government in the work of giving these people homes and employment. During the period of eight years of Mrs. Chisholm's stay in Australia, she cared for and settled over eleven thousand souls. Her memory can never die from the hearts of the Australian pioneer and his descendents. She returned to England in 1846, and continued her good work in behalf of the colony until her death.

Notwithstanding the adverse conditions under which the colony passed, yet throughout the administration of Governor Gipps it made progress. It recovered largely from the embarrassment arising from the depression of trade, and ultimately entered upon a career of prosperity.

The Governor's health failed him towards the end. He was recalled in 1846, and soon afterwards died.

Interregnum.

Sir Maurice O'Connell administered the government from 12th July till 2nd August, 1846.

CHAPTER XVII.

GOVERNOR FITZROY.

1846-1855.

SIR CHARLES FITZROY, the Governor, arrived on the 2nd August, 1846, and entered upon his official duties on the 3rd. He was born in 1796, hence was in his fiftieth year. He formerly was Governor of Prince Edward's Island, Canada, and in 1841 was Governor and Commander-in-Chief of Antigua and the islands of West Indies.

He was affable and courteous in his bearing towards all, and in this respect gave great satisfaction to everyone who came in contact with him. He was not only a gentleman born, but had all the nobler qualities of refinement and gentleness that one looks for in the character and bearing of a man whose education and instruction were under the very best influences.

One of the first subjects submitted to his consideration was that of railways. The people of the colony had begun to discuss their importance, and accordingly a meeting had been assembled, and had appointed a committee to wait upon the new Governor, and present to him their views that they had embodied in a set of resolutions favourable to the undertaking.

The Governor received the resolutions with much approval, and promised his assistance in attaining the desired results.

At a very early period in his administration the subject of reviving the system of transportation engaged the attention of the colony, and gave color to much of the legislation of his time.

There had been considerable feeling manifested on the subject for several years. Ever since 1837 the Home Government had practically ceased sending prisoners, in accordance with a recommendation made in a report of a committee of the House of Commons, which closes in the following words: "That transportation to New South Wales should be discontinued as soon as practicable"—a notice of which was printed in the *Gazette* in November, 1837: "That it was the intention of Her Majesty's Government to discontinue the assignment of convicts to private individuals." One of the strongest reasons urged at that time was the fact that such services came in conflict with the labour of the workman class, and the Government ought not to encourage that plan. This was followed by the announcement made first in May, 1839, and more fully provided in May, 1840, "That from and after the 1st August, 1840, the island of Van Dieman's Land and Norfolk Island and islands adjacent thereto should be the places to which felons and other offenders in the United Kingdom then being, or thereafter to be, under the sentence of transportation should be conveyed."

This was sufficient to settle the matter in the minds of most people in the colony. The question, however, was again raised in a communication from W. E. Gladstone, Secretary for the Colonies, in which was suggested the revival of the system. There was coupled with this intimation the assurance that nothing should be done in the matter, without the full concurrence of the colony.

It was very apparent that a considerable number of the wealthy land-holders, who had formerly profited by the free-labour system of convict assignment were anxious to have restored to them the advantages that it brings. The poorer classes, who were much more numerous than the former, were decidedly opposed to its restoration on the ground (1) that they would not get the benefit, but that it would all naturally pass into the hands of the wealthy, who had practically the control of the legislature; (2) that the whole system was demoralising in that it came into conflict with the working man who had a right to look both for employment and a fair remuneration for his labour. Strong men advocated each side of the question. Those in favour of it took the position that, inasmuch as Van Dieman's Land and Norfolk Island were to be places to which they would be sent, from thence hundreds would find their way over to New South Wales, and the evils of the system would be perpetuated without the benefits.

The Legislative Council were disposed to yield, and did give their assent to a modified restoration of the system, but Parliament could not settle such a question for the people. They assembled in large numbers all over the colony, and they determined on a direct appeal by petition over the heads of the members of the Council, and were graciously assured by the Governor that, as far as he was concerned, he held it to be his duty to forward their petition to the Home authorities, and to see that they had every chance of being fairly heard. This act of the Governor gave him great popularity with the people, who became thoroughly satisfied with his fairness towards all classes. This feeling, however, did not last. It was soon made apparent that the Governor was in full sympathy with those who were favourable to the revival of the transportation system. No doubt his bias in favour of its restoration was due to the fact that the Home authorities were desirous of continuing it under certain modifications, as may be inferred from the despatch sent by W. E. Gladstone, who was then Secretary of State for the Colonies, and strong men in the Council such as Wentworth, Dangar, and Macarthur favoured it. The great mass of the people were opposed, and manifested such a spirit of determination that it was difficult to carry such a measure against the voice of the people. Committees and anti-transportation leagues were formed all over the colony, and in the other colonies as well, and unified all efforts. The favourable action taken by the Legislative Council induced the Home Government to believe that the people were favourable to the scheme, and accordingly the ship "Hashemy" was despatched with two hundred and twelve male convicts on board, and arrived on 11th June, 1849. A monster meeting of determined citizens protested, and were disposed to resist their landing; but to avoid a conflict they were permitted to go to the interior of the colony. They were the last that ever came. The several colonies united in forming one grand party under the title of "The Australasian Anti-transportation League," and embodied their sentiments in a series of resolutions that were intended to effectually check the efforts of the Home Government in reviving the system :—" (1) That they engage not to employ any persons thereafter transported. (2) That they would use all the powers they possessed to prevent the establishment of English prisons or penal settlements within their bounds, and to seek the repeal of all regulations, and the removal of all establishments for that purpose. (3) That they would support in every way all who might suffer in the lawful promotion of this cause." The English Government and the Colonial Council could send the prisoners, but they could not force the people to employ them. This firm stand made by the masses settled the question, and prevented its revival.

Early in 1846 the question of the coal supply agitated the minds of all. The valuable mines of Newcastle had been worked by Government until 1828, when the entire coalfields of the colony were leased to the Australian Agricultural Company on terms which gave that company a perpetual monopoly of the entire coal trade. The increasing demand for coal in steam navigation, manufactories, etc., had the effect under the terms of the lease of giving them an annual return of many thousands.

In 1847 The Australian Agricultural Company gave up their lease, after being satisfied with the terms of compromise.

The new squatting regulations were received in July, 1847. There were three classes of lands—(1) The settled lands ; (2) the intermediate ; (3) the unsettled. The settled comprised the original nineteen counties, and East and West Macquarie ; all lands within twenty-five miles of Melbourne, fifteen from Geelong, and ten from many other towns ; all lands within three miles of sea, and within two miles from the Glenelg, Clarence, and the Richmond Rivers. The intermediate districts, the counties Bourke, Normanby, Grant, Auckland, and Gippsland, and any counties that may be fixed and proclaimed before 31st December, 1848 ; unsettled district, all besides. The unsettled lands could be leased for fourteen years; the intermediate, leased for eight years ; the settled, leased for one year. This prevented the alienation of the lands from the people. The colonists were satisfied with this regulation, and as a result immigration revived, and general prosperity followed.

The death of Lady Fitzroy at Parramatta, on 7th December, was the occasion of much melancholy and sadness. She had been thrown from her carriage, and, from injuries received, died.

In 1847 the chief subject that occupied the attention of the Parliament and the people was the separation question. Port Phillip for a considerable time had been agitating this subject. They had succeeded in obtaining a favourable reply from the Home authorities, notwithstanding the efforts of the Sydney district in opposition ; but a change in the administration at Home brought into power a class of persons not at all familiar with the pressing wants of the colonist, and consequently a delay in treating the question with that earnestness needed to bring about its accomplishment at once. The agitation was revived from year to year by the people of Port Phillip, and urged with a persistency that was bound to win in time. A favourable period came in the latter part of 1850. The question of responsible Government was earnestly urged upon the attention of the Home Government at the same time. The two questions were being pressed with great vehemence on the Colonial Secretary, Earl Grey, who solved the matter in an Act entitled, " An Act for the Better Government of the Colonies," which he introduced into the British Parliament, and which passed in due time, and was communicated to the Government of New South Wales.

This Act granted to New South Wales power to change or modify its own constitution, to create two Houses in its legislature, one or both of which could be elective, or one elective, and the other by nomination and appointment for life or a limited period. All salaries, except that of the Governor and judges, to be under the control of the legislature. The Act contained also provision for the separation of Port Phillip, South Australia, and Tasmania (Van Dieman's Land) into independent colonies, with like powers. New South Wales, in the exercise of the powers conferred upon her, adopted a constitution, which created a responsible Parliament of two Houses—the one elective and representative, and the other by nomination, holding office for life—as nearly after the model of the Home Government as the circumstances would admit of.

Changes in the constitution were the chief topics of interest in the discussions both in and out of Parliament during the years 1848 to 1851. The growing sentiment of the colony in favour of a representative and responsible Government had begun to modify the attitude of the Mother Country towards the colony. The colonists were beginning to assert their intention to be heard on all questions affecting their interests, though there were a few of the leaders in politics in favour of creating a titled class, and were also disposed to deny the franchise to the poor, and would have been glad to shape the constitution so as to give themselves and their descendants a monopoly of privileges; yet the people were quick to discern these insidious acts of injustice. Their protests were earnest and frequent, and had their effect on the Home authorities. They resisted all attempts to encroach upon their rights as full-fledged members of a free country, and in a public meeting assembled in Sydney in January, 1848, they expressed emphatically their sentiments in the following resolutions :—" (1) That the meeting viewed the proposed change in the constitution of the colony indicated by the despatch of the Secretary of State with the utmost apprehension and dismay; (2) that the proposed measure would have the effect of depriving the colonists of the elective franchise, which the meeting maintained was their inalienable right as British subjects; (3) that in consequence of the wide dispersion of a large portion of the inhabitants of the colony any measure for establishing municipalities similar in principle to the district councils, which it was attempted to create by the Act of Parliament 5 and 6 Victoriæ, would be so repugnant to the wishes, and so adverse to the interests, of the community that it was utterly impossible it could ever be brought into effective operation ; -(4) that the colonists protested against this being made the subject of theoretical experiments in legislation, and were anxious to enjoy a form of government founded, as nearly as circumstances would admit, on the principles of the British Constitution; (5) that the creation of Port Phillip into a separate colony afforded no sufficient reason for such innovations." These resolutions were extensively endorsed by the people, and copies forwarded to England. It was during the first session of the new Colonial Parliament that a new excitement awoke the ambition and interest of all—the question of transportation. Taxation and separation were questions now of the past. Port Phillip had gained her independence, and under the name of Victoria was entering upon her new colonial life, South Australia and Van Dieman's Land were doing likewise, and New South Wales had just entered upon the honor and burden of its legislative duties, when the report came of "gold in the mountains." The *Morning Herald* of May, 1851, startled the city of Sydney and the continent with the announcement in a brief paragraph, but in terms which left no doubt on the minds of the people, although Governor Fitzroy expressed some doubt when he sent the despatch to Earl Grey announcing its discovery near Bathurst. His doubts, however, soon became dissipated when he was assured by a Mr. Stutchbury, who wrote from Summer Hill Creek confirming the report, and that "four hundred persons were hard at work washing gold in tin-dishes." The year was chiefly remarkable for the excitement its discovery had upon the colony and the world. There had for a long time existed in the minds of many the conviction that gold would be discovered in paying quantities in the mountainous regions of New South Wales. It had been reported by one of the early convicts, but not credited. Shepherds from time to time had found pieces, notably one Macgregor, who had been in the habit of coming to Sydney with small pieces found in the upper country. A Mr. Smith, who was employed in the vicinity of Berrima two years previously, showed specimens to the Colonial Secretary, but refused to reveal the place where it was found. It was, however, through a Mr. Hargraves that the discovery of gold in Summer Hill Creek was first made and announced. The gold excitement of California had drawn thousands from Australia two years previously. Among them Mr. Hargraves, who went in search of the precious metal across the Pacific. Though unsuccessful in finding the coveted wealth yet he acquired skill as a prospector, and returning to Australia, through his knowledge acquired in America he was led to believe that gold existed in the mountains of his native land. A brief search was rewarded by the discovery of rich auriferous deposits. The Governor claimed it as the Queen's prerogative, but the people laughed at his claim, and rushed to the mountains. As a necessary accompaniment to the discovery of gold, a branch of the Royal Mint was founded in 1853. This was mainly due to the earnest advocacy of Sir James Martin.

In 1852 the University of Sydney was inaugurated. It was the first institution of the kind in the colonies. The wealthy and more aspiring had previously to go to England or abroad to complete their collegiate education. This, for a long time, was felt to be a great drawback to the youth of this country. The erection of this noble University was favoured by the people generally, and has done much to infuse a spirit of rivalry among the various educational circles of the colony. The benefit of this institution is beginning to be widely felt in all the professions.

The respect in which the Governor was held by the people of New South Wales may be inferred from a farewell address which passed the Legislative Council almost unanimously:—" (1) That this Council, on the eve of its prorogation, and of the departure for England of His Excellency Sir Charles Augustus Fitzroy, desires to report its deliberate opinion of the practical ability, sound judgment, and eminent success, which, during a period of more than eight years, have characterised His Excellency's personal administration of the Government of this colony. (2) That this Council more especially desires to express its sense of the frank, cordial, and truly constitutional spirit on all occasions manifested by His Excellency in his communications with this branch of the legislature—a course which has been attended with the happiest results, and has in no slight degree tended to confirm that love of order and those feelings of loyalty and of attachment to the Parent State which pervade all ranks of the community. (3) That in bidding him farewell, this Council desires to convey to His Excellency the assurance of its best wishes, and to express its hope that His Excellency's administration of the Government of this colony may ensure to him a continuance of the confidence and favour of our Most Gracious Sovereign. (4) That the foregoing resolutions be embodied in an address to His Excellency the Governor-General, to be presented to His Excellency by the House to-morrow." These sentiments were not entertained by all the members of the House. An amendment was offered by the Rev. Dr. Lang, to the effect "That His Excellency's administration had been throughout a uniform conspiracy against the rights of the people; that from the inefficiency of the Government the colony had fallen from the leading position in the group, and become only second in the list; that the funds of the colony had been lavishly expended in the maintenance of unnecessary offices and the payment of extravagant salaries, while urgent public works had been postponed and neglected; that no such efforts as were necessary had been made to supply the colony with an industrious population of the working classes from the Mother Country; that no efforts in the way of geographical discovery had been made; that Leichhardt had been left to perish miserably in the central desert of Australia; that instead of relaxing the oppressive character of the land system, in accordance with the obvious intent and spirit of the Orders-in-Council, His Excellency had voluntarily exceeded the powers entrusted him in rendering that system still more oppressive; and that the moral influence which had emanated from Government House had been baneful to the interest of the community." This amendment was advocated with most bitter vehemence, but was lost on a division of twenty-eight to six, and the address carried by the same, showing beyond any question the feelings of the House. The country was very much of the same opinion. The action of the legislature embodied in the above commendator resolutions were widely endorsed by the Press of the country, and opposed by a very limited portion of it.

The Governor retired from the Administration of New South Wales on the 17th January, 1855, and on the 28th of January he set sail for England.

The following statistics we quote from the official history. They show the rapid progress made by the colony in all branches of industries:—

In 1846 the population of the colony was 196,704; in 1850 it was 265,503; and in 1851, Victoria having been separated from the colony of New South Wales, the population was 197,168, but in 1854 it had reached 251,315.

Land under cultivation in 1846 was 183,360 acres; in 1850 there was 198,056 acres; 1851, after separation, 153,117 acres; 1854 there was a falling off to 148,851.

The revenue in 1846 amounted to £352,778; in 1854 to £1,004,467; expenditure in the same years £290,092 and £966,569. The imports of 1846 were £1,630,522, and of 1854, £5,981,063. The exports in 1846 were £1,481,539, and of 1854, £4,050,126. Horses in 1846 were 88,126, horned cattle 1,430,736, sheep 7,906,811, and pigs 45,600; and in 1850, just before separation, horses 132,437, horned cattle 1,738,965, sheep 13,059,324, and pigs 61,631; and in 1854, after having somewhat recovered from the loss occasioned by the separation of Port Phillip District, New South Wales had horses 148,851, horned cattle 1,576,750, sheep 8,144,119, and pigs 68,255. The above figures plainly reveal a history of continuous prosperity; and when we take into account that it covers a period embraced in the gold excitement when all classes were drawn away from the farming and pastoral enterprises, it is matter for congratulation that the natural products of the soil contributed so largely to the prosperity of the times.

CHAPTER XVIII.

SIR WILLIAM DENISON.

1855-1861.

SIR WILLIAM DENISON, who was Governor of Van Dieman's Land, was appointed successor to Governor Fitzroy.

One of the first questions the new Governor was called upon to deal with was the consideration of a new constitution. The people of Sydney were not satisfied with the one they had adopted in 1851, and resolved to better it if they could. A large meeting of the citizens held in Sydney had adopted a petition praying the Governor to dissolve the Legislative Council, with the object of making some changes in the constitution. This the Governor refused. The Governor, in his speech to the Parliament, adverted in complimentary terms to the munificence of the colony in providing an endowment for the University and affiliated colleges, but urged their favorable attention to a bill for the further encouragement of education in providing for primary schools as well.

The restoration of steam communication with England, which had been broken off on account of the English war with Russia, was an important subject for legislation.

During this year a Steam Postal Communication Bill was passed by the Council, and again was established a steam service between the colonies and the Mother Country that greatly facilitated communication and the commerce of the country.

This measure received the favourable attention of the Council, but was reserved for the first Parliament of responsible government to act upon. The recent war with Russia had been brought to a successful close, and the colony was enjoying the brightest prospect of a revival of trade.

An important series of resolutions, expressive of the loyal sentiment of the colony, was introduced by Mr. Henry Parkes, and passed by the Council on the 6th November, 1855, which very much tended to show the almost universal sentiment of good feeling that existed towards England :—
"(1) That the progress of the war in which England and her allies are engaged against Russia has been anxiously watched by the people of this colony, who fully concur in the justice of the cause sustained by the allied Powers. (2) That this Council, entertaining the same patriotic sentiments which animate all classes of the community, feels a warm pride in the loyalty, valour, and fortitude displayed by our countrymen in arms. (3) That this Council, on behalf of the colony, deeply deplores the loss of the brave men and distinguished commanders who have fallen in battle, or died in the course of the war by pestilence and disease, and desires to express its earnest sympathy with great Britain in these national bereavements. (4) That this Council, on behalf of the colony, views with unspeakable gratification the increasing cordiality which marks the alliance between Her Majesty the Queen and the Emperor of the French, from which it hopes for an early and enduring peace, and a succession of other benefits scarcely less valuable to mankind." The princely liberality of the people of the colony had previously been exemplified in large contributions made towards the widows and orphans of fallen soldiers in that war, and was the subject of commendation by the Governor in his speech in reply on the presentation of these resolutions.

The opening of the railway to Parramatta was formally made in September. A large concourse of people assembled on the occasion, and joined in the inauguration of this enterprise.

In the latter part of this year the Governor announced to the Council the assent of Her Majesty to a bill conferring a constitution on New South Wales. The colony had most earnestly contended for a responsible government. The powers conferred by the Home Government to the colonies in 1850 had conceded the privilege of representation, but it had reserved to the Governor the right of selecting his ministers of advice. They were entirely under his control, and responsible alone to him. What the colony contended for was a Ministry holding office only so long as they retained the confidence of the Parliament, and in this respect an imitation of the Home Government. On the 27th November the Speaker of the House announced that Her Majesty's assent to the Constitution Act was granted.

The Constitution Act called into existence a new legislature, composed of two Chambers and a responsible Ministry.

On the 19th December the Legislative Council was prorogued; but prior to this act the Governor, in a speech of considerable ability, referred to the satisfactory adjustment of many matters of interest to the colony, among which was the restoration of steam communication with England, the encouraging legislation in regard to railways, the feeling of loyalty that generally prevailed, as evinced in their expressions of good-will shown towards the orphans and widows of our fallen soldiers, and more especially in the new powers of self-government granted to the colony, in the exercise of which he hoped to see unmeasured prosperity follow.

On this occasion the Governor-General's commission and instructions, under the new constitution, were presented to the Council, revoking the former commission, and re-appointing Sir William Denison Governor of New South Wales.

The Governor, in January, 1856, honored Mr. Stuart Alexander Donaldson with the duty of forming the first responsible Ministry. After considerable difficulty he succeeded as follows:—Stuart Alexander Donaldson, Colonial Secretary; Thomas Holt, Colonial Treasurer; William Montague Manning, Attorney-General; John Bayley Darvall, Solicitor-General; George Robert Nichols, Auditor-General and Secretary for Lands and Works; William Colburn Mayne, Representative of the Government in the Legislative Council. The first parliament assembled on the 22nd May, 1856. Sir Alfred Stephen was appointed President of the Legislative Council, and Mr. Daniel Cooper was elected Speaker of the Assembly. This Ministry continued in office until the 22nd, when Mr. Donaldson informed the House that the want of support given to the measures the Government had proposed led them to the belief that they had not the full confidence of the House, hence they tendered their resignation.

The Governor sent for Mr. Cowper, and on the 26th August, 1856, the following Ministry was announced :—Charles Cowper, Colonial Secretary ; Robert Campbell, Colonial Treasurer ; Terence Aubrey Murray, Secretary for Lands and Works ; James Martin, Attorney-General ; Alfred Lutwyche, Solicitor-General and Representative of the Government in the Legislative Council. The Legislature met on the 16th September. The only business they were enabled to do was the passing of resolutions congratulating the Queen on the peaceful relations she sustained to France. A vote of censure, moved on the 17th, and debated for five days, relieved this Ministry from further duties on the 22nd. Their resignation was accepted on the 2nd October.

Mr. Henry W. Parker was entrusted with the task of forming the third responsible Ministry. The new Ministry consisted of—Henry Watson Parker, Premier and Colonial Secretary ; Stuart A. Donaldson, Colonial Treasurer ; John Hay, Secretary for Lands and Works ; William M. Manning, Attorney-General ; John Bayley Darvall, Solicitor-General ; Edward Deas-Thompson, Representative in Legislative Council. The first Parliament was prorogued on the 18th March, 1857. On that occasion the Governor, in his speech, referred to the frequent changes of Ministry, which prevented much of the proposed legislation, but that Parliament had been successful in passing some useful measures. Changes in the Government were to be expected. The colony had not yet the necessary experience in independent government to avoid all blunders; and it would require time to call out the ability of its leading politicians, and prove their adaptability to the work assigned them.

The second session of the first Parliament assembled on the 11th August, 1857.

The Government introduced an Electoral Bill, intended to increase the number of members, and regulate the election of the same. On this they were defeated, and tendered their resignation on the 4th September.

On the 8th September a new Ministry was announced as follows :— Charles Cowper, Colonial Secretary ; Richard Jones, Colonial Treasurer ; Terence A. Murray, Secretary for Lands and Public Works ; James Martin, Attorney-General ; Alfred J. P. Lutwyche, Solicitor-General ; John Dickson, Representative of Government in Legislative Council.

During the year 1857 a terrible disaster befel the colony in the loss of a noble ship and one hundred and twenty lives at Port Jackson Heads. The night was dark, and the sea storm-tossed. The mountainous billows that dashed their angry surf against the bold but half concealed cliffs that guarded the entrance to Port Jackson had been lashed into fury by a north-east gale that had prevailed for days. The captain had ordered the ship to tack about for a time in search of the entrance, but was baffled in the attempt by the thundering roar of waters that answered from the gloom. A momentary rift in the surging mass of foam deluded the captain into the belief that he had found the harbour, and turning the vessel towards the supposed entrance all were made happy in the expectation of reaching home and friends. The happiness was but a momentary joy. In a few minutes the "Dunbar" was violently dashed against the hidden cliff that frowned from above upon the wailing mass of humanity that struggled in vain for life. One hopeless shriek and a despairing groan mingled their sad voices with the mocking foam that surged back the terrible answer that all had sunk. Early next morning tidings of the wreck wrung the hearts of friends and strangers alike with grief. Thousands hurried from Sydney to the scene only to add their tears to the universal sorrow. One survivor only remained to tell the pitiful story. He had been washed up, and lodged on a ledge of the cliff. A young man volunteered to be let down by a rope, and thus save the man. It was found that the wreck was occasioned by mistaking a low break in the rocky coast called the Gap for the open entrance to Port Jackson. An electric revolving light of greater magnitude than any in the world was erected forthwith as a beacon to warn the mariner of danger, and at the same time to be an everlasting monument of the young nation's grief.

Early in the year 1857 there was a strong sentiment aroused in the northern district in favour of an independent colony. The interests of the Moreton Bay District were so distinct from that of the rest of the colony of New South Wales that several petitions were forwarded to the Home authorities praying for separation, and it was reported that there was a request forwarded with some of these petitions by the "squatocracy" of that district for the restoration of transportation, as it was impossible to secure from the aborigines or other sources efficient service for the care of their increasing flocks.

On the 14th November Mr. Parkes moved the following resolutions, which were carried unanimously:—(1) "That this House, with feelings of sincere and unmingled gratitude, recognise in the act of Her Most Gracious Majesty, by which the transportation of British criminals to these Australian colonies was made to cease and determine, the concession of a great and complete measure of justice, which was sought by the unanimous prayers of the colonists, and has been productive of general and permanent satisfaction. (2) That in the opinion of this House the compliance of Her Most Gracious Majesty with the prayers of the colonists in the settlement of a question so long agitated, while it has confirmed the feelings of loyalty and attachment to the Mother Country, which happily exist in these communities, has led to the most beneficial results in their vastly improved social condition, and their rapid progress in political character and commercial prosperity. (3) That in the opinion of this House any steps on the part of Her Majesty's Government to revive the transportation of convicts to the northern portion of New South Wales, or to any part of Eastern Australia or the islands adjacent, would be regarded as a breach of faith by the colonists, would create universal discontent, and lead to consequences greatly to be deplored. (4) That the foregoing resolutions be embodied in an address to the Governor-General, with a request that His Excellency will be pleased to transmit them to the principal Secretary of State for presentation to Her Majesty." The effect of the above on the Home Government appears to have been salutary, as the revival of transportation seems to have been dropped. Nevertheless, the Imperial Parliament was disposed to listen to the prayer of the northern district, in so far as to propose to give them a separate colony, and to fix the southern boundary on a line south of latitude 30°, thus including the New England and Clarence River districts, which called out the opposition of the New South Wales Parliament, for on the 6th November they passed the following resolutions:—"(1) That this House has learnt, with regret, that it is the intention of the Imperial Government to fix the southern boundary of the proposed new colony of Moreton Bay at a line south of the thirtieth parallel of south latitude. (2) That as the interests of the various districts proposed to be included in the new colony are not identical, this House is of opinion that in defining the future boundary line of the colony of Moreton Bay it is the duty of the Imperial Government to consult the wishes of the several districts proposed to be included in that colony. (3) That while this House does not feel called upon to dispute the propriety of the Imperial Government erecting the districts of Moreton Bay and Darling Downs into a separate colony, if in accordance with the expressed wish of the majority of the inhabitants thereof, it submits that on the same principle it will be unjust to the inhabitants of New England and the Clarence River to include those districts in such colony, if averse to their being so included. (4) That in the opinion of this House the interests and commercial connection of New England and the Clarence River are now, and will continue to be, so completely identified with the colony of New South Wales, and distinct from those of the districts of Moreton Bay and Darling Downs, that if the question whether the first-mentioned districts shall be included in the new colony be referred to the inhabitants of those districts a very large majority will be found opposed to their being so included; and in support of such opinion this House refers to the petition signed by 1,551 inhabitants of New England and Clarence River, praying for the establishment of an Assize Court at Armidale, in which petition they assert that they do not desire to be included in a section of the northern districts which may be separated from the present colony of New South Wales. (5) That this House requests that the Imperial Government will defer the final settlement of the southern boundary-line of the new colony until the opinion of the inhabitants of the districts of New England and the Clarence River is ascertained upon the subject. (6) That the foregoing resolutions be embodied in an address to the Governor-General with a request that His Excellency will be pleased to transmit them to Her Majesty's Secretary of State for the Colonies at the earliest opportunity."

On the 15th January, 1857, a despatch from Her Majesty settled the disputed question of the title by which the members of the Legislative Council and the Speaker of the Assembly should be recognised by stating it to be Her Majesty's pleasure that they should be entitled to the designation of " Honorable."

Sir Alfred Stephen resigned the office of President of the Council, and John H. Plunkett was appointed to fill the vacancy.

Parliament was prorogued on the 18th March, 1857: thus terminated the first session of the first Parliament. The frequent changes of Ministry during this first session somewhat retarded the progress of legislation.

GOVERNOR DENISON. 135

However, the country enjoyed prosperity and peace. During this session an Act amendatory to the constitution granted to the legislature the right of making changes to the constitution without the two-thirds majority, and re-apportioned the membership thereof on a more equitable basis.

The second session of the first Parliament assembled on the 11th August, 1857. The Treasurer's (Mr. Donaldson) budget showed a gratifying condition of finance and trade, considering the interruption occasioned by the war of Great Britain with Russia, the effects of which had not yet passed. The Parker Ministry was defeated on their "Electoral Bill," and resigned on the 4th September. Mr. Cowper was charged with the duty of forming a Ministry, which he did as follows:—Charles Cowper, Colonial Secretary; Richard Jones, Colonial Treasurer; Terence A. Murray, Secretary for Lands and Works; James Martin, Attorney-General; Alfred Lutwyche, Solicitor-General.

Many questions of an intercolonial character had sprung up even since the separation of Victoria, South Australia, Tasmania, and the Moreton Bay District, which had been looking towards a separation from New South Wales, and called for some legislation that would meet the approval of each of the colonies. On the 19th August Mr. E. Deas-Thompson brought the matter before the Legislative Council, who appointed a select committee, and who reported favorably and recommended that delegates from the several colonies might devise a place of General Assembly for the colonies, in view of which the following resolutions were passed unanimously on the 6th November:—" (1) That it is expedient that a Federal Assembly should be established, invested with the necessary power to discuss and determine all questions of an intercolonial character arising in the Australian colonies generally. (2) That the best means of originating a Federal Assembly would be by inviting a conference of delegates from the respective colonies, to which belong the duty of determining upon a plan of union, and for this purpose that the legislatures of Victoria, South Australia, and Tasmania should be requested to select three delegates each—one of whom might be a member of Council, and two members of Assembly—to meet three delegates from this Council to be similarly appointed. (3) That these delegates, assembled in confidence, be empowered to propose a plan of federation, to be afterwards submitted for approval to the legislature of the respective colonies. (4) That the expenditure incident to the conference should be borne by the respective colonies in whatever proportions may be fixed by the conference itself. (5) That the conference shall hold its meeting in whatever place the majority of the delegates may determine, their decisions being interchanged in writing within a month of their elections being completed.

For the next few years bills of importance were discussed, and enabled the colony to assert her views upon all subjects affecting her well-being. Educational reform was very much needed, especially in the primary departments. A favourable consideration finally put educational matters upon a firm and liberal basis. Parliament put on record her conviction that both Houses should become elective, by the almost unanimous passage of a resolution to that effect in 1857. Steam and mail communication was established by a monthly service with England through the Peninsular and Oriental Steam Navigation Company.

In 1858 an Electoral Act was passed through Parliament which conferred manhood suffrage and vote by ballot. This Act increased the membership of the Assembly to eighty, and gave every adult male of six months' residence in any electorate a vote. This measure was a wise one, for nothing tends so much to the good government of a people than the sense that each man has a share in the government of the body politic. With this theory the education of the people has to go hand in hand. A true democracy will ever see that the educational advantages of the nation are co-extensive with the privileges of self-government. Hence, with the increased privileges under the new Electorate Act came the question of extended facilities looking towards the universal enlightenment of all classes of the community. The spirit that accorded the one was not slow in recognising the need of the other, and therefore each succeeding Ministry that came into power freely granted every encouragement to the schools of the colony.

The new Electoral Act having come into force the second Parliament was dissolved on the 11th April, 1859.

The third Parliament assembled on 30th August, the members having been elected under the new Electoral Act. Sir Daniel Cooper was chosen Speaker. The Governor, in his opening speech, congratulated the Government on the condition of the country, expressed the hope that in the interest of the people there would be established a Free Public Library, alluded to the separation of the Moreton Bay District, and that the finances were in a healthy condition.

The question of the separation of the Moreton Bay District into an independent colony had long been entertained by the people of that portion of the country. Year after year their representatives had urged it upon the attention of the New South Wales Parliament, but they were opposed by nearly all the politicians of note of that day. The district had an able advocate in the person of the Rev. Dr. Lang, who in former years had successfully fought the battle of separation for the Port Phillip district, and never ceased the contest until it was constituted an independent colony under the title of Victoria. With an equal zeal, and even with greater persistency, he labored for the same result on behalf of the Moreton Bay district. The inhabitants had long felt they were too far removed from the centre of Government, and that their remoteness therefrom barred them from being properly appreciated by "the powers that be," and that they could scarcely hope for great prosperity until they had accorded to themselves the right of collecting their own revenues and disbursing the same in improving their own position. The Home Government was pleased to endorse their view of the question, and accordingly granted their petition. The announcement was made by the Home authorities in July, 1859, and was received with universal gladness. This had the effect of infusing new hopes in regard to the possibilities of the colony. Many of the early settlers there had unbounded faith in its rapid development; if they were untrammelled by what they were pleased to term the old fogey ways of a selfish mother who sought to rule her infant child with a rod of iron, and whose supreme thought seemed to be that no other course than a stern repressive one would serve her interests. The people of the district thought otherwise, and were restive under the yoke that the mother colony was pleased to impose. The Parliament at Sydney acted as if the entire district was chiefly adapted for penal purposes ; or at best it was an appendage to the mother colony desirable only as a paddock where she might pasture her flocks, and where her aristocrats might obtain large areas at a nominal sum, and thus secure an inheritance without money or price. Taking the most favorable view of the matter, there is no question that growth and rapid development could not be secured as long as she remained an insignificant part of New South Wales. Their interests were not in common, and it was impossible for their representatives to form such a faction of the parliament at Sydney as to make their presence felt or their demands imperious. Independence and self-government are the watchwords of all peoples who feel their oppression, and the principle is sure to win because it is based on the inherent rights of manhood; and it is a standard around which all people of intelligence will rally, and from which they are never disposed to budge. The dogged determination of Englishmen, so well educated in its value by a thousand years of historic experience, is not easily satisfied with anything short of their personal and family rights in regard to property, person, and life; and responsibity for their protection and care, will lead them to sacrifice life itself. Happily the contest in this instance did not demand extreme measures. It was one of politics only, and its accomplishment rested with the authorities at home. The English Government for many years has evinced a determination to yield all rights of the kind to her people. The only assurance the Imperial Parliament seems to exact is, that the rights of all her citizens should be equally guarded, and that upon the broadest basis of personal freedom consistent with the good government of all concerned. The entire population of the Moreton Bay district, at the time of its separation from New South Wales and its erection into the colony of Queensland, was only about 25,000 souls, rather a small number to constitute a nation. But numbers were not the only facts regarding it. The immense country embraced within its boundary limits, and its known fertility, had great weight with those who could look beyond the present and scan the future. The Queen, on the advice of her Ministry, was graciously pleased to grant the desired boon. The wisdom of her act has more and more appeared as the years have brought increasing multitudes to her territory, where homes and happiness alike have waited on the labor of the industrious.

CHAPTER XIX.

PENAL EXPANSION.

Prior to separation the Moreton Bay district was by no means an unimportant section of the original colony. It had made its presence and power felt for many years. The class of people that had emigrated thither both from the old country and the settled districts round Sydney, were of the intelligent and industrious sort; they had gone there for business and the special purpose of building up for themselves and families such homes as they could not expect to find elsewhere. It is easy to understand that the rugged manhood that would dare the wilderness, could speak out also on its own behalf when necessary, and they never failed to do so. No doubt among the causes that led to the separation was the discussion throughout the country on the Lands Bill, that had been introduced by John Robertson (now Sir John Robertson), and had been growing in interest for several years. This had been for a long time before the people. Under the Imperial Regulations of 1843, given to the respective colonies to guide them in the disposing of their lands, the price fixed for all country districts was 12s. per acre, payable within one month from the purchase. The lands could not be selected beyond certain limits, and then not till after survey. Under such a method it was not possible to obtain good lands until the existing authorities saw fit to place them in market, and when they were so placed, friends of those in official position had the advantage of knowing the valuable tracts before they came into market. They very easily managed to give themselves and their near friends the advantage of any good purchase, and thus there had grown up a gigantic wrong that the whole power of the administration was committed to. The bills introduced proposed to give parties anxious to till the soil the right to go anywhere and make a selection of the best lands they could find, even before survey, and make payment thereon at the rate of 5s. per acre, and the balance in three years, and even then the balance could be deferred from year to year at an interest of 5 per cent. These proposed changes did not meet with so hearty a reception at the hands of the upper branch of the House as was desired by the people, that House being largely interested in the squatting interests that had been spread all over the colony. The lordly stationmasters, who had an undoubted control of the action of the Upper House, had made it almost impossible to obtain the desired legislation in this respect. The "squatocracy," so called, of the Moreton Bay district were the predominant element in their section. It was, therefore, to their personal interest to separate, and thus secure an extended lease of the privileges secured to them by the Imperial Land Policy—that, in their opinion, should not be disturbed. It became quite evident that the popular will of the people, as expressed in the Lower House in the Legislature at Sydney, pointed to the speedy passage of the bill, notwithstanding the almost unanimous opposition of the Upper House, a prediction which was fulfilled in a very short time, and hence the earnestness and persistency of people in control of the politics of the Moreton Bay district, who asked for and obtained separation.

Queensland, or the Moreton Bay district, has a Centennial History, although her practical development does not date back more than sixty-five years. Captain Cook, on his first trip of exploration, sailed along the coast of Australia, visiting Moreton Bay in his ship "Endeavour," and naming the bay after the Earl of Moreton, who was at the time President of the Royal Society. Captain Cook's knowledge of the country was exceedingly limited, as he simply touched upon some of the more prominet points going northward. He named, however, several of the chief bays and principal promontories. Running aground on a coral reef, his vessel sustained an injury which necessitated repairs, for which purpose he entered a river which he named "The Endeavour," after his ship, and

PENAL EXPANSION.   141

on which is now situated Cooktown, named in honor of the event. The next exploration of this territory was made by Lieutenant Flinders, in 1799 in the ship "Norfolk." He was commissioned by the New South Wales Government to make thorough exploration of the north-eastern coast and the Gulf of Carpentaria, and to make maps of the coast line, noting its rivers and bays, together with a fuller description of the character of the country. His first point of interest was Moreton Bay, which he extensively examined, but in which he failed to discover the entrance of any river. Landing upon Brisbie Island, which lies outside of the bay, he endeavored to hold intercourse with the natives, but they showed a disposition of antagonism, which led to an encounter, and resulted in a skirmish between his men and the natives, hence the name applied to the place, Skirmish Point. Proceeding further north he discovered and examined nearly all the bays that up to the present time are found marked upon our maps. Pursuing his investigations around Cape York, he sailed through the Gulf of Carpentaria. The report of Lieutenant Flinders concerning this region represented the coast as being low, swampy, and marshy, and unfit for human habitation. Not being favorable, the Government at Sydney paid little or no attention to this portion of the country for many years. The next visit made was by Lieutenant King in the ship "Mermaid," who in 1817 was commissioned to pursue the investigations previously made, and to discover more thoroughly the nature of the country inland, in view of its adaptation for a penal settlement. He succeeded in enlarging the surveys and maps of Captain Flinders, and added much valuable information. However, he did not succeed in gaining much additional knowledge of the interior. The first real occupancy of the territory was in 1823, when it was found necessary to secure additional settlements for penal purposes. Under advice from the Home Government the authorities at Sydney instructed Lieutenant Oxley to proceed to Port Curtis with a view of finding out its adaptation to such a purpose. This gentleman being dissatisfied with that region, made a thorough exploration of Moreton Bay and discovered the Brisbane River, which he named after the Governor of that day. Oxley sailed as far north as the Bowen, and made an examination of all points of interest, between Sydney, along the coast, but found, in his opinion, the Brisbane River as offering the greatest advantages in that respect.

The overcrowded condition of Sydney and Port Macquarie with prisoners made it desirable to find new locations for their settlement. It was part of the penal policy of those days to multiply centres of operation remote from each other, and from which the prisoners could easily be despatched to the several works that were being carried on—bridges, roads, and other things that were necessary in developing the new country. Lieutenant Oxley was directed to examine Port Curtis thoroughly, as that was supposed to be the most appropriate for the upper district. All previous reports had represented Moreton Bay and the surrounding country to be of a low marshy nature; hence, without further examination, it was not regarded with favor as a suitable place. Oxley's thorough examination of Port Curtis, in 1823, revealed the fact that it was unsuited, and thence abandoning that, he directed his course southward and came to Moreton Bay, and by a mere accident came in contact with two men, whose story of shipwreck was thrilling beyond description, and whose accidental discovery on Brisbie Island was beyond all doubt the chief means by which Oxley was led to the discovery of the Brisbane River. Although this bay had been thoroughly explored by previous parties, as yet there was no knowledge on the part of the authorities of any river emptying into it. The men above referred to bore the names of Pamphlet and Finnigan. Their story was to the effect that they formed a portion of a crew of four, who had been engaged in timber business along the coast, and were carried out to sea and shipwrecked upon the island, the crew consisting of Parsons and Thomson, together with themselves. When they were driven to the island they were received and treated kindly by the natives, and through them reached the mainland, and became in that way cognisant of the existence of a large body of fresh water. These men were in a condition of semi-starvation, and hailed with delight the approach of Oxley and his party. Upon their report a thorough exploration was made by Oxley of the Brisbane River and its resources. They were delighted with the appearance of the country. The river was found to be broad and deep, and the country on either side in every direction fertile and well wooded. Oxley named the magnificent stream the Brisbane River, after the Governor. He discovered and named Oxley Creek running into it, Lockyer Creek being named by Allan Cunningham, who shortly afterwards, in conjunction with Lockyer, had discovered it further up the river, when they had more thoroughly explored the region that had been so favorably reported on by Oxley. The words of his report are worth here recording :— "When examining Moreton Bay, we had the satisfaction to find the tide sweeping up a considerable inlet between the first mangrove island and the mainland. A few hours ended our anxiety, the water became perfectly fresh and no diminution in the size of the river. After passing Scareach the scenery was peculiarly beautiful : the country along the banks alternately hilly and level, but not flooded, the soil of the finest description of good brush land, on which grew timber of great magnitude, some of a description quite unknown to us, amongst others a magnificent species of pine. Up to this point the river was navigable for vessels not drawing more than sixteen feet of water—the tide rose about five feet, being the same at the entrance. We proceeded about thirty miles further, no diminution having taken place in either the depth or the breadth of the river, excepting one place, for the extent of thirty yards, where a ridge of detached rocks extended across the river, not having more than twelve feet upon them at high water. From this period to Termination Hill the river continued of nearly uniform size. The tide ascends daily fifty miles up the mouth of the Brisbane. The country on either side is of a very superior description, and equally well adapted for cultivation or grazing." On the strength of Oxley's report, Governor Brisbane established a penal settlement the following year, in 1824. He selected for this purpose a prominent point on the Moreton Bay, north of where the Brisbane empties into it, and named it Redcliffe. A small band of prisoners were established here, and immediately set to work to erect rude houses, huts, etc., for their accommodation ; but after having occupied the same for the space of a few months only, it was found to be a very miserable selection. On account of the absence of good soil in the vicinity, and a sufficiency of fresh water, they abandoned the place and moved twenty miles higher up the river, and selected the site upon which has grown up the City of Brisbane. The natives, upon discovering the vacated huts at Redcliffe, set fire to them, exclaiming, "Humpy bung," which means huts (humpy) extinguished (bung), which is interpreted by some to mean also "houses of the dead. The name has clung to the place ever since, and Humpy Bung continues only to proclaim the existence of its past short-lived glory. It is a point of interest to the visitor who is pleased to gaze upon the first step of Queensland's civilisation. This was the beginning of the convict era in the Queensland portion of the continent; its prosperity was rapid, if we may regard prosperity from the standpoint of increase in numbers of convicts sent to the region. For four years afterwards, in 1828, the reports claim 1000 convicts, guarded by 100 soldiers, as being located at Moreton Bay. This class of people here laid the foundations of the future growth and development of this region. As in most other portions of the Australian Continent, the building of roads, bridges, courthouses, gaols, the clearing of lands, and other improvements, preparatory to the occupancy of the section by white and free people, were essential pre-requisites, and the honor and glory of our present civilisation must, to a large extent, be accorded to those unfortunates who many years ago sowed the seed from which we are deriving a bountiful harvest.

CHAPTER XX.

THE GENESIS.

THE pre-colonial history of the Moreton Bay district embraces the period between 1824 and 1859—that is, the portion of her existence that antedates the time when, as a full fledged colony, she began to administer her own affairs. It includes what has been termed the penal era, which embraces the years between 1824 and 1840, and the settlement era, or that embraced within the years when free white emigrants were induced to come to the country and to begin the development of the same for the purpose of making homes for themselves and families. It is needless to say much in regard to the penal era, other than so far as to place on record some of the more salient points to which the future generations may with profit refer. That it was not a paradise of happiness or of bliss goes without saying. In fact, the type of serfdom that existed in the earlier years of colonial life among the unfortunate members of the body politic who were in condemnation was of a kind most repulsive to all such as are actuated by humanitarian sentiments. Having been chosen for the care of the worse "sort of fellows," it is not a matter of surprise for us to learn that the utmost severity characterised the discipline under which these persons were ruled. We are scarcely qualified by our superior advantages and education to judge of the roughness characteristic of those masters who were placed over the penal population of Moreton Bay during the years above-mentioned. Our judgment scarcely finds excuse for the brutality that was frequently used in the administration of discipline, so-called, but which may be truthfully characterised by the term tyranny. The old English mind, especially the military portion thereof, was drilled in the severest sort of schools, and it is therefore probable that the severity under which their military education was obtained had the effect of blunting their sense of mercy and rendering them blind to all sentiments of compassion. At all events, the stories told of early convict life in the colonies are such as would stir the blood of all flesh, even the most barbarous of the nations of the present day. Pulpits, press, and schools all cried out in detestation and condemnation of the prisoner. The lash was the common mode of discipline, the chain and ball and dungeon and the horrors of a state of semi-starvation were the toys in the hands of the commanders of those times. To give the reader a faint idea of the popular sentiment that prevailed at a much later date in the Parliament of the mother colony concerning prisoners, we give a series of resolutions passed in 1861, and which called forth, before they became law, a vast amount of discussion which extended over many years, and which numbered among its opponents historic names that figure largely on the pages of colonial life and times. The resolutions expressed the better sentiment of the people, and were brought about by the terrible condition of barbarity into which the penal institutions had fallen, not in one part, but in all parts of the Australian Continent. Reform in their management became imperative. There were few, however, who interested themselves in this department of benevolence; the great bulk of humanity took it for granted that the prisoner only got his deserts, and therefore they seldom concerned themselves as to whether those entrusted with the care of the unfortunate prisoner administered their trust in the spirit of guardians who exercised a feeling of benevolence in the restoration of the condemned, or in the spirit of an assassin whose aim is to compass his death or ruin by a legalised course of torture under the plea of discipline. Sir Henry Parkes, who was then without a title and in comparative obscurity was among the most noted advocates of reform and led the discussions which resulted many years afterwards in the passage of the following resolutions, which only became law in that colony after the period of separation. They were as follows:—First: Every prisoner should receive a reward for good conduct in the shortening of his sentence. Second: An Inspector of Prisoners should be appointed to have entire supervision of the prisoner. Third: That secular and religious instruction should be accorded. Fourth: That suitable labor should be provided so as to develop habits of industry in the prisoner and fit him for honest toil when free. And Fifth: That all should be provided with decent clothing when discharged. It was sought also to abolish capital punishment. A resolution to that effect being offered and supported by many of the leading people of those days. A lengthened and earnest debate followed upon the presentation of this question, but all failed to effect this noble reform. There are few portions of the earth that have risen to the grandeur and effectiveness of such a policy. We have no doubt that in the not distant future the world over will yet see this to be the more excellent way. It is not human to admit the element of mercy into Governments; men choose rather the harsher methods—the vindictive spirit that would destroy in its wrath. It was altogether a divine thought that conceived the power of graciousness even in human affairs. "Away with him," is an earthly cry; "Spare him a little longer," is the teaching of him who knew the power of love, and it is equally the language of all human hearts in the closest bonds of brotherhood; and when we have all graduated out of the narrow limits of estrangements and are cast into the broad fellowship of a universal brotherhood we too will more readily cry "Spare the offending member."

There were several detachments or bands of prisoners stationed at as many centres, Brisbane being the head-quarters. The smaller companies that were assigned to the supervision of a subordinate officer, called a superintendent, were utilised at different places throughout this region in the construction of several works of a public character. One of these bands was employed at Ipswich in the making of lime—hence the early name the place bore—"Limestone Ridge." The district was densely peopled by the black natives; the magnificent river with its shoals of fish, the extensive bay with its many islands and moderate climate, made it a spot which was peculiarly suited to the wants of the blackfellow. Every step that was taken by the new class of settlers was an infringement of the natives' rights, yet be it said in their praise, that the many acts of kindness shown by this race towards the shipwrecked or half-starved explorers that found themselves cast among this people revealed the fact that before the white man forced his vices upon them they were animated by the kindest sentiments of sympathy and interested in the well-being of such as appealed to them for help. It was only a few years later when a spirit of enmity existed between the races that quickly ripened into distrust, cruelty and murder. The aborigines hailed the advent of a white man, but their ways were neither honest nor politic; the white man wronged the native, and especially the native "gin," and thus sowed the seeds of rancor and death. Conflicts became the common sport of both. The native with his superior cunning, and the white man with his superior weapon, kept the district in a perpetual broil and fermentation; but it was an unequal contest. The poor native was compelled to retire and to submit to the abominable wrongs the white man chose to perpetrate; there was no help for him; the great British nation was behind the white man. It was true the authorities did not on paper countenance the white man's crimes; they wrote against them, and the pulpits of England spoke against these evils, but they still continued to send them rum, and still took a white man's word in preference to that of a blackfellow, and still went on stealing these peoples lands and gave them nothing adequate in return. They, in other words, forced their civilisation upon them, and gave them whisky and bullets until they cried out, "It is enough."

The persons placed by authority in command were Captain Miller and Captain Bishop, from 1824 to 1825; Captain Logan, from 1825 to 1830. Captain Logan was murdered in this latter year by prisoners who were goaded on to desperation by his severity. Captain Logan was a man of herculean strength and energy. His chief concern was to keep the men under his command employed as much as possible, and this he did with a severity that sometimes amounted to a cruelty. He had two purposes in view—first, the moral reform of the prisoner by his physical occupancy; and, second, a desire to accomplish as much towards the comfort and development of the new settlement as possible. He, perhaps, did not always estimate the physical ability of those from whom he exacted the task, and these men were frequently found to be unequal to the amount of labor that was imposed, owing to the physical weakness incident to a sparse diet. He made work, in fact, a punishment, and it had the effect of exasperating the worker. The modern policy adopted in some penal institutions of other lands, making work an element of happiness, thus leading up to reward and teaching the prisoner that a man is a fool who does not work, was never dreamed of in Captain Logan's time. His was the voice of a commander, and his commands must be enforced by the lash laid on to the verge of death, or the heavy chains and balls, or even death itself. This treatment was almost in universal practice, and could result in only one thing—that is, the destruction of both the ruled and the ruler. There were very few who pursued any other, and the legitimate result was sure to follow—men sighed for death when driven to desperation; they frequently struck dead some companion for no other reason than that both the slayer and the slain might escape the further tortures of a living death—the one by speedy hanging, and the other by the hand of his friend. It was under such a condition of things that Captain Logan came to his death in 1830, and thus was brought to a close a life of one whom the prisoners regarded as the impersonation of all that was cruel, and one whom the authorities were wont to uphold as an exalted type of British discipline and honor. It is well that final judgment is reserved to one Judge, who alone can understand man's ways, and whose judgment is just.

To accord honor to whom honor is due, it becomes us to mention that Captain Logan was indefatigable in his efforts to explore the surrounding country. He never consulted his own case; he was as active as any man in the settlement, and succeeded in making valuable discoveries within a radius of 150 miles of Brisbane. He discovered the Logan River and the rich country through which it flows. He caused many excellent farms to be cleared and put under cultivation; he erected many serviceable buildings both for the prisoners' comfort and the public service. He made roads through new regions, and opened the country for pioneer life. A windmill erected in his day still exists to remind one of the past. It occupies the most elevated knoll in the city of Brisbane, and is now used for a signal station. His death, so tragical, had the effect of awakening, both in the colony and at home, a discussion upon the question of penal discipline, in which the learned and experienced took part, and which had the effect of modifying in a measure the administration. Humanitarians came to the front and urged upon the authorities the propriety of trying a more excellent way, and the change that has come over the sentiments of the people in this regard is deemed to be one of the hopeful signs of the times.

Captain Clunes succeeded Captain Logan, and he administered from 1830 to 1835. He was succeeded by Captain Fyans, who administered from 1835 to 1837. He in turn was succeeded by Major Cotton, who administered from 1837 to 1839. Lieutenant Gravat succeeded Captain Cotton, and continued from May, 1839 to July, 1839. The last of these commanders was Lieutenant Gorman, who administered from 1839 to 1840, the year which witnessed the termination of the penal settlement and the removal of the prisoners from the same.

The discovery of fine sections of agricultural lands and pastures led the white free element to seek its occupancy at a very early date. Allan Cunningham, a botanist of good repute, was one of the most valuable of all the early explorers, and did much towards giving the public a knowledge of the interior of this portion of the country. It was through this gentleman's efforts that the Darling Downs, the Dumaresque River and its tributaries, the Peel Plains, and the Canning Downs were reported. His account of this region made from time to time to the authorities at Sydney was of a most satisfactory nature and soon led the farmers in the vicinity and the pastoralists of the interior to go out to the new territory in search of pastures and farms. Governor Brisbane, whose interest in the extension of colonial enterprise was real and constant, made an early visit to the new settlement. In 1825, within one year after it first became a penal settlement, he visited Brisbane and surrounding country, and was much pleased at the selection, and also at its future prospects.

The favorable reports of Governor Brisbane, added to those of the few visitors who had seen and reported on the character of the country, induced some to take their flocks over to the Darling Downs, and their families to the more convenient places that had been written about. Yet it was not possible, before 1840, for any white man to settle in the regions occupied by the convicts. The law prohibited all such from visiting the district without a special permit, and such was only given to people who would not be likely to investigate penal matters too closely, and who would maintain silence concerning anything they might see. It was also unlawful for any person to settle within fifty miles of any convict station, so that practically up till 1840 the penal settlement at Moreton Bay, on the Brisbane River, was cut off from the knowledge of the outside world. Among the early visitors to this region may be recorded that of Mr. James Backhouse and George Washington Walker, two quaker friends, who left England for the purpose of visiting the penal settlements of Australia, and preaching to the prisoners the Word of God as they might see fit to interpret it. Their benevolence, no doubt, awakened in them a desire to investigate for themselves the treatment to which this class of people were subjected. There can be no doubt that these people were animated by a laudable desire to do them good. However comforting the Gospel may be to the enslaved, there are conditions under which it is of very little benefit; and the experiences of the convict class to whom these good people sought to minister, were of such a kind as to unfit them to receive any consolation from a religion that seemed to endorse such a vindictive spirit as ruled among them, just as at the present time the advocacy of capital punishment by the clergy is a sad comment on the spirit of Christianity, and robs religion of its chief charm; so the advocacy of the cruelties that were practised on the prisoners by nearly all religious people in those days unfitted these visitors to be Gospel bearers to any profit. Backhouse and Walker, no doubt, were good people in the general acceptation of the word, but there are times when people need bread more than sermons, shoes more than doctrines, and a practical Christianity rather than a theoretical one. It does not appear from any of the records, that the above "gospellers," as they are sometimes styled, added any star to the crown of their rejoicing by plucking any brands from the burning. Their report of what they saw was very much relied upon by the governors and authorities of that day, and possibly did much towards bringing to the knowledge of those who governed at home the facts in relation to the treatment of these people.

Among the first white settlers may be properly noted Patrick and Walter Leslie. They had received from Cunningham's own lips a full account of the rich Darling Downs, and therefore, on the 10th March, 1840, accompanied by his assigned servant only, Patrick Leslie set out to investigate the same. He and his servant reached the Darling Downs in the early part of March, and being more than satisfied with the appearance of the country, Mr. Leslie hastened back again to the New England district, where his brother Walter was in waiting with his flocks and cattle, and they, accompanied by twenty-two assigned servants—concerning whom Mr. Leslie said in a letter to the authorities that they were "worth any forty men he had ever seen since "—set out for Queensland, and reached it a few weeks later. The above testimony, which Mr. Leslie bore to his servants, is abundantly established by many other witnesses in regard to the bulk of the assigned servants of those early days. That the great majority of them were valuable aids to the pioneers in developing the resources of the new district and the care of their extensive flocks, and the husbanding of their effects, is beyond any question. Very soon after this others found their way to the country north, and it became filled up by a class of diligent industrious people, who sought out the rich valleys along the streams, and occupied the Downs with cattle and sheep, so that when the first official report was made from the district, it was found to contain, in 1844, forty-three stations, and as it is the first official report from the district, it will be deemed of sufficient importance to make a record of the same in this centennial work. The report represents the district to have contained, of free settlers 471, horses 660, cattle 13,295, sheep 184,651, and a large amount of cotton, nearly 1800 bales in all having been exported from the district up to that time, revealing the enterprise of its people in testing the adaptability of the soil for the growth of that product. The first sales of town lots in that district was made in 1841, thirteen acres having been sold for the sum of £4,687. Governor Gipps made a visit to the place, and helped in directing the survey and laying out the town of Brisbane, and in the year 1845 the first sale of town lots was effected there. Captain Wickham, R.N., was appointed Police Magistrate for the new town in 1841. Thenceforth it entered upon a career of growth and development, whose rapidity was alike a surprise to the authorities in Sydney and a gratification to the pioneers of that new country. Dr. Simpson was appointed Commissioner of Crown Lands in the Moreton district around Brisbane, and Christopher Rolliston for the Darling Downs. The latter was born in Nottinghamshire in 1817, and was educated under private tutors, arriving in New South Wales in 1838. He engaged in farming on the Hunter River for about five years, gaining colonial experience, and a knowledge of the agricultural resources of the country, when he received the above appointment. In February, 1853, he went to England on leave of absence. In December, 1854, he returned to the Colony of New South Wales, and was appointed Private Secretary to Sir William Denison in February, 1855. In March of the following year he was made Registrar-General, to whom we are indebted for the inauguration of the present system of registration. In 1858 the statistical branch of the Colonial Secretary's Department was transferred to the Registrar-General and the Statistical Register was first published. In the same year the registration of deeds was transferred from the Supreme Court to this department. In 1862 the Real Property Act was passed, and its introduction devolved upon him. His experience, while in the Crown Lands Department in Queensland, was of much service both in the Moreton Bay district and subsequently elsewhere. He acquired a large knowledge of the wants and necessities of the farming community.

Among the white settlers, whose connection with early times is an important factor in the commencing of the new settlement, must be mentioned that of Mr. Andrew Petrie—a young Scotchman of good education and rugged manhood, who was sent to the settlement in 1837 as clerk of works, under Colonel Barney, and whose continuous residence in the colony from the above date through the many changes and conditions through which it passed, and only terminating a few years ago, gave him an opportunity of witnessing the horrors of penal times and the gradual unfoldment of civilisation and the development of all the enterprises that have gone on since the removal of all penal restriction in 1840 to the present time. Mr. Petrie's own experience with the natives is most thrilling, and the narrow escapes it has been his good fortune to make from robbery and murder on several occasions when in pursuance of his duties, which sometimes led him up and down the coast, with sometimes a very scanty supply of food and clothing, and which was always an object of attack on the part of the natives, is sufficient to fill many chapters of a book ; but a mere mention of the fact will suffice to satisfy our readers, who will have to content themselves with a short statement rather than a minute account of individual experiences. Among the native tribes there were found from time to time white men who, as convicts, had escaped from the penal settlements, chosing rather the freedom of savage life than to submit to the barbarities of penal servitude and what it implied. Among those found by the white settlers was one named Durramboi. His English name we will not mention, as he is at present a respectable and well-to-do citizen, and entitled to the confidence and good opinion of his fellow-townsmen. When discovered among the savage tribe he was blackened and lived as the natives did, and had won among them universal esteem. What is marvellous to relate is that he had lost the use of his mother tongue and had acquired the native dialect. He is bent and old in appearance, and the sight of the old man, as he attends daily in silence upon his routine of business, is sufficient to make a strong man weep in sympathy as he calls up the

the terrible memories that his turbulent life suggests. It can be easily imagined that the early white settlers who had flocks and cattle would be constantly annoyed by the blacks, whose hunger would lead them to steal sheep and cattle for food. A condition of turbulence and revenge, murder, and waste followed upon the mutual attacks that were made. Various stratagems were resorted to by the whites to protect their own property, which are said to have not always been of the most Christian character. A story runs that a whole tribe was poisoned on one occasion by two lonely shepherds, who, in their anxiety to protect their property, could think of no other means than to poison a whole tribe. This they attempted to do by placing arsenic into a quantity of flour, which was placed where it would be stolen by the natives. That they were poisoned in large numbers is a fact beyond any question, and as a result the enmity and revenge of the tribes became so furious that they murdered the shepherds and continued their attacks on innocent individuals in different parts of the country with impunity. The story is told of a Mrs. Fraser who was captive among a tribe for eighteen months before she was rescued. A vessel by the name of "Stirling Castle" had been wrecked on the great Sandy Island, now named Fraser Island, in Wide Bay, at the Mouth of the Mary River. Captain Fraser, with his young wife and crew, escaped from the waves, but fell victims to native barbarity, and all were murdered most cruelly except Mrs. Frazer, who was taken captive and reduced to the lowest condition. Tidings having reached the white settlements, a party was sent out to rescue her, which they succeeded in accomplishing only by the aid of a convict absconder by the name of Graham, who had been living with the blacks for twelve years, and through whom intelligence was communicated, and who used his acquired skill and cunning in aiding the crew in accomplishing her deliverance. It is not necessary to pursue these incidents to any great length, as the above is a fair specimen of the hundreds of like cases that came under the notice of the early pioneers.

When the new Lands Regulation Bill had passed, and the lands of the Moreton district were placed in the market at 12s. an acre, there were multitudes who stood ready to acquire possession of the same. Free settlers began to pour into the district with great rapidity, and in 1843, when responsible Government or a pseudo-representative Government was accorded to the Colony of New South Wales, the district of Moreton

THE GENESIS.

Bay became entitled to a representative at Sydney in the Parliament of New South Wales, and Mr. Alexander McLeay was chosen as their first representative, so that we may, for all practical purposes, regard the period embraced between 1842 and 1859 as the pioneer period of Queensland. The question of penal servitude was one of the things of the past. They had now begun to lay the foundations of a growing country, and had inaugurated many of the enterprises that would grow and develop into permanent institutions, the benefit of which future generations would inherit. One of the first questions that came before the Parliament at Sydney was the treatment of the natives who were reputed to have suffered much at the hands of the whites; but it was not until Queensland had secured separation, and thus obtained a responsible Government of her own, that a thorough investigation of this question was obtained.

Through the efforts of the Rev. Mr. Schmidt, the earliest missionary among the German immigrants, supported by Dr. Lang, who had all along given the district a great deal of his personal attention and care, an investigation was made that revealed a condition of things which called for legislative action more thoroughly to repress the whites in their treatment of the natives, and thus secure a degree of peace that could not be attained by the adoption of any other policy. From all these sources of information it would appear that murder, treachery, and brutality were practised on both sides, but from the sparseness of the white settlement, and the unreliability of the testimony of both blacks and whites, it was almost impossible to arrive at a correct and full knowledge of the facts. Touching the injuries inflicted, or the real causes of the depredations committed upon the flocks and families of many of the earlier pioneers, it was contended by some of the white settlers that they should, on permission being obtained from a magistrate in their district, have unlimited license to shoot down and exterminate any tribe even a part of whom should have been detected in the act of murder or robbery. Nothwithstanding the perils that threatened the advance of civilisation, it was during this period that most of the important explorations took place. Messrs. Russell and Petrie had done much toward the exploration of White Bay and the region known as Bunyah-Bunyah, and through all that country extending between the head waters of the Burnett River and the Darling Downs.

Another fact in the pioneer period was the systematic emigration that gave to the district some of the noblest specimens of manhood. If the reader imagines that the early settlers were of an inferior type of starved-out Europeans, who were forced in abject poverty to forsake the land of their birth, and go in search of an existence in the new country, they will have conceived a very erroneous view of the fact. Dr. Lang, from the commencement of its development, endeavoured to secure the best classes of mechanics skilled in their respective trades, scholars of a sturdy type competent to fill any position that demanded scholarship, and strong healthy men, most of whom were married, and thus well equipped for pioneer life. It was his special aim to induce such a class to come and take hold of the problems of a new country with an enthusiasm worthy of their ancestors. They were not without a little money, and many of them had a fair supply. There was a universal demand for labor, convictism, with its system of assigned servants having passed away. Assigned servants being no longer available made the labor market one of imperious demand without an adequate supply. The Government of New South Wales endeavoured to meet the want, and sent to the district in 1843 the ship "Artemesia" with 240 emigrants. These all found positions awaiting them, and still the demand was increasing. Flocks and cattle were without shepherds and herdsmen. They demanded care, and they were multiplying so rapidly that thousands and tens of thousands were yearly added to their number, and began to cover all the rich plains of the Downs and to occupy the valleys in the neighbourhood of Brisbane. Dr. Lang inaugurated his system of emigration, and in quick succession the ships "Fortitude," "Chasley," and the "Lima" brought some of the sturdiest specimens of manhood and womanhood to the place that Scotland and the North of England could spare, and nearly all became prosperous and contented in their new sphere. Many of these became noted in the history of their adopted land, and the descendants of many of them still living with a few of the original toilers fill the honorable stations in the political and commercial enterprises that exist in the Colony to-day, among whom may be mentioned the Petries, Wickhams, Cribbs, Ballantynes, Leslies, Russells, Hodsons, Elliotts, Kings, Sibbleys, Gregorys, Adams, Alands, Bulcoxes, Douglases, Grahams, Grays, Griffiths, Rymes, Hallorans, Hassels, Jordans, Lillies, Raffs, McMasters, Pettigrews, Sheridans, Turners, and a host of others, many of whose biographical sketches will be found elsewhere in this work. Nations grow by the individual achievements of men who apply themselves to their respective tasks and accomplish them. To write fully the history of Queensland would be to write the individual deeds of all its successful men and women. This would be impossible, for their name is legion. To one who has watched its gradual progress since the commencement and the rapid strides it has made, it must be a marvel to contemplate; and the early pioneer who risked his life either as a shepherd or explorer is worthy of a high place among the prominent men who figure on the pages of history, and for this reason Cunningham, Leichhardt, Mitchells, Russells, Leslies, Petries, Kennedy, Walker, Dalrymple, Gregory Bros., and many others who dared the hardships of the wilderness and conquered the waste places of the continent, and thus prepared for us of the present homes of quiet and plenty, should have a place in the nation's heart and their lives be treasured for the inspiration of the future generations who may yet come and go.

The exploration of this period that was both active and extensive and opened to the pastoralists of the continent the vast capabilities of the plains and the many valleys of the interior, had the tendency of drawing from the older parts of the continent tens of thousands of cattle and sheep. Capital flowed in from England, and many of the scions of aristocratic houses became squatters, traders, and speculators, until within a very short period the entire colony became covered over with flocks and herds, and the "humpty" became the welcome abode of both the "kidded" sort, who perchance spent his infancy under the luxury and surroundings of wealth and case, and the common laborer whose life was one of hardship and toil; both of them meeting on common grounds and having an equal chance in the struggle of life, and frequently the lordling being outstripped in the race by his companion of rougher manners. The ease with which lands in large areas were obtained on lease from the Crown was an inducement to early occupancy, and the stubborness with which the class of squatters who had obtained these leases resisted all efforts on the part of the farmers who desired to occupy small areas of land for agricultural purposes came to be the most perplexing of all questions, and was not easy of solution for the reason that the squatting interest had largely built up the Colony. The product of wool, canned meats, hides, etc., formed no inconsiderable part of the wealth of the young Colony, and therefore had a strong claim on the Legislature for protection. The squatters interested in this enterprise embraced within their number many of the wealthy colonists and capitalists who were non-residents, and hence the poor immigrant who longed for a home of his own found it no easy task to compete with the wealthy squatter in gaining the ear of the Legislature, much less in securing what he thought was the birthright of every honest man coming to these shores, namely, the right to occupy and till the soil. These respective interests began to make themselves felt at a very early date in Australian history, and have continued to force themselves upon the respective Parliaments in these colonies. The question involved in their discussion has found advocates pro and con. The Press has never ceased to take up one side or the other, and give the people the light of its intelligence. Governments have been created and overturned in the contests that have engaged the respective parties on this question. The extent of territory in this Colony has given the squatters an influence and importance relatively that the same class in other colonies do not possess. The impartial reader must see that a great deal of judgment is required to solve the problem justly.

It was during this period also that the gold excitement in Australia was at its highest point of frenzy chiefly in Victoria and New South Wales. The discovery of gold in these two colonies had the effect of so completely absorbing the attention of the people that all other things were secondary considerations. The active ambitious men from all the colonies hastened to the goldfields to strike for fortune, and as an immediate result the hum of industry was hushed all over the land. Those who did not catch the fever were considered drones and imbeciles. Queensland shared in the general stagnation that ensued, and for the years between 1851 and 1858 a condition of paralysis had seized her enterprises. It was during this period that she was knocking loudly at the Imperial door for Separation. Victoria, who had won an Independent Government of its own in 1851, and at once discovered gold and drew to her shores millions of wealth and multitudes of people had entered upon a career of prosperity unparalleled in history; and it was natural to attribute much of this to her superior legislation and political independence, but which it was that gave it the advantage, its legislators or its goldfields, the Moreton Bay district did not take time to consider. Victoria got Separation and prospered. Moreton Bay must have Separation ere it can prosper was the argument that prevailed with its politicians, and was accepted by all its people. In 1858, a year before Separation came to them, gold was discovered within her own boundaries, in the far north, on the Fitzroy River. The intelligence was borne all over the continent as quickly as the wires and mail routes of that day could bear it, and Keppel Bay soon became crowded with vessels from all parts of the world. At a point about seventy miles up the river, called Canoona, a city of 15,000 diggers sprang up within a few months. The gold was found to be limited, and, disappointed and crushed in spirits, the masses of the diggers became reduced to a point of starvation and wretchedness beyond description. This was the picture that appealed to the sympathies of the outside world. Assistance was sent them from Sydney and Victoria, and many of the miners were glad to return to their friends. A goodly number of the braver sort settled upon rich lands in that part of Queensland, and the town of Rockhampton was founded. Out of the distress and want came in a few years prosperity and trade that has given to that part of the country a pre-eminence among the cities of the north. Separation came at length, the announcement to that effect having been made in July, 1859, and on the 10th December the first Governor, in the person of Sir George F. Bowen, read the proclamation that inaugurated a new condition of things in that part of the Australian Continent. That it was a just request on the part of the Moreton Bay district, and a wise act on the part of the British Government to concede it, is abundantly proved by its subsequent history. The growth and prosperity of the Colony have been the marvel of the world, and its possibilities in the same direction none can fully measure. Its valleys and its downs have been found suitable for the culture of all products—cotton, tobacco, and fruits of all sorts, wheat, maize, oats, barley, and other cereals are grown abundantly on the high tablelands; while every clime and quality of land awaits the toiler and brings to the industrious a bountiful harvest.

The prospect of progress that presented itself to all who were acquainted with the internal wealth of the Colony was bright indeed. The monetary circles of Europe were beginning to show great activity in regard to Queensland securities; in fact, the tide of prosperity had already begun to rise. A good season had already blessed them with signs of increase, and therefore to themselves there appeared no reason why they should not march onward and take their place side by side with the more prosperous colonies of New South Wales, Victoria, and South Australia. Indeed, the very exultation they experienced, when they came to realise their freedom, gave them the indominitable courage that has been characteristic of their history since. There is nothing like a sense of freedom to develop latent powers—a sense of slavery or serfdom crushes manhood and unnerves the arm of even strong men; but when men are free, and conscious that they control their own destiny, how differently they enter upon the task of life. Existence becomes a lasting joy, and doubtless to the thrill of gladness that filled their hearts on their realisation of independence, are due largely the hopefulness and great activity of these subsequent years of their progress.

CHAPTER XXI.

THE GOVERNORS.

QUEENSLAND entered upon the task of governing her own affairs from the 10th December, 1859. The boon which the people of the Moreton Bay district had so earnestly desired for so many years came to them at an opportune moment—just after and at the time when the vast resources of the Colony were beginning to be known. Already a class of energetic workmen, who were both skilled in mechanism and well educated in the schools of England, Ireland, and Scotland, had come to the Colony, and had made considerable progress in laying the foundations thereof. These were men of herculean strength and undaunted by the trials of pioneer life. They entered upon the task of self-government with an intelligence worthy of the Queen whose name was conferred upon the new Colony by herself, and was an honor they appreciated and endeavored to honorably bear.

Sir George Ferguson Bowen, K.C.M.G., was a comparatively new man in colonial matters. He was, however, a trusted servant of the Crown of some years experience—a scholar of eminence, and therefore one who would be likely to act cautiously and with intelligence in the manipulation of all the delicate questions that were sure to come before the new Parliament. He had spent several years in the Presidency of the University of Corfu—a position that demanded the strictest discipline and large scholarship, and therefore not one likely to be at the disposal of a novice. The satisfaction he gave in that institution led to his translation to the Secretaryship of the

Ionian Islands, in 1854, where he continued to discharge the somewhat responsible duties imposed by the Crown until the year 1859, when he was transferred to the more responsible and delicate task of launching the new Colony of Queensland upon the sea of responsible government, and so shaping her initial policy as to avoid the dangers of conflict with the mother land on the one hand, and that of clashing interests among her own people on the other. One of the first acts of his administration was to discontinue aid to religious bodies. This question had been one of long and serious contest in the mother colony, and occasioned a great deal of religious discussion, and a class prejudice which the new Colony desired and determined to avoid. Governor Bowen was spoken of as a "new-chum," implying that coming to such a country as Australia was, he was necessarily ignorant of the wants and ways of a new land, and that he would have much to learn. At the same time his popularity amongst the rough people of the Colony was universal at first. When we use the word "rough" in regard to the people generally we do not use it in any sense reflecting either on their intelligence or manners. In both these respects the reader must be informed that there has ever been in these colonies people of greatest intelligence, scholarship, and refinement, and this has not been confined to the few only, but it has been, and is to-day, characteristic of the masses. A few years residence under these changed conditions induces the general abandonment of what in European society is deemed to be an evidence of refinement. Kid gloves, swallow-tail coats, and huge starched fronts are not considered a *sine qua non* in social circles in this new land. The people soon learn the propriety of laying aside the black coat and donning a white one, of going in their shirt sleeves, if necessary; in fact, without losing any true sense of dignity or manhood the immigrant to Australia soon acquires the disposition to consult his own personal comfort rather than the stupid rules of etiquette that may be justified in European circles, but under the blazing sun of the Southern Hemisphere are out of place. To a "new-chum" this appears odd and wanting in self-respect—rough and uncultured, but, as a rule, he soon joins his southern cousins and acquires the same air of freedom and independence.

The type of Government under which the Colony of Queensland started was that of New South Wales, the mother colony, and consisted of two Houses of Parliament, an Upper one or Legislative Council nominated by the Crown, and the Lower House or Legislative Assembly elected by the people. The Governor strove to make himself agreeable and to adapt himself to the new conditions under which he found himself. He visited the outlying stations and sought by commingling with the people to acquaint himself with their wants and secure their confidence. His popularity was almost universal from the beginning of his residence in the Colony. He encouraged the industries of the country. That of cotton culture gave promise of great profits. Early in his administration large areas were put under culture, and it was found to be a profitable enterprise. Two causes led to this result—first, the American War had interfered with the culture of cotton in the Southern States of America, and lessened the supply that was demanded by the English market; and the second was the large demand at home for the product arising out of the increased desire by her people for the fabric itself, and also the partial failure of the crops in other quarters of the world. These causes raised the price of cotton in this Colony four-fold, and made its culture one of the most profitable in which the colonists could engage. The labor problem was one of great difficulty. The removal of prison labor from the district, and the inadequacy of the assigned servants who had been previously accorded, together with the growing industries that were being multiplied on every hand, rendered the supply of labor scarce and its price very high. The Governor had not, however, a bed of roses to lie upon during his entire official residence in the Colony. He was charged with being parsimonious and stingy. Some said that his benevolence was restricted; that in his domestic affairs he was mean; and many who in former times cried " Hosanna " now cried " Away with him." That his intimacy was confined to a very few, and those of a political class with whom he was intimately associated and to whom he had to give his confidence, is a circumstance that may have grown out of the arduous burdens of state that rested upon him, rather than to any disposition to slight any of the people. We must acknowledge that it was no easy task to manage the affairs of State in such a manner as to avoid suspicion; that some interests were more constantly protected than others. On the 4th January, 1868, after an experience unlike anything he had had in his former career, and after having accomplished considerable good in the Colony, his relation to the same ceased, and the administration passed into the hands of the President of the Council, Colonel Maurice Charles O'Connell. Governor

Bowen's administration was characterised by great energy, unswerving integrity, and a lofty purpose to serve his Queen.

Colonel O'Connell, who succeeded to the Administration, filled the office from January 4th until August 14th, 1868—a period of more than seven months. O'Connell was a man of some note. He was a son of the O'Connell who married the daughter of Governor Bligh, and rendered good military service to Queen Isabella in Spain. He was of Irish parentage—a military man—of a somewhat pompous style, but of a warm generous heart. He was universally liked for his generosity and kindliness towards the poor and unfortunate. He was appointed member of the Legislative Council in Bowen's administration. His interest in military matters was a distinguished feature in his colonial life, and he gave all encouragement within his power in forwarding the volunteer movement in the colony with which he became officially identified. His administration was characterised by an urbanity that made him a favorite with all classes. As a matter of course he was not expected to assume all the responsibilities incident to the position of Governor. In such a place he might have found it a difficult matter to retain his popularity. He was succeeded by Colonel Samuel Wensley Blackall on August 14th, 1868.

No Governor ever enjoyed such universal esteem as Governor Blackall. He was a gentleman well up in years. A man of ripe scholarship, and a heart brim full of all those exquisite qualities that endear the aged to all ranks and conditions. No man could have evinced more enthusiasm in undertaking the arduous tasks of governing in a new land, and especially at a time which involved so serious a question as that of labor. The Polynesian Laborers Act was passed early in the first year of his administration. It had long been a question as to how the labor demand should be met. The multiplication of flocks and cattle herds, and the extension of stations into all parts of the vast territory, the discovery of mines in the different portions of the colony, the opening up of new enterprises, and also the increasing activity of every department of the country had completely exhausted the supply of labor, and to meet this increasing demand some had imported coolies from India, China and other countries, from the Islands of the seas, and in this last there had grown up rivalries and wrongs in connection with a semi-slavery, all of which necessitated legislation on the part of the Government to guard individual rights, and to prevent abuses that already had sprung up in connection with the trade, hence the passage of the above act. Governor Blackall intimated to a friend that he should leave his bones in the Colony, a prediction that was fulfilled, for he died on the 2nd January, 1871—only about two years after his coming to the Colony. He was buried in Amity Cemetery, Toowong. His gubernatorial days in the Colony were brief in duration, but in the short space of time allotted him he stamped his superior nature upon many of the institutions of the Colony. It is impossible to estimate fully the value of a good man's influence until after death has put a stop to his life, and "that his works will follow him" is a fact borne out by more than divine teaching. It was when laid in his grave that the people of the Colony began fully to feel how large a place he had in the hearts of his people and how potent an influence for good was the life that was now gone. He had done much towards harmonising the discordant elements in the body politic, and he had in a very quiet way accomplished reforms whose chief benefit appeared in subsequent times. Colonel Sir Maurice Charles O'Connell, Knt., succeeded to the administration on 2nd January, 1871, and continued till 12th August, 1871. Another seven months of responsibility gave him an opportunity of demonstrating his disposition to treat all classes with becoming courtesy, and during these months he added to the regard in which he was previously held.

The Most Honorable George Augustus Constantine, Marquis of Normanby, Privy Councillor, assumed the reins of Government on 12th August, 1871, and continued in the office until 12th November, 1874. The Marquis is regarded to this day as one of the noblest specimens of manhood the colonies have yet seen. He was a man of the world—fond of manly sports, such as horse racing, boating, cricketing, and riding, and gave general encouragement to all such amusements. He was a shrewd politician, who knew how to maintain the dignity of his office and administer the affairs of State with a quiet resoluteness that was at once a menace to the presumptuous and an encouragement to the timid. His predecessor, Governor Blackall, was of a very delicate physique, whose health was never good, and among some of the more aggressive politicians he was regarded as a weakling; but in the Marquis of Normanby no politician dared assume any such opinion. He was a fine specimen of a sturdy English gentleman, whose heart was kind, but whose spirit was proud and lofty, and who did not flinch from any duty his country saw fit to impose upon him. His word was law, but his strong good sense never led him to use words rashly. Strong common sense, combined with a long experience in political matters and a good knowledge of mankind, made him a safe and valuable adviser of the Crown and a trustworthy exponent of British ideas in their application to Colonial Government, and in which he ever evinced a disposition to give due weight to all reasonable requests that came from the people in a constitutional way. To give the reader a glimpse into his private character, the story is told that on an occasion, when he was driving through the Darling Downs over some rough country, his wife complained very much of the roughness of the roads, and, continuing her grumbling, the Marquis, in a blunt way, said, "D—n it; I cannot help it." And to the end of the journey peace and quietness was restored.

When the Marquis ceased his administration, on 12th November, 1874, he was succeeded for a short time by the President of the Council, Sir Maurice Charles O'Connell, Knt., whose term lasted only from the above date until 23rd January, 1875, when William Wellington Cairns, C.M.G., assumed the reins of Government. His administration was of very short duration, extending only over a period of two years. Governor Cairns was a recluse, and mixed very little with the people, and for that reason he made very little impression upon the Colony during his short residence. His habits were those of the student. He was reputed to be a lover of books, and, like many of his Scottish countrymen, was wedded to scientific and literary subjects much more than to questions of State policy. It must not be inferred from this that he evinced no concern in the progress of the Colony. There is no doubt that he had its well-being constantly at heart, and strove in his own way to give all measures coming before him the closest kind of study, and, doubtless, the mental concern bestowed upon the questions that from time to time came before him for solution was as great and as intelligent as that given by his predecessors. Nevertheless, he did not succeed in so impressing the fact upon the minds of the people, and when the time of his departure came, on 14th March, 1877, he went away regretted by very few. Neither political party succeeded in obtaining his friendship or confidence beyond the coolest recognition they sustained to the administration. Neither the one party nor the other could charge his administration with any fault save that of want of sociability. He was conscientious and just in his bearing towards all, and his natural reserve of manner must be taken as an idiosyncrasy of a scholar rather than as any slight sought or intended to be put upon the people.

Sir Maurice Charles O'Connell, Knt., again for the last time succeeded to the administration, which lasted only for one month, or from 14th March till 10th April, 1877. He died in 1879, and was buried at the old cemetery at Milton, his funeral being an occasion of national mourning and regret. He bore to the grave the esteem of nearly every one. Friend and foe in politics alike vied in their offices of respect to one who, though vain somewhat of his rank and record, could be justly pardoned and revered for the acknowledged worth that dwelt within a heart that was always open in its frankness and generosity. His best monument is the brightness and cheer that accompanied him through life. His many kindly offices of charity and goodwill made his pathway redolent with their rich perfume, and both memory and record will hold the treasure in freshness for many generations to come.

On the 10th April, 1877, the administration passed into the hands of Sir Arthur Edward Kennedy, K.C.M.G., who was transferred from Hongkong to fill the vacancy occasioned by the translation of Governor Cairns to South Australia. Governor Kennedy was a descendant from the ancient Scottish family of Kennedys, at the head of whom is the Earl of Cassilus. He was born in 1809, and is the third son of Hugh Kennedy, Esq., of Culha, County Down, Ireland, who married Grace Dora, daughter of John Hughes. He was educated at Trinity College, Dublin. In 1827 he entered the army as an ensign in the 11th Regiment; was lieutenant in 1832; and captain in the 68th Light Infantry in 1840. He retired from the army in 1848 to accept civil employment, having been selected two years previously to fill the office of County Inspector under the Board of Works, and serving continuously as Inspector under Sir John Burgoyne. He was Relief Commissioner, and afterwards Inspector of Poor Laws until the office was abolished in 1851. In 1839 he married Miss Georgina McCartney, by whom he had one son and two daughters. Captain Kennedy left the army and entered the Colonial Department of the Civil Service. His reputation and influence secured him the important position of Governor and Commander-in-Chief of Vancouver Island and its dependencies in British North America. He was Governor of Western Australia from 1854 to 1862. His administration was commended by the Imperial Government, and as a mark of approval of his Sovereign he received the honor of knighthood in August, 1867. On 7th January, 1868, he was appointed Governor of a West African possession. After serving in that position for some time, he was appointed at Sierra Leone in the courts of mixed commission with foreign powers for the suppression of the slave trade. He was afterwards Governor of Hongkong, where he administered from 1872 to 1877, from which date he was transferred to the Governorship of Queensland. His administration was characterised by a straightforward course of action that revealed him to be a man of great self-reliance and conscious power. He could never be charged with vacillation or a spirit of "time serving." He honestly endeavoured to maintain the honor of the Colony, and showed great wisdom in the treatment of all parties in political life, his official bearing towards all being just and fearless. The years of his administration were characterised by great activity and development; emigration had largely increased; the population and capital had poured in and developed local enterprises. As a rule, he was very much liked, although there was one circumstance that conflicted with the people's notions of propriety—a large retinue of Chinese servants that constituted his domestic help was an eyesore that the Colony could not brook, they having been taken from Hongkong, where he had learned to appreciate the qualities of Chinamen in the relations of household servants. He carried with him a small army of such, and had every position in his household filled with "helps" of that nationality. The Colony was at the time, and had for many years previously been, trying to solve the problem of how to get rid of Chinese cheap labor, and how they could put a stop to the importation of the semi-slavery that had been carried on from the contiguous islands of the sea. The prejudices amongst the colonists towards foreign cheap labor was very intense, and the fact of its being encouraged by the Governor in his domestic arrangements brought down upon his own head the anathemas of the masses—a feeling shared in by many of the wealthier classes also, who were adverse to the institution as being destructive to the dignity of labor and tending to the demoralisation of the class of emigrants from their own motherland who were largely dependent upon labor for their sustenance and support, and being out of harmony with the exalted democratic policy that had for many years been growing in all portions of the Australian colonies. There were many Acts of importance passed during Governor Kennedy's administration.

There was no especial regret expressed at his departure except by a few friends who had shared largely of his society.

The Hon. Joshua Peter Bell succeeded, during the absence of Governor Kennedy, to the administration, which he filled from 19th March till 22nd November, 1880, the Governor having been granted leave of absence to visit England. Mr. Bell was a well-tried colonist, who had acquired great wealth as the reward of industry and careful speculation chiefly, in the squatting interests of the Colony. He at the time was the President of the Executive Council, and had filled that position since the death of O'Connell, on 23rd March, 1879, and in which office he had won the confidence of all political parties, and had grown in popularity. Mr. Bell was born in County Kildare, Ireland, in 1826. His family emigrated to New South Wales in the year 1830, when the subject of this sketch was only four years of age. He was educated first at the Sydney College, completing his education at the King's School, Parramatta. In the beginning of 1847 Mr. Bell came to the Moreton Bay district, Queensland, and with his father and brothers acquired a magnificent property, known as Jimbour, near Dalby, where they attained considerable fame as wool growers, taking the leading prizes at the Intercolonial Exhibitions in the colonies against all comers in one year, and commanding best prices in the English markets. Mr. Bell first entered the Parliament of Queensland in the year 1863. He accepted office in the McAllister Ministry in May 1866, and again in the McAllister Ministry on 7th August, 1866, continuing therein until 15th August, 1867, during which time he delivered some sound common-sense financial speeches, which were highly eulogised by the Press. He represented Dalby uninterruptedly in Parliament till his appointment as President of the Legislative Council in March, 1879. He married Miss Dorey, the daughter of Dr. Dorey, by whom he has several children.

When Governor Kennedy resigned, on 2nd May, 1883, the Government was administered by Sir Arthur Hunter Palmer, K.C.M.G., who continued in office until 6th November, 1883. In some respects Sir A. H. Palmer is the most wonderful instance of success and self-reliance to to be found in the colonies. He was born in Armagh in

1819, and came to New South Wales in 1838, and was engaged in pastoral pursuits as manager of Mr. Dangar's stations in the north of New South Wales. In 1845 he went to Queensland. In 1866 he was returned to Parliament, and in the following year became Colonial Secretary in the McKenzie Ministry, and successively Minister for Public Works and Minister for Lands in the same Cabinet. After holding office for thirteen months the McKenzie Ministry resigned, but Mr. Palmer again came into power in 1870, and formed the Palmer Ministry, which held office for nearly five years. In January, 1879, Mr. Palmer joined Mr. McIlwraith and formed a combination, taking the office of the Vice-President of the Board of Lands and Works, which gave him greater prominence and larger opportunity of displaying his powers as a clear-headed politician and active administrator. He is a large station owner in Queensland, and is identified with the squatting interests of that Colony. He married a daughter of Mr. Mossman, of Sydney. By dint of hard work, from which he seemed never to shrink, he rose step by step until he has reached the highest point it is possible to reach in the Colony. That real worth and intrinsic merit are the elements that have given him favor with the people are evidenced by the fact that in his nature there is no fawning at the footstool of authority or sycophantish obsequiousness in his manner towards those in social or political stations. His manner has always been abrupt, though not lacking in true kindliness. Sham in politics, religion, or business has always met in him a stern rebuke, while he has ever been ready to give a warm, helpful hand to all those who show an earnest desire to succeed. It is said by his political opponents that "where he cannot convince by argument he can by vim." He was elected to the Presidency of the Legislative Council in 1883.

Sir Anthony Musgrave, G.C.M.G., entered upon the duties of Governor on 6th November, 1883, and continued therein until the day of his death, on the 8th October, 1888. The late Sir Anthony Musgrave had a remarkable career.

In 1850 he was Private Secretary to the Governor of the Leeward Islands, was afterwards appointed Treasury Accountant in Antigua, and subsequently made Colonial Secretary thereof. In 1860 he was appointed Governor of St. Navis, and in 1861 was promoted to St. Vincent. In 1864 he was removed to Newfoundland, and from there, in 1869, was appointed

Governor of British Columbia, then appointed Governor of Natal, and, on Sir James Ferguson being removed to New Zealand in 1873, was made Governor of South Australia, which appointment he held until 1877.

During his term of office he sought in every way to identify himself with the interests of the Colony. Possessed of a good education, and being a man of honorable record, his connection with the Colony in the capacity of Governor has extended the interests of the Colony. Circumstances tended very much to depress him during the last year of his administration, one incident of which was the attitude he assumed towards a prisoner by the name of Kitts, who was recommended for Executive clemency by the Ministry as a proper person upon whom to exercise the royal prerogative of mercy, which act he refused to do until forced by an appeal to the mother country by the present Ministry, who held his action to be indefensible, and therefore not in the interests of peace and good Government; and other things that revealed a want of unity between him and the Legislature.

The termination of his career was sudden and painful to a degree. A stroke of appoplexy cut his days short in a moment, and terminated his administration in the Colony of Queensland without warning and amid the heartfelt grief of the nation and regret of a large majority of the colonists. That the sympathy of the nation was deeply stirred was evinced in the expressions of regret and the tone of the Press throughout the colonies, and which expressed itself in a public funeral, which by its numbers and evident signs of sorrow showed the regret of all classes.

Governor Musgrave was a man of superior education, and socially was very much appreciated by his friends; but he failed in popularity among the people on account of his disinclination to hold intercourse with the people generally, and was regarded by many to be out of sympathy with the present democratic policy of the Colony. In private life he was a gentleman, but ill-fitted both by education and preference to govern a colony of this type. As Commander-in-Chief, His Excellency the late Governor was accorded full military honors. His remains were buried in Toowong Cemetery, on 10th October, 1888. The funeral procession left Government House at 11 o'clock, the streets being lined with thousands of spectators; every point of vantage was occupied, and the sailors on every point of the river climbed to the mastheads. The departure of the cortege from Government House was announced by the discharge of seventeen guns from the Queen's Park Battery. It proceeded to St. John's pro-Cathedral, where the service was conducted. When the gun-carriage, with its sad burden, arrived, the coffin was lifted on the shoulders of six of the Permanent Force, who bore it into the church. As the slow procession wound its way, headed by the choir and clergy, the solemn tones of Canon Glenny rose above the hum of the moving bodies repeating the opening words of the Anglican service, "I know that my Redeemer liveth." Following the coffin were the pall-bearers and the great party leaders, who sank all differences, and side by side Sir Thomas McIlwraith and Sir Samuel Griffiths walked in their homage of grief to the departed. As the choir entered the chancel, the words of the hymn, "My God, My Father While I Stray," burst forth. This hymn had been selected by Lady Musgrave herself, for it indicated so clearly the spirit of resignation which had its hold upon her. The refrain of each verse, "Thy will be done," was noticed as coming with special emphasis by the large congregation which crowded the church to the utmost limit. After the preliminary service was read, the solemn tones of the organ pealed forth "The Dead March in Saul," and the coffin, with its load of white flowers, was removed from the church and re-placed on the gun-carriage. The procession having been re-formed, moved along the north quay by the river and Cemetery Road to the Toowong General Cemetery, where the body of the late Governor was consigned to its last resting-place. The closing portions of the burial service were read by Archdeacon Dawes. It was estimated that not less than 40,000 people witnesses the procession, which was said to be over two miles in length.

In the Assembly a resolution of condolence was moved by Sir Thomas McIlwraith (Premier), and seconded by Sir Samuel Griffiths (ex-Premier), as follows, and subsequently sent to Lady Musgrave:—"We, the members of the Legislative Assembly of Queensland assembled, desire to express profound sympathy with you in the irreparable bereavement you and your family have been called upon to suffer in the lamented death of your husband, the melancholy suddenness of whose decease deeply affected the whole community over which he so ably presided. We desire at the same time to express our regretful sense of the loss we and the public have sustained in the removal from amongst us of a presence so gracious and an influence so elevating as those of our esteemed Governor, and to place on the records of this House the tribute of our mournful regard for the memory of his noble example of fidelity to the high ideal of duty." Letters of like condolence were sent from the respective Governors of the neighbouring colonies. At a meeting of the Committee of the Australian Economic Association the following day there was moved and seconded and carried unanimously:— First: That the Executive Committee of the Australian Economic Association desire to place on record their deep sense of the loss sustained by the death of His Excellency Sir Anthony Musgrave, G.C.M.G., Governor of Queensland, who, though recently elected a corresponding member of the Association, had expressed his cordial sympathy with and a desire to cooperate with its work, and to acknowledge with feelings of admiration the strong interest manifested and ability displayed by him in the discussion of economic questions ; and, secondly, that the above resolution be respectfully communicated to Lady Musgrave with an expression of sympathy in her deep affliction.

Immediately subsequent to the death of the late Governor the announcement was made from the Home Colonial Office that Sir H. A. Blake was nominated as his successor. This appointment met with almost a universal protest, which was urged first upon the ground of his limited colonial experience, and, secondly, and chiefly on account of his supposed connection with the coercion measures in Ireland. The opposition by the Irish element in the Colony, who had been the chief supporters of Sir Thomas McIlwraith, no doubt had its due weight in causing Sir Thomas to urge the protest with feeling and persistency. The Home Government withdrew the appointment, and subsequently announced the appointment of General Sir Henry Wiley Norman, who is a gentleman of sixty-two years of age, and who has had a most brilliant career, standing sixth on the list of generals in the active list. Major-General E. D. R. Ross, who was a fellow-subaltern, and served with him in India, speaks of him in the highest terms as an administrator. He is expected shortly, and before these pages will have been published, Governor Norman will have arrived, and have assumed the reins of Government. He will receive a hearty welcome, not alone in the colony, but also by the Australian Governments.

CHAPTER XXII.

THE MINISTRIES.

RESPONSIBLE Government is attended with difficulties of its own, and among the greatest are the numerous changes that are sure to take place in the conduct of its business and the personae of its constitution, but such a difficulty is not to be regarded as an unmitigated evil. It is attended with much good, in fact. It is a question concerning which there has been much debate as to whether the frequent changes incident to a type of government in which the people have a direct interest in every act of legislation is not a great benefit, inasmuch as it forces the masses to read continually on all matters affecting the legislation, and also inasmuch as it gives the country an opportunity of calling into prominence its brightest intellects available. Whatever may be said concerning the want of refinement on the part of some of our modern legislators, it cannot be questioned that the people are gaining from year to year greater advantages, and that, compared with more autocratic types of Government, they are infinitely more progressive and have better opportunities of rising from poverty to affluence, and, as a matter of fact, enjoy greater protection to life, property, and person. It is for these reasons the most eminent statesmen the world have ever witnessed have come from the ranks of the people. The hope that is engendered in the breast of every young man that he can, or may, rise in influence and wealth, and that the obstacles in his way are not insurmountable inspires him with a laudable ambition to better his condition. It moreover gives him a loftier view of the grandeur of life; its possibilities are such as to lead him on and on in a more honorable career, and his achievements become additional reasons why he should act well his part. In looking at the many changes that have occurred in the Governments of Australia, one, at first sight, would be disposed to regard it as an evidence of instability, but such is by no means the case; the opposite of this is the fact, and if proof were needed we would only have to point the reader to the fact that business institutions are becoming better established every year, and the credit of the colonies continues to increase abroad, and gradual improvement in the condition of the masses is apparent on every side. The changes that have taken place in colonial Governments are the most hopeful signs of the times, for it precludes stagnation, and stagnation is death. The constant see-saw movement among the respective political parties, in which one is now up and the other down, causes the whole community to investigate the reason of things. The highest intelligence is sure to express itself, and the greatest gifts are pressed into service, not always in Government offices, for eloquence can be much more serviceable in mass meetings than in the daily routine office work and vice versa. The best arguments of the scholar and the ruder common sense of the man uncultured in letters have their due share in making the laws of the country and in choosing the representatives entrusted with this task, and therefore we have reason to congratulate ourselves on the fact that responsible Government is restless, sensitive, and always keenly on the alert for sentiments of popular approval or of discontent, and seeks to know what can be said on each side of every question affecting the body politic, and therefore has to test its merits by appealing both directly and indirectly to the intelligence of the people. We are sometimes amazed with the frequency with which Ministries are changed both in their leadership and in their composition. The leader of to-day becomes the follower of to-morrow, and the friends of the present were the antagonists of the past; and thus while in apparent instability tosses the ship of State hither and yonder in a most threatening manner, filling the timid with alarm, yet the experienced mariner has long since learned that there is nothing at sea so much to be dreaded as a calm, and that the contrary winds and frequent storms are nature's methods of accomplishing her work most fittingly, and that the storm is alike profitable when her laws are duly obeyed, and the wise intelligence of the seamen can adjust the vessel to the requirements of the breeze.

THE MINISTRIES.

The first Ministry entrusted with the administration of the Government was called the Herbert Ministry, and consisted of Robert George Wyndham (Colonial Secretary from 10th December, 1859, to 1st Februrary, 1866), Ratcliffe Pring (Attorney General from 10th December, 1859, to 30th August, 1865, succeeded by John Bramstone from 31st August, 1865, to 11th September, 1865, who was succeeded by Charles Lilley from 11th September, 1865, to 12th July, 1866), Robert Ramsay McKenzie (Colonial Treasurer from 15th December, 1859 to 4th August, 1862, who was succeeded by Thomas Delacy Moffat from 4th August, 1862, to 2nd October, 1864, who was in turn succeeded by Joshua Peter Bell from 22nd December, 1864, to 20th July, 1866); and without portfolio, Maurice Charles O'Connell (from 21st May, 1860, to 28th August, 1860), John James Galloway (from 28th August, 1860, to 10th November, 1860), and William Hobbs (from 30th April, 1861, to 14th January, 1862); St. George Richard Gore (Secretary for Lands and Works from 14th January, 1862, to 21st March, 1862, who was succeeded by Arthur McAllister from 21st March, 1862, to 20th July, 1866); and without portfolio, John Bramstone (from 3rd July, 1863, to 1st February, 1866).

It was one of the first concerns of Governor Bowen to surround himself with advisers with some experience in colonial matters, and at the same time who would be willing to accord a reasonable devotion to the wants of the new Colony in an unselfish manner. His selection of the first Premier was one who was a stranger to the Colony, being himself a new chum, and being a resident in the Colony only a sufficient number of days to entitle him under her laws to all its privileges, and, indeed, came to the Colony, no doubt, at the request of the mother country, for the express purpose of giving shape to the policy of the new Colony, and for the further reason that he was known to be a man of considerable intelligence and education, and would be a safe man in the office of Colonial Secretary. Robert George Wyndham Herbert, K.C.B., D.C.L., the at present permanent Under-Secretary for the Colonies, and at the formation of Responsible Government in the Colony of Queensland was made Colonial Secretary and first Premier, is the son of the Hon. Algernon Herbert. He was born on 12th June, 1831, and was educated at Eton, and afterwards at Balliol College, Oxford, where he took high honors. In 1855 he was appointed Private Secretary to the Chancellor of the Exchequer, the Right

Hon. J. D MOREHEAD,
Colonial Secretary.

Hon. W. E. Gladstone. He was called to the bar of the Middle Temple in 1858, and in 1859 was appointed Colonial Treasurer and Premier of Queensland, at the same time becoming a member of the Legislative Assembly of the Colony. These offices he retained until 1865. From 1868 to February 1870 he was one of the Assistant Secretaries to the Board of Trade, and in the latter year was appointed Assistant Under-Secretary of State for the Colonies, and Under-Secretary, on 1st May, 1871, which position he still holds. The billet Sir Herbert first occupied in the Colony was said to have been offered to Captain Wickham, and upon his refusal, the position was forced upon Sir Herbert. While this form of procedure may have been followed, it was evidently the intention of the Home authorities that Herbert should be entrusted with the responsibility.

The Attorney-Generalship was entrusted to Ratcliffe Pring, who occupied that position with marked ability for nearly six years. His eminent qualifications as an Attorney fitted him, in a remarkable degree, for the duties of the office; but his independence of spirit, and his strong opinions upon many questions that came under the consideration of the Cabinet, and the forcible way in which the Hon. Mr. Pring was accustomed to express himself, brought him frequently in conflict with his associates and with the politicians of his day. He resigned the position, and was succeeded by John Bramstone, a man of scholarly attainments, and who had graduated at Balliol College, Oxford, in 1854, being elected Fellow of All Souls in 1855. He was called to the Bar in 1857. In 1859 he went to Queensland as Private Secretary to Sir George Bowen, and which office he resigned in 1861. He was a member of the Executive and Legislative Councils from 1863 to 1866, and from the former till 1869. He went to England in 1867, and was Assistant Boundary Commissioner for Devon and Cornwall, under the Reform Act of that year. He returned to Queensland in 1868, and was called to the post of Attorney-General in the Lilley Ministry, and filled the same from 12th November, 1869, to 3rd May, 1870. He represented the Burnett district from April 1871 till December 1873, at which last date he resigned his position in the Assembly, and was appointed Attorney-General at Hong Kong, acting as judge from February to May, 1874. He was subsequently appointed as Assistant Under-Secretary, 30th June, 1876. His occupancy of his position of Attorney-General in the first Ministry lasted only a few weeks, when its duties were committed to Charles Lilley, at that time a prominent young barrister, and now occupying the position of Chief Justice of the Supreme Court. The importance of the office at that time may be inferred from the amount of legal advice sought and required on all questions that came before the young Colony for discussion. It is not to be wondered at that friction would be frequent, and the office would be more or less one of perplexity and discomfort. Charles Lilley was eminently qualified to fill the position, for he at once had all the advantages of a ripe scholarship, and an independent spirit.

Mr. Charles Lilley, now enjoying the title of Sir Charles Lilley, K.C.M.G., was born at Newcastle-on-Tyne, England, and received the greater part of his education at University College, London. He was articled to an eminent London solicitor, and arrived in Moreton Bay in 1856. He re-entered upon the profession of the law as an articled clerk to Mr. Robert Little, Crown Solicitor, and was joint lessee of the *Moreton Bay Courier*. On the separation of the Colony from New South Wales, Mr. Lilley was elected member for Fortitude Valley, which he continued to represent until the end of his Parliamentary career. In 1861 he was called to the Bar, and appointed Q.C. in 1865. In the same year he became Attorney-General in the Herbert Ministry, holding the same office in the following year under Mr. McAllister's Premiership. He was himself Premier and Attorney-General in 1868, and Colonial Secretary in the following year, when he established free education throughout the Colony. In 1870 he resigned, in consequence of Parliament having objected to his having ordered the building of the steamer Governor Blackall without Parliamentary sanction. In 1874 he was appointed a judge of the Supreme Court, and Chief Justice in 1879. Sir Charles Lilley has always taken a very active part in educational matters, and is at present Chairman of Trustees of the Brisbane Grammar School, an institution he was mainly instrumental in founding. He was Chairman of the Royal Commission on Education, which resulted in free secular and compulsory education. He was also the means of the Queensland Judicature Act being passed, and has been for many years at the head of the movement for the establishment of a Queensland University.

Robert Ramsay McKenzie, to whom was entrusted the folio of Treasurer, was a man of independent spirit, a squatter whose interests were large and prosperous. He was a large owner of the new farm suburbs, and lived in that delightful part of the city of Brisbane, enjoying a good share of the comforts of life. He died in Scotland, when on a visit there to see a sick brother. His relationship to Governor Bowen was said to have been not of the most harmonious character. He was a prominent defender of the squatter party, and a politician of more than ordinary power. His successor in the office was Thomas De Lacy Moffat, and he was succeeded by Joshua Peter Bell, an epitome of whose life is given in our last chapter.

The Lands and Works Department was a very important folio to fill; in fact, it is at all times; but more especially was it the case in the new Colony, when it was desirable to adopt the policy that would meet with the endorsement of the people and be a benefit to the Colony at large. The first called to the task was Sir George Richard Gore, whose life and record were that of a high-toned gentleman, yet who frequently came in conflict with his associates on the question of what is the best policy for the Colony. Mr. Gore had the esteem of the people generally. He was succeeded by Mr. Arthur McAllister, an eminent lawyer, who had a part ownership in the establishment of the Ipswich *Herald* — now the *Queensland Times* — a paper started in 1859. At the time of separation he was the earnest advocate of the Liberal Policy.

Mr. McAllister, who was afterwards known as Sir Arthur McAllister, C.M.G., was born in Glasgow, and educated for the law. After spending some years in New South Wales, in 1850 he went to Queensland and took a leading part in advocating Separation. He was subsequently returned for Ipswich, for which he sat until Queensland became a separate colony. He accepted a seat in the first Herbert Ministry as Secretary for Lands and Works, which he filled from 21st March, 1862, until 20th July, 1866. In 1866 he was Premier, and again in 1867, and subsequently from 1874 until 1876, when he resigned his post and became Agent-General for Queensland in London. He was an eminent lawyer and a scholar of considerable learning, a great favorite with the sex, and on all suitable occasions expressed his appreciation of them. He was not wealthy, although his profession brought him a liberal income; yet he found it scarcely adequate to supply all his wants. He was affable and pleasant in his manner, and hence was popular socially. He died in London a few years ago.

The second Ministry was called into power on 1st February, 1866, and lasted only until 20th July, 1866. Its organisation was entrusted to Mr. McAllister, and consisted of himself as Secretary for Lands and Works; Colonial Secretary, Robert Ramsay McKenzie; Attorney-General, Charles Lilley; Colonial Treasurer, Joshua Peter Bell; and John Douglas as Postmaster-General. The new element introduced to this Ministry was John Douglas, who was a hard-working man, but who was said to be of too yielding a nature to be entrusted with the duties of public office. He was born in 1828, and educated at Rugby School and Durham University. He arrived in New South Wales in 1851, and received the appointment of Goldfields Commissioner. Subsequently he engaged in pastoral pursuits, and sat in New South Wales Parliament as member for Darling Downs, and subsequently for Camden. Mr. Douglas returned to Queensland in 1863, and represented Port Curtis in the Legislative Assembly. In 1886, on being appointed Postmaster General in the McAllister Ministry, he entered the Legislative Council. He, however, re-entered the Lower House, and sat in the Assembly as member for Eastern Downs. On his appointment as Treasurer, Mr. McAllister resigning that position, he afterwards took the leadership in the Council, and in 1869 he went to London as Agent-General. In 1875 he once more entered Parliament as member for Maryborough, and in the following year was made Minister for Lands in the Thorne Ministry, and the next year, in 1877, on Mr. Thorne's resignation, he became Premier, resigning on the defeat of the Ministry in 1879. In 1885 he was appointed Government Resident of Thursday Island, and Acting High Commissioner for New Guinea on the death of Sir Peter Scratchley. Mr. Douglas now holds the position of Her Majesty's special commission for the protected territory of New Guinea.

The McAllister Ministry was short-lived, and was succeeded on 20th July, 1866, by Robert George Wyndham Herbert, who endeavoured to discharge his task by calling into service an entirely new list of men, with the exception of Attorney-General Pring. The men Mr. Herbert selected for his colleagues were men of prominence, though unknown in this important relationship to His Excellency. The Ministry consisted of Robert George Wyndham Herbert, Premier; without portfolio, George Raff; Ratcliffe Pring, Attorney-General; John Donald McLean, Colonial Treasurer; George Elphingstone Dalrymple, Colonial Secretary; John

Watts, Secretary for Lands and Works; Thomas Lodge Murray-Prior, Postmaster-General.

George Raff, who was without a folio, was entitled to all the honor of his new position. He had been identified with the Colony from the year 1851, and was actively engaged in all the contests that marked the early history of the Colony when she was struggling for her independence, and subsequently when she was endeavouring to form a policy under responsible Government that would be for her best interests. During his Parliamentary career, which was unbroken from the period of Separation, in 1859, until 1866, he was distinguished for his straightforward advocacy of the policy of the Liberal party. He was in favor of throwing the lands open to occupancy on the most liberal terms. He was adverse to all extravagance in pushing public works that were beyond the wants of the people. An extract from the Queensland *Times* of 1867, just after his retirement from public life, will give the reader a true insight into Mr. Raff's character :—

"We make no excuse for devoting a considerable portion of our space for the publication of a slightly-abridged report of the address delivered by Mr. Raff to the North Brisbane electors; his remarks being well weighed and deliberately uttered, will abundantly repay a very serious and careful perusal. Standing aloof now as this gentleman does from the present struggle, his observations on public affairs are especially deserving of attention. Mr. Raff never was a claptrap orator, and never condescended to court popularity. Nevertheless of this he had his share, and he was entitled to it by his stern consistency, his unflinching adherence to principle, his unquestionable sincerity, and his ardent yet disinterested patriotism. He had never anything to gain by politics, yet none of our unpaid representatives has worked harder as a politician, and his serious voice of warning against extravagance and reckless expenditure of the public money was raised persistently year after year, but raised in vain. He now stands aside to gaze sadly on calamities which he foresaw, and would have averted but that his warning voice fell on deaf ears. He retires from the arena of public life."

The occasion of this estimate of his public service was an address by Mr. Raff to his constituency and the public, in which he gave an account of his stewardship, and concerning which one of the papers of that date,

20th July, 1867, that was opposed to his public policy, said: "That Mr. Raff is unquestionably an able man, one whose social position, high personal character, and intimate acquaintance with the public affairs of the Colony give him an influence which is not possessed by many among us. As a leading merchant in the neighbourhood, he is in all respects, save one, the best, or at least one of the best, men to be found as a metropolitan member; but that one little objection is a fatal one. He evidently does not represent the feelings of a majority of electors on any single question of importance. As a member for the Leichhardt, Kennedy, or some purely squatting electorate northward, Mr. Raff would be in perfect accord with his constituents, because from what we can learn they also believe in immediately rushing the whole of the unalienated Crown lands into the market, disposing of them by auction sale at any price they will fetch; but as a representative of an agricultural or mercantile constituency he would be utterly out of place."

In the estimate that both these papers put upon his character as a man, there is a harmony of opinion. The Polynesian question or slave trade, as some clergymen of that date were pleased to call it, gave Mr. Raff considerable prominence. The labor question has always been a difficult one to solve. While the high prices of cotton and sugar continued, labor was not so serious an item of consideration, but at the close of the American War, when cotton and sugar fell in the market, it became necessary to find some cheaper substitute for the white laborers. The abolishment of the present system had cut off that supply, and the general scarcity in the labor market induced many of the planters of sugar and cotton to seek the natives from the Islands of the South Seas. The practice of employing the Kanakas, as they were called, became popular, and was relied upon as the chief source of labor supply. This class of laborers generally worked for a year or two, when they were returned to their island homes with about £10 of value, which consisted of clothing, knives, hatchets, beads, and other trinkets. This system afforded too much temptation to unscrupulous persons; first, in giving them as remuneration for their service a less amount of trinkets than they stipulated in their contracts should be granted; also, it encouraged many unscrupulous captains of trading vessels to engage in the traffic of securing natives, which they were not always careful to do by agreement with them, but frequently compelling them by force, and landing them in the Colony against their will. In order to accomplish these nefarious designs, the sailors would frequently appear in the disguise of missionaries, and in this way induce them to board the vessels, when they would be carried off to a strange land. This resulted in a prejudice against the clergy, and on the part of the ignorant Islanders the prejudice was so great as to result in the murder of some who were engaged in their legitimate missionary work. These evils were not endorsed by the people of Queensland. As a rule, with very few exceptions, the planters were disposed to treat honorably these laborers, and discharge every obligation implied in their contract in a kindly manner. This led to the passage in the Queensland Parliament of what is known as the Polynesian Laborers' Act, which was passed in 1868, and was intended to regulate the labor traffic. The Act required each captain who brought to the Colony laborers a document signed by a missionary or British Consul, stating that they individually left of their own accord. It required also a Government agent or inspector to accompany every vessel so employed, who should see that they were well treated on the voyage, and that, upon returning, each laborer had his stipulated amount of goods as remuneration for his toil. While these regulations checked much of the abuse practiced in former days, yet other abuses sprang up. In some cases a present to the king of the island by the sailors was sufficient to induce him to cause his people to express before a missionary their willingness to go; being afraid of their chief, their expression of free will was easily obtained. Even the Government agents on board the vessels were at times bribed, and in other ways the wholesome purposes of the Act were evaded. In course of time the clergymen of the Colony, and of the neighboring colonies, got up mass meetings in condemnation of the traffic, and represented it to be semi-slavery, and to be carried on with the approval and knowledge of these masters and planters in the upper country. Mass meetings were held all over the Continent, and it was charged, among other evils—first: That these laborers were kidnapped by the traders, and that, when landed in Queensland, were enslaved by the masters, who not only neglected their spiritual interests (for most of the Fijians are Christians), but also ill-treated them. Mr. Raff, being one of the masters, and a very large employer of Polynesian labor, became prominent as one of the abettors of the system, and his testimony before a Parliamentary Committee appointed to investigate the charges was relied upon to a very large extent. In obtaining the facts of the case an exhaustive inquiry, that extended over a lengthened period, and that resulted in disclosing much that was wrong in the trade so far as the traders were concerned, and led to the abolishment of the system, disclosed the fact that Mr. Raff's plantation, among many others, was carried on in a most honorable way, and that the native islanders in his employment were better cared for physically, socially, and morally, than in their own island home, and that at the end of their contract period, the terms of agreement under which their labor was secured were carefully carried out. It is impossible to deal more largely with this question; Mr. Raff was the leading spirit in defending the system, or rather in presenting the facts as they were viewed on the side of the masters, it is but just to say that his utterances in reply to the charges made were accepted as the truth by the Commission.

The honorable character sustained by Mr. Raff gave his word authority on the question. That abuses were frequent there can be no doubt, but that these were exaggerated in the charges preferred by those interested in exciting the public against them cannot be doubted either. The passage of the Polynesian Labor Act was intended to control the trade, and bring it within the rules of just Government, and did check abuses that had been so common previously, but failed to prevent others growing up. The moral sentiment of the Colony has always been against these pernicious practices and abuses.

John Donald McLean, who was entrusted with the Colonial Treasury, was a man of thorough commercial capabilities, whose honesty and efficiency were unquestioned; yet from various causes his term of office, expiring in a few days with the resignation of the Ministry and resumed for a few weeks in the subsequent one of McAllister, was of short duration.

John Elphingstone Dalrymple was chosen for the responsible position of Colonial Secretary, involving duties for which he was eminently well adapted.

John Watts, Minister of Lands, and Public Works, held office in this and the McAllister Ministry that followed, but beyond the brief term of about one month in both Ministeries never served afterwards in a position of public trust. As Postmaster-General, Thomas L. Murray-Prior,

HON. W. M. PATTISON,
Minister without Portfolio.

in this, and subsequently from 15th August, 1867, to 25th November, 1868, discharged the duties of his office with efficiency. This Ministry was only in office seventeen days, and was succeeded by the fourth Ministry formed by McAllister, and which consisted of Arthur McAllister, Colonial Secretary; Charles Lilley, Attorney-General; John Donald McLean, Colonial Treasurer, who was succeeded first by John Douglas on 19th December, 1866, and who in turn was succeeded by Thomas Blackett Stephens on 21st May, 1867; Joshua Peter Bell, Secretary for Public Lands; John Watts, Secretary for Public Works, succeeded by John Douglas on 21st May, 1867; without portfolio, George Raff; and St. George Richard Gore as Postmaster General.

The new men who were called upon to fill the important positions assigned them were Thomas Blackett Stephens, who as successor in the Treasurer's Department to John Douglas, and who in Queensland political circles has left a record without a stain, enjoyed a reputation unsullied from the first. The Hon. T. P. Stephens was born at Rockdale in 1815, and came to New South Wales in 1849, and was for a few years with Mr. Atkinson, carrying on business at the Circular Quay, Sydney. A few years before separation he settled in Brisbane, and commenced the fellmongery business near Cleveland. About the year 1862 or 1863 he gave up that, and started fellmongery business on the Burnett Swamp, on the Logan Road, near South Brisbane, to which he gave the name of "Ekibbon." Subsequently he added the tannery business, which speedily grew and prospered until it became the largest tannery and fellmongery establishment in that part of the colony. About the time of separation of Queensland from New South Wales, Mr. Stephens became the proprietor of the *Courier*, the oldest newspaper in the Colony, and held it until 1869, when it passed into the hands of a company, of which he was a shareholder. Mr. Stephens' connection with the *Courier* terminated about 1873, when the property was sold to the present proprietors. He was intimately connected with the *Queenslander*— a paper in which he took the greatest interest, and whose success is largely due to his energy and scholarly attainments. Mr. Stephens was elected an alderman of the Municipality of Brisbane soon after it became a Municipality, and held the office for several years. In 1862 he was elected Mayor. He represented South Brisbane in the Legislative Assembly from the period of Separation until he retired from public life. Shortly before his death, which occurred on 20th August, 1877, he was nominated to a seat in the Legislative Council. He served on several occasions in the Ministries. This Ministry continued in existence for only one year; the fifth was entrusted to the Premiership of Robert Ramsay McKenzie, and lasted from 15th August, 1867, until 25th November, 1868, being a little over a year. It consisted of Robert Ramsay McKenzie, Colonial Treasurer; Arthur Hunter, Colonial Secretary, who subsquently took the office of Secretary for Public Works, and was succeeded by Arthur Hodgson on 10th September, 1868; Ratcliffe Pring, Attorney-General; Edward William Lamb, Secretary for Public Lands, who was succeeded by Arthur Hunter Palmer on 10th September, 1868; and Thomas Lodge Murray-Prior, Postmaster-General. The new people introduced to Ministerial office were Mr. Arthur Palmer, whose history is given elsewhere, Mr. Arthur Hodgson, and Edward Lamb. Mr. Arthur Hodgson, subsequently known as Sir Arthur Hodgson, K.C.M.G., arrived in Sydney in 1840, and was not long in Australia before he and others were attracted to the district of Moreton Bay. He was among the first to settle on the Darling Downs. It is said that near the place of his first camping he found a knife, the maker of which was known to him when at Eton, and in commemoration of the circumstance he called his homestead "Eton Vale." Previous to separation he represented the Darling Downs of New South Wales. In 1856 he was appointed General Superintendent of the Australian Agricultural Company. In 1862 he represented Queensland at the London Exhibition. After the separation of Queensland he represented the electorate of Warrego. In 1874 he returned to England. He was knighted in 1878.

In 1868 Charles Lilley, now Chief Justice of the Supreme Court of Queensland, was charged with the formation of the sixth Ministry, which consisted of Charles Lilley, Attorney-General; Thomas B. Stephens, Colonial Secretary, succeeded by Arthur Hodgson, who was subsequently succeeded by Charles Lilley; Thomas Henry Fitzgerald, Colonial Treasurer, succeeded by Mr. Stephens; the Hon. Arthur McAllister, Secretary for Public Lands and Public Works and Goldfields; James Taylor, Secretary for Public Lands when they were assigned departments by themselves; Ratcliffe Pring, Attorney-General; John Douglas, Postmaster-General, who was succeeded by Richard Gore. Thomas Henry Fitzgerald, Treasurer, and James Taylor, in the Office of Public Lands, were new to Ministeral duties.

After a period of about eighteen months, and several exchanges in the Cabinet, the seventh Ministry was formed by Mr. Palmer, who called to his assistance several new men, who were chosen for their strong common sense rather than for any superiority over the tried men of the former Ministry. Robert Ramsay as Treasurer, William Henry Walsh, Charles James Graham, and John Malbon Thompson brought qualifications to their respective offices which rendered the Premier good service during his continuance in office. So firm was the hold this Ministry had on the confidence of the people that it continued in office for four years, during which time much activity was displayed in the railway and agricultural interests of the Colony. First among the active elements of the Ministry is to be mentioned William Henry Walsh. He was born in Oxfordshire, England, in 1825, and arrived in New South Wales in 1844, soon after which he entered upon pastoral pursuits. After serving in the Parliament of New South Wales before separation he was returned for Maryborough in the Queensland Parliament, receiving his first appointment (Minister for Public Works) in 1870, which position he resigned in 1873. He was returned as member for the Warregal in 1874, and was elected Speaker of the Assembly. In 1879 he was appointed to a seat in the Legislative Council.

On 8th January, 1874, the eighth Ministry was formed, the Hon. Mr. McAllister being entrusted with its construction. Following the successful plan of his predecessor, he chose as his associates many new men, who had been well tried in the various enterprises of the Colony, but whose public services were of a more modest character, and consisted of the Hon. Arthur McAllister, Colonial Secretary ; Thomas Arthur Stephens, Secretary for Public Lands, succeeded by William Prior ; William Hemment, Colonial Treasurer ; Edward O'Donnell McDevit, Attorney-General, who was succeeded by Sir Samuel Walker Griffith ; Thomas McIlwraith, Secretary for Public Works and Mines, succeeded by the Hon. Arthur McAllister, Henry Edward King, and James Robert Dixon, in the order named ; George Thorne, junr., Postmaster-General ; William Prior, a man of superior business qualifications, and successor to that most remarkable of all politicians, Mr. Stephens, Secretary for Public Lands ; and Mr. Hemment, whose commercial standing was a tower of strength. In his selection of Mr. O'Donnell McDevit and Samuel Walker Griffith was evinced a clear-sighted knowledge of the fitness of men abundantly justified in their subsequent career ;

and for the Public Works and Mines his selection of McIlwraith and Henry Edward King was a wise one. The public service of the former of these men forms a very large part of the history of this Colony in its late years, and that of Mr. King being identified very largely with the mining development of the country and its railway projects. Mr. King was the eldest son of Captain John W. King, of the Fifth Northumberland Fusiliers, and was born 9th June, 1832. He received his education in the College School, Gloucester, and having passed his examination in 1850, he was gazetted as 2nd Lieut. in the 5th Fusiliers in March of that year. He retired from service by sale of his commission, and sailed for Australia in 1852, landing first in Sydney. He visited the goldfields, and worked in various parts with very little success. In 1853 he came to Brisbane, first seeking colonial experience in the interior upon a station. In 1854 he accompanied William Arthur, Esq., upon an expedition, and visited the district of Port Curtis. In 1858 Mr. King married and purchased the station on the Dawson. In 1860 he sold the station and removed to Rockhampton. As leader of a prospecting party, he visited the Port Curtis Ranges, discovering small quantities of gold and copper, but abandoned the same. In 1862 he was appointed Government Surveyor and Commissioner of Crown Lands for the district, surveying the first runs on the Marcoo and Constant Rivers. In 1864 he was transferred to Leichhardt, and in 1865 he was sent to Gympie as the first Gold Commissioner there. In May, 1870, he resigned this position, and was returned to Parliament as representative of the Wide Bay district. He was re-elected at a subsequent date. In 1874 he accepted office as Minister for Works, and was elected for Ravenswood; but in May, 1876, he resigned his portfolio, in consequence of a difference with his colleagues respecting the policy of railway extension, and immediately thereafter was elected Speaker of the Assembly. In 1878 he was returned for Maryborough, and again chosen as Speaker, from which, in 1883, his public career terminated. Mr. King was always a Liberal in politics, a firm supporter of the Lilley Ministry, and opposed to the squatting party.' On his retirement from the office of Public Works and Mining, Charles R. Dixon was chosen to fill the vacancy.

Mr. Dixon was born at Plymouth, Devonshire, England, in 1832, and educated at the High School of Glasgow. He was a financier of great knowledge and experience, having been largely connected with the Scotch

Banks. Mr. Dixon arrived in Victoria in 1854, and in Queensland in 1862. He entered the business of auctioneer, in which he was very successful. In 1873 he entered Parliament as representative of Eunogera, and has continued to represent that electorate ever since. In 1873 he accepted the above office, and when the Liberal party was re-organised under Mr. George Thorne, he was appointed therein Colonial Treasurer, which he held until 1879. Mr. Dixon led the Opposition in the Assembly during the absence of Mr. Griffith in England in 1881. He was one of the representatives of Queensland at the Federal Council held at Hobart in 1886.

George Thorne, as Postmaster-General, had an opportunity that falls to the lot of few, but he was equal to the demands of the times. Mr. Thorne is a native of Sydney. His father (Mr. George Thorne), who died in 1876, was the oldest inhabitant, and the founder of the town of Ipswich, Queensland. He had been many years in the army, and was much esteemed by Sir George Gipps. The subject of our sketch was born at the end of 1838, and received his education in private schools, in King's School, Parramatta, and in other institutions, graduating from the University of Sydney in 1858. Mr. Thorne took a course of nine years in pastoral life, thus acquiring a good knowledge of Queensland, and becoming familiar with the political questions of his day. In 1867 he was returned as one of the members for West Moreton. In the general election of 1873 he was returned for Fasifern. A new Ministry having been formed by Mr. McAllister shortly after the meeting of Parliament, Mr. Thorne accepted the portfolio of Postmaster-General and a seat in the Council as representative of the Government in that Chamber in 1874, and immediately applied himself to the task of Postal and Telegraphic connections. He pushed with great energy the lines and stations throughout the Colony, and identified himself with the Conference for the laying of cables connecting New Zealand and New South Wales, and extending the communication to Singapore and Europe, via Normanton. In 1876 he became Premier and Minister for Works, resigning his position in 1877, and visiting Europe in 1878. He was elected member for Queensland Legislative Assembly from the Dalby electorate in 1879. His excellent service in the Postal and in the Public Works Departments brought him so prominently to the front that he was selected by the Governor as Premier of the ninth Ministry, which consisted of himself as Secretary for Public Works and Mines; John Douglas, Secretary for Public Lands; Samuel

THE MINISTRIES.

Walker Griffith, Attorney-General and Secretary for Public Instruction; James Robert Dixon, Colonial Treasurer; Robert Mewter Stewart, Colonial Secretary; and Charles Stewart Mein, Postmaster-General.

This Ministry continued but a few months in office, and was re-organised under the leadership of the Douglas, or tenth Ministry, as follows:— The Hon. John Douglas, C.M.G., Secretary for Public Lands, and subsequently Colonial Secretary; Samuel Walker Griffith, Attorney-General and Secretary for Public Instruction, resigning the former office, which was then filled by James Francis Garrett; James Robert Dixon, Colonial Treasurer; Robert Mewter Stewart, Colonial Secretary, who was succeeded by William Miles; Samuel Walker Griffith, Secretary for Public Works; George Thorne, Secretary for Public Works and Mines; James Francis Garrett, Secretary for Public Lands and Mines; Charles Stewart Mein, Postmaster-General, with several incidental changes in the re-assignment of the respective folios. The personæ of the Thorne Cabinet was retained, but many new names were added in this Ministry.

Charles Stewart Mein as Postmaster-General rendered efficient service to the colony. He was born in Maitland, New South Wales, on 14th June, 1841, and received his education in Mr. Cape's School, Darling-hurst, Sydney, subsequently at the Sydney Grammar School, graduating from the Sydney University in 1862, being a fellow-student of the Hon. Sir S. W. Griffith. Subsequent to his graduation, he was Private Secretary to the Attorney-General of New South Wales, but came to Queensland in 1867, and was admitted a solicitor of the Supreme Court at the end of 1870. He was nominated to the Legislative Council on 9th May, 1876, and was appointed Postmaster-General and representative of the Government in the Council on 8th July, 1876. He was again appointed Postmaster-General and representative of the Government in the Upper House on 24th June, 1884. In 1885 he was appointed Minister of Public Instruction. On the death of the late Mr. Justice Pring, he was raised to the Bench of the Supreme Court on 17th April, 1885. Mr. Mein has represented the Colony on two occasions at the Intercolonial Conference — first in Sydney in 1877 with Mr. Griffith as associate, afterwards in Melbourne in 1878. Mr. Mein has for many years past taken an active interest in the maintenance of the Defence Force, being Commander of the 1st Regiment with the rank of Lieutenant-Colonel. He is President of the National Agricultural and Industrial Association of Queensland, and of the Brisbane School of Arts, and of the Queensland Turf Club.

Mr. Charles F. Garrick rendered good service, first as Attorney General, and subsequently in the Lands and Mines Department. He is at present Agent-General for Queensland in London, and enjoys the distinguished title of Q.C., K.C.M.G. He was born in Sydney, New South Wales, where he received a liberal education. He came to Queensland soon after separation, and carried on a successful business as solicitor, being associated with Chief Justice Sir Charles Lilley. After several years experience in Brisbane he went to England, where he was called to the Bar of the Inner Temple, thereafter returning to Brisbane. Previous to his visit to England he was elected to a seat in the Assembly for East Moreton, and took an active part in politics throughout his colonial career. At the last general election but one he was returned for Moreton and entered the Griffith Ministry as Attorney-General holding the office for a short time only, subsequently being appointed Postmaster-General with a seat in the Legislative Council, where he represented the Government. He has been Minister for Lands in the Douglas Ministry and acted as Treasurer in the absence of Mr. Dixon. He was one of the Queensland representives of the Intercolonial Conference in December, 1887. He was knighted in 1886.

The eleventh Ministry was entrusted to Sir Thomas McIlwraith in January, 1879, and consisted of Thomas McIlwraith, Colonial Treasurer, succeeded by Archibald Archer, who was also Secretary for Public Instruction from January, 1882, to 13th November, 1883; Arthur Hunter Palmer, as Colonial Secretary and Secretary for Public Instruction, who was succeeded by Thomas McIlwraith as Colonial Secretary, both of which gentlemen were knighted during this term; John Malbon Thompson, as Minister of Justice, who was succeeded by the Hon. Ratcliffe Pring, Q.C., Attorney-General, who was succeeded by Henry Rogers Beor, Attorney-General, who in turn was succeeded by Pope Alexander Cooper, and at last succeeded by Charles Edward Chubb; Charles Hardy Buzacott as Postmaster-General, succeeded by Boyd Dunlop Morehead, who was succeeded by Francis Gregory; John Murtagh Macrossin as Secretary for Public Works and Mines, succeeded by Albert Norton and Patrick Perkins, as Secretary for Public Lands. The new people brought into this important position were Archibald Archer, Henry Roger Boer, Pope Alexander Cooper, Charles Edward Chubb, Charles Buzacott, whose sketch appears elsewhere, and Morehead, A. C. Gregory, J. M. Macrossin, Albert Norton, and Patrick Perkins. This Ministry was confronted with a new political power in the person of Griffiths, whose policy was liberal, and who championed the cause of moral reform, a liberal land policy, and who combated the squattocracy in what he conceived was a selfish policy of monopoly, and in his judgment tended to check the progress of the Colony.

On the 13th November, 1883, the twelfth Ministry was formed, with Samuel Griffiths as Premier, and consisted of the Hon. Sir Samuel Walker Griffiths, Q.C., K.C.M.G.,as Chief Secretary, who subsequently assumed the office of Colonial Treasurer, having previously, for a short time, been head of the Board of Public Instruction, but was succeeded in this by Charles Stewart Mein, and afterwards was succeeded by Berkeley Basil Moreton; William Isles as Secretary for Public Works and Mines, who died while in office, and was succeeded by C. B. Dutton, who resigned December 12th, 1887, and was succeeded by W. C. Hodgkinson; C. B. Dutton was appointed Secretary for Railways when that office was created 12th December, 1887; James Francis Garrick as Colonial Treasurer, succeeded by James Robert Dickson, who resigned August 9, 1887, when the folio passed into the hands of the Premier; James Francis Garrick, Postmaster-General, which folio passed quickly from the hands of Charles Stewart Mein, R. B. Sheridan, Hon. S. W. Griffiths, Q.C., Hon. Berkeley Basil Moreton, P. McDonald Patterson, and Hon. W. H. Wilson, in the order named; Charles Bodell Durron as Secretary for Public Lands resigning that position when he assumed the above office, and was succeeded by Henry Jordan; Arthur Rutledge as Attorney-General. Its term of office continued until January, 1888, when on the Imperial Defence Bill question it was defeated, and was succeeded by the thirteenth Ministry under the Premiership of McIlwraith, who called as his associates the Hon. J. M. Macrossan, as Minister for Mines and Works; the Hon. H. M. Nelson, Minister for Railways; Hon. B. D. Morehead, Colonial Secretary; Hon J. Donaldson, Postmaster-General; Hon. M. H. Black, Mr. N. Pattison, without portfolio; Hon. A. J. Thynne, Minister of Justice; and Hon. A. Norton, Speaker, a sketch of whom appears in another chapter.

Hon. A. NORTON,
Speaker.

CHAPTER XXIII.
CELEBRATION.

THE latter part of the first century of Australian History is one of display and rejoicing. It was natural that as her Centennial was approaching she should feel some ambition to show the world what she had accomplished during her brief existence—that she had boundless resources and great wealth was already known to a limited number of her own people and a few in the commercial centres of the world. In 1877 the first Exhibition of an international character was held, to which other British colonies were invited to join. Exhibits were sent from New Zealand, Ceylon, Fiji, and the Dominion of Canada, one of the most remote of Her Majesty's Colonies. The initiatory steps to accomplish this result were taken by Mr. Augustus Morris, who was a Commissioner to the Centennial Exhibition of the United States in 1876, where Canada's excellent productions led him to seek commercial relations between that country and Australia.

The Hon. John Young, of Montreal, was chosen to represent that country in this Exhibition. He was a man universally esteemed at home, and well fitted by a long life of commercial experience and prosperity to represent honorably the interests entrusted to his keeping. He examined every portion of the continent, every source of wealth she possessed, and was good enough to express astonishment at the infinite variety of our resources and the enormous advantages of the climate as compared with the colder regions of the North American continent, and predicted a great future for this country. That Exhibition proving to be a great success, we were encouraged to show our neighbours by others of a like character much wealth and power of production that were as yet hid from the commercial knowledge of the world. At the same time we learned how valuable a freetrade with other portions of the British Empire would become. Projects were before our people to exhibit at Paris, in 1878, and to hold an International Exhibition at Sydney, in 1879, and still another in 1880 in Melbourne. All of these were endorsed by the Colonial Treasurers, and invitations were sent out to all nations to join in these Exhibitions, and there came favorable responses from all parts of the world. France, Germany, Austria, Hungary, Belgium, Italy, Switzerland, Holland, the United States of America, Canada, and all the Australian Colonies, the Islands of the Seas, and not least, Great Britain and Ireland, all were eager to see this new nation of the South that had so rapidly sprung into existence, and to bring their own treasures of Art, Science, and Culture, not in the spirit of rivalry but in the spirit of brotherhood, and to link a younger sister in the bond of universal fraternity. The gathering together from the ends of the earth the best specimens of their handiwork was a revelation and an inspiration to all Australians, and equally so was our continent as it burst upon the gaze of the world outside. With mutual wonder and admiration each looked on the works of another, and found an exquisite pleasure in the contemplation that in the future there was room for grander results and a sublimer inspiration to lead us on.

An occasion that called forth the loyalty of the Australians occurred in connection with the Soudan War. The Soudan expedition may or may not have been ill advised. The sentiment of the country was pretty much divided upon the subject. The leading journals took opposite sides; some praised, some condemned, and more were disposed to regard it as the natural expression of a young nation's enthusiastic desire to do something that would call forth a mother's praise and recognition. The immediate cause of this loyal outburst was the death of the gallant General Gordon, a brave, christian soldier. Whatever the opponents of the Soudan Contingent may say respecting the wisdom of organising an expedition of men untrained, they cannot surely condemn England's desire to put an end to the cruel slave trade and check the oppression under which the Soudanese existed. The Colonies had followed the story of General Charles George Gordon's expedition from its commencement, early in 1884, and with all other English Dependencies, took a lively interest in the expedition.

The slave-trade carried on among the Soudanese by the sub-officials of the Egyptian rulers was a cruel wrong that would seem to justify Mahomet Achmet in rising up under the title of "Mahdi" the prophet, and under *the inspiration* of good-will towards his oppressed countrymen, call upon them to resist the unjust and tyrannous acts of their rulers. The wretched and miserable condition of society, in which children were torn from their parents, and friends separated for the purpose of satisfying the cupidity of an aristocratic horde of semi-officialdum, is without parallel or justification. It was but a natural thing, and in accordance with the great law of self-preservation, that these downtrodden, tax-ground Soudanese should strike back at the inhuman assassins, whose delight was intensified by the sorrow they could wring from the cries of the wretched slaves under their lash. The awful grandeur of an oppressed people rising up *en masse*, listening to the voice of a leader whom we may call a "false prophet," yet who has a true prophet's "inspiration," awakens our sympathy and admiration. It was not the first time that Egypt had put her tyrannous heel upon the oppressed. A prophet came to them, and thundered at the Court of Pharoah the stern command, "Let my people go," and from out their bondage they followed until he led them to a land of deliverance; and why should not the Soudanese, ground into slavery, listen to a leader who came to them, and who cried out to the weeping sons and daughters of Soudan, "Arise and follow me, and I will be your saviour." Such is the Soudan side of the question. The "Mahdi," with the masses, fought for their family altars; they fought for their liberty, for the very life of their brothers and sons. They struck at their despoilers. It is true that their enemies were their "constituted" rulers. To strike back was to rebel against law and order. By "the code of nations" they had no right to rebel. According to the same standard their duty was to endure the wrongs and await the slow march of time for changes in the organic law. The English side of this question must be considered from a somewhat different standpoint. There is reason to believe that England was as anxious as the Soudanese to put down the cruel slave-trade that was the chief cause of the rebellion. She had appointed first Mr. Baker as Governor, and subsequently General Gordon, with the special duty of checking it, and entirely delivering the people from its existence, but in this she failed, and in disgust at the treachery and opposition of some of the shieks, these noble Christian men and brave officers returned to England, Mr. Baker about the year 1878, and General Gordon in the latter part of 1881. With their departure was revived the unholy traffic, and within a very few months all the horrors of slavery and the unjust wrongs of former years were repeated with increased cruelty, and hence the rising of the people to redress their own wrongs and free themselves from the oppression. England had vested rights in Soudan, her merchants were under the sworn protection of Egyptian authority, England's commercial interests were jeopardised by the success of the Soudanese rebellion, and hence England's commercial prosperity was best served by putting down the rebellion, and restoring peace and order. General Gordon was appointed "to report on the military situation in the Soudan, and to provide in the best manner for the safety of the European population of Khartoum, and of the Egyptian garrisons throughout the country, as well as for the evacuation of the Soudan, with the exception of the seaboard." His real object was to effect reforms in the Government of Soudan. He began the task by discharging the prisoners who had been incarcerated for non-payment of unjust taxation. He sought to remove wrongs under which the people were crushed; at the same time he wished to put down all rebellion, and bring about such reform as would tend to the peace and order of the country, and at the same time be a safeguard to his own people. Both England and the Soudanese aimed at the same results, but the "Mahdi" and his people having been frequently deceived by the treachery and injustice of pasha and shiek came to regard their ally as being equally opposed to them, and hence when they surrounded Khartoum and hedged in Gordon and other British officers and soldiers the Soudanese knew not that they were fighting against their best friends. General Gordon fell in the unequal conflict. England's help did not come with sufficient despatch to afford relief, and the entire nation mourned the loss of a truly great and noble-minded soldier. When the tidings of his assassination reached England and her colonies it was the occasion of heartfelt sorrow, and aroused a universal sentiment of loyalty and devotion, and to give expression to this feeling in some tangible shape Canada was quick to respond to the call that seemed to come from Khartoum in the hour of her deep grief and need; and equally so Australia, moved by a common sympathy, was impatient to do likewise. Sir Edward Strickland, under the impulse of loyal enthusiasm, wrote to the *Sydney Morning Herald*,

CELEBRATION. 197

calling upon the colony to follow in the footsteps of Canada. . . . "A grand opportunity is now offered to Australia of proving, by performing a graceful, a loyal, a generous act, that she yields not to Canada or to any portion of the British Empire in loyalty and affection towards our Mother Country. I would suggest that a regiment, one thousand strong, be raised in Australia as speedily as possible, and be placed at the service of Her Majesty the Queen to aid her troops already in bitter war both in North and South Africa." The letter, from which is taken the above extract, was read all over the colony, and had the effect of arousing the country in that direction. Immediately after its publication the subject was seriously discussed in the Cabinet, on the motion and earnest advocacy of Mr. Dalley, who had previously consulted with the chief commandant of the forces in New South Wales, Colonel Richardson, and also Colonel Roberts, who was officer in command of the New South Wales Artillery, and others prominent in the civil as well as in the military service. There was a wonderful unanimity of sentiment both outside and more especially among the members of the Cabinet, who embodied their feelings of loyalty in a resolution offering help to the Mother Country. The following despatch was immediately sent to Sir Saul Samuel, Agent-General of the Colony, in London, on the 12th February, 1885 :—" The Government offers to Her Majesty's Government two batteries of its Permanent Field Artillery, with ten 16-lb guns, properly horsed; also, an effective and disciplined battalion of Infantry, five hundred strong. The Artillery will be under the command of Colonel Roberts, R.A.; the whole force under the command of Colonel Richardson, the commandant, and undertaking to land the force at Suakim within thirty days from embarkation. Reply at once." After much preliminary consultation by the parties most concerned in the War Department of the Home Government, a favourable reply came in the following words :—" Her Majesty's Government accept, with much satisfaction, offer of your Government upon the understanding that the force must be placed absolutely under orders of General commanding as to duties upon which it will be employed. Force of Artillery is greater than is required; only one battery accepted. Transport should call at Aden for orders. If your Government prefer the immediate despatch of your contingent, War Office does not desire to delay it. Press comment very favourable upon your splendid offer." From nearly all the colonies came gracious words of approval, and among the many leading journals of this country and England there were but few who did not approve of the offer. It was accepted as the expression of loyal devotion to England. There were a few journals, however, of a high order who disapproved of the act, and questioned the motive. Both journals and men of mark and distinction did not hesitate to stigmatise the movement as puerile, and the motive prompting it as simply a childish craving to be baptised in the popular current of Royal benedictions, which being interpreted means the ingenious arrangement of the larger letters of the alphabet, so as to feed those more matured in the art of diplomacy with chaff made palatable by the Royal " well done." Those who opposed the movement were few in number at that time. The mass of people spoke in terms of approval. People of wealth stood ready and anxious to supplement the action of the Cabinet with their money. Among the larger donors who came forward with their material help may be mentioned £1,000 a year from Mr. James Reading Fairfax, and the same amount from his brother Edward Ross Fairfax ; the same amount from Mr. Daniel Cooper, son of Sir D. Cooper; and from the *Evening News* Company, Thomas Walker, of Concord, Mr. B. W. Levy, of West Maitland, each £1,000 per year; and Mr. James Tyson £2,000 a year; and many other smaller gifts. Such was the enthusiasm that there came offers of goods, storage accommodation, and volunteers beyond the number needed. Ladies and gentlemen offered their services as nurses, attendants, etc., until the Government said, "We have enough." Seven hundred and forty-three men were announced as the strength of the Contingent Force, and in addition to accompany these five hundred and thirty-two were chosen as an Ambulance Corps. Nothing can be imagined like the excitement that was aroused by this outburst of loyalty and devotion to the cause of England, not alone by those who had volunteered their services on the battlefield, but by those who had made an equal sacrifice by giving up their brothers, sons, and husbands in the hour of England's need, and whose sacrifice was all the more real because it was spontaneous, and made without the hope of any personal gain, except such glory as surrounds a soldier's grave, or the scanty provision that is usually made for the worn-out veteran, who, tottering home when his task is done maimed and blind, is tossed aside to make room for the more active, stirring sons of toil, who in manhood's vigor pursue their several ways, unconscious of the price paid by others in their behalf. The scene surrounding the "embarkation" was appalling in its grandeur. It was not possible for the great heart of the people to be unmoved while the "Contingent" was astir. The thrill of sentiment was a universal impulse. Even such as opposed the methods were none the less loyal and true in their attachment to the interests of Englishmen involved in the conflict—they too joined in the universal demonstrations of sympathy and good-will. From the remote interior the swarthy herdsman came, the miner laid down his pick and shovel, and the sturdy farmer let his oxen rest, while he joined his fellows in the general tramp to the city. One could scarce conceive how widespread was the feeling of sympathy with the brave soldier and his friends. It was apparent to everyone that no idle curiosity prompted this pilgrimage—nothing but a common impulse in the cause of a common brotherhood. The city for days before the departure was filled with strangers and friends alike; from points remote and nigh they came, the youth stirred by the bugle's call, and the aged by memories of the past, and wives, sisters, and mothers by a sentiment too sacred and beyond the power of human pen to write or words express. The city was alive with visitors. A general commotion attested the uncommonness of the occasion. It was unlike the ordinary holiday. There was bustle and stir and tramping to and fro, but amid the din there was the hush of suppressed gloom. Each face wore the lines of sadness and anxiety, save the schoolboy, whose whistling notes and incessant clatter never fail to assert his supremacy where the crowds do congregate. While the ships "Iberia" and "Australasian" were awaiting the "embarkation" of the "Contingent" in the Circular Quay, and all hands on board making ready for their reception, the reader can scarcely realise the picture of "the parting." The aged and the young, wives, mothers, sisters, and brothers mingled their tears together as they said "farewell." His Excellency Governor Loftus arose and addressed the members of the Contingent in words of solemn congratulation and sympathy, the closing sentences of which were characterised by pathos, and a sublime recognition of the great service about to be rendered to his country, whose greatness was due to the unity of its action and its trust in God. . . . "In your ranks are numbers who are voluntarily leaving the paths of fortune, worldly advantage, the comforts of home, and the sweetness of domestic life for heroic service in a bloody war in which already many brave men have been stricken down. You are doing this to show to the world the unity of the mighty and invincible Empire of which you are members. Your country charges itself with the care of those dear ones whom you leave behind. All that generosity, tenderness, care, and gratitude can do to care for them, to succor and console them, will be looked upon as a labor of love by the nation. (Cheers.) Soldiers, you leave us amidst the acclamations of your fellow-citizens, whose hearts will be with you in your camps and your conflicts, amidst an enthusiasm of admiration and sacrifice unexampled, with the sympathies of every true citizen of the Empire, with our earnest hope that it may be your glorious privilege to share in the triumph as in the service, and to come back to us crowned with England's gratitude, as you are now encompassed with her sympathies. Soldiers, on the part of your fellow-citizens, I now say to you 'farewell!' and may God ever have you in his holy keeping." (Loud and prolonged cheering.) Colonel Richardson, commandant, made the following reply :—" My Lord, on behalf of the officers, non-commissioned officers, and soldiers of the Contingent, I beg to return my sincere thanks for the inspiring and kind address which you have given us this day. If anything were wanting to complete our loyalty to Her Majesty the Queen, it has been done by Your Lordship's speech this afternoon, for every man who has volunteered in this service is determined to do his duty, not only to Her Majesty the Queen, but for the honor of the colony. I again thank you, on behalf of the officers, non-commissioned officers, and men." (Cheers.) This part of the programme was the official "farewell," but now came the personal "farewell," accompanied with sobs and the lingering caresses. The State can, amid pomp and splendor, calmly speak its words of compliment and praise for loyal service done, and heave its national sigh without a tear, but the individual heart under the strain of grief and love speaks its words of farewell with a far different accent. It cannot have respect to rule, save the rule of its own omnipotent self. The mother holds the form of her soldier boy in a mother's embrace long after the officer in authority has given the stern command, and the bugle calls to duty. Her silent grief and gushing heart utters its "farewell" in a language only a mother's soul can understand.

On the 3rd March, 1885, at half-past four p.m., the ships "**Iberia**" "**Australasian**" moved away with the New South Wales Soudan

Hon. J. M MACROSSAN.
Minister for Works and Mines.

contingent, while the bands played "Auld Lang Syne," and the guns at the fortifications thundered their salutation as they passed up the harbor and out at the Heads. They reached Aden on 27th March, and on the 30th disembarked at Suakim. Their service on the battle field was of brief duration, and involved but little inconvenience. The evacuation of the Soudan shortly after their arrival rendered their prolonged stay unnecessary. On 17th May they were ordered to return, having received the commendation of the Queen, whose message expressed in fitting terms the appreciation of the nation, as follows :—"The Queen commands to be conveyed to the officers, non-commissioned officers, and men of the contingent her thanks for their services during the recent campaign, and expressed her great satisfaction that her colonial forces have served side by side with British troops in the field. Her Majesty wishes them a prosperous voyage home." Lord Wolseley, Commander-in-Chief, in his farewell address to them said :—"I feel that Australia, in putting such a fine body in the field, is a warning to any quarrelsome nation that they will have to fight not only Great Britain and Ireland, but also England's most distant colonies. Speaking for myself, I hail your presence with the greatest pleasure. I have been delighted with your physique and manly, soldierly bearing. I shall feel proud to see the same contingent in the field again." They returned to Australia, where they were welcomed back by every demonstration of rejoicing, and bore their honors with pride and loyal devotion. While this act had the effect of arousing much loyal feeling, the question still remains, "Is it wise for the colonies to rush into and share with England the burthen of her quarrels?" Will the fact that Australia and Canada sent to the Soudan their contingents lead England to stand ready on all occasions to do likewise; and, if so, would the military preparations and expense needed to be in a position of constant readiness involve a greater outlay than most of the colonies would find it convenient to pay? And, lastly, would not the fact of the colonies taking part in the mother country's wars rather invite attack than otherwise? The more democratic a people becomes, and the smaller their military force, the less liable are they to be molested from without. A "contingent" force implies a willingness to make the first assault, and it is human nature to strike back. One of the strongest elements in the American Republic is not the size or quality of her armies, and the consequent burden of taxation needed to maintain them, but it is the smallness of her standing army and the largeness of her loyal heart, that relies not so much upon the professional soldier and the titled officer as upon their personal interest in the success of their own affairs. The years 1887 and 1888 have been prolific of interest to every Australian. The jubilee of Her Majesty's reign marks the one, and the centennial of our country's history marks the other. No more interesting portion of her history could engage the pen of the writer, and none more worthy of record. There is no brighter page than that which tells the story of a nation's joy as she enters upon the celebration of the jubilee of her Queen, whose rule has been marked by kindliness and goodwill, save that which tells the story of a nation's birth, growth, and manhood. Both are pages of our history, written on the loyal hearts of nearly four million souls, who do homage to the name of the one and are the honored inheritors of the other. It was a natural thing that in England, the mother land, there should be every demonstration of joy during the jubilee year, in acknowledgment of which Her Majesty was pleased to scatter with a liberal hand honors, titles, and other expressions of good will to her people whose worth had been prominently presented to her notice. The demonstrations of loyalty that characterised the masses upon the occasion of her jubilee celebration were the grandest and most pronounced that had ever greeted any monarch in any land. The Press described the line from Buckingham Palace to Westminster as being a scene of enthusiastic loyalty unequalled in the history of England; but we have to do chiefly with that which characterised the event in the colonies. In Victoria, New South Wales, Queensland, South Australia, Western Australia, Tasmania, and New Zealand there was a universal expression of gladness and thanksgiving, in which the Churches forgot not to assemble themselves and to give thanks. It was an occasion for those in the so-called higher circles of society to express their joy in levees and balls and merriment; the military forces in reviews in our public parks. Monster picnics and vast assemblages of people in all manners and forms united to do homage to their Queen. All the cities were ablaze with lights; while flags, banners, and bands of music expressed the universal sentiment of goodwill to Her Gracious Majesty.

The historical fact of the year 1887 that stands out in bold relief is the event of the jubilee celebrations. In all celebrations there is epitomised a whole history of circumstances, events, and sentiment. Celebrations express more than the vista and results of the past. They equally express the relationship of the present, and tend to bring out into prominence the sentiments and benefits derived from the life or fact celebrated. "The Queen's Jubilee" was the occasion of national rejoicing. Every part of her vast Empire united to do honor to her name. It was not simply the fact of Her Majesty's reign of fifty years that called forth the warm expressions of fealty and gladness, it was rather the people's recognition of the grand results that had come from a rule that has been characterised by an earnest solicitude for the well-being of every part of her vast dominions. All through a long career of fidelity to the interests of her people, the Queen had evinced a most benevolent and sympathetic tenderness in dealing with problems affecting the welfare and elevation of her subjects. No question of reform or policy of liberal ideas looking towards the amelioration of any class of individuals failed to obtain the Royal approval. Her ascent to the throne was hailed with universal joy. Though but an infant, still she was one matured in Christian principles, and possessing all those graces of mind and heart for which her life has been remarkable. Her early training and culture had been placed in wise hands, and all the circumstances surrounding her infant years were of such a type as to conduce to the developement of a model Queen. Not only was her advent to the throne received with every mark of gladness, but each succeeding year since 1837 has added to the affection and regard entertained towards her by her three hundred and twenty millions of people. It was a fitting thing that at the close of the fiftieth year of an eventful and important reign her grateful people should review the incidents in a life so remarkable, and a character so ennobling in its example and real worth. When she came to the throne in 1837 the mails were carried at the rate of ten miles an hour, and that was deemed the utmost speed possible. Now the mails are carried at the rate of thirty miles in the same time, and by means of telegraphic lines we become cognisant of what every part of the world is doing within a few hours of its occurrence. The voyage that then was made in six months from England to Australia is now being made in less than six weeks, and with corresponding comfort. England, at that time, had not more than twenty-four million inhabitants, including Scotland, Ireland, and Wales. Now she has more than thirty-five millions, notwithstanding in that period over twenty millions of people have emigrated to America and other parts of the world. From official sources we learn that at present she rules one-fourth of the people of the world, and who can tell what influence she does not exert upon the balance of mankind. Her ships carry on three-fifths of the trade of the world.

It is affirmed that her import and export trade is nearly £800,000,000 per year. How rapidly every department of learning has grown we scarcely need record. All the more important improvements and discoveries of modern science have been made during her reign, the telegraph, railroad construction, telephonic facility, steam for purposes of navigation, propulsion, manufacturing, and general mechanism, electricity in its many branches, modes and purposes of application, education in its relation to the masses. There were then but few of the common people who had the advantages of obtaining a liberal education. The wealth of her people was confined to a very limited number. Now it has become extensively distributed, and the distribution is largely due to the great change affected by the supremacy of the great principle of "Free-trade" that came to be applied in the early part of her reign, and that has worked such marvellous results for the benefit of her working people. The England of 1837 and the England of 1887 present a great contrast in the finish and architectural excellencies of her public and private buildings. Changes in this department alone have been greater than have been effected in any two centuries previously. The castles of former times, gloomy, solid, and forbidding, have been largely changed into bright palaces of comfort. The merchants' dingy home of fifty years ago has been exchanged for the princely suburban villa; the hut or cabin of the poor has given place to the cottage, clean and tidy. The cities of that time were pictures of gloom, misery, and squalor by day, and a scene of carnage, revelry, dissipation, and the flickering lamp-light by night. All this has given place to streets of cleanliness, comparative sobriety and industry, with the marks of wealth and growing prosperity on every side apparent, and the streets lighted up by night, making its cheerfulness vie with the splendor of the day; lines of transit bearing to and fro to suburban villas the masses morning and evening anxious to reach the places of their toil at the beginning, and as glad and full of expectation to enjoy the rest and companionship of their homes at the end of each day's work. We need not add words to justify a nation's joy and gladness as it pauses and reviews a period in its history so fraught with changes and reforms. It needs no further argument in its behalf that in no country in the world has there been so much done in the people's behalf, and under no other royal administration has there ever been accomplished so much for the well-being of every class and section of the English Empire. The culture of the high, the education of the masses, and the increased and growing rights and privileges of the poorer people, all found a fitting occasion in this Jubilee year, not merely to eulogise the Queen, though that was well deserved, but to remind us all that our lot has fallen in goodly times, and under conditions that render it possible for each one to achieve the great ends of a prosperous life and a useful career as an integral part of an Empire the grandest and most powerful in the world, and which has reached that position by her adherance to principles of right, by her high and exalted notions respecting the rights of others. The defence and protection which she seeks to give to every citizen, and the general virtues that have marked her history, and of which her queenly character has been a true embodiment and fair example for fifty years, have tended largely to bring about a condition of society that would foster and abet every enterprise and effort that aimed at the elevation and relief of the poor, the care of the sick, the protection of the young, the guidance of the outcast, and perhaps more than all other things the growing faith she has in a religion of good works in behalf of all who are in need, and a decreasing faith in a State religion of dignity and earthly power.

There would be little gained by a Jubilee whose demonstrations reached no further than the noisy revelry of the bacchanalian feast, or the brilliant pyrotechnic whose blazing flash lights up the heavens for an exultant moment, and then suddenly dies and leaves behind a midnight gloom. The nation would have been wanting in a true sense of its own personal dignity were it to fail in rendering all honor to the name of one who has been associated with every beneficial change affecting the citizens' political standing—changes which have gradually given him increased powers of self-government, and which have tended to make him more and more loyal to the Throne.

The life of Queen Victoria has been from the beginning an eventful one in every aspect from which it may be viewed, and the review of a acreer so intimately connected with every part of the Empire cannot fail to inspire each citizen either at Home or in the Colonial dependencies with gratitude and reverence.

When Alexandrina Victoria was born at Kensington Palace, 24th May, 1819, it was scarcely dreamed that in her hands would be placed the destiny of England. Yet it was but a short time afterwards when it became apparent that to her would be committed the reins of government, in view of which her widowed mother, the Duchess of Kent, without husband or father to sympathise with her in her loneliness, and now leaning on the love and wisdom of her devoted brother Leopold, Prince of Coburg, resolved to devote her life to the honored task of training England's Queen. How much the excellence and nobility of her character is due to the personal oversight and motherly instruction accorded by the Duchess herself will doubtless appear to those who have read the testimony of the Earl of Liverpool, when he moved in the House of Lords that the sum of £6,000 a year should be placed in the hands of the Duchess for the maintenance of Victoria. He says: "The conduct of the Duchess of Kent is unexampled for propriety, domestic affection, and moral purity." A character of such high worth could not fail to leave its impression for good, and mould the life of one whose entire public career has reflected honor upon the mother, and alike honor upon the nation who has witnessed through fifty years of Royal administration, every virtue of daughter, sister, wife, mother and Queen, and, we will still add, friend. We cannot dwell upon the many incidents of her domestic and private life, revealing the broad sympathies of her heart and the religious fervor of her spirit; it is with her public life that the historian has more especially to do.

Alexandrina Victoria succeeded to the Throne on the 20th June, 1837, and was crowned a year afterwards, on the 28th June, 1838. The pomp and splendor of the occasion gave clear proof of the nation's great joy upon the event of coronation. Westminster Abbey, in all the centuries of its existence, had not witnessed a more awe-inspiring ceremony. Special boxes and galleries had been erected within the large edifice, all the city of London was astir early in the morning, and all England was in the city. A drizzling rain gave a sombreness to the morning hours—a fitting prelude to the solemnity of the occasion. Just before the procession started, at ten o'clock, the sun shone out in all its glory, and, as they marched along "from Buckingham Palace up Constitution Hill, down

Piccadilly, St. James' Street, Pall Mall and Whitehall," the streets, crowded with loyal hearts, gave proof of their warmest love. The great Abbey itself was "carpeted with tapestry of gold and green, and purple and crimson in bewildering confusion—the peers in their robes and coronets, the peeresses in their diamond tiaras; Marshal Soult, white-haired and soldierly, in and out of his wonderful carriage, the observed of all; the Duke of Wellington, welcomed with continued cheers, quite grim and alert-looking, quite overpowered in his voluminous mantle; a five-hour ceremony of the most impressive character, during which the Queen sat in crimson velvet, furred with ermine, and bordered with gold lace—now in the stone-seated chair of St. Edward, and now in the gilded chair of homage, she makes an oblation of an ingot of gold; the Archbishop of Canterbury administers the oath, and performs the anointing; then follows the presentation of the spurs, the sword, the investment with the cloth-of-gold dalmatia; the orb is placed in her hands, the ruby ring put upon her finger, the sceptre with the cross placed in the right hand, and another with the dove in her left, and then the crown, the last symbol of authority, made specially for the Queen, sparkling with its gems, is placed upon her head, while trumpets sound, guns fire, and drums beat; peers and peeresses put on their coronets, the bishops put on their caps, the heralds wave their batons, and all the people join in a mighty roar 'God save the Queen.'" Such is a faint picture of the pomp and splendor of the ceremony that inaugurated, and was hoped to symbolise, the reign of Her Majesty, Queen Victoria, whose "Jubilee" we now celebrate with equal pomp and splendor; they, with hope, we in fruition; they looked forward, and wondered if the solemn obligations of her coronation she would remember, and the spurs, and robe, and orb, and sceptres, with cross, and dove, and crown, would be to her the gaudy toys of a vain display, or the signs of a regal life. We look back upon a queenly life, linked by personal merit and heartfelt solicitude to every part of her growing Empire, and are constrained to join in the universal jubilant, and echo back the tones that have never ceased to vibrate in every portion of her dominion since first her people sang "God Save the Queen."

It is a profitable task to read the history of one trained under a mother's fond keeping, dutiful, earnest, and kindly, and evincing in her youthful life a Christian sense of dependence upon her Creator. Her memorable words addressed to the Archbishop of Canterbury on the occassion of his hurried visit early in the morning, in company with the Lord Chamberlain, to announce to her the death of William the Fourth—it having occurred at twenty minutes past two o'clock that same morning—and to communicate to her that she was Queen, "I beg Your Grace to pray for me," will ever be quoted as showing that her mind and heart had been thoroughly trained during her infancy to look upon her royal estate as a great trust to be valued for the opportunities it afforded of doing good.

The description given by Secretary Greville of her appearance and manner at her first Privy Council at eleven o'clock of the morning of the death of the King is as follows: "Never was anything like the first impression she produced or the chorus of praise and admiration which it raised about her manner and behaviour, and certainly not without justice. It was very extraordinary, and something far beyond what was looked for. Her extreme youth and inexperience, and the ignorance of the world concerning her naturally excited intense curiosity to see how she would act on this trying occasion, and there was a considerable assemblage at the palace, notwithstanding the short notice which was given. She bowed to the lords, took her seat, and then read her speech in a clear, distinct, and audible voice, and without any appearance of fear or embarrassment. She was quite plainly dressed, and in mourning. After she had read her speech, and taken and signed the oath for the security of the Church of Scotland, the Privy Councillors were sworn—the two Royal Dukes first, by themselves; and as these two old men, her uncles, knelt before her, swearing allegiance, and kissing her hand, I saw her blush up to the eyes as if she felt the contrast between the civil and natural relations, and this was the only sign of emotion she evinced. Her manner to them was very graceful and engaging. She kissed them both, rose from her chair, and moved towards the Duke of Sussex, who was farthest from her, and too infirm to reach her. She seemed rather bewildered at the multitude who were sworn, and came one after another to kiss her hand; but she did not speak to anybody or make the slightest difference in her manner, or show any in her countenance to any individual of any rank, station, or party." The impression the youthful Queen made upon her people then has never changed in all these years.

Hon. M. HUME BLACK,
Minister for Lands.

Her marriage occurred on the 10th February, 1840, with Prince Albert, the second son of Ernest, Duke of Saxe-Coburg Saalfield, his mother being Louisa of Saxe-Gotha Altenberg. He was born on the 26th August, 1819, and hence was three months younger than the Queen. He was a young man of most excellent character and liberal education and ideas, and made a fitting companion for his royal cousin Victoria. Much of the success of her reign was due to the superior good judgment he evinced on every occasion. He was honored with the title of Prince Consort after years of waiting, a title that finally gave him a social standing at Court that in his earlier years of married life he did not possess. The estimate the Queen herself held the Prince Consort in may be learned by a perusal of the book written by herself, entitled "Our Life in the Highlands." Though a foreigner by birth, yet his identity with the interests of the nation was one of the most prominent facts of his life, and the great service he rendered to the Queen as her closest adviser was duly appreciated and acknowledged by the nation. The married life of Queen Victoria and the Prince Consort was a happy one. To them were born four sons and four daughters, all of whom were trained in the same simple fashion that marked that of the parents, and has borne fruit in the domestic felicity that has characterised the married life of each one.

For twenty-one years the domestic life of the Queen was unclouded. She had lived in an atmosphere of perfect contentment and happiness until the death of the Duchess of Kent, which occurred in March, 1861. A heavier sorrow befel her in the latter part of the same year in the death of Prince Albert on the 14th December. This was a circumstance that changed her entire life, socially. The nation joined her in her sorrow, and keenly felt the loss of one who was more than royal consort. He was emphatically the friend of the poor, and the honest patron of art, science, letters, mechanism, and agriculture, thus linking himself and the royal house with every interest in the realm. Though this last sorrow fell like a blight upon her youthful life it did not mar her excellencies as Queen. The social world felt the shock, and mourned with hollow selfishness her enforced retirement from its gaieties for the last twenty-seven years. The solitude of her retirement has been fruitful in giving depth to the affection of her people, who have never ceased to mourn with her the loss both she and they have sustained. A mutual sorrow has cemented the bond between the ruled and ruler. Every church and synagogue throughout the realm has in heartfelt sympathy breathed the prayer "God Save Our Gracious Queen and the Royal Family," while she has stretched the ægis of her protection to them all, irrespective of the shades of difference in their religious beliefs, and has said in the language of her King "well done." Fifty years of such a Queen could not fail in giving to the realm peace and prosperity, and in return a nation's tribute of thanksgiving. 1887 will be for ever memorable in the annals of history for its universal "Jubilee." The Motherland and her many dependencies were of one mind. All united in the agreeable task of sending their grateful tribute to the Queen, not because she possessed virtues of any special nature, but because in her life were apparent all those excellencies of character that in any one is a charm, but in a queen is unmeasured in the far reaching nature of its benefits, and does much towards establishing the nation in righteousness. Too often it happens that elevation in official dignity tends to a corresponding baseness of manners— not that there is in the trust itself any compulsion to wrong-doing, but the exaltation brings flattery and a multitude of temptations that few are disposed to resist. Even those who regard themselves as proof against all evil influence, perchance fall an easy prey to the wiles of the designing or to the pride of self-sufficiency or to the manifold follies of social life.

Efforts were made in each of the colonies to organise societies for the permanent benefit of her people. In New South Wales a meeting was convened at Government House, to consider the importance of celebrating the Jubilee by the creation of some permanent fund. On the invitation of Lady Carrington 100 ladies were present, and at her suggestion and request they resolved that the highest compliment they could pay to Her Gracious Majesty would be the creation of a Women's Jubilee Fund for the relief of distressed women, and that a congratulatory address should be sent to the Queen by the women of the colony. No suggestion could be more in accord with the feelings and sympathy of Her Majesty. Her own life having brought her into close contact with the sorrowing, in the afflictions that befel her own domestic circle, has awakened and intensified a nature that all through her career has been characterised by a tenderness towards all in distress. This movement was heartily endorsed by the women of the colony, and was entered into heartily, for the reason that the object contemplated was one that would for ever remain and be a perpetual bond of sympathy between the women of the colony and the Queen. A response came from all quarters ; the ladies with one accord joined in the work, and as the result of their mature thought, they resolved upon holding an exhibition under the title of the "Women's Art Exhibition," in which their handiwork might be gathered together, exhibited, and sold for the above purpose. The result of the effort was over £6,000, and made a nucleus that would serve to stimulate future efforts in the same direction. In Queensland an effort of a somewhat similar character resulted in the inauguration of a fund for the education of worthy girls who were not in a position to defray their own expenses. This idea met with the hearty response of the ladies and leading gentlemen in the Colony of Queensland, and was successful in raising a considerable sum towards the object. In South Australia they conceived the idea of putting their loyal feeling into active service by the inauguration of a Jubilee Exhibition, whose object was—(1) to mark the Jubilee of their own foundation as a colony—the pioneers of that colony having established themselves in Adelaide fifty years ago ; (2) to bring the products of Australia together where they could witness the progress made, and acquaint themselves and the world with the substantial benefits arising therefrom ; (3) that they might be impressed with the capabilities of their country and be stimulated to active exertion in developing the undeveloped resources of the future; (4) that the result of their Jubilee effort might remain with them and afford a perpetual memorial of their past history of struggle and triumph; and (5) be the means of celebrating in the most intelligent and auspicious manner the reign of Her Most Gracious Majesty.

Two questions in connection with these Jubilee rejoicings were brought prominently before the people of these Colonies for their consideration and acceptance, viz., the "Imperial Federation" and "Naval Defence." It was deemed by the authorities to be an opportune time in which to introduce subjects of such vast import, and that were likely to awaken a good deal of discussion, pro and con ; when the minds of the people were filled with the gladness of this festive occasion, nothing was supposed to be easier than to influence the masses favorably in regard to the Imperial idea which had for many years been the dream of some of our leading statesmen : that England and her Dependencies in all parts of the world should be bound together by stronger ties. This was a movement that was somewhat in conflict with the growing democratic tendencies of the colonies, and during the Jubilee rejoicings it was made a matter of consideration by the Imperial Council, that were summoned together on 4th April, 1887, and which was composed of delegates from the respective colonies and representatives of the Home Government, and whose ostensible purpose was to consider, among many other subjects, the Colonial Defences, Penny Postage, Land Transfer, Enforcement of Colonial Judgments, Extradition of Absconding Debtors from the Colonies, the New Hebrides, New Guinea, the Transportation of Récidivistes, Cable Communication, Investment of Trust Funds in Colonial Stocks, the Deceased Wifes' Sister matter, and Imperial Federation. Of these many subjects the first and the last-mentioned ones seemed to occupy the entire time of the committee's deliberation. It was not the purpose to grant this delegation any power to commit the colonies to any of its conclusions. However important the above subjects may have been in the eyes of the colonies, the conference seems to have lost sight of all of them except the Naval Force scheme and the Imperial Federation question, and judging from the unreasonable length of time devoted to these two, one is almost disposed to give credence to the suspicion that it was the main object of the conference to secure their passage and adoption, the one being a necessary adjunct of the other. Queensland was the only colony of the Australian group that rejected them, and possibly therein she shows her good sense. No doubt she did a little calculation on her own account, and came to the conclusion that if she had to pay £35,000 interest on the cost of the cruisers, which would place the cost at £700,000, she could, with more profit to herself, borrow the above amount at four and a-half per cent. instead of five, and own her ships at a profit to herself of £3,500 per annum over the Federation plan, the cost of maintenance being the same in both cases.

The Naval Force Bill recommended by this Imperial Conference, and adopted by most of the colonies, provides that not more than £35,000 interest on the first cost of five cruisers and two torpedo gunboats, and in addition not more than £91,000 for expense of maintaining this royal luxury, will be required. The above estimates will no doubt be found to be a few shillings greater than will be actually needed. This bill is but part of a scheme hatched in the Imperial Council. It is ostensibly to unite all the colonies of the British Empire in the enjoyment of a portion of the

Naval Force, and as a matter of justice, to tax each portion of the Empire with the expense of maintaining the same, in consideration for the security their presence would be against foreign attack. The proposition meets with a very doubtful reception throughout the Australian Colonies, and has awakened a considerable sentiment in favor of an Australian National Party. It is very generally supposed that it is a part of the scheme of Imperial Federation, a plan somewhat popular among a very limited class of politicians that are somewhat afraid of disintegration growing out of the increasing spirit of self-government that in nearly all the colonies dares to assert itself.

To hug into unity by coercion is a very questionable policy in view of events not yet faded from the memory of English statesmen. The surest bond between the several parts of the Empire is the love and harmony that are sure to come from a due recognition of the rights of each. Let England continue to foster the genius of self-government among her colonies, honor manhood and lift her working people, and not seek to foist her broken down useless scions of an ancient nobility of very questionable renown upon a struggling people, and not a citizen throughout her wide extent but would respond to England's call in time of need; but grind her people with the burden of an ancient aristocracy, crush out the manhood from the spirit of her sons, throw her half-witted progeny of a useless aristocracy on the toiling masses to sustain, under the pretext of a much-needed "naval force," and you batter down the strongest bulwark of a nation's strength—the nation's heart and sense of manhood. There is scarcely to be found a man of common sense in all the Australian colonies who believes that the little fragment of a naval force proposed to float upon her waters in time of peace would be of any value in time of war, should any of the Great Powers send even one of her modern "floating engines of destruction" to claim our homage. The loyalty born of fair treatment is the only tie that will bind the colonies to the Motherland with an indissoluble bond of affection and co-operation. The plan under which the above Act has been passed was one adopted by an Imperial conference held in London, made up of naval authorities at Home and representatives from the colonies, and is as follows:

"Without reducing the normal strength of the naval force on the Australian station, an additional force of five fast cruisers and two torpedo boats is to be maintained in these waters; three cruisers and one gun-boat to be kept always in commission, the remainder to be kept in reserve. These vessels are to be paid for out of Imperial funds, but the colonies will pay interest on their prime cost at the rate of five per cent., such payment not to exceed the annual sum of £35,000. The total sum payable by the Australian colonies is to be £126,000 per annum, and the contributions will be made on the basis of population. This Imperial sentiment resulted in the organisation in the Queensland colony of the Queensland National party, whose policy, as announced in their organisation, is meant to embrace members in every part of the colony, and their motto is "Alliance, not dependence," and whose objects are thus set forth :—First : Cultivation of Australian national spirit with respect to all matters affecting education, trade, labor and law. Second : The federation of the Australian colonies into a united dominion, with provision for a system of Australian national defence. Third : Energetic vindication and protection of civil and political liberties, rights and obligations of the people, and the adoption of the principle that laws passed by the Australian Legislatures shall not require Imperial sanction to render them operative. Fourth : Fostering of protection of Australian industries. Fifth : Exclusion from Australia of Chinese and other servile races, and the preservation of the entire continent as a home for white men. Sixth : Exclusion from the islands and waters of Australasia and the Western Pacific of all foreign convicts. Seventh : Active promotion of all legislative measures calculated to—(1) check wasteful expenditure of public monies, prevent the levying of oppressive taxation and against the abuse of political patronage ; (2) to repress injurious monopolies, allay sectional jealousies, and prevent the creation of privileged classes ; (3) to stimulate settlement upon land and develop its mineral and other resources ; (4) to carry on reproductive public works to conserve the rainfall, improve natural watercourses, and tap the subteranean waters of the country ; (5) to remedy all abuses in law, to repeal barbarous and obsolete acts, and to reduce the cost of law proceedings. Eighth : To return members to the Legislative Assembly pledged to carry out the foregoing principles and objects. At the last elections the National party went to the poll on these issues and were successful, with Sir Thomas McIlwraith as their leader and representative, against Sir Samuel Griffith, who was committed to the views of the

Imperial conference on the question of the Naval Defence Bill and Imperial unity.

Following the festivities of the Jubilee an epoch still more marked in the history of the Australian colonies was the Centenary of their existence. An event so important in the history of the continent could scarcely fail to engage the serious attention of the country, and impress the several Governments thereof with the importance of marking in some way the fact. It was but natural that New South Wales, the mother colony, should take the lead in this respect, all the colonies joining to carry out her arranged programme, by which she sought to give expression to their feelings of joy and gladness upon the occasion. The ordinary methods of celebrating historic events, such as illuminations, picnics, sports, music in its various forms, racing, cricketing, and the indulgence in all other pastimes by which the colonies are accustomed to express their joy, were indulged in universally. The policy, however, of the mother colony was, in addition to these, to inaugurate several substantial enterprises. The Premier proposed that the colony should begin several works of a substantial nature that would be permanent monuments of the nation's progress. After much debate and a good deal of opposition, it was resolved—(1) to erect a State house Mausoleum in connection with the creation of a public park, also it was resolved to hold an Intercolonial Exhibition, embracing especially live stock, agricultural produce, industrial products, and many other things, that the people might witness for themselves the results of the toil, energy, and resources of the Southern Hemisphere. It was resolved to hold an intercolonial banquet at which the leading representatives of the several colonies should be entertained. The issue of new postage stamps. To carry out these special details, which were designed to be of an Australian type rather than that of one colony, a committee of trustworthy and experienced leading men was appointed, who in due time were pleased to witness the successful realisation of their purpose.

The Centennial Banquet to the Press.

Though not embraced in the official programme the gathering together at the Town Hall on Wednesday night, 25th January, 1888, of representatives of the Press of Australasia must be deemed one of the most important entertainments of the hour. It cannot be denied that the influence of the Press of this country has been on the side of right and justice. We do not claim that it is unblemished. Occasionally it has been the perpetrator of most cruel wrongs. Its tyrannous hoof has oftentimes crushed the helpless, while for money it has not hesitated to dip its trenchant blade in blood, and laugh to scorn the victim's feeble groan. The Press has usually been found upon the side of the oppressed. How grandly she fought the battles of the people of this colony during the past fifty years is within the memory of even our middle-aged men. Our former rulers used to muzzle the Press; they did not like to have the people know all that was going on. The genius of those past times was to say only upon the printed page what was bright and pleasant, and what would not offend. The Press of modern times takes hold of facts after a different fashion. It speaks out its Anglo-Saxon words in terms of plainest denunciation and rebuke. Where wrong exists and injustice profits thereby, the Press erects a tribunal without ermine, scales or wig— issues its warrants to all concerned. At its bidding kings, priests, governors, politicians, judges, lawyers, doctors, all professionals, artisans, and workmen come, and as a full-fledged court tries and condemns or acquits without prejudice or partiality. Mr. Bennett, of the *Evening News*, did a worthy thing to invite on this important occasion those who were the representatives of a free unfettered Press, and give them an opportunity to interchange thoughts and expressions, review the past, and pledge themselves to the grander future. About three hundred from the journals of the colonies joined in this part of the celebrations. The invitations were very widely sent out and generally accepted. Among those present were several leading members of the Government and Parliament. The speeches on the occasion were direct, plain, and manly. It is impossible within our limited compass to give even extracts from the many excellent things said upon the occasion. We merely insert a letter which expresses the universal sentiment:—

"To the Editor: Sir,—The splendid success of the banquet at the Town Hall last night must have been in the highest degree gratifying to the generous and hospitable donors as it certainly was to the guests. As one of the latter, I beg to sincerely thank the proprietors of the *Evening News* for affording me this unique opportunity of meeting so many men of "light and leading" from all the colonies.

Hon. A. J. THYNNE,
Minister for Justice.

"My principal object in writing, however, is to ask whether we cannot take advantage of the present gathering of a large body of men fairly representative of the intellectual ability of the Press writers of Australia, and do something more than drink each other's health, and form for the time being a kind of Mutual Admiration Society.

"I cannot imagine anything calculated to have a better effect upon the interests of the Press, of politics, and of the general public, who have to depend upon journalists to so large an extent for their information upon all subjects of interest than a conference of all the newspaper men now in Sydney and discussion of a few of the most important political questions engaging the serious attention of each or all of the colonies, such questions, for instance, as free-trade and protection, the land laws, local government, colonial federation, and that most important of all questions, which underlies all the others, which will soon engage the earnest attention of the whole civilised world, and which is so little understood even by a large proportion of newspaper editors—I mean land nationalisation. Such a conference, in which each speaker would bring to bear on the subject, the local coloring, and special local knowledge resulting from his own experience, would surely be a fitting termination to this new departure in journalism, so happily conceived, and so ably carried out.

"In order to give practical shape to my proposal, I would suggest that on the steamer to-morrow a committee should be formed to draw up a list of subjects for discussion and a few rules for the control of the proceedings. Of course, each question should be discussed not exhaustively but on general grounds, and each speaker limited as to time; which last might form hereafter a useful precedent for our legislators.

"I merely throw out a general suggestion; if it be entertained, others will no doubt improve upon it.—I am, etc., R. MURCHISON."

To describe all the entertainments embraced in the programme would be neither profitable nor possible. Each locality offered the best demonstration their circumstances would justify, but we cannot close without saying a word upon the Centennial Banquet, for at this were grouped Australians of every class.

The State Banquet was intended to be the most important occasion of all the Centennial festivities. The purpose was to bring together the

Governors and leading representative people from all the colonies of Australasia, and in a friendly gathering to express their gratification at the work of the past century, and to put on record their ambitions for the future - The Exhibition Building, Prince Alfred Park, being the largest in the city was chosen as the only suitable one capable of entertaining so large a number. Seating accommodation for nine hundred and thirty-one guests was provided. All that art could do in the way of decoration was done to make the building gay and festive; and judging from the din, noise, and outbursts of acclamation one must conclude that the original purpose was fully realised. As the guests were all representative men, and the occasion was meant to be historic, we could scarcely expect to be excused were we to omit mention of the excellent speeches that expressed the sentiment of all present. A full list of the guests will be found in the closing chapter.

No banquet would be complete without the after-dinner oratory. It seems to be an Englishman's way of returning thanks. The Frenchman and the Italian express their joy in song, but the banquet always has the effect of unloosing the tongue of the Englishman. We are largely imitators of the English, and in this respect are said to be their equal; at any rate our best speeches are after dinner. It is after dinner all the time in Parliamentary circles, and possibly this will account in a large measure for the stupendous exhibition of oratory that one listens to in that Chamber, sometimes under the spell of which he becomes oblivious to all questions of legislation save "the adjournment of the House." We would not intimate that the excellency of the table had anything to do with the inspiration that moved each of the speakers to speak flatteringly of the colony in its present and its past. A telegram from the Queen was received by Lord Carrington, and read as follows:—

"The Queen warmly congratulates the Australian colonies on the splendid material and social progress achieved during the past hundred years. She deeply appreciates their loyalty, and she has watched with sincere interest the excellent administration of their Governments, and she prays that their prosperity and close attachment to the Mother Country may continue to increase as hitherto."

It was the signal of an enthusiastic outburst of cheers. Toasts to Her Majesty the Queen and Prince of Wales and Royal Family were given in true colonial fashion. Lord Carrington then proposed, with becoming modesty, the health of the *other* Australasian Governors, which was responded to by Governor Loch, of Victoria, Sir W. F. D. Jervois, Governor of New Zealand, Sir Anthony Musgrave, of Queensland, Sir William Robinson, of South Australia, Sir Robert Hamilton, of Tasmania, Sir F. N. Broome, of Western Australia, and Sir Charles Mitchell, of Fiji. It was a pleasant thing to see all the vice-regal heads of the respective colonies join on this occasion with our own much-respected Governor, and review with pride not armies and their conquests, but the work of earnest toilers, who, by sweat of brow and expense of muscle, built the foundations of a nation that is sure to rank in the next one hundred years with the great Powers of the earth.

The toast "Australasia, her trials and triumphs in the past, her union and progress in the future," was above all others best calculated to call forth the wisest and best sentiments of the assembled greatness of the colonies. This was proposed by Sir Henry Parkes, and it is only proper that our pages should record the words as spoken, for manly utterance and comprehensiveness and faithful portrayal of all that is worthy of celebration, we commend this oration as the historic review of the past and keynote of the future. Upon rising he said: "Your Excellency, My Lords, Your Excellencies, and Gentlemen,—Great as is the honor of being permitted to stand before an Australasian gathering of representative men like this, I can honestly assure you that I would gladly have escaped the duty and the responsibility. I have to ask you to drink a sentiment which I trust will have some influence in uniting these young Australian states. On 26th January, one hundred years ago, a small band of men landed only a few yards from where we are assembled now. In that quaint old book written by David Collins we get the first glimpse of whom those men were, and in that book we are told that they had just arrived under the blessing of God after a voyage happily completed in eight months and one week. Perhaps no passage of history can present to the mind a stronger and more clearly defined contrast to the present day. Eight months and one week this band of exiles had been journeying across the world to plant the great Empire of Australasia. They arrived, as you all know, at a bay only a few miles from here, and as we all know, they left to find a more commodious harbor and a safer anchorage; and Collins tells us that they found a spot 'at the head of the cove near the run of fresh water which stole silently along under a very thick wood.' That is the place where, there is all reason to believe, the British ensign was first hoisted, and that is the place so long known to us as the Tank Stream ; and the cove is the beautiful cove known as the Cove of Sydney to this day. Then we have the very graphic description by Captain Watkin Tench, who was in charge of marines, of how these poor exiles landed. Tench tells us in his journal :—

" 'Our passage to Port Jackson took up but few hours, and those were spent far from unpleasantly The evening was bright, and the prospect before us such as might justify sanguine expectation. Having passed between the capes which form its entrance, we found ourselves in a port superior in extent and excellency to all we had seen before. We continued to run up the harbor about four miles in a westerly direction, enjoying the luxuriant prospect of its shores, covered with trees to the water's edge, among which many of the Indians were frequently seen, till we arrived at a small snug cove on the southern side, on whose banks the plan of our operations was destined to commence.'

"I hope you will pardon me for reading these extracts because I know of no better way of doing what I desire to do—to bring as vividly as possible before your minds the helplessness of the founders of this great Empire. The first blow struck by the axe of those English exiles on the rough ironbark was in reality the salute of civilisation in a new world. Whatever adverse colors shrouded the assemblage of that poor group of men, they unconsciously were laying the foundation-stone of what I believe will be the greatest Empire in the world. I will, with your permission, before I conclude, give you the reasons why I think the future Empire of Australasia will be superior to all that has gone before us ; but just for a moment I must dwell upon the progress of this one colony, and only for a moment. Twenty years after the landing of Captain Phillip and his band of exiles, the population was only 10,000 souls. For forty-one years the colony of New South Wales was the only representative of civilisation. About forty-one years after the foundation of the settlement the colony of Western Australia was founded, and a year after that event the colony had still only 97,912 souls. In 1843, which is the memorable year when representative government was first introduced, the population of the colony was only 165,451 souls. In 1856, when we first obtained our present constitution, and when the other colonies obtained theirs, the population of this country was only 286,873 souls.. Last year the population of our colony was 1,044,000 souls. At the close of last year the shipping of this one colony numbered 1,128, of which 485 were steamships; their tonnage was 128,544 tons, and their value £2,265,000. At the present time Australasia has at least three and a-half millions of population. From a calculation which I believe is based upon the most trustworthy data, at the end of another generation the population of Australasia will be 12,000,000 souls—say in the year 1922. Now I have done with New South Wales, and I have done with our past history; except that I will say this—that we have no reason to turn away from the peculiar character of our early surroundings. We have no reason to blush, or for a moment to desire to avoid comment upon those early years of exile; and I venture to say that during those early years many heroic things were done which go intimately into the foundation of nations. Let it be always remembered, when we turn to the early history of this one colony, that so long as the offenders of England were sent here, the offences for which they were sent were such as bear no punishment at all to-day. Many a man was sent here for offences which could hardly be said to affect his moral character. We have examples of most heroic suffering, the most complete repentance and the most noble fortitude in many of the unknown exiles who laid down their lives in those dark days. But pass from all that to the heroic deeds which the early founders of Australia performed in times of deep trial, bordering on starvation, to the enlightened objects they sought and accomplished in planting new industries on this continent; and taking all in all we have no cause to turn away from a calm and quiet contemplation of those early years. That then is all I can say. We stand now on a different footing altogether. We are seven—five on this continent, the tight little island of Tasmania, and the coronet of isles, New Zealand—making seven young states, who may be said at noon of night, after the close of this banquet, to start on a new race for another hundred years. It will be for us not to turn back to the hundred years that are past, but to look steadily to the future over the hundred years that lie before us; and it is my belief that at the end of that hundred years the population of this country will be at least 60,000,000 of souls. You talk of the growth of America with her

55,000,000 to-day, including her negro population; but the conditions of life are so favorable here, the conditions for the propogation of the race are so favorable that we should show an increase of population which has never been seen in any other part of the world. We have none of the biting snowstorms, none of the iron frosts that are so hurtful and detrimental to the progress of human life in many parts of the United States of America; but go where you will, to the north or to the south, penetrate throughout the forests of our interior, you can hardly reach a place where the conditions for life are not eminently favorable—more favorable than in any other part of the world. Then there should be no ravages upon us from without, and may we not hope that there will be no internal disorders to shorten human lives; and I expect to see the human race more rapidly increase here—indeed I am sure that it will be the case—than we have ever seen it in any country in any age of the world. Whatever the United States may have done in the increase of population, we should do much more; and as surely as the sun rises upon the first day to-morrow of another century, so surely at the close of that century we should be one of the greatest people on the face of God's earth. It matters little, and I say this before the representatives of our beloved and august Queen—it matters little to us what is the form of our future governments. We shall be loyal Britons still under whatever form it may be, but in all reasonable probability we shall never in trying to solve the problems of Government find a happier connection than a union with the old parent State. But what we have to do, above all other considerations, is to be loyal to the trust which God has imposed upon us here, in doing the best we can for the development of our resources—doing the best we can for building up a stalwart people—doing the best we can to preserve and extend the liberties which happily we possess, without bloodshed, almost without struggle, and to a large extent by the enlightened beneficence of the mother State. This brings me then to the future of these countries, and I trust that we shall in the course of a very short time be able to tread under foot all paltry rivalries, and in a broad spirit of Australasian union, join together, not to work out a better fortune for Victoria, or for this country, or for South Australia, or for Tasmania, but to work out a high, grand, and enduring destiny for the whole of Australia. Clearly this day is to be the time of a new departure to a more firm advance, to a more powerful nationality, and if the robust and vigorous colony of Victoria, and if Queensland, with the force of her boundless resources, and if South Australia, with her wealth and power, will only unite one and all to maintain the interest of a United Australia we cannot go wrong. When we rise from these tables to-night it will be no ordinary rising. Most gatherings of this kind bring men together to make a few speeches, to enjoy each other's company, and to depart and think no more about it. But we are here to-night fairly representing the whole of these great colonies, and when we leave this hall it is not to forget the teaching which the remembrance of it ought to bring home to every one of us, and that teaching is that we should live and act more for our common country than ever, for its defence and prosperity. We are old enough to take this high course. We have sufficient of national spirit with us now to enter upon this greater career of political greatness, and if we lay aside all paltry jealousies, if we seek to consider each other's interests as equal to our own, if we enter upon the path of the next century with these broad views and this resolute spirit, then our destiny is in our own hands. The changes which lie before us are so manifest that we ought not to close our eyes to them. There must be great changes, and that very soon, in the condition of Europe, and in these changes the Mother Country cannot expect to be entirely untouched; but whatever changes take place in other parts of the world there will be great ones in this young world of ours. Our riches are so boundless, our application of power is so completely in our own hands, that if we do not become rich and prosperous, as well as free, the fault will be at our own doors.

"England has shown one thing beyond all doubt that what she wants us to do most is to guide ourselves in a political course to an honorable destiny. She has shown beyond all doubt or possibility of suspicion in the past that she desires in no way to interfere with us. We are, in fact, so many republics without the dangerous polity of a real republic. We have in the temperate monarchy of the present day a greater freedom than we ever could enjoy in any form of republican government known in the world. The bonds that unite us to the Imperial power are bonds of silk. The bonds that are to unite us together must be made of steel. While we remain different colonies I trust we shall at all times, in season and out of season, in times of prosperity and in times of adversity so act that we shall sustain our Governments on the lines of the British Constitution. There are no teachers of ancient or modern times equal to the teachers of our own country; there are no guides equal to what we may find under the shadow of the British Constitution in our future course, and, if we adhere in this spirit to the firm purposes of working out our own destiny in connection with the Mother Country, whatever may happen we shall have the assurance of having fashioned our course well, and depend upon it, if the time of danger should arrive to the Empire, we shall be in a position to be her worthy colleagues and defenders. I for one make no boast of my attachment to the British Constitution, and at the same time seek to shirk my just responsibility. If we are to be part and parcel of the Empire we must be prepared to take our fair share in all its burdens and dangers, and we are entitled to have a share in all its honors. It is in that sense I will seek to maintain our position in the future as a thorough Australian, and being a thorough Australian a most consistent and patriotic Briton.

"I am glad to think that at this gathering to-night we have representatives of the great colonies which belong to the group, and I trust that the feeling of unity now experienced will not be suffered to die out. One word more and I shall detain you no longer. Let us hope that as time rolls on we shall be able to agree on the policy which by its essential principles will unite us as well as does the feeling of kindred. At present we are one by a feeling of kinship chiefly; but the railroad which has been made through several of these colonies has had the effect of still more closely uniting us, and if we can only agree on lines that shall be applicable to all the colonies alike and of broad national policy then our prosperity is assured. If the colonies by another generation contained a population as I have said of 12,000,000, then we shall be able at any time, if attacked from without, to sweep the invaders into the sea. Even now, if we had wise military organisations, if we had organisations that would press all the force of our young men into the service of the country, we could raise an army against which no foreign invaders could stand. I think it was Sir William Jervois who told us that government was nothing, that prosperity was nothing without a proper system of defence. Well, the defence of these free countries ought to consist in the right arms of our young men, and we have now a youthful

Hon. J. DONALDSON,
Postmaster General and Minister for Education.

population sufficiently numerous, sufficiently brave for all the purposes of public defence, and we could easily organise the men to defend our soil against the invader. I do not consider it my duty to detain this great company longer, but I now propose 'Australasia : Her Trials and Triumphs in the Past, Her Union and Progress in the Future.'"

With the closing of the banquet we pass the line that marks our first century. What marvels a true history would unfold were it possible to record every fact in its true light! The early years of toil and hardship witnessed brutality and wrong upon the helpless. We dare not write our historic page in the full sunlight; we would rather sketch a picture in the gloaming while yet the scattering rays reveal the truth, but hide their hideous forms from view; we have reached an altitude we never reached before; we look back and down upon the past. It has been a struggle, a struggle against desperate odds; our companions, where are they? Away in the valley beneath. Let us lift the clouds that encircle the base. What a motley multitude—shackles, fustian, and purple, the dim and sparkling eye looking up the difficult ascent; some hopeful, most despairing; some waiting for the morning, and others conscious that their sun had set never to rise again. The blanched visage and the bony form tell us too plainly of half-rations and the weight of the iron chains; the gloom darkens; we can see no more; but, hark! We can hear voices away down the mountain side. Is it the tones of merry-making as of yesterday, where children picnic and artisans shout hurrah, and lords and ladies banquet? Nay, nay, it is the commingled voices of the sorrowing and the glad; perchance from the dungeon cell, and from the Christian temple, where the priest and his slave both offer sacrifice by the shedding of blood—the one at the altar, the other at the "whipping post." Let the vista pass, as the pale horse and his rider claims the Empire.

We look again, this time a new generation has assumed the task. They are of a restless kind; they toil and bear the burdens of the past. Their eyes are on the future, where we stand; they explore and build and conquer. They are a stalwart race; they climb and climb, and still they climb. Every step they take in the difficult ascent is a step planted firmly upon the way. To these earnest toilers comes the stern command, "Thus far, and no farther." Again "death," on his "fiery steed," claims a conquest, the smoke of battle dims our vision, and the picture fades from view. We look again, and lo, a third generation has come upon the scene—this time a race of giants, and they battle for the rights of manhood, and they win; they strike a fettered Press, and break its chains; they speak to the throne, and transportation ceases; they speak again, and royalty, in recognition of their maturity and manhood, hails them as co-workers in the great cause of self-government. What a royal race of men! How they fought for liberty of speech; how they wrestled with the problems of life. They linked themselves in close fellowship with science, arts, letters, and mechanism, and as a result they pushed out roads of modern type into the remote interior, and stretched lines between the most distant points; they multiplied school-houses with all the appliances of modern instruction; they gave the lands to the people; they sacrificed time and life, and have reached the summit, and with us stand to-day in the flood-tide of our Centennial rejoicings. Many of them sank on the way; many have lived to partake of the fruition of their hopes. Their whitening locks and feeble forms speak to us, their sons, in words of earnest counsel and patriarchal wisdom. We are called upon to take up the work so nobly inaugurated by our fathers, and may it be our highest ambition to leave behind for our sons to contemplate a record as bright as that which has gone before.

We cannot close this chapter without mentioning the fact that 10,000 of our worthy poor were remembered by the gift to each of substantial benefit. It may seem to many like a small thing compared to the crushing poverty that some have to struggle against in this world, but it was like the friendly hand of sympathy in time of need. The cheering sunshine brings out the warbling songster with sweeter song when the cloud has passed by, so have the joys of this festive season been heightened by the relief given to those in need.

CHAPTER XXIV.

THE CONSTITUTION.

THE crowning fact in colonial history was the passage of the Act securing responsible government. It took thirty years of a desperate struggle to bring about this most desirable reform.

The first meeting, held for the purpose of discussing the need of a constitution for the colony, was held on the 23rd October, 1825. A committee, consisting of Messrs. D'Arcy and W. C. Wentworth, Thomas Raine, W. J. Browne, and Daniel Cooper, was appointed to prepare a petition to the Governor, asking for the establishment of a House of Assembly of one hundred members.

On the 26th January, 1827, a public meeting held in Sydney appointed a committee of twenty-four of the leading citizens to prepare and present to the Home authorities a petition asking for trial by jury.

On the 9th February, 1830, a public meeting was held to petition the Imperial Parliament for the right of trial by jury and a representative Legislature.

In 1831 a meeting was held in Sydney for the purpose of sending a congratulatory address to William IV. on his ascension to the throne of England. They expressed the hope that His Majesty would "extend to the only British colony that was bereft of the rights of Britons a full participation in the benefits and privileges of the British Constitution."

The next meeting on this subject was held in Sydney on the 26th January, 1833, Sheriff McQuoid in the chair. Mr. Wentworth moved, and Mr. Lawson seconded, a resolution in favor of a petition to the King and

Parliament that a representative Assembly might be instituted for the colony, and that they should have the right of levying and appropriating their own taxes.

On the 8th December, 1835, a meeting of the Patriotic Association was held in Sydney for the purpose of discussing the sort of Parliament they should ask the Home Government to grant. Two forms were discussed, one consisting of Upper and Lower Houses, and the other of one House only, consisting of fifty members, ten of whom should be nominated by the Government, and the remaining forty elected by the people.

Another meeting was held in 1841 that urged by petition to the Queen the importance of having a representative Legislature that would consult the wishes of the colonists. Dr. Bland occupied the chair, and threw into the movement all the energy of which he was capable. All over the colony meetings to the same effect were held, and the demand for a new constitution was urged with vehemence.

The largest meeting ever assembled for such a purpose was held in Sydney in the latter part of 1841, and adjourned to meet on the 16th February, 1842, at which a petition was drawn up, that set forth :—" (1) That they were free subjects, forming a population of 10,000 persons. (2) That their movable and immovable property was estimated at £30,000,000, and the property annually created by them at £2,500,000; that the maritime commerce of the country during the preceding ten years amounted to £22,500,000; that the community raised for Government purposes an annual revenue of £350,000; that besides the consumption of British manufacture and the employment of British shipping, the colony relieved Great Britain of a surplus population of 57,000 souls, at a cost to the colonists of £1,250,000. (3) That notwithstanding their numbers, wealth, the importance of their commerce, the high rate of their taxation, and the magnitude of their revenue, the community had no control over their taxation, no voice in the management of their affairs, no representation in the local Legislature, and thus they were destitute of those free institutions which every Briton was taught to prize as the safeguard of his liberties, and as the invaluable birthright of his race."

The sum of £81,000 reserved from the control of the Council for the payment of the salaries of the Governor, the Superintendent of Port Phillip, of the judges, and civil and religious list gave great offence,

A new Constitution Act was passed by the Imperial Parliament on the 29th July, 1842, and was received with general rejoicing. The contest of the colony that had been going on for many years resulted in the granting of a responsible Government, in part at least.

This Act granted the colony a Legislative Council consisting of fifty-four members, thirty-six of whom were to be elected by the people, and eighteen were to be nominated by the Crown, six of whom to constitute a Ministry—namely, the Colonial Secretary, the Colonial Treasurer, the Auditor-General, the Attorney-General, the Commander of the Forces, and the Collector of Customs.

The qualifications of an elector was a freehold of the value of £200, or an annual rent of £20 per annum. The qualifications of a member was a freehold of £2,000, or income of £100 per annum. The Act took effect in January, 1843.

In 1849 the Council petitioned the Queen for a reduction of qualifications to an annual household of £10, or freehold of £50, or an annual leasehold in Sydney of £5.

The Imperial Parliament yielded to the continuous petitions that were being sent by the colonists, and passed in 1850 an Act for the better government of Her Majesty's colonies. By this Act New South Wales was granted enlarged powers in the direction of free government, and on the 5th August, 1850, elective privileges were accorded to Victoria, South Australia, Van Dieman's Land, and West Australia; and to Victoria an independent Legislature. The qualification of electors in the colonies of New South Wales were reduced to £100 freehold, or £10 leasehold. A civil list of £73,500 was fixed for New South Wales.

Power was given the Queen by this Act, by which the Imperial Parliament could erect into separate colonies the territory lying north of the thirtieth degree of south latitude.

The above Act did not satisfy the colonists. A petition was drawn up by Mr. Wentworth, and received the sanction of the Council, to the effect that if there was a surrender to the Colonial Council of all revenues, territorial as well as general, and a constitution granted similar to that in Canada, they would provide for the whole cost of the internal government of the colony, whether civil or military, and they would also provide a civil list during Her Majesty's life, and five years after her death.

A protest against the New Constitution Act was entered upon the minutes of the House of the Legislative Council, and copies forwarded to the Home authorities.

A committee was appointed by the Council to prepare a constitution for the colony, consisting of W. C. Wentworth, S. A. Donaldson, E. Deas Thompson (Colonial Secretary), J. H. Plunkett (Attorney-General), J. Macarthur, C. Cooper, J. Lamb, J. Martin, T. A. Murray, and Dr. Douglas.

In 1852 this committee brought in two bills, one to grant a civil list to Her Majesty, the other to confer a constitution on New South Wales.

A despatch was received from the Secretary of State for the Colonies (Sir John Pakington) announcing that the control of Customs and the administration of the lands should henceforth be in the hands of the local Legislature, that transportation to Tasmania should cease, and that it was the desire of the Imperial Parliament that the Council should establish the new Legislature on the basis of an elective Assembly and a Legislative Council nominated by the Crown, the Council to fix the number of members.

A committee was appointed to draft a constitution, consisting of Mr. Wentworth, E. Deas Thompson, J. Macarthur, J. H. Plunkett, Cowper, Martin, Donaldson, Macleay, Thurlow, and Murray. This committee brought up a report that did not meet with the approval of the Council. It proposed the creation of an Upper House, whose membership should have conferred upon them hereditary titles, who should have the power to elect from their own class the membership of this House. A meeting of the citizens was held at the Royal Hotel, at which the above proposal was condemned in unmeasured terms, and "The Celebrated Constitution Committee" was appointed on the 3rd August, 1853. The chair on this occasion was occupied by Mr. John Gilchrist, a merchant. Speeches were made by Messrs Darvall, Robert Johnson, Henry Parkes, Montifiore. J. W. Blyth, Denichy, Mort, Archdeacon McEncroe, John Browne, Piddington, and E. Flood. They passed a series of resolutions condemning the attempt to foist upon the colony a constitution in violation of the people's rights. Notwithstanding this outside protest Mr. Wentworth and his Legislative Committee, after a contest of seven days, carried the objectionable bill through its second reading, and it was made the order of the day for its committal on the 6th December, 1853. A mass meeting assembled on

Circular Quay to express their dissent, and to petition the Queen to withhold her assent, and that no constitution except one based upon British liberty would ever receive the sanction of the colony. The pressure was so great that when the objectionable bill came up in committee it was modified in its offensive features, and passed its third reading by twenty-seven to six. The bill established a Parliament of two Houses—the Legislative Council to consist of not less than twenty-one naturalised or natural born subjects, the President to be nominated by the Crown; the Legislative Assembly to consist of fifty-four members, to be elected for five years.

The contest was a severe one. The people contended earnestly and long for responsible government, and their voice in the matter could not be ignored. A deputation, consisting of W. C. Wentworth and E. Deas Thompson (Colonial Secretary), was appointed to go to England and watch the progress of the bill. In due time it received the sanction of the British Parliament, and became the law, governing the Legislature of the colony.

The Constitution Act.—An Act to Confer a Constitution on New South Wales.

Whereas by the thirty-second Clause of the Imperial Act passed in the Session holden in the thirteenth and fourteenth years of the reign of Her present Majesty intituled An Act for the better Government of Her Majesty's Australian Colonies it was among other things enacted that notwithstanding anything thereinbefore contained it should be lawful for the Governor and Legislative Council of this Colony from time to time by any Act or Acts to alter the provisions or laws for the time being in force under the said Imperial Act or otherwise concerning the Election of the Elective Members of such Legislative Council and the Qualification of Electors and Elective Members or to establish in the said Colony instead of the Legislative Council a Council and a House of Representatives or other separate Legislative Houses to consist of such Members to be appointed or elected by such person and in such manner as by such Act or Acts should be determined and to vest in such Council and House of Representatives or other separate Legislative Houses the powers and functions of the Legislative Council for which the same may be substituted. And whereas it is expedient that the powers vested by the said Act in the said Governor and Legislative Council should be exercised and that a Legislative Council and a Legislative

Assembly as constituted by this Act should be substituted for the present Legislative Council with the increased powers and functions hereinafter contained Be it therefore enacted by His Excellency the Governor of New South Wales with the advice and consent of the Legislative Council thereof as follows :—

1. There shall be in place of the Legislative Council now subsisting one Legislative Council and one Legislative Assembly to be severally constituted and composed in the manner hereinafter prescribed and within the said Colony of New South Wales Her Majesty shall have power by and with the advice and consent of the said Council and Assembly to make laws for the peace welfare and good government of the said Colony in all cases whatsoever Provided that all Bills for appropriating any part of the Public Revenue for imposing any new rate tax or impost subject always to the limitation contained in [clause sixty-two] of this Act shall originate in the Legislative Assembly of the said Colony.

2. For the purpose of composing the Legislative Council of New South Wales it shall be lawful for Her Majesty before the time to be appointed for the first meeting of the said Legislative Council and Assembly by an Instrument under the Sign Manual to authorise the Governor with the advice of the Executive Council in Her Majesty's name by an Instrument or Instruments under the Great Seal of the said Colony to summon to the said Legislative Council of the said Colony such persons being not fewer than twenty-one as the said Governor and Executive Council shall think fit and it shall also be lawful for Her Majesty from time to time to authorise the Governor in like manner to summon to the said Legislative Council such other person or persons as the said Governor and Executive Council shall think fit and every person who shall be so summoned shall thereby become a Member of the Legislative Council of the said Colony Provided always that no person shall be summoned to the said Legislative Council who shall not be of the full age of twenty-one years and a natural born subject of Her Majesty or naturalised by an Act of the Imperial Parliament or by an Act of the Legislature of the said Colony Provided also that not less than four-fifths of the Members so summoned to the Legislative Council shall consist of persons not holding any office or emolument under the Crown except Officers in Her Majesty's sea and land forces on full or half-pay or retired officers on pensions.

Hon. H. M. NELSON,
Minister for Railways

THE CONSTITUTION.   233

3. The Members of the first Legislative Council of the said Colony who shall be so summoned by the Governor with the advice of the Executive Council shall hold their respective seats therein for five years from the date of the first summonses to the said Legislative Council but all future members of the said Legislative Council who shall be summoned thereto after the expiration of the said five years by the Governor with the advice of the Executive Council as aforesaid shall hold their seats therein for the term of their natural lives subject nevertheless to the provisions hereinafter contained for vacating the same and for altering and amending the future Constitution of the said Colony as established by this Act.

4. It shall be lawful for any Member of the Legislative Council to resign his seat therein by a letter to the Governor and upon the receipt of any such letter by the Governor the seat of such Legislative Councillor shall become vacant.

5. If any Legislative Councillor shall for two successive Sessions of the Legislature of the said Colony fail to give his attendance in the said Legislative Council without the permission of Her Majesty or of the Governor of the Colony signified by the said Governor to the Legislative Council or shall take any oath or make any declaration or acknowledgment of allegiance obedience or adherence to any Foreign Prince or Power or shall do concur in or adopt any act whereby he may become a subject or citizen of any Foreign State or Power or whereby he may become entitled to the rights privileges or immunities of a subject or citizen of any Foreign State or Power or shall become bankrupt or take the benefit of any law relating to insolvent debtors or become a public contractor or defaulter or be attainted of treason or be convicted of felony or of any infamous crime his seat in such Council shall thereby become vacant.

6. Any question which shall arise respecting any vacancy in the Legislative Council on occasion of any of the matters aforesaid shall be referred by the Governor to the said Legislative Council to be by the said Legislative Council heard and determined Provided always that it shall be lawful either for the person respecting whose seat such question shall have arisen for Her Majesty's Attorney-General for the said Colony on Her Majesty's behalf to appeal from the determination of the said Council in such case to Her Majesty and that the judgment of Her Majesty given with

the advice of her Privy Council thereon shall be final and conclusive to all intents and purposes.

7. The Governor of the Colony shall have power and authority from time to time by an Instrument under the Great Seal of the said Colony to appoint one Member of the said Legislative Council to be President thereof and to remove him and appoint another in his stead and it shall be at all times lawful for the said President to take part in any debate or discussion which may arise in the Legislative Council.

8. The presence of at least one-third of the Members of the said Legislative Council exclusive of the President shall be necessary to constitute a quorum for the despatch of business and all question which shall arise in the said Legislative Council shall be decided by a majority of the votes of the Members present other than the President and when the votes shall be equal the President shall have the casting vote Provided always that if the whole number of Members constituting the said Legislative Council shall not be exactly divisible by three the quorum of the said Legislative Council shall consist of such whole number as is next greater than one-third of the Members of the said Legislative Council.

9. For the purpose of constituting the Legislative Assembly of the said Colony it shall be lawful for the Governor thereof within the time hereinafter mentioned and thereafter from time to time as occasion shall require in Her Majesty's name by an Instrument or Instruments under the Great Seal of the said Colony to summon and call together a Legislative Assembly in and for the said Colony.

10. (In regard to the number of Members of the Assembly which was fixed at fifty-four.) This was repealed by 22 Vic. No. 20 sec. 2, and eighty Members substituted and one for the University when it became entitled to it by the graduation of a certain number which it reached in 1876. See Electoral Law.

11. (Qualification of electors.) It was repealed by 22 Vic. See Electoral Law.

12. (Joint-owners and occupiers shall be entitled to be registered as voters and to vote.) Also repealed by 22 Vic. See Electoral Law.

13. (Division of the Colony into Electoral Districts.) Repealed by same.

14. (Electoral lists.) Repealed by same.

THE CONSTITUTION. 235

15. It shall be lawful for the Legislature of the Colony by any Act or Acts to be hereafter passed to alter *(a)* the division and extent of the several counties districts cities towns boroughs and hamlets which shall be represented in the Legislative Assembly and to establish new and other divisions of the same and to alter the apportionment of Representatives to be chosen by the said counties districts cities towns boroughs and hamlets respectively and to alter the number of Representatives to be chosen in and for the Colony and in and for the several Electoral Districts in the same and to alter and regulate the appointment of Returning Officers and make such new and other provision as they may deem expedient for the issuing and return of Writs for the election of Members to serve in the said Legislative Assembly and the time and place of holding such elections Provided always that it shall not be lawful to present to the Governor of the Colony for Her Majesty's assent any Bill by which the number or apportionment of Representatives in the Legislative Assembly may be altered unless the second and third readings of such Bill in the Legislative Council and the Legislative Assembly respectively shall have been passed with the concurrence of a majority of the Members for the time being of the said Legislative Council and of two-thirds *(b)* of the Members for the time being of the said Legislative Assembly and the assent of Her Majesty shall not be given to any such Bill unless an address shall have been presented by the Legislative Assembly to the Governor stating that such Bill has been so passed.

16. (Qualification of Members of Assembly.) It was repealed and changed by Electoral Law 22 Vic. No. 20 sec. 2.

17. No person being a Member of the Legislative Council shall be capable of being elected or of sitting or voting as a member of the Legislative Assembly.

18. Any person holding any office of profit under the Crown or having a pension from the Crown during pleasure or a term of years shall be incapable of being elected or of sitting or voting as a Member of the Legislative Assembly unless he be one of the following Official Members of the Government that is to say the Colonial Secretary Colonial Treasurer Auditor-General Attorney-General and Solicitor-General or one of such additional Officers not being more than five as the Governor with the advice of the Executive Council may from time to time appoint by a notice in the

Government Gazette declare capable of being elected a Member of the said Assembly.

19. If any member of the said Assembly shall accept of any office of profit or pension from the Crown during pleasure or for term of years his election shall be thereupon and is hereby declared to be void and a writ shall forthwith issue for a new election Provided that nothing in this Act contained shall extend to any person in receipt only of pay half-pay or a pension as an Officer in Her Majesty's Navy or Army or who shall receive any new or other commission in the Navy or Army respectively or any increase of pay on such commission or to any of the Official Members of the Government or other Officers referred to in the last preceding clause of this Act who may accept any other office.

20. (Disqualifying ministers of religion.) Afterwards repealed by 22 Vic. No. 20 sec. 2 See Electoral Law.

21. (Duration of Assembly.) Repealed by 37 Vic. No. 7.

22. The Members of the Legislative Assembly shall upon the first assembling after general election proceed forthwith to elect one of their number to be Speaker and in case of his death resignation or removal by a vote of the said Legislative Assembly the said Members shall forthwith proceed to elect another of such Members to be Speaker and the Speaker so elected shall preside at all meetings of the said Legislative Assembly except as may be provided by the Standing Rules and Orders hereinafter authorised to be made.

23. The presence of at least twenty Members of the Legislative Assembly exclusive of the Speaker shall be necessary to constitute a meeting of the said Legislative Assembly for the despatch of business and all questions (except as herein is excepted) which shall arise in the said Assembly shall be decided by the majority of votes of such Members as shall be present other than the Speaker and when the votes shall be equal the Speaker shall have the casting vote.

24. Upon any General Election the Legislative Assembly shall be competent to proceed to the despatch of business at the time appointed by the Governor for that purpose, notwithstanding that any of the Writs of Election (not exceeding five) shall not have been returned or that in any of the electoral districts the electors shall have failed to elect a Member to serve in the said Assembly.

25. It shall be lawful for any Member of the Assembly by writing under his hand addressed to the Speaker of the said House to resign his seat therein and upon the receipt of such resignation by the Speaker the seat of such Member shall become vacant.

26. If any Member of the Assembly shall for one whole Session of the Legislature without the permission of the Assembly entered upon its journals fail to give his attendance in the said House or shall take any oath or make declaration or acknowledgment of allegiance obedience or adherence to any Foreign Prince or Power or do or concur in or adopt any Act whereby he may become a subject or citizen of any Foreign State or Power or become entitled to the rights privileges or immunities of a subject of any Foreign State or Power or shall become bankrupt or an insolvent debtor within the meaning of the laws in force within the said Colony relating to bankrupts or insolvent debtors or shall become a public defaulter or be attainted of treason or be convicted of felony or any infamous crime his seat in such Assembly shall thereby become vacant.

27. (Election to take place on vacancies.) Repealed by 22 Vic. No. 20 sec. 2. See Electoral Laws.

28. Any person who shall directly or indirectly himself or by any person whatsoever in trust for or for his use or benefit or on his account undertake execute hold or enjoy in the whole or in part any contract or agreement for or on account of the Public Service shall be incapable of being summoned or elected or of sitting or voting as a Member of the Legislative Council or Legislative Assembly during the time he shall execute hold or enjoy any such contract or any part or share thereof or any benefit or emolument arising from the same and if any person being a Member of such Council or Assembly shall enter into any such contract or agreement or having entered into it shall continue to hold it his seat shall be declared by the said Legislative Council or Legislative Assembly as the case may require to be void and thereupon the same shall become and be void accordingly   Provided always that nothing herein contained shall extend to any contract or agreement made entered into or accepted by any incorporated company or any trading company consisting of more than twenty persons where such contract or agreement shall be made entered into or accepted for the general benefit of such incorporated or trading company.

29. If any person by this Act disabled or declared to be incapable to sit or vote in the Legislative Council or Legislative Assembly shall nevertheless be summoned to the said Council or elected and returned as a Member to serve in the said Assembly for an electoral district such summons or election and return shall and may be declared by the said Council and Assembly as the case may require to be void and thereupon the same shall become and be void to all intents and purposes whatsoever and if any person under any of the disqualifications mentioned in the last preceding section shall whilst so disqualified presume to sit or vote as a Member of the said Council or Assembly such person shall forfeit the sum of £500 to be recovered by any person who shall sue for the sum in the Supreme Court of New South Wales.

30. It shall be lawful for the Governor of the Colony for the time being to fix such place or places within any part of the Colony and such times for holding the first and every other Session of the Legislative Council and Assembly of the said Colony as he may think fit such times and places to be afterwards changed or varied as the Governor may judge advisable and most consistent with general convenience and the public welfare giving sufficient notice thereof and also to prorogue the said Legislative Council and Assembly from time to time and to dissolve the said Assembly by proclamation or otherwise whenever he shall deem it expedient.

31. There shall be a Session of the Legislative Council and Assembly once at least in every year so that a period of twelve calendar months shall not intervene between the last sitting of the Legislative Council and Assembly and the first sitting of the Legislative Council and Assembly in the next session.

32. The Legislative Council and Assembly shall be called together for the first time at some period not later than six calendar months next after the proclamation of this Act by the Governor of the said colony.

33. No Member either of the Legislative Council or of the Legislative Assembly shall be permitted to sit or vote therein until he shall have taken and subscribed the following oath before the Governor of the Colony or before some person or persons authorised by such Governor to administer such oath *(a)* For the oath now substituted. See 33 Vic No. 11 and whensoever the demise of Her present Majesty (whom may God long

preserve) or of any of her successors to the Crown of the United Kingdom shall be notified by the Governor of the Colony to the said Council and Assembly respectively the Members of the said Council and Assembly shall before they shall be permitted to sit and vote therein take and subscribe the like oath of allegiance to the successor for the time being to the said Crown.

34. Provided that every person authorised by law to make an affirmation instead of taking an oath may make such affirmation in every case in which an oath is hereinbefore required to be taken.

35. The said Legislative Council and Assembly in the first Session of each respectively and from time to time afterwards as there may be occasion shall prepare and adopt such Standing Rules and Orders as shall appear to the said Council and Assembly respectively best adapted for the orderly conduct of such Council and Assembly respectively and for the manner in which such Council and Assembly shall be presided over in case of the absence of the President or the Speaker and for the mode in which such Council and Assembly shall confer correspond and communicate with each other relative to the votes or Bills passed by or pending in such Council and Assembly respectively and for the manner in which Notices of Bills Resolutions and other business intended to be submitted to such Council and Assembly respectively at any Session thereof may be published for general information and for the proper passing entitling and numbering of the Bills to be introduced into and passed by the said Council and Assembly for the proper presentation of the same to the Governor for the time being for Her Majesty's assent all of which Rules and Orders shall by such Council and Assembly respectively be laid before the Governor and being by him approved shall become binding and of force.

36. Grants the Legislature constructed by this Act power to alter any of its provisions Provided each Bill passes through its second and third readings and receives the concurrence of two-thirds of the members of the Legislative Council and Assembly respectively Provided every such Bill shall be reserved for Her Majesty's assent and for thirty days be laid before both Houses of the Imperial Parliament.

37. Lodges all power in the hands of the Governor with the advice of the Executive Council in appointing all Officers under the Government of the Colony except Officers liable to retire on political grounds who shall

be appointed by the Governor alone and excepting also minor offices in the several departments which are to be filled by the heads of the departments.

38. By this section judges are made continuous notwithstanding the demise of Her Majesty or any of her heirs.

39. It shall be lawful nevertheless for Her Majesty her heirs or successors to remove any such judge or judges upon the address of the Council and Assembly of the Colony.

40. Secures their salaries during the continuance of their commission.

41. Establishes all existing laws except such as are changed by the Act itself or that may hereafter be changed by the operation of the Act.

42. Establishes all existing courts and commissions except such as may be abolished by the said Act.

43. Gives Legislature power to make sale of waste lands and laws regulating the same.

44. Makes it impossible for the Legislature to impose any duties or restrictions on supplies for Her Majesty's Forces or to violate any existing treaty Her Majesty may have concluded with any Foreign Power.

45. Gives power to impose duties on goods of foreign manufactory but restricts it in the matter of differentiating

46. Fixes the boundaries of the Colony of New South Wales.

What follows has reference to the civil list.

Preamble.

And whereas the Legislative Council of New South Wales constituted under the Imperial Act passed in the Session holden in the thirteenth and fourteenth years of the reign of Her present Majesty intituled an Act for the better Government of Her Majesty's Australian Colonies are desirous that Her Majesty should owe to the spontaneous liberality of her people in this Colony such grant by way of Civil List in lieu of the provision contained in the schedule to that Act as shall be sufficient to give stability and security to the Civil Institution of the Colony and to provide for the adequate remuneration of able and efficient Officers in the Executive Judicial and other departments of Her Majesty's Colonial Service the granting of which Civil List belongs constitutionally only to Her Majesty's faithful people through their Representatives in the said Legislative Council and Her Majesty's most dutiful and loyal subjects the Members of

the said Legislative Council in council assembled being desirous that a certain competent revenue for the purpose may be settled upon Her Majesty (to whom may God grant a long and happy reign) as a testimony of their unfeigned affection to Her Majesty's person and government have accordingly freely resolved in lieu of the aforesaid statutable provisions for the like purpose to grant to Her Majesty her heirs and successors a certain revenue payable out of the Consolidated Revenue Fund of this Colony Be it therefore enacted as follows :—

47. All taxes imports rates and duties and all territorial casual and other revenues of the Crown (including royalties) from whatever source arising within this Colony and over which the present or future Legislature has or may have power of appropriation shall form one Consolidated Revenue Fund to be appropriated for the Public Service of the Colony in the manner and subject to the charges hereinafter mentioned.

48. Provides that out of said Revenue Fund all charges and costs of collection shall be paid.

49. Provides for the payment of Civil Lists as per schedule "A" "B" and "C" said amounts not to exceed £64,300 per annum.

50. Civil List to be accompanied by surrender of all revenues of the Crown.

51. Provides for the payment of pensions to Judges of Supreme Court pensions to certain Officers liable to removal from office on political grounds.

52. Provides for superannuation pensions to certain other Officers not liable to removal for political reasons To be regulated by Superannuation Act 4 and 5 Wm. IV c. 24.

53. Consolidated Revenue to be appropriated by Act of the Legislature Debentures or any other charges on Consolidated Revenue Fund not to be affected by such consolidation.

54. Provides that no money vote or Bill is lawful unless recommended by the Governor.

55. Provides that no part of public revenue shall be issued except on warrants from the Governor.

56. Provides that this Act shall be proclaimed within one month after its reception by the Governor of the Colony and shall take effect from date of proclamation.

57. The definition of the term "Governor."
58. Provides the limits and force of this Act etc.

Schedule A.

	Salaries Payable while present Incumbents are in Office.	Salaries to be Paid in Future as Vacancies Occur.
To be placed at the disposal of Her Majesty for the salary of the Governor-General if Her Majesty sees fit, otherwise to revert to the Consolidated Revenue Fund	£7,000	£7,000
One Chief Justice	2,000	2,000
Three Judges, including one for Moreton Bay	4,500	4,500
Colonial Secretary	2,000	2,000
Colonial Treasurer	1,250	1,250
Auditor-General	900	900
Attorney-General	1,500	1,500
Solicitor-General	1,000	1,000
Governor's Private Secretary	400	400
Master in Equity and Curator of Intestate Estates and Chief Commissioner of Insolvency Estates	1,000	
Chairman of Quarter Sessions and Commissioner of Court Requests	800	
	£22,350	£20,550

Chief Justice's salary is increased to £2,600, and Judges' to £2,000 each by 20 Vic. No. 8, and Colonial Treasurer's to £1,500 by 20 Vic. No. 18.

Schedule B.

Pensions to Judges on ceasing to hold Office, etc.	£4,550
Pensions to existing Officers of the Government liable on political grounds to retire, etc.	5,000
Pensions to Officers not liable on political grounds to retire, etc.	3,500
	£13,050

Schedule C.

Public Worship	£28,000

Several subsequent Acts have modified some of the above features, which will be noted in subsequent chapters.

This forms the basis of all colonial constitutions and, hence, is given in its original entirety. Each colony, after obtaining a separate existence, has modified the above to suit its own ideas. These changes are noted in another chapter.

CHAPTER XXV.

INTERIOR EXPLORATION.

FOR nearly thirty years after the first settlement very little was done towards the exploration of the interior. During all these years the colonists were in almost total ignorance of the country, on whose eastern coast they had settled. They were content to occupy the lands in the immediate neighbourhood of Port Jackson. A few of the more adventurous spirits had gone up and down the coast, and rendered valuable service to geographical science by the charts they had rudely drawn of the coast and some of its characteristics. Notably among these are to be mentioned Bass, Flinders, Clarke, and Baudin. This latter was a Frenchman, who made his explorations from his own country, and took to himself the credit of being the first to discover and make charts of the southern coast. Exploration was made to a very small extent in every direction from Port Jackson, but was rendered unsatisfactory by the mountainous range that ran north and south parallel with the coast, and only distant about forty miles, and whose eastern aspect was bold and rocky, rendering ascent impossible up to the time that Lawson, Blaxland, and Wentworth, in 1813, discovered a pass that to more timid spirits would appear impossible to travel, but to this trio afforded sufficient encouragement to lead them on to search for brighter regions beyond. To these names justly attaches the honor of being the first explorers who have given us an intelligent picture of the interior beyond the Blue Mountains. Their report to Governor Macquarie on their return was of the brightest character. They not only succeeded in finding a passable route over the mountains, but had found valleys of the most luxurious pasturage and soil of the richest character, and in extent what appeared to be limitless. This discovery, made during a destructive drought, was welcomed as a godsend. The cattle everywhere had been starving, and the numerous flocks that had of late years been rapidly multiplying had spread over every available acre of pasturage on the eastern stretch, embraced between the mountains and the coast, and which had become exhausted by over-stocking. The colonists had for a long time been anxious to find new pasture fields and agricultural lands. This territory beyond the mountains was a timely discovery.

The Governor lost no time in availing himself of the advantages to be derived from the early occupancy of such a region, and immediately employed a large force of labour to build a road through to the plains. The Government Surveyor, Mr. Evans, was charged with the task of making a more thorough exploration of the new land of promise, and accordingly made an extended investigation of the route discovered by Blaxland, Lawson, and Wentworth, and beyond, and was even more enthusiastic in his description of the valleys and streams that gave evidence of such boundless extent and richness that in the judgment of Mr. Evans and his party contained sufficient pasturage and lands to supply the wants of the colonists for "one hundred years to come." By January, 1815, a magnificent road was built to the little settlement, which was afterwards called Bathurst by the Governor when he made a tour of inspection in the following May. The two rivers bearing the names respectively of Lachlan and Macquarie were discovered by Mr. Evans in 1814, and named after the Governor. In a very few months after the road was opened the entire country became covered with squatters and their flocks. For months the road presented a most lively appearance. Tens of thousands of sheep were driven slowly westward to find more suitable nourishment, and Bathurst became a centre of no small importance. The success in this direction made the colonists ambitious to find new territory yet beyond. Governor Macquarie was in his element when engaged in new enterprises. He was pleased to give encouragement to every movement that in any way tended to open up and develop this new country.

The discovery of the two rivers Macquarie and Lachlan in these valleys and plains, and the fact of their rapid divergence, one going in a north-westerly direction, and the other south-west, awakened a desire to

INTERIOR EXPLORATION.   245

trace them to their exit. Their course suggested the theory of an inland sea into which they emptied. Oxley, the Surveyor-General of the colony, became thoroughly interested in the discoveries made by his colleague and deputy, and at the request of the Governor was very willing to undertake the task of more thoroughly exploring this region. Accordingly in 1817 he organised a party of four in addition to himself, consisting of Mr. Evans, a surveyor, Mr. Allan Cunningham, a botanist, Mr. Fraser, and Mr. Parr. All were scientific men, and entered upon their work—not through any feeling of curiosity, but from a desire to add to the scientific knowledge of the country. They started from Sydney in April, 1817, and soon reached Bathurst. At that point Oxley resolved first to follow the course of the Lachlan River, that being much the larger of the two. As they made progress they found fish in abundance, and lands of a very varied type. Here and there it was somewhat undulating, but generally flat and barren. The river itself seemed to spread out into a marshy region that was little better than a vast swamp. After having travelled to the south and west until they reached longtitude 145° and latitude 34°, they gave up the search in that direction, retraced their course along the Lachlan for a time, and then turning northward they crossed the country in the hope of reaching the Macquarie. In this they were successful, for after having passed through a tract of red sandy loam soil they came upon several fine streams that ran through a country which gave them much promise, and was well wooded and rich in pasturage and other signs of fertility. Mr. Oxley's impression of the country through which the Macquarie ran was most encouraging, and his report of its capabilities was such as to awaken the colonists to desire more thoroughly to explore a region that most of them were inclined to believe was of a valuable character.

In 1818 Mr. Oxley fitted out another expedition to more thoroughly explore this country. Mr. Evans, Dr. Harris, twelve men, and several horses, with six months' provisions, constituted the preparation for a journey they expected might last several months. They began this expedition by examining the country through which the Macquarie traversed. · For a time they were delighted with the prospect. Rich valleys and luxuriant pasturage and considerable timber in places led them to hope that they had discovered a country of immense distances and value for pastoral and agricultural pursuits; but as they continued to follow westward into the unexplored depths they were frequently met by difficulties that dampened their expectations. Sometimes they had to cross immense tracts of swamp, into which the horses would sink up to their knees, and which had the effect of exhausting the animals in a very short time; and at times they were forced to cross rough, rugged portions of country that was equally trying to man and beast. Finally they reached a vast extended level plain through which the Macquarie slowly flowed, and speedily the river spread out into a low marshy swamp of unlimited extent, through which they were unable to penetrate. After making a somewhat brief investigation of the surrounding country they were forced to direct their course eastward, and crossed the New England Range. Oxley was sent to explore the Moreton Bay District in 1823, and proceeded up the Brisbane River, and located the present site on which has grown into a city of importance the present capital of Queensland. His report to Governor Brisbane represented the region called Moreton Bay District to be of the best quality of land, well timbered, and capable of growing all kinds of tropical fruit and vegetables.

Allan Cunningham, who accompanied Oxley in his investigations on the Lachlan and Macquarie rivers, and who was an eminent botanist, followed up the examination of this district so successfully inaugurated by Oxley, and made valuable discoveries, among which were the Liverpool Plains and the Darling Downs, besides many botanical specimens both rare and valuable. This country soon became occupied as a pastoral district, and has continued ever since to be one of the most valued on this account. Mr. Cunningham became the first botanist in charge of the Botanical Gardens of Sydney. A monument is erected to his memory in the Gardens, and stands in one of the ponds, surrounded by water lilies and other swamp vegetation, thus symbolising his life work by which he achieved great renown as a scientist.

Captain Stewart had but a brief experience as an explorer, though he was very enthusiastic in his examination of the geography of the country. He among many others was of the opinion that there existed a large river that had its origin in Lakes Bathurst and George, and emptied into the sea on the eastern coast, and hence was of the opinion that when found would afford water communication to the interior plains surrounding those lakes, and Captain Stewart was accordingly commissioned to explore the coast in search of the mouth of such a river, and to follow it up to its source. The captain and his party never returned to report their experiences. In after years Lieutenant Johnson, R.N., was sent on the same mission, and if possible to learn the fate of Captain Stewart. He succeeded, after much investigation, in learning that the ill-fated explorer was seized and murdered by the natives of Twofold Bay. Johnson, on this trip, discovered a river which he called the Clyde.

Among coast explorers none is more worthy of mention than Captain Phillip Parker King, son of Governor King. Captain King made his first cruise around the coast of Australia in 1817. Among the assistants that were granted him was Mr. Allan Cunningham, who, as botanist, after having had considerable experience with Oxley in the interior, was more desirous than ever to add to his knowledge of Australian botany, and therefore was glad to embrace the opportunity of going into the western portion of the continent. Captain King made four voyages of exploration to the western and north-western coast, each time accompanied by Mr. Cunningham. Conjointly they were successful in obtaining a very correct knowledge of the coast and the character of the vegetation found in that portion of the continent. Captain King became in time an honorable member of the Legislative Council.

In 1824 one of the most important explorations of the interior was effected by Hume and Hovell, who went overland in company with six convicts, who were offered a full pardon if they were successful in making the entire journey from Sydney to the ocean on the South. Hamilton Hume was a young man of great bravery and daring, born at Parramatta in 1797. Captain Hovell was a man of learning and perseverance, and was well-fitted to become one of this band who were anxious to contribute to the geography of the country, and rendered valuable service in this expedition. They first discovered the Murrumbidgee which they described as a large river that swiftly flowed through magnificent lands heavily wooded. To cross this stream was a task most difficult to accomplish. The wood on its banks was like most of the Australian woods, so heavy that they could not construct rafts that would float at all. Finally they made a punt out of one of their carts, by taking off the wheels, and covering it with a tarpaulin, into which they packed their goods and supplies. They attached to it a rope, and Hume, having taken the other end thereof in his teeth, managed to swim the river, and gaining the opposite side was enabled to draw over the supplies in this crude scow. The party accomplished this most hazardous feat without loss of either cattle or of any of their number. They were soon compelled to abandon their wagons and carts on account of the roughness of the country. They loaded their oxen and horses with their effects, and leading the animals they were enabled to cross mountains and scale difficult heights, and from elevations reached they gained views of most magnificent country, which stretched out in every direction into valleys of richest verdure and plains of vast extent. Soon afterwards they came upon the banks of a more rapid stream. To the left of them they saw not far distant the snow-capped mountains, since called the Australian Alps, and to the right of them stretched forests of gum-trees. The river that confronted them was two hundred and forty feet in breadth. The task of crossing this body of water was not easy of accomplishment. They had now no cart out of which to construct a scow. The ingenuity of the party was equal to the occasion, and having first made a sort of basket of wicker work in form of a flat-bottom boat they covered it with a tarpaulin, and thus were able to float over their effects with comparative ease and safety. One of the six servants accompanying Hume and Hovell, known by the name of Thomas Boyd, is credited with being the first to have crossed the river. His claim to this honor rests not only on his own testimony, but upon that of others. He is still living at Tumut, in the southern portion of the colony. They called the river Hume (now known as the Murray) in honor of their leader. Thus encouraged the brave band directed their course in a south-westerly direction through a country more lightly timbered. Their progress on this account was more rapid and pleasant. Almost each day they were delighted by the freshness and beauty of the country through which they passed. On their way they crossed a river they called the Ovens. A few days later the Goulburn, which they named the Hovell, a name it bore for many years. Hume and Hovell now separated from the rest of the company for a few days that they might ascend a lofty hill in the vicinity from whose summit they felt assured they could see the southern ocean. In this expectation they failed, and called the peak Mount Disappointment. They rejoined their companions, and continued their march southward through a country of surpassing loveliness and beauty. They finally reached an expanse of water that was called by the natives Geelong, and which Hovell contended was Western Port, while Hume maintained that it was Port Phillip. The party returned to Sydney by the same route, and were rewarded by Governor Brisbane. To the leaders, Hovell and Hume, were granted twelve hundred acres of land each, and to their servants a full pardon. The results of this expedition were of the most satisfactory character. A country of beauty and excellence was brought within the knowledge of the colony, and inaugurated colonisation in a part of the country that since has developed into one of the most fruitful portions of the continent.

On the 10th of September, 1828, an exploring expedition was organised under the direction and leadership of Captain Sturt, an officer in the 39th Regiment. The party consisted of Sturt, Hume, Dr. McLeod, an army surgeon, two others, with eight prisoners as servants. The long-continued drought that had prevailed for two years suggested to Governor Darling the practicability of exploring in those regions where Oxley was prevented by vast swamps, and hence their first attempt was to follow up the Macquarie River. They soon reached the point where Oxley was compelled to return. The drought had turned the marsh into a hard solid region, where all vegetation was withered and dead. Desolation and barrenness made up the complete picture of the country in this locality. It was in the summer months that this journey was taken, and the heat was excessive. Sturt resolved to follow the course of the Macquarie no longer, but directed his way westward, and passed through a region where shells and claws of crayfish gave evidence of inundations. They soon came upon a broad river, which through part of its bed was now in a series of ponds. The river he called the Darling in honor of the Governor. They followed its course for about ninety miles, discovering the Bogan, which empties into it. This river they passed up for about fifty miles. He returned to Sydney after having satisfied himself of the fallacy of the theory of a great inland sea. At least some slight knowledge had been gained by this trip of a region that had puzzled the geographers of that day.

Sturt was again sent in 1829 to explore the country in the more southern districts. This time he had a naturalist by the name of Macleay. They reached the Murrumbidgee at Yass Plains, and proceeding down its course they discovered the Lachlan at its junction with the Murrumbidgee. This they followed until they reached a large river which he named the

Murray in honor of Sir George Murray, the Minister for the colonies at that time. They sailed down until they came to where a large river entered on their right. This was the Darling River which he had previously discovered in its upper portion. They went up this stream for a considerable distance, and, returning, they proceeded down the Murray through its entire length until they came to a lake, which they called Alexandrina after the young Princess Alexandrina Victoria. Retracing their steps they sailed up the Murray, and thence by the Murrumbidgee, and finally reached home exhausted and worn out by the arduous task, but bearing back to their countrymen laurels no other explorer had ever been able to win. Subsequent examinations of all the regions over which they passed only confirmed Sturt's report. Macleay's services were invaluable in the department of botanical science. Sturt became blind, and though he partially recovered from this affliction he never regained his full health. He lived for many years, and was honored for the heroic service he rendered to his country.

The next expedition was undertaken by Major Mitchell in 1831. His ambition was to explore the north-west. He set out on his first expedition with fifteen convicts, and provisions sufficient to last them several months. They reached the Upper Darling, and there tarried for supplies that were left in charge of two of his men. After waiting a considerable period in vain he finally learned that his stores were plundered by the natives, and the two men in charge murdered. Mitchell was compelled to return, having first buried the dead bodies of his friends. Nothing daunted, he undertook the task in 1835, accompanied by George, a brother of Allan Cunningham, who had previously accompanied Oxley. They took the direction of the Bogan, but made little progress, Cunningham having separated became lost, and was cruelly murdered by the natives. This circumstance terminated the expedition. The following year Major Mitchell, undertook a third expedition; this time down the course of the Lachlan, and across the Murray southward. His party consisted of himself and twenty-five convicts. They met several hostile natives, who showed a determination to resist their advancement. The men were well armed, and soon put the natives to flight. They passed through some of the most beautiful country they had ever beheld. They crossed the Avon and Avoca rivers, and reaching the Glenelg they explored one of the richest pastoral districts of the south, and finally reached the Messrs. Henty settlement established just three years previously. They were entertained here for several days. Major Mitchell returned by the same route. His observations in the Port Phillip District were so satisfactory that he was led to give to it the name of "Australia Felix," an appellation which it bore for many years, and which in many respects is characteristic. On the strength of the report of Major Mitchell large tracts of land in that district were placed upon the market, and brought fabulous sums; and thus began its colonisation, although a few years previously the Henty's, Falkner's, Batman's, and a few others had settled around Port Phillip, and in the neighbouring localities. Major Mitchell was knighted for this service, and bore the honor with becoming dignity and grace until the date of his death, 5th October, 1855.

Captain Grey and Lieutenant Lushington made an exploration of the west and north-western coast of Australia in 1837. At that date what was known of the continent was confined to the eastern portion. The west was a comparative blank. A deep interest was felt in regard to that region by the Home Government. The great triumphs achieved in recent years by Sturt and Mitchell in bringing to light vast portions of country of a nature most suitable for flocks and agriculture had induced many to believe that tracts of equal extent and value were concealed from view in the west awaiting the ambition and bravery of some new adventurer. When the above offered themselves to the British Government they were immediately accepted. Captain Grey, of the 83rd Regiment, was placed in charge of the expedition with Lieutenant Lushington to assist him in the undertaking. They reached the coast of Western Australia, and anchored in Port George. From this point Captain Grey, taking with him a few dogs and men, began the examination of the country. This attempt was a failure. The hostile character of the natives and the exceeding heat of midsummer unfitted them for their arduous task. His second attempt was not much more successful. He proceeded first to Timor to obtain horses. These he found to be unsuited to the task. The natives were hostile, and Captain Grey, relying more upon the effectiveness of his firearms than upon any acts of diplomacy, had several bloody encounters with them. He received three wounds, but flattered himself that the record he made in the numerous deaths among these native bands did not at all reflect upon his bravery as a British soldier. His purpose was to thoroughly investigate the region through which the Swan River flowed. They were, however, successful in passing through much country of a most picturesque character, through which flowed many beautiful rivulets, and on the banks of which stretched immense meadows of great luxuriance. Grey's health prevented further exploration for a time, but in 1839 he made another attempt. This time he intended to proceed to Shark's Bay, about six hundred miles to the north of Swan River. Before he reached the place of landing a storm at sea shattered his vessels, and his stores having been mostly lost he was compelled to return to Perth, thence to Adelaide.

The next explorer worthy of mention is Strzelecki, a Polish Count, a young man of great learning, and an enthusiast in botanical and mineral science. To this young scientist is due the discovery of that portion of Victoria bearing the name of Gippsland. In 1840 Strzelecki travelled all through the eastern portion of that district, climbed the mountains called the Australian Alps, and first reported the discovery of gold. He called the attention of the Governor to the rich mineral deposits, and also to the fact that the entire district, which he named Gippsland in honor of the Governor, was one of the most enchanting spots in Australia; that its flowers, ferns, and vegetation were most beautiful, and the richness of the soil was unsurpassed. His investigations were made in the years 1839 and 1840.

In 1840 an exploring expedition was undertaken by Edward John Eyre, the expense of which was half borne by himself, the Government of South Australia bearing a part, and the balance by private donation. He first made a tour of the country in the immediate neighborhood of Lake Torrens. Going northward about two hundred miles he reached Lake Eyre, in character similar to the Torrens, barren and desolate. He reached an elevation, from which he commanded an extensive view of the surrounding country, but the prospect was anything but cheerful. In every direction, as far as the vision could reach, were to be seen desolation and a dreary stretch with no water in view. This he named Mount Hopeless. He now returned to Spencer's Gulf, and thence directed his course towards Western Australia, his purpose being to follow near the coast around the Great Australian Bight. He struck out into that great waste, and three times was forced to return for water supplies. He was urged to give up the task. He resolved to reduce the number of his band, lessen the amount of his supplies, and then quickly push forward.

His experience, as related by himself during the terrible march was most painful, never did explorer encounter more fearful suffering from thirst, starvation, and exhaustion. His little band entreated him to return, but nothing could induce him to abandon his cherished project of traversing the great unknown bight. On the way Baxter died, and Eyre and Wylie (his black servant) alone remained to complete the journey. They reached King George's Sound and the little town of Albany. The citizens esteemed his visit to be a great honor. They cared for them, and entertained them like princes worthy of the greatest reverence. After resting for a time they were carried back to Adelaide in a sailing vessel, and received the encomiums they had so dearly earned from their fellow citizens, who never ceased to recognise the greatness of the service rendered to their country.

In 1844 Sturt, who had been so successful in the exploration of the country watered by the Murray, Lachlan, and Darling, organised an expedition to cross through the very heart of the continent. He had in his company Mr. Poole, surveyor, Mr. Browne as surgeon, and Mr. J. McDouall Stuart as draughtsman. They followed up the course of the Darling to Laidley's Ponds; thence to Lake Cawndilla; thence in a north-westerly direction into the interior. They reached a mountainous region, which they called the Stanley Range in honor of Lord Stanley, Secretary for the Colonies; thence to another, which they named the Grey Range. The excessive heat of the summer months compelled them to remain during the hot season at a place they named Rocky Glen Depôt. Here Mr. Poole, surveyor of the party, died. He was buried on a hill, which they named Mount Poole. Their sufferings during these summer months is graphically told by Sturt in his diary. Describing the intensity of the heat he says: " Under its effects every screw in our boxes had been drawn, and the horn handles of our instruments as well as of our combs were split in fine laminæ. The lead dropped out of our pencils; our signal rockets were entirely spoiled; our hair, as well as the wool on the sheep, ceased to grow; and our nails had become as brittle as glass." They decided to return, and on their way they discovered Cooper's Creek, made memorable by the bitter experience of Burke and Wills years afterwards.

In 1844 an important exploration of the eastern coast of New South Wales and part of Queensland was made by Dr. Leichhardt. At the same time while Sturt was occupied in pushing his investigations in the interior,

Ludwig Leichhardt undertook an expedition along the coast belt from Port Jackson to Port Essington, and examined the country east of the great dividing range. Although large and prosperous settlements had been established for years on the banks of the several streams that ran eastward from the mountains to the sea, yet there were large tracts of territory on which the foot of a white man had not rested, and still under the sway of the savage tribes that had their huts and villages on the streams and bays along the entire length of the continent. He and his party encountered great opposition from the natives. Mr. Gilbert, the naturalist of the party, was killed in an attack made upon them soon after they started. His company now consisted of but four men beside himself. He continued his explorations, and discovered the Mackenzie, Burdekin, Fitzroy, Dawson, Mitchell and Gilbert rivers, and explored the country to a considerable extent through which they ran, and finally reaching the Gulf of Carpentaria was delighted with the capabilities of the country through which many of these streams passed. He then proceeded forward towards his destination, discovering on his way the Roper and the Alligator rivers; thence to Port Essington or rather to Van Dieman's Gulf, where they were taken on board a vessel, and by which they sailed to Sydney. Dr. Leichhardt's success on opening up to the world this vast tract of country was such as to awaken the wildest enthusiasm among the citizens of Sydney. He was welcomed back, and received, as a mark of appreciation for his great services, £1,000 from the Government, which was supplemented by a donation from the citizens of £1,500 in addition. He made his second trip in 1847. This time he failed in accomplishing much, for having wandered about in the vicinity of the Fitzroy Downs for several months he abandoned temporarily the task, and returned to Sydney. His third expedition, and his last, was made in 1848. He intended crossing the continent from east to west. He made ample preparations for a lengthy march. His great ambition was to discover the heart of the continent, and tell the story of his experience with his own lips. He started from Moreton Bay, and proceeded as far as the Condamine, from which point he sent a letter to a friend in Sydney. He announced his intention of pushing westward. This was the last ever heard of him or his party. What his fate was remains to this day a mystery. He and his companions probably perished at the hands of some hostile tribe. Several parties have been organised and sent in search of him, but all have failed. His fate remains a mystery beyond the ability of all recent explorers to unravel. His ambition was greater than his genius. His desire to investigate was so ardent that he lost sight of the dangers to which he was exposed, and became forgetful of his own safety.

In 1848 Kennedy, an assistant surveyor, who had accompanied Mitchell in his explorations through Queensland, especially that portion of it traversed by the Culgoa and the Warrego rivers, was sent on a tour through the Peninsula of Cape York. The large cape extending like a peninsula about three hundred miles northward, and forming the eastern boundary of the Gulf of Carpentaria, was a mystery. Up to this date nothing was known of its character other than was obtained from the slight examination made of the coast from time to time by the passing ships that occasionally did a little trading with some few of the natives. The region surrounding Kippel Bay had been explored by Leichhardt, and already the town of Rockhampton had assumed the appearance of an embryo city. It was a busy station for purposes of trade, and many of its people had begun to have a vague notion respecting the country for many miles around. Through the natives who came there to trade they had gained a vague idea of the interior, but Cape York was over three hundred miles to the north, and intervening was a land infected by barbarous races of most savage people with whom it was dangerous to come in contact, and hence to undertake an expedition like the present one evinced a heroism and bravery of no ordinary character. Kennedy possessed all the elements necessary to organise and bring to a successful issue an expedition of this kind. He had with him a party of twelve chosen men, one of whom was a blackfellow named Jacky Jacky, a faithful body servant, and who rendered good service to his master and the cause of science as well. The party was first landed at Kippel Bay, from which point they were to proceed overland to Cape York, where the sloop "Albion" would be in waiting to receive them, and to furnish supplies that they might complete their task, which contemplated an investigation of the coast bounding the Gulf. They began their pilgrimage from Rockhampton, taking with them what supplies they thought they would require. Their course was through a dense thick growth, through which they had at times to cut their way. They could only accomplish a few miles each day. They encountered many swamps and dense foliage that made their progress slow and unsatisfactory. When they reached Weymouth Bay they were very much exhausted, and believing the work could be accomplished much better with a less number, and with less difficulty, Kennedy left all except Jacky and three men. One of the men having received a wound accidentally, which made it impossible for him to proceed further, was left in the care of the other two, and single-handed, with Jacky alone, Kennedy determined to push forward and reach his destination, and return and rescue his party. He had not gone far when he encountered a native tribe of most desperate and treacherous character, who stealthily followed them for days, when finally he was pierced in the back, and fell. A hand to hand encounter ensued, when Jacky, who was a skilled marksman, fired a fatal bullet that caused one of the leaders of the hostile blacks to writhe in the agonies of death. This caused the rest of them to rush away in terror. The faithful Jacky was left but a few moments with his dying master, who had time only to direct his servant to bind up some important papers, and carry them to the ship. Kennedy died in a few moments, and was buried by his weeping friend, who stripped from his own person his garments to cover the grave of his master. Jacky, after much difficulty, succeeded in reaching Cape York, when being observed by the ship, was rescued, naked and almost starved. The ship hastened to the spot, Weymouth Bay, in search of the wounded man and his two guards, but they could find no trace of them; thence to the place where Kennedy was buried, but not a vestage remained to mark the spot, nor yet could they find the papers that Jacky had hid in the hollow of a tree. They hurried to Weymouth Bay to relieve the eight men that were left behind at that point, and here they confronted a horrible spectacle —the dead bodies of five, and two crawling skeletons alone remained of all the band of whites that, under the guidance of Kennedy, attempted the task of exploring the great North. All that posterity can do for such heroes is to record their deeds and write their names. Their noblest deeds are beyond our vision. Their greatest sacrifices are the daily experiences through which they passed, and of which there can be no record.

One of the more important expeditions of this kind was organised in Melbourne under the command of Burke and Wills in 1860. The expeditions previously sent out from the different chief cities of Australia accomplished a great deal, but there was so much to be done in the same direction that almost every year found some one anxious to contribute towards the work

of exploration. A Mr. Kyte made the generous offer of £1,000 towards equipping an expedition to explore Central Australia. This was immediately supplemented by the Victorian Government in the further sum of £3,000. The Royal Society of Victoria, anxious to make the expedition as effective as possible, took the matter in hand, and through their well-directed efforts succeeded in obtaining from the Government a second sum of £6,000, and through private subscriptions £3,400 more, making in all over £12,000. They secured twenty-seven camels from India, and twenty-eight horses. The party consisted of Robert O'Hara Burke, who was placed in command, Mr. Landells in charge of the animals, Mr. Wells, surveyor and scientist, three Hindoos to conduct the camels, and thirteen men. As far as human foresight could judge, the party was thoroughly equipped for a journey across the continent. They started from Melbourne on the 20th August, 1860. In consequence of some disagreement between Burke and his second officer, Mr. Landells resigned, and Wills was appointed in his place, and a man by the name of Wright secured to take general charge of the camels. They reached Minindie, on the Darling, and establishing a depôt at that point Burke took part of his company, including Mr. Wright, and moved on towards Cooper's Creek. After having satisfied himself that there was an abundance of water and grass for the animals in the interior, Burke sent Wright back to camp at Minindie to bring up the remainder of the men and stores, and to have the main depôt established on Cooper's Creek. Almost immediately on Wright's arrival at the camp a messenger arrived in hot haste from Melbourne to announce that McDouall Stuart had nearly crossed the continent. Wright forthwith despatched two men to overtake Burke if possible, and acquaint him of the fact, so that he might avail himself of the route taken by Stuart in the event of his not being able to proceed in the direction he himself had marked out. Wright remained at Minindie awaiting the return of the two men. Weeks passed, and no return. Messengers were sent in search of them, but in vain. Not the least trace of them could be found. The searchers all returned, horses wearied and broken down by starvation and the excessive heat, for already it was approaching the summer season. Wright then thought it was time to move the men and stores to Cooper's Creek, which he was sent back by Burke to do, but which he had, on his own judgment, assumed to delay until the return of the two messengers which he had sent out. This change in the programme occasioned considerable confusion. Burke was anxiously waiting at Cooper's Creek for the part of the camp that he had left at Minindie, and wondered what could have occurred to delay them. He never dreamed that his plans would be changed or interfered with by his subordinate officer. Such, however, was the terrible fact—a circumstance that led to no end of perplexity, miscalculations, and disaster. The summer, with its scorching sun and oppressive heat, was upon them. The thermometer was registering 130° F. in the shade. The grass was being burned up, and the rivers and rivulets drunk dry. The multitude of little streams that danced joyously through the verdant meadows a few months before, and encouraged Burke to send back Wright to bring up the rear, had now all vanished before the burning rays of the sun. The earth was parched and dry; even the birds that were wont to mingle their song-notes with the murmuring waters had gone. Desolation and barrenness had claimed universal sway; horses were worn out, and had to be left on the desert to die; men sickened, became despondent, pallid, ashy, and faint for want of water, footsore and exhausted, and unable to trudge along. The whole caravan was compelled to halt, and give the men a chance to recover. Even the camels, which are noted for their ability to endure privations and fatigue, became lank and unfitted for their task.

In the meantime Burke and Wills had waited long beyond the time allotted for the appearance of Wright with the remainder of the expedition. They could wait no longer, and taking six camels, one horse, and provisions sufficient for a three month's tour, and leaving the remainder in charge of a man by the name of Brahe, with two men, Gray and King, they resolved to start out across the country toward the Gulf of Carpentaria. They left word that if they did not return within three months Brahe was to consider them lost, and that he was then at liberty to return to Melbourne. Burke and his three companions followed up the course of Cooper's Creek for a considerable distance, on account of the water and grass being abundant in that locality; then striking northwards, on the 140° meridian, they pressed rapidly on until they struck a stream, which they named Eyre Creek, and which they continued to follow for several days, the grass being abundant, and the water supply very much needed to sustain the animals. When the creek took an eastern direction they were compelled to leave it, and go directly north. After six weeks of travel through a country of varied character—at times well wooded, an abundance of excellent fodder for their camels and horse, and at times through a region of sand, rocks, and barrenness—they finally struck a river, which they named Cloncurry. Its water flowed in a north-easterly direction, which seemed to give them hope that it must be a branch of some of the rivers that emptied into the Gulf, or was itself such a river. They followed it until it joined a much larger body of water, which Burke afterwards found to be the Flinders. There was an abundance of palms and verdure. Burke and Wills left Gray and King on the banks of the Flinders in care of the worn-out animals, while they pressed with all haste to the Gulf; and returning immediately they reached the camp where they had left Gray and King. The camels had greatly gained in strength by the rest and the abundant grazing they had enjoyed for several weeks, but the provisions had become well-nigh exhausted. It needed the utmost care and subdivision to make them hold out until they should reach the main depôt on Cooper's Creek, which was left in charge of Brahe, and to which, by this time, Wright had without doubt come with his abundant supplies from the Darling. Their provisions were now scant, and could last but a few days longer by using the utmost economy. Gray was sick, and nigh exhausted; so were they all. They trudged wearily onward day after day. Their food was now all gone. It was still in the beginning of March, and six weeks of a trying journey before them. They killed one of the camels, dried its flesh, and upon this they subsisted. This also very soon was consumed. They now killed their only horse. Gray succumbs, and dies on the desert, and is buried in a rude fashion. Burke, Wills, and King are all of them sick, weary, and half-starved. They are not far distant from plenty on Cooper's Creek, if only their strength and courage holds out. They are brave and hopeful, and gathering up all their energy they brace themselves for the struggle. At last they succeed in reaching the camp, but oh, the fearful disappointment! all had departed. Like ancient Israel, who having travelled "three days into the wilderness" without water are cheered by the appearance of a spring in the desert far in the distance, to which they rush in their eagerness and thirst, but when they taste the water they cry "marah," for they are bitter. There was written upon the heart of each of this band "marah"—disappointment and bitterness. As they looked around in their despair they discovered the word "dig" in large letters carved into the bark of a tree. They lost no time in obeying the command, and digging they came upon a small supply, and a brief statement of the cause of their departure. They learned that Brahe had remained there for almost a month and a-half over the period he was instructed to stay, that Wright had not put in an appearance from the Darling, and that he only left when his own supplies had become so nearly exhausted as to make further delay dangerous. Brahe had just gone that morning, and was now on his way to the depôt on the Darling.

Burke, Wills, and King ate a hearty meal, and rested several days, but the small remnant of provisions warned them of the importance of reaching without delay some point of relief. A contention arose between Burke and Wills as to the course they should now pursue. The distance to the Darling was three hundred and fifty miles. Wills desired to take that course, because they knew it, and it was watered. Burke contended that Mount Hopeless was only one hundred and fifty miles distant, and there was on it a large sheep station, and the journey could be effected in a comparatively short time. Burke's plan was adopted. They set out along the course of Cooper's Creek until it spread into a wide marsh impossible to pass through. After wandering about in hope that they might see the peak of the mount on the horizon, they were disappointed; though within not more than fifty miles, it escaped their notice. Weary, footsore, and hungry, they were compelled to retrace their steps back to the camp. They killed their last camel, and drying its flesh they had a supply of food that would serve them for their return journey. They reached Cooper's Creek exhausted and sick. Wills was too ill to bear much more. While they had been gone Brahe had met Wright on his way from the Darling, and both came to the old camping ground to see if they could afford any relief or obtain any tidings of Burke and his party. They came when it was too late. They hurried back to the Darling, thence to Melbourne to announce their sad fate. Burke had learned, in his wanderings, of a small seed called "nardoo" which the natives used for food. He went in search of some tribe who could teach him its use, and how to collect it. They were successful. Having found a native camp, they were received in a friendly way, and were taught the manner of obtaining this food. Upon it they subsisted for some time. The natives showed them many acts of kindness. They broiled fish for them, helped Wills, who was very weakly, by carrying his bundles for him on the journey, and in other ways showed their good heart towards the wanderers. On this food they lived for several weeks. It could not last. It did not afford sufficient nourishment to sustain their strength. Wills was speedily sinking. In their extremity Burke and King resolved to go in search of some native tribe. They had to leave their sick companion behind in their rude hut. Wills wrote a letter to his father, gave them his watch, and bade them adieu. His friends, Burke and King, collected, and placed near his head, all the nardoo they had in store, as the last token of esteem they could give to their dying friend, and then departed. Burke and King struck out as wanderers in search of some blacks, who, in their extremity, they could appeal to for help. On the second day out Burke succumbed to the overwhelming burden that had crushed his manly spirit. He could go no further. He laid down sick, weak, and utterly prostrated. He had not the power of will to rally. King gathered a few bushes together to make for his companion a dying bed as soft as the hard conditions of the wilderness would afford. On this he placed him. Burke gave King his watch and pocket-book to carry to his friends in Melbourne, and then bade adieu to earth. He died, and passed from the hardships he was called upon here to endure. King hurried back to the creek only to find that Wills, too, had given up in death. He buried him, and then went in search of a native's hut. He fell in with a tribe that were kindly disposed towards the weary wanderer. King became a great man among the natives, whom he cured of some of their diseases, and to whom he taught the art of shooting birds and animals. It was not a life of luxury that he enjoyed, nor did he expect it. It was one of anxious waiting and hoping against hope. The natives were kindly, but their tenderness was not suited to his aching wants. He gradually became weaker and more delicate. Wright and Brahe had returned to Melbourne, and announced the loss of their chiefs—that they were still wandering in the wilds of the desert they knew not whither. No time was lost by the people of the colony. The Press took up the broken story of the expedition, and told it in a manner that aroused every heart, and stirred the nation in sympathy. Search parties were organised all over the continent. The Royal Society that had sent them out ten months previously now sent Mr. A. W. Howitt to search in the region of Cooper's Creek and all the country around. A party was sent by Queensland to search in the neighborhood of the Gulf of Carpentaria, under the direction of Landsborough.

South Australia sent McKinlay northward, through the region of Lake Torrens, Lake Eyre, Mount Hopeless, and Cooper's Creek Walker, with a Queensland party, was sent across the country to explore the region lying between Rockhamton Bay and the Gulf. These all made diligent search, and many other smaller parties had taken upon themselves a similar task. Mr. Howitt's party went direct from Melbourne to Cooper's Creek, on the theory that if any of the party of Burke and Wills were alive they would most surely endeavour to reach that point, it being their main depôt. In prosecuting their search along the creek they discovered camel's tracks, and thus gaining a clue they sought from the native blacks to obtain further knowledge, and were rewarded by being brought to one of their huts where King was sitting sick, and ready to die. He was taken charge of by the rescue band, who ministered to every want. Under the care and attention he received he speedily rallied, and regaining his strength was enabled to relate the story of the expedition from the beginning to the end. How remarkable a providence it was that preserved King amid all the dangers and deaths that occurred. Had this one link in the chain been severed the world would have been in total ignorance concerning this, the most remarkable discovery ever made by any one band of explorers. King not only had been able to preserve and give a verbal account of the terrible journey, but was the instrument in the preservation of those remarkable records made by the pen of Wills himself, whose faithful recital of their experiences from day to day in their most minute details have preserved for the world a true and full picture of the bitter experiences through which the men passed, and also records the hopes, ambitions, and triumphs that accompanied their great sacrifices. The party returned to Melbourne with King in November, 1861. Another party was immediately organised, and sent to bring down the bodies of Burke and Wills for interment. This party was expected to make investigations of the country through which they passed, and succeeded in rendering good service in the interest of science as well as bearing back the remains of their fellow citizens. They arrived in Melbourne, *via* Adelaide, on the 28th December, 1862, and Burke and Wills were accorded the honor of a public funeral. A monument was subsequently erected in the centre of the city of Melbourne to perpetuate the memory of these heroes, who voluntarily left home, comfort, and friends in the interest of their country, and sacrificed life and all its possibilities—

for they were yet in their prime of manhood—for the good of the generations to come. King was voted an annuity by the Government of Victoria of £180 per year. He died on the 15th January, 1872, of a disease that owed its origin to the exposure and privations through which he passed on the desert.

John McDouall Stuart will ever stand in history, associated with her chief explorers, one of the most honorable and successful. His long experience with several expeditions of historic value, and his personal efforts in more limited spheres of investigation, have made him an important factor in the many efforts made in the opening of the interior. His experience with Sturt in 1844, when they crossed the Stony Desert, gave him an insight to the difficulties and dangers the explorer of that period had to encounter, and thus prepared him for the hardships through which he was destined to pass in subsequent years. He inaugurated several small expeditions to explore portions of South Australia in the immediate neighborhood of Torrens and Eyre Lakes, and discovered many localities that have been occupied as sheep runs with immense advantage. In fact, his reports have been relied upon by the Australian Governments more than upon any other living geographer. His observations have been characterised by an exactness that gave them great value. His frequent excursions within a limited radius from Adelaide made him invaluable to the squatting interests of that colony, for all his minor attempts in examining the capabilities of the soil were prolific of success. At his instance, and on his judgment, scores of prosperous runs have been established all over the South Australian colony. But an explorer of such genius and ambition could not be circumscribed within the narrow limits of any division of the continent. His ambition was as wide in its grasp as the continent, and hence his work was co-extensive with the commands of Australia itself. He made several attempts to penetrate to the centre, and to explore outwards. He was desirous of crossing the country from one side to the other. In this arduous undertaking he was successful, and his chief success in this regard is perpetuated in the great overland telegraph line which runs from Adelaide to Port Darwin, and thence connects with submarine lines that afford us the means of communication with London, Europe, and in fact with all parts of the world.

His first attempt to cross the continent was in 1859. South Australia had offered a reward of £2,000 to the first who should accomplish the feat.

He did not undertake the expedition for the reward simply. His heart was in the work, but doubtless it made some difference in the extent and completeness of the outfit. He pushed northward from Adelaide, and made satisfactory progress through the untravelled waste of Central Australia until he came within five hundred miles of Van Dieman's Gulf, when he was compelled to return, more because of the overwhelming number of blacks that opposed his progress than from any failure on the part of his men. He made another effort the following year, and succeeded in reaching a point within two hundred and fifty miles of the northern coast. A failure in his supplies compelled him to return. It was a report of this expedition that was sent to Burke and Wills when they were waiting at Cooper's Creek for Wright, who was expected from the Darling. It was received by Wright, and sent to Burke and Wills by the two messengers whom he commanded to return, and for whose return he waited beyond due time. Stuart made his great triumph in 1862, a year later than Burke and Wills' successful, though fatal, expedition, and in entire ignorance of it. Having made more complete arrangements he pressed along quickly by the same route as his former attempts and reached Van Dieman's Gulf, and returning by the same reached Adelaide the very day that Howitt and his party bore back the remains of Burke and Wills. Though these latter were the first to accomplish the transcontinental pilgrimage, yet the Adelaide Government justly considered that their offer of £2,000 were due to, and fully earned by, their fellow townsman, Stuart, and to him it was paid as an acknowledgment for services that cost not only time and money, but a great deal of hardship as well. Out of the results of these expeditions grew the enterprise of constructing a telegraph line across the continent from Adelaide to the Van Dieman's Gulf, which was accomplished in 1872; and immediately following this enterprise the entire country was utilised in the interests of sheep-raising, so that in a very brief period large stations were established at wide intervals along the line.

The question of exploring from the centre to the western coast engaged the deliberations of the many who were interested in the development of geographical science. The construction of the overland telegraph had the effect of awakening an intense desire to extend their investigations. This general interest in the question called to the front a number of men who were prepared to forego personal ease and pleasure for the sake of the

honor and advantage that the increased knowledge of the interior would bring. Among these is to be mentioned Warburton, who undertook the task of travelling through to the western coast from the centre. His expedition consisted of himself and son, two white men, and two Afghans, seventeen camels, and provisions sufficient to last for eight months. He started from Alice Springs, which is situated in the midst of an oasis of beauty and foliage, near the Tropic of Capricorn, and is itself a valley of loveliness in the mountain range along the route of the telegraph line. The country westward was of a sandy, barren character. Here and there were to be seen on the weary track only a few tufts of grass—the sandy stretch of country having very limited areas in which foliage appeared. About four hundred miles westward they had to cross ridges of red sand, which had a terrible effect upon the eyesight, and which years before intercepted the progress of Gregory, who was compelled to abandon the attempt to cross them because of lack of water, and their great power of retaining the heat. Warburton, however, was better prepared for the work, and persevered and accomplished the task, after having endured the greatest hardships and suffering, the loss of fifteen camels, only two out of the entire number surviving the journey Although his men were brought to the verge of the grave at times, still they rallied, and at last succeeded. The expedition reached Oakover River, and sailing from that point they were returned to Adelaide whence they had departed, nine and a-half months previously. During the latter part of their journey they were forced to subsist on the dried flesh of their camels, and what chance game they could obtain from the natives.

Ernest Giles, in 1873, made an unsuccessful attempt to accomplish the same feat. Warburton's expedition, though successful in crossing the plains, did not realise the expectations of the country in regard to pastoral interests. He had found no good grazing lands, and young Giles was confidant that vast areas must be in the unknown territory of Western Australia, and making moderate preparations he started from the transcontinental telegraph, and going westward passed through a country so completely barren and destitute of animal and vegetable life that he was compelled to abandon for the time being the task of crossing it. Mr. Giles made a second attempt in 1875. This time he was successful. His experience on a former occasion made him cognizant of the necessity of being thoroughly equipped for such a task, and hence his preparations consisted of eighteen camels and ten men. In the comparatively short space of six months they succeeded in crossing from the telegraph line in South Australia through to Perth. They took a route mostly along the thirtieth parallel. They found this region to be covered with a dense scrub without water. Here and there, at immense distances, were to be found small streams, but insufficient for pastoral purposes. The expense of the outfit was borne by Sir Thos. Elder, of South Australia, as was that of Mr. Warburton's in 1872. This gentleman, who owned a large number of camels, evinced great generosity and interest in geographical science in expending much time and money in fitting out expeditions for service in this department.

Another name worthy of mention in this connection is that of John Forrest, and with him is associated that of his brother Alexander. John Forrest was Government Surveyor, in the service of Western Australia, and became deeply interested in the expedition of Dr. Leichhardt. The results of the search made by the several colonies in his behalf failed to satisfy him. He scarcely believed they were sufficiently thorough, and he could not rid himself of the idea that in all probability Leichhardt reached the western portion of the continent, and if not murdered might be a wanderer or captive among some of the hostile bands of the interior. He went in search of the lost explorer in 1869. They left Perth on the 16th April, and went in a north-easterly direction through a country that they reported to be barren, and unfit for occupancy. They returned in about three months and a-half without gaining from the natives any information respecting the lost Leichhardt.

In 1870 both John and his brother Alexander were sent out by the Government of Western Australia to examine more thoroughly the coast of the Great Australian Bight. Eyre's remarkable expedition in 1840 only served to give a general knowledge of the coast. The Forrest brothers expedition was intended to make a more thorough examination thereof in view of its possibilities for pastoral purposes. They succeeded in making the trip along the coast in five months, reaching Adelaide on the 27th August. Their report to the Government confirmed that of Eyre's published thirty years previously. Their next expedition was made in 1874, and its main purpose was to become better acquainted with the character of the country between the western coast and the South Australian settlements near Lakes Torrens and Eyre. The journey was accomplished with very few incoveniences other than those arising out of expected exposure to the suns rays on the Sandy Desert. They found all along the Murchison River a fine stretch of good pastoral lands, and a number of kangaroos, emus, bronzewing pigeons, parrots, cockatoos, black swans, and ducks. They reached the telegraph line in South Australia, having passed through a country which, as a whole, is of little value. Throughout the vast extent of waste there are oases of beauty and value, but so limited that it is scarcely to be expected this desert can ever be utilised as an abode for man, unless the future may discover methods of irrigation unknown to modern genius.

The Gregory brothers, both Augustus and Frank, contributed somewhat to the exploration of the great north-west, and although they were baffled in their work by the difficulties of the way, they succeeded at least in satisfying geographers that intervening between the western coast and the telegraph line of Central Australia there extended plains of sand and desolation that entitles that region to the designation that already attaches to it—"The Great Australian Desert."

Exploration thus far has established the fact that the most valuable areas of the continent are confined to the eastern half. What future exploration may develope is beyond our ability to prophesy. There doubtless are vast areas of land and mines and wealth that lie concealed awaiting the advent of some new generation yet unborn. Nature has always locked within her bosom treasures that are meant to be the reward of earnest investigation on the part of each succeeding generation. She will never cease to have new wealth to confer upon her toiling sons as they each come and prove themselves worthy of her bounty. The gems of the past generations will shine dimly when compared with the sparkling brightness of those precious stones that will deck future crowns. There will never come a time when nature shall cease to have new wonders wherewith to astonish her children, to gladden their hearts, and to reward them for their industry. Is it just for us to think that all that nature has to give her grand heroes who endure hardship and sacrifice their lives is a cold marble slab, or the written page, or the artist's crude lines as the reward? We would rather believe that not one act that has contributed to the individual or the general good will ever fail.

CHAPTER XXVI.

AUSTRALIAN RESOURCES.

THERE is nothing that interests the general reader of history so much as the sources of a country's wealth—the means by which its people live and gain a competency. It is true there are classes who value a country for other reasons. The soldier reads history from the standpoint of warfare. The bloody page possesses a charm to him that the agriculturist cannot appreciate. The story of a contest in which figures the thundering cannon, the glittering sword, the clash of arms, and the shout of victory are the chief things that make up history suited to the soldier mind. The plough-share and its triumphs figure as the chief factors in the esteem of the farmer. A clergyman counts the churches, while the doctor estimates the country's strength by the state of its pulse. The masses are more concerned about the means of obtaining bread, clothing, and personal comfort, and value a nation more on this account than they do for any so-called heroic deeds of bloodshed.

Australia attaches more importance to her pastoral, agricultural, mineral, and commercial interests than to any other. She is one of the leading pastoral countries of the world. Her magnitude in this respect is not properly understood even by her own people, and much less by those outside. She is the first among the nations in the production of wool, and America comes second. Relying upon figures taken from the *Washington Republic* the comparison would stand thus: "The value of wool in Australia per annum will represent £20,000,000 ; that in the United States of America, £14,500,000; the Argentine Republic, £9,000,000; Russia,

£8,500,000; Austria-Hungary, £7,500,000; France, £6,000,000; and Germany, £5,500,000." The above figures are all taken from the source mentioned, except that of Australia, which are copied from our own official reports, and hence the comparison may be relied upon as being approximately correct. The rapidity with which this enterprise has developed is a marvel to contemplate. It is just one hundred years since the first sheep were introduced to the continent, and although the official reports tell us that there were forty-four sheep brought with the first settlers, the first census taken in the May following tells us there were only twenty-nine in the colony. From this small beginning they have multiplied until they have reached, according to the official reports in 1887, the inconceivable number of over 86,000,000, and distributed among the several divisions of the continent as follows:—New South Wales has 39,168,304; Victoria, 10,770,403; Queensland, 9,690,445; South Australia, 6,696,406; Western Australia, 1,809,071; Tasmania, 1,608,946; and New Zealand, 16,677,445. The past year has been one of the most favourable ever known, from which we are justified in adding to the above figures merely the ordinary increase, which will give us at this date not less than 100,000,000 sheep. The immense flocks that one meets on the plains astonish the traveller unaccustomed to a pastoral country. In every part of the continent, remote from civilisation as well as near, are large runs called sheep stations, and flocks sometimes numbering three or four hundred thousand. Formerly the flocks were taken care of by shepherds. More recently they are inclosed by wire fencing, and removed from one enclosure to another as occasion may demand. The attention to sheep-farming is on the increase. The number of stockholders registered at present is over 110,000. Small holders of land, as well as the squatter or man who leases from the Government thirty or forty thousand acres of land, finds sheep-raising to be profitable. The room for increase in the colonies is practically unlimited. The area occupied at present in this enterprise is greatest in the colony of New South Wales. Out of the 200,000,000 acres of land comprising the colony there were, in 1886, 142,927,493 acres held under lease for pastoral purposes, most of it for sheep-farming. In Queensland there is room for the greatest increase. In this colony there has been very rapid growth in the last ten years, although the excessive drought of the three years preceding 1886 had the effect of checking their growth, and in some parts largely decreasing their numbers, but grazing facilities and width of area is to be found to a greater extent in Queensland than in any of the other colonies. Victoria has her available tracts pretty nearly all occupied by squatters. South and West Australia have considerable room for extension, while New Zealand, both North and South Island, have leased out most of their territory for this purpose. The area under lease no doubt will bear a large increase in the number it is capable of carrying, there being allowed at present about three and a-half acres to each sheep.

A drought for two seasons (which is a rare occurrence) is attended with great loss; in many parts, especially those remote from the large rivers, it will be fifty per cent. The country of late years has felt the importance of conserving the waters, and considerable has been done in this direction.

A great deal of attention has been given to the improvement of the breed. Those engaged in this department have spared neither time nor money in bringing up the quality of the wool. Thousands of pounds have been paid for imported breeds of known excellency, and the result has been a quality of wool that commands the first prices in the markets of the world. When it is remembered that fortunes are made in the course of a few years from this source, and that ordinarily flocks will double and treble in the course of three or four years, at the same time yield an average of five pounds of wool per sheep during the period of increase, at a cost of not more than tenpence per year for rental, care, and all other expenses, one cannot wonder that the aristocracy of the country—the richest men in the colonies—are those who have devoted attention to the sheep industry.

Cattle.

The raising of horned cattle is an industry only second to that of sheep. The grasses are favourable to the development of this source of wealth. In former years, in fact, it was deemed by many to be a more certain source of profit. Beef was always in demand at fair remunerative prices, and their tallow never failed to command a good market value. Many pastoralists of wealth deal exclusively in this kind of stock, and have made it pay largely upon the capital invested. This industry is most prosperous in the colony of Queensland. Though they have only about one-third the population of either New South Wales or Victoria they have more than three times the number of cattle. In fact, she has as many as all the other Australian Colonies put together. New South Wales had, twelve years ago, more than double the number of cattle that she has now. There is to be noted a steady decrease from year to year in their number. In 1876 New South Wales had 3,134,086 horned cattle, and in 1887 she had only 1,367,844—not one half of the former number. On the other hand, there has been as steady an increase in the colony of Queensland, her northern neighbor. The facts only indicate that Queensland is better adapted to the raising of cattle, while New South Wales obtains the best results from the product of her flocks of sheep. Throughout the Australian continent in all the colonies, irrespective of the imaginary lines that mark their boundaries, and separate one colony from the other, live stock of every description thrive, as the official reports clearly show, and the capabilities of the soil in this respect is beyond the ability of anyone to calculate.

Horses.

Horses, from the beginning of the colonisation of the country, were introduced, and found to be profitably raised. Perhaps no country in the world can present at their Agricultural Shows such a display of fine horses as are to be seen in these colonies. New Zealand is doubtless taking the lead in draught, and the other colonies in race and coaching breeds. The colony having among her first settlers many Englishmen of the leisure class who were familiar to the racecourse at Home and having lived in such an atmosphere carried here a great love for the horse, naturally sought to create the same sentiment in this clime. The isolation of the continent from all other parts of the world induced her people to look to her own resources for enjoyment. She soon got the habit of relying upon herself for all her pleasures, and has thus brought her sports and products to a very high degree of perfection. It is said that the American is never so happy as when he gets on one of his railway coaches, and goes somewhere—he does not care much in what direction, as long as he gets away from home; the millionaire will leave his palace, and go into some rude hut for a month or two; and the artizan will exchange cottages with his fellow for a time; they all want change; they strive to get away from themselves and their own. The whole nation gets on a Pullman palace car, and travels, it matters little where; they simply wish "to go." It is not so with the

Australian. He believes emphatically in himself and in his own. He relies on what he has got, and bends all his energies in making it better, and soon comes to believe it is the best. His sun and moon are the brightest and warmest that shine; his land is the most prolific; his sheep grow the choicest wool; his cattle produce the best beef; and his horses beat the world. Her draught horses have for many years been in demand in America, and have commanded the highest prices in that market. A good draught horse is not to be found in all portions of the continent. In fact, this class of horses have not had all the attention they ought to have had in former times; still, during the few past years there has been more care taken in the development of a class suited to the dray. The horse that has come in for the largest amount of consideration in these colonies is the race horse, and in this respect some of the fastest runners on record are to be found here. The racecourse is the chief sport of the nation. Every town and county almost has its racecourse, and every locality has its special breeders for the turf. Even the remote portions of the country, where there is nothing but sheep runs and stations established at distances of ten, twenty, and thirty miles apart, and at each station perhaps a group of a dozen families constituting the entire settlement, there are to be found the local racecourse and the purest breed of blooded stock. Men, women, and children all talk "horse," and bet upon their favorites with a zest and interest that dwarfs all other subjects. It is their chief sport, and not confined to one sex. Men and women, boys and girls, all evince a fondness for the animal beyond that known in any other part of the world. The whole nation worships the horse. There is no city or municipality that will tolerate abuse of the animal. Cruelty towards it is punished severely, and the sentiment is so universally inculcated in the education and sentiment of the people that I have seen a little child of five years of age work itself into a towering rage on witnessing a man on the street whip his horse because of its balking at the foot of a hill. The child but reflected the universal feeling. The Australian is pre-eminently a horse-loving people. Nowhere in England or in America will one see such sights as at Flemington and Randwick, the two chief racecourses in the colonies. Though these are located, the one at Melbourne and the other at Sydney, they are in no sense local. They belong to, and have been made by the Australian without respect to the colonial boundary that divides the one colony from another.

On "Cup" day 150,000 people will go to Flemington from all portions of the continent, and join in the general holiday. "For every man training in England or America there are six in New South Wales, Victoria, and Queensland" was what a jockey said the other day to his friend who was on a visit from America, and who expressed astonishment at the universal interest there was manifested in training of horses on every hand. It is not to be wondered at that among the live stock of the continent there is such a showing. The last report gives the number of horses in the Australian colonies to be 1,372,756, making one horse to every three inhabitants, counting men women, and children. There is no future of Australian civilisation more pleasant to contemplate than this one. Moralists may deplore the widespread practice of betting that has grown up in connection with this sport; but is not the evil more than offset in the moral sentiment that has permeated all classes through the kindly feeling that has been developed by the universal regard and esteem in which the horse is held.

Pigs.

Though a very profitable enterprise, the raising of pigs has not kept pace with the general growth and increase in other departments of live stock. They are easily raised, but the absence of wild nuts and suitable roots and grasses for the development of this animal has confined the industry to the immediate wants of the people themselves. The pig is not grown here for the foreign trade, but simply for home consumption. To make good pork in this climate requires the animal to be fed on cereals, and the cost would be more than would be found profitable. The largest yield in the Australasian Colonies is from New Zealand, where there are raised about two hogs to every three inhabitants; the average in Australia being less than one to three. The smallest average is in Queensland, where it is one to six, the heat of that region being unfavorable to their development. When the country comes to devote its attention particularly to the cultivation of the soil, and use the power thereof in the production of cereals, hog-raising will become not only profitable, but one of the most paying industries of Australia.

Agriculture.

The capabilities of the soil in regard to its power of producing crops is yet in its infancy. There has been comparatively little done in this respect. The Australian has found during the past one hundred years that it did not require any extraordinary effort to secure a livelihood by watching his sheep and cattle grow, and his horses win at the racecourse. He has not concerned himself very much about the more difficult science and art of good farming. We do not mean to say that there is no good farming to be found in Australia by any means. There are agriculturists of the most advanced type, who have not only experimented with her soil, but who have grown rich from its products, and the number of them is increasing year by year; but as long as wool commands such prices, and cattle thrive on such easy conditions, and mines are so prolific, the incentive to the somewhat laborious routine of a farmer's life is wanting, and therefore the progress will be slow. It is estimated that there are not more than perhaps 43,000 holders of the soil in New South Wales, about an equal number in Victoria, about one-half as many in Queensland, and a proportionate number in the several colonies, the largest proportion being in New Zealand. The large leaseholders employ their lands for sheep and cattle.

The whole area under cultivation in 1887 was less than a million acres in New South Wales, there being less than an acre to each inhabitant. This limited area is not because of any lack of soil of the most paying quality, but because her people believe life can be obtained on easier terms. They are not disposed to exhaust their energies in toil that they have not yet found the need of.

Large portions of the continent are well adapted for all kinds of agricultural pursuits, and when a farmer class shall have immigrated to this country, and shall have adopted agricultural methods in treating the soil, it will be found that few countries possess the productive excellencies which she possesses to the same degree. But the great want of Australia is a class of intelligent farmers. Such are to be found here, but not in sufficient numbers to give character and repute to this special department. The density of her vegetable growths along her streams and the luxuriance of her foliage indicate the vitality of her soil and its wonderfully productive power.

Wheat.

The average yield of wheat in New South Wales is reported to be, for the past twenty-six years, $13\frac{1}{2}$ bushels per acre, and for the last fourteen years 15 bushels. Such an average has never been reported in any of the wheat-growing countries of the world outside of Australia. In America the average per acre for the same period was less than 9 bushels; in Austria and in Russia less than 10 bushels. In the other colonies of Australia the average during the same time is exceedingly different. In Victoria the average was 12.02; South Australia, 8.16; Queensland, 10.37; West Australia, 11.54; Tasmania, 18.19; and New Zealand, 26.09. This latter colony has a class of Scottish and English farmers of most practical and scientific type who follow this vocation, not alone for the wealth it brings, but for the luxury and sense of independence that are enjoyed by the owners of the soil, and that cannot be experienced by any other class. Tasmania follows close upon the former, and the result there is due largely to the same circumstances. It is true the climate and temperature of both New Zealand and Tasmania render them more suitable for the culture of wheat, but while these circumstances are factors in the production of these large averages, they are not the only factors. The skill and painstaking attention to latest improvements in agriculture and the intelligent study of methods and means of obtaining the best results will account chiefly in this or any other country for a numerical standard as high as that referred to in the above figures. The virgin soil in the more southern or colder climates almost invariably yield from 28 to 40 bushels of wheat, but crops taken year after year from the same lands for twenty years or more can only result in a decrease of average until perhaps not more than 7 bushels will be returned, and then it ceases to be profitable. There are millions of acres of the finest wheat-lands unoccupied, and awaiting the advent of such as have ordinary intelligence, and are not afraid to work.

Maize,

commonly known as Indian corn in North America, from the fact that the Indian or native American of very remote times used it as his chief article of diet. The practice of using the green unripe corn (or maize) by roasting it on the ear in the hot ashes was universal among them, and is esteemed by the European American to this day as the most relishable vegetable dish in its season. Its successful culture requires plenty of heat and moisture, and hence the more northern or warmer portions of the Australian continent are much better suited to its culture, although it grows to perfection in almost any part. About 4,000,000 bushels are at present produced, and the greater part in the more northern districts. It does not always command a very high price, but as the country grows older and the agriculturist begins to realise its superior pork-making qualities and its value for feeding horses and cattle, both for milk and beef purposes, there will doubtless be a more pressing demand for it, which will surely tend to increase its culture. As an article of human consumption it is not yet appreciated. The people in these colonies are entirely ignorant of its use, except in the form of starch, and as food for horses. The "Johnny cake" is a luxury to which they are strangers, and as for porridge made from its meal, or "puddings, gems, and fried flaps" from the same, they have not the most remote conception, and are quite content to drift on to eternity without a knowledge of its bone, muscle, and brain-giving energy. The largest quantity of maize is grown in the Queensland colony. Last year nearly 2,000,000 bushels were raised, making an average of about six bushels per head, whereas in the entire continent there is one bushel to each inhabitant. There are a few maizena manufactories engaged in the preparation of thereof. In time its use will increase its value, and tend to develop its culture.

Barley

is grown on the continent to great profit. The portions of the colonies that give the best results are in New Zealand, Victoria, South Australia, and New South Wales. Queensland, Tasmania, and Western Australia have not yet gone very extensively into its culture, although the soil and climate are suitable for its production even here. The demand has chiefly been for brewing purposes, although as hay it has been utilised to some extent. Different varieties are needed for these purposes. A moist climate is best adapted for this cereal, and hence the coast districts and Tasmania and New Zealand being islands subject to frequent rains and fogs are peculiarly adapted to the production of this grain.

Oats.

The oat grain is grown in many parts of the continent with very great success, and much profit. As an article of food for horses it cannot be surpassed. This grain requires a very large amount of moisture. A dry season is almost certain to be destructive to it, and for that reason farmers in the interior parts of the colony cannot rely upon it. Drought is so liable to come that it would be very unwise for the farmer to depend entirely upon this cereal. New Zealand and Tasmania, together with the coast regions of the main continent are the localities most suited to its growth. The circumstance of moist and dry climate has led to the cultivation of two classes of grain—the white oat and the brown Calcutta—this latter being the only kind that is at all certain in the dry season, the white oat requiring a moist climate. There are many varieties of the white oat that grow to great perfection. The New Zealand product is held in highest esteem.

Rye.

Rye is grown to some extent. It could be cultivated almost anywhere in Australia, especially in those regions where the soil is poor. The demand is so very light that few experiments have been made with a view to profit. The entire yield for the year ending 1887 was 16,739 bushels for New South Wales, and less than 50,000 in the entire continent.

Millet.

Millet is not extensively cultivated, though it grows abundantly. The demand is limited. It has not been grown for exportation. If the demand should increase, the grain can be cultivated with ease and profit. In 1885 the acreage sown to millet was 119, and the yield 1,843 bushels, about 15¼ bushels to the acre.

Hay.

The preparation of hay differs very materially from that adopted in England, Canada, and the Eastern and Northern States of America. The above all cut their hay from certain grasses. Australia, like the Pacific States of America prepares its hay crop principally from oats, wheat, barley, and rye. This forms the most nutritious fodder when cut while it is yet green.

Grass hays are to a very limited extent used. Clovers are being introduced with some considerable success. The alfalfa or lucerne of the western and southern portions of the United States, we think, ought to be cultivated with great profit. As many as seven crops of this clover have been mown in one year, and its milk-producing qualities render it most remunerative. Cattle and horses thrive well on it.

Pasture Fields.

In a country like this, where pastoral interests are, and must continue, to be the chief industries of the country, a great deal of attention will yet be paid to the culture and development of grasses for grazing purposes. The growing industry of dairying in all its branches of milk supply, cheese, butter, and butter-canning and condensation must soon have the effect of developing good pasture fields within circumscribed limits. While the open plains in all their magnificence and extent are well adapted for beef-making, they are not suited for the dairy, and hence the importance of producing a grass for grazing purposes.

In the coast regions in Queensland, New South Wales, Victoria, and South Australia, New Zealand, and Tasmania there have sprung up large dairy industries of late years, and through these firms many experiments have been made with the different grasses, and valuable knowledge has been gained in this way which will result in a complete revolution in grass-farming in the colonies. Almost the same conditions of climate and soil have developed the culture of alfalfa in the Pacific States of America, which has been relied upon as the basis of good grazing in that country. When mixed with other grasses, there is produced a crop that will stand a longer period, and carry a larger number per acre.

Dairy Farming.

The superior advantages enjoyed in Australia by the pastoralist in the large tracts of lands he can secure by low rental from the Government, and by purchase on most favorable terms, have rendered every encouragement to the dairy industry. The particular care exercised by many of our leading farmers in developing the milking quality of our cattle has been noticeable for many years, and within the last ten years there have been several dairy factories started, all of which have been very successful—not merely in a financial sense, but in producing articles of consumption that compare favourably with the products of any other country, and which in a large measure have taken the place of the imported article. Butter and cheese are being largely produced in the coast districts, both south and north, and the reputation these articles have obtained in the London market has stimulated this enterprise to a very great degree. Cheese factories on the mutual or co-operative plan are being established among the farmers of more limited means. They are thus enabled to derive all the profit accruing from the business. This industry is increasing rapidly of late years, and taking its growth in the recent past as an indication of its future development, we have every reason to believe that it will become one of the chief sources of the nation's wealth.

Tobacco.

Tobacco culture has grown into some importance during the few past years. In some parts of the colony of New South Wales and Queensland its development has been rapid and profitable. In fact, it has seldom failed in giving good returns on the capital invested. This industry is yet in its infancy, and it is scarcely possible to estimate its importance in relation to the future of the country. That it can be grown in several portions of Australia has been time and again demonstrated, and that it can be made to pay has also been made apparent, but for some reason it has not yet attained the reputation necessary to make it valuable in the markets of the world. Having never been in the habit of using this luxury of savage and civilised life, we are bound to acknowledge our inability to judge of its intrinsic value, but we are told by experts, who are considered by themselves to be first-class in their ability to discriminate between the Colonial and American brands, that the Australian tobacco is not equal to that of American production, unless it is stamped with a Virginia label, in which event it is said to possess all the merits of the American weed. It is very amusing to witness some of our Yankee cousins, with an air of Washington independence and self gratification, puff our colonial tobacco, and speak of its superiority over every other when it is manufactured under the label of the Stars and Stripes. The cultivation of tobacco must come to be a very extensive industry in the colonies, for the reason that our people almost universally use the article. They are second only to the American, who has been known to say, sacriligiously, that he believed "tobacco has been the means of saving more souls than the churches," and to give color to the correctness of this doctrine is to be mentioned the fact that the clergy of late years have become its warmest patrons, and thus teach its virtues, by example, to those whom they are expected to train. The plant requires a peculiar soil for its profitable production, but this condition seems to be well met in the following localities, all of which have cultivated it to their satisfaction and profit. Small farms in the vicinity of the Paterson River have been prolific in the growth of tobacco of a very superior quality, also about Glendon Brook, Wollombi, Jerry's Plains, Singleton, Scone, and Tamworth. The labour necessary to take care of this crop is not more than is needed in the cultivation of maize, and is attended with double the profit.

Large manufactories have sprung up all over the colony. In every important city there are to be found several carried on by heavy companies, besides smaller ones in the immediate neighborhood of its culture. In the Hunter District there are nearly a dozen giving employment to thousands of hands. The first tobacco factory was established at West Maitland, New South Wales, by Wolfe, Gorrick, and Co., in the year 1841, an American firm, whose extensive experience with the plant and its culture enabled them to offer much valuable information regarding soil and methods of developing it. It has been found to be one of the most remunerative industries. Three-fourths of a ton has frequently been raised to the acre, and it commands about £50 to the ton.

Peas, Beans, and Vetches.

The dryness of the interior portions of the continent will for ever bar the culture of the "green crops" embraced under the above caption. Plenty of moisture is imperative in their successful culture, and hence they can only become the products of New Zealand Islands, Tasmania, and a limited portion of the coastal valleys. Their great value in the feeding of pigs and for domestic use has not yet impressed the Australian. Food of all kinds has been so abundant, and obtained with so little effort from the soil that the necessity for experimenting with all kinds of possible crops has not been the rule. Peas, beans, and tares or vetches can be cultivated here with a success equal to that in any other country, and doubtless will be when the production of cheap food becomes a question of importance.

As an article of domestic diet these crops have not yet been appreciated. There is no better substance for the table than the bean, in some of the finer varieties. The Boston baked bean is a dish of universal merit and reputation, but in this country it is little known.

Roots.

All the ordinary roots that are cultivated in Europe and America grow here without difficulty. Potatoes, beets, turnips, carrots, and parsnips yield returns prolific as elsewhere, especially in the more southern localities. In New Zealand, Tasmania, Victoria, and the lower coastal portions of New South Wales they grow to greater perfection than in the warmer latitudes, and *vice versa* the quality of the sweet potato attains a greater degree of perfection in Queensland than in Tasmania.

The turnip can only be grown satisfactorily in a moist soil, but there are sufficient areas to make this profitable when its value for feeding cattle shall have been felt.

The beet and mangelwurzel is a crop of very great worth, and is grown in many parts of Europe and America as a sugar industry. Whether it can ever compete with the sugar-cane in this climate is a question that is not likely soon to be solved.

Vine Culture.

At a very early period in the history of Australia the adaptability of its soil and climate to the growth of grapes was tested and proved, and through a long series of years every variety of vine has been tried. The conditions that are found suitable in other countries are not always unerring guides to its culture in new lands. The vine culturists of this continent have learned more from experience than from the methods adopted in other countries. The first experiment made here was as far back as 1828, when on a moderate scale were planted a few acres, and from which was manufactured wine of a very passable quality. This much has been demonstrated that the character of the climate cannot always be tested by the thermometer. That instrument can test the warmth and chilliness of the air, but it cannot detect every ingredient in its composition in relation to the growth and development of the vine. The temperature of the champagne district may be the same as that of Burgundy and Madeira, but there is a peculiar bouquet imparted to the one that is distinguishable from that of the others. This circumstance alone requires time and skilful experimentation to analyse and take advantage thereof. Nothing but experience can ever adapt the known variety to the special locality. It is found that the vine that grows to the greatest state of perfection in one place will not always thrive and do well in another that possesses the very same conditions of climate; and what is true respecting the climate is even more so in regard to the soil. Soil is a very difficult matter to understand without experimentation. Even when the main constituents are very nearly the same, there are so many minor circumstances that make it different. We cannot always go out and select the appropriate field for any special vine. This takes time, but it is time alone that will ever be able to discriminate between soils, climate, and varieties. The apparent long period that has elapsed since the grape was first introduced to this country will give an historic value to the reports made in recent years concerning this industry. There have been many failures in different portions of the country, and in many instances where one variety has utterly failed another has been found successful.

In a new country like Australia it would scarcely be fair to count the failures as so much evidence contraindicating its growth. The wine interests of the world have been built up by ages of most systematic study, experimentation, and change, and the grand results remain to attest the fidelity of the first laborers. Taking such a view of the history of this industry in these colonies, we have everything to congratulate ourselves for. Every year adds to the character and value of this product. We have reached not the first place, but among the honorable places in the list of wine-producers. Our wines need age to give them all that intrinsic merit that makes them marketable with wine consumers. The fact that our native manufacturers are yearly receiving increased orders from Europe, and not among the least is to be classed France, who is herself one of the largest and best wine-producers among the European countries, is evidence of its excellence. All the best varieties of vine known in Spain, Portugal, France, Italy, and Switzerland, and elsewhere have been tried in the localities deemed most suitable to its culture, and the knowledge obtained has been most satisfactory.

Both for table use and for wine, Australia must some day rank with the first nations of the earth in the extent and quality of its vineyards. It is contended by many moralists that with the rise of this industry will come a reform among her own citizens in respect to her drinking customs that should be hailed by all lovers of sobriety and good government. "So mote it be" would be our prayer if we were sure of the premises, the truth of which we are neither prepared to affirm or deny, although we confess that the position looks plausible. The drinking customs of this country are by no means light, as may be judged from the last report of the specially appointed commission, who, in their returns to Parliament, pointed out as a fact that the liquor traffic of New South Wales represents nearly £5 per head each year. The people drink excessively of whisky, rum, gin, brandy, champagne, and colonial beer. If the culture of the vine should result in changing these customs to the drinking even of the same quantity of wine, and the entire or even partial abandonment of the former, then would we say "May God speed the day." As an industry it is one of great promise; both climate and soil being well adapted to its culture. The area under cultivation, according to the report of 1887, was 5,840 acres, about two-thirds of which is used in the manufacturing of wines, the remainder used on the tables of her own people. The average yield per acre is about 200 gallons of wine. Special varieties of the vine flourish in every colony. Each portion is found to be suited to the development of some particular species, which fact cannot fail to be taken advantage of by European vineyardists, whose lands of late years have failed to give their former returns. The ordinary pest of the vine, phylloxera, has not yet proved a foe to its culture in these parts. Victoria, South Australia, Queensland, and New South Wales have large and successful vintages, which will claim special consideration when we come to note the local industries of each colony.

Minor Products.

The great number of soil products that have been tested here and constitute a part of the industries that have been found profitable preclude the possibility of particularising. We must therefore group many of them in the closing paragraphs of this chapter. The wide range of climate found in Australia, passing from that of the frigid to the torrid, has had the effect of inviting people of every part of the world in trying the cultivation of plants peculiar to each climate. The fact that the settlers in Australia came from every nation, and had among their number those who were not only familiar with the nature of the different plants, but many that were experts, gave the continent the greatest advantage in experimenting intelligently upon the agricultural possibilities of the nation. Flax, though not yet extensively grown, can be produced abundantly, especially in the moister portions along the coast and on the many islands. The soil most suitable for its culture is alluvial or sandy loam, or a loose marl. It will not grow on dry clay or gravelly soils.

Chicory is cultivated very successfully in the moist portions, and where irrigation is abundant. In fact, the best results are obtained in the dry regions where there are facilities for frequent irrigation. It is easily grown and very profitable, as much so as any other product of the soil. The difficulty of eradicating it once it has taken root is the chief objection to its culture. It is like the mustard and horse-radish plant, once it becomes an occupant of the soil it remains, and like the Australian "squatter," it requires most radical measures to upset its assumed claims of permanent ownership. This industry is capable of great extension.

Broom Corn has only of very late years received the attention that its importance demands. The ease with which it is grown in America, and its great abundance, has cheapened the article as one of import to a degree that was supposed to render its culture here a matter of no importance; but its value as a fodder induced some to speculate on its introduction. The result has been most satisfactory. The area of soil suitable for this plant is very extensive both in New South Wales and Queensland, only a very limited portion of which has been utilised for this purpose. When tried it has been remunerative to a large degree, both for broom manufacturing and for cattle. When it becomes important to raise fodder for stock, this industry will become one of the most flourishing.

Arrowroot is grown very extensively in the colony of Queensland. The loamy soil that is frequently met with in that colony is the most congenial. The value of arrowroot in commerce is so universally appreciated that one is led to look upon an industry of this kind as among the most important sources of a country's wealth. The enterprise is young on this continent, but one that has never failed in bringing satisfactory returns on the small capital invested. It is the small farmer of a few acres that can make this profitable, for the reason that its culture is simple and inexpensive. The soil is of the same character, and needs the kind of preparation that would secure good returns from the potato. The roots are divided and planted in rows, and then cared for in the same manner that potatoes are. The root is taken up, grated, and washed in water, and the sediment, when dried in the sun, becomes the arrowroot of commerce. The method and production is similar to that of potato starch. The yield per acre is enormous, sometimes reaching one thousand pounds.

The Sunflower is not extensively cultivated, and yet it is one that can be grown on all alluvial soils in this climate. It is an industry that must in the near future become very extensive. It is the best fowl food ever known. It requires less than a gallon of seed to an acre, and one acre will feed six hundred hens.

The Castor Bean, though a native of the West Indies, is suitable for this climate. The few experiments made have been satisfactory where tried. The method is simple, being very similar to the culture of Indian corn or maize. It requires an alluvial soil. The crop is both abundant and remunerative, and must become an industry of great value, unless mothers cease feeding the pernicious stuff to their helpless babies.

Sugar.

The sugar-cane is cultivated in the northern portion of New South Wales, and very extensively in Queensland. Nearly thirty years ago the experiment of sugar-cane growing was made in the neighborhood of the Clarence River. Its success from the beginning was not only complete, but it was beyond the sanguine expectations of the most hopeful. At that time there had been little progress made towards the settlement of that portion of the colony of New South Wales, but as soon as the fact was announced that it was destined to become a sugar-producing centre a general rush was made to that locality. The lands were extensively purchased both by speculators and the *bona fide* planter. Land speculators made extensive use of the Press to work up an enthusiasm in regard to it. The result was that a large area was at once placed under cultivation, and the industry became established as one of the leading enterprises that invited capital. The Clarence, Richmond, and Tweed rivers all ran through districts that soon became occupied by sugar plantations. Large refineries were established. Some of the finest plants in the world are here to be found. The industry extended so rapidly that land in that region was soon all taken up for the purpose of sugar culture. The industry spread to Queensland, where it found even a more congenial climate, and a wider range of area suitable for its culture. The exceeding cheapness of sugar for the few past years—selling as low as twopence per pound in the market—has checked its extension; but it is still paying largely, and is one of the firmly established industries of the northern portion of the continent, and doubtless will continue to be a source of great revenue.

Honey.

The almost universal profusion of flowers at all times of the year in bloom suggested bee-culture as an industry most likely to be profitable. The experiments made in this direction have met with a varying result. Some have been very successful, and many have been total failures. The flowers, though remarkable for their beauty, are not distinguished for their sweetness, and bees very readily find that out. The climate is not sufficiently cold to make it imperative for the bee to toil and lay up in store for the severity of the winter months. They soon learn that in a country like this life is obtained on too easy conditions to induce its kind to toil and fly, and search alone for man's happiness, and being wiser than even Solomon's bee, they have learnt the art of living without much work. Notwithstanding these drawbacks considerable has been done. The imported clovers and the cultivated flowers of suitable fragrance have been introduced, and have in a great measure taken the place of the native plants. It is an industry of considerable worth, although not as extensive as the wants of the country, yet its product is large and increasing.

Garden Fruit and Vegetables.

The garden is one of the chief incidents of an advanced civilisation. New countries are not expected to develope all the possibilities of the garden at once, and it is not to be supposed that our gardens can compare favorably with those of Europe or America. The people here have been too much occupied in tending their flocks and herds, and building houses, roads, and have been content as a rule to get along with the plainer and more substantial articles of diet, and hence you will find most of the farmers and artisans of Australia well satisfied with good beef, mutton, bacon, bread, potatoes, sugar, tea, and very little coffee as constituting their ordinary diet. The products of the garden are luxuries that they neither relish or hanker after, and hence it is a rare thing to see a well regulated garden connected with the large station of the " squatter " or " selector." This lack must not be taken as any evidence of unfruitfulness of the soil. Gardens are in sufficient numbers, and have attained such proportions as to have demonstrated the fact that all the ordinary products thereof can be cultivated, and are grown here in abundance, and are found on the tables of many of her people; while gardening has not claimed the attention of the Australian to any great extent, yet they are to be found around all cities and towns of importance. The Chinese are our chief gardeners, and to that class is to be accorded the honor of having developed garden products to the degree of perfection to which they have attained. Our markets at all times display a wider range of vegetation than perhaps can be seen in any other country in the world, and developed to a higher degree of perfection, among which may be mentioned—asparagus, artichoke (globe), artichoke (Jerusalem), cabbage, cauliflower, capsicum, celery, cress, cucumber, egg plant, garlic, gourd (like pumpkin), leek, lettuce, melon, mustard, onion, parsley, parsnip, pea, pumpkin, radish, rhubarb, squash, tamato, sugar maize, vegetable marrows, spinach, shallot (onion), watercress, herbs (sage, thyme), sweet marjoram (savory), mint, and all kitchen vegetables.

The Orange.

The orange has been cultivated in the country almost from its first settlement. The Rev. Mr. Johnson, the clergyman who came to the settlement with the first fleet in 1788, and who continued in the colony for eleven years, was the gentleman who introduced it. A few seeds obtained from oranges, brought from Lisbon he planted in his garden on the Parramatta, and they grew with such rapidity that in years afterwards he ate ripe oranges plucked from his own tree. From time to time he planted cuttings, and thus extended his orangery each year until his oranges were not only found in the Sydney market, but for many years were recognised as the choicest fruit to be had. Their growth was rapid, and the immediate result of his enterprise was to give to the early colonist a foretaste of the excellent fruit that is so abundantly raised in the colony to-day. The Rev. Mr. Johnson at that early date was more highly appreciated by the "wicked" people for his oranges than for his church services, though he was universally acknowledged to be a "godly and sincere man." The orange culture grew very rapidly around Parramatta at an early period, and still continues to flourish as one of the characteristic industries of the country. Oranges in some of their varieties are grown in all portions of the continent. Over eight million dozen oranges were grown last year, besides an equal number that, falling from the trees, were rendered unfit for the market. The trees grow to a very great size, some as high as forty feet, and over two feet in thickness. Over eight thousand acres were under cultivation in 1887.

The extent to which this country can be utilised in the culture of nearly all kinds of fruit is yet not fully known, but this much is apparent, that both in climate and soil it is marvellously adapted to nearly all fruits that can be raised elsewhere. Good yields have been attained from the pear, quince, persimmon, plum, lemon, peaches, apricots, passion fruit, strawberries, gooseberries, raspberries, walnut, almond, and many others. In fact there is scarcely any fruit or product of the soil but what can be produced abundantly in one or another part of the continent. The full capacity of the soil can only be estimated from the facts that have been made plain during the past one hundred years. Comparatively speaking we are still in our infancy, and it will require hundreds of years to come to make even an approximate demonstration of its full power of production. Not alone can be mentioned the products of cultivated fields above mentioned, but who can conceive how vast are her timber resources. Some of the most valuable species of wood are grown on the continent. Upon this question we need not dwell or do more than mention the fact.

Our achievements during the past century are worthy of admiration and congratulation. There are people who are ready to tell us we have no history because we have had no wars or serious bloodshed, in connection with which no names have figured largely on our annals. Our pride and glory is that our history is not one of carnage; it is the more glorious one of conquest without armies. It is the history of toil and its results—the grander story of the daily struggle of our fathers, mothers, brothers, and friends. Oh, who can do justice to the many lives that have all along the line done their part nobly and well in the quiet retreats of home, and also in the public walks of life—the one as an important factor in our history as the other? What record can be made sufficient to chronicle their heroic deeds? They placed themselves upon her virgin soil, and made the continent respond to their wishes; they wanted homes, and here they found them; they asked for lands, and the continent spread her millions of acres at their feet; they have changed the wilderness into a garden, and "made the desert blossom as the rose"; they have built cities and hamlets, manufactories and industries of infinite variety, and success has been their reward. The history of Australia has been a record of ordinary diligence and honest labor in her thousand avenues of trade.

Mineral Resources.

For many years after the first settlement was made the country looked to her pastoral and agricultural facilities as her main dependence. The character of her people was that of a pastoral and agricultural community. Their highest ambition was directed towards the acquirement of lands and the building of homes. Their chief efforts were expended in bringing their farms to a high degree of perfection. The wealth of the community was measured by the acreage under cultivation. It is true there were whisperings and occasional reports concerning sources of fabulous wealth concealed beneath her mountains, but they were deemed to be only the dreams of mad scientists or the tricks of speculators. For the last forty years of colonial history we have had ample demonstration of the existence of mineral wealth without limit or bound. While exploration was busy penetrating the trackless desert, scouring the mountain ravines, following the river courses, and bringing to light new stretches of country to gladden the pastoralist and tiller of the soil, the explorer of the depths, the mining engineer, the expert prospector, were busy investigating the possibilities of her mines, and the secret avenues that lead the delver to untold treasures of coal, gold, silver, copper, tin, lead, iron, shale, antimony, bismuth, manganese, cobalt, and precious stones innumerable. There came with these discoveries a craze that drew the masses from their flocks and their farms, and ever since has divided the attention of the people between the wealth of the field and the wealth of her mines, both enormous in their extent, and commanding the homage of the world.

It is impossible in the small compass of a chapter to give the reader a full view of all that has been accomplished in this department. The colossal fortunes that have been realised from her mines in the past forty years are the best explanation of their value. One meets with multitudes of people in this country who have surrounded themselves with every circumstance of wealth. They have horses and cattle and flocks; houses of splendid appointments and comfort; they have gardens of luxuriance and beauty; they dress in "fine linen and purple, and fair sumptuously every day," all of which attest the boundless wealth that has been dug from her mines and gathered from her fields.

Coal.

Coal was discovered in Australia in the year 1796, at Port Stephens, and in the following year at Port Hunter, or Newcastle. Lieutenant Shortland was sent by the Governor to investigate a report made by some members of a wrecked crew who, being cast on the coast, made a fire of coals that cropped out of the bank near the mouth of the river Hunter. Upon examination the report was found to be correct. Lieutenant Shortland found a seam of coal six feet thick. He then passed up the river for a considerable distance, and named it Hunter after the Governor. Subsequent investigations have revealed extensive coal deposits in several localities near the Hunter, in the Blue Mountains, and at Hartley. The coal regions may be divided for convenience into three districts. There is the Hunter River District, the chief depôt of which is the city of Newcastle, at the mouth of the Hunter River. This district comprises forty-five out of the seventy-three mines that are being worked under official inspection. There is the south coast district embracing Illawarra, about twelve mines being worked, and the western district extending into the western plains along the Castlereagh, embracing Marulan, Berrima, and mines in the Lithgow Valley. Queensland and New Zealand have found coal beds of considerable extent, but have not yet developed them. For many years this industry made very slow progress, but of late years the annual product of the above mines have reached three million tons, and are yearly increasing. The average price of the coal is nine or ten shillings, at Newcastle. The number of men employed in the mines in 1887 was 7,847. The quality of the coal is of the best. Up to the year 1829 the entire amount of coal taken from the mines was less than 50,000 tons, but up to 1887 there have been over 40,000,000 tons, at a value of £18,352,669, and adding the output for the years 1887 and part of 1888, we have a total of more than twenty millions of pounds sterling as the product of this one source of wealth. About sixty per cent. is exported to the other colonies, and to America (North and South), China, Japan, and Java. The future of this enterprise is beyond the ability of anyone to estimate. In extent the coal area is said to embrace 23,950 square miles, the seams of which vary from three feet to twenty-five feet. Practically, it is without limit. Each year we obtain from the official records new discoveries. The demand is increasing yearly from all directions. Manufactures are multiplying, and add to the demand. It is therefore apparent, that one of the chief resources of a country's wealth being the cheapness and abundance of its fuel, we cannot fail to grow and prosper.

Gold.

The king of all metals is gold. We might add with all truthfulness that the king above every other king is gold. Nothing can be compared to it. Mankind, as a rule, pays profounder homage to this one part of creation than all else put together. No god commands such universal adoration. The kings of the earth bow to it. All potentates acknowledge its supremacy. Commerce, trade, science, art, religion, and philosophy offer their costliest sacrifices at its shrine. It gives prominence and honor and influence to all that possess it. Its voice is heard at every court, and its commands obeyed. Every earthly benediction comes trooping in its train. It measures all other earthly blessings—the standard by which all things are judged. Churches, theatres, universities, halls of learning, stock boards, banking houses, insurance societies, printing establishments, and the mart estimate their respective prosperity by the favors its liberal hand bestows; and humanity generally estimates a country by the same rule.

In 1851 the first grand rush to the goldfields was made. Australia suddenly became known to the world, and then all eyes were turned towards her, and she became great among the nations of the earth because she had gold reputed to be in extent as boundless as her dominion. We rank third among the nations, according to an international report of the comparative product of 1886 taken from a foreign source. Russia comes first with 54,217,600 dollars (£10,843,320); America second with 30,800,000 dollars or £6,160,000; and Australia third with 21,000,000 dollars, or about £4,200,000. Gold is found in every portion of the continent. It is impossible to say how far this one source of wealth extends. Each year brings to light new discoveries in this field, which will no doubt continue for years to come. Immense fortunes have been made, and so have large sums of money been sunk in speculation. Stock gambling and wild speculations have been carried on to a great extent, and have involved thousands in ruin, as is the case in every gold-mining country in the world. Disappointed people are found in every city and part of the continent. Thousands have come to this country with all they possess, and have, in their eager thirst for gold, put every penny in some half-matured scheme or bogus mining firm, and after losing all, they have returned to the land whence they came with a dark picture of the misery endured by the average miner in Australia. Nevertheless the facts remain that untold wealth has been dug from her soil, and millions more await the digger.

The Mount Morgan mines of Queensland are to-day giving forth returns on capital invested as large as Ballarat, Bendigo, and Mount Alexander, in Victoria; Summerhill Creek, Turon River, Orange, Mudgee, Abercrombie, and Araluen, in New South Wales. Queensland promises to be the most fruitful portion of the continent in the production of this metal. Up to the end of 1886 she had produced £18,293,257.

Silver.

Silver was first discovered in 1862 in the Moruya district, but little was done. In 1872 the mines at Boorook, in the New England district, were discovered, from which was taken considerable silver. On the western slope at Sunny Corner, near Bathurst, silver was taken in large quantities, but the chief argentiferous district is on the Barrier Range, in the western portion of the Riverina district. For many years this was regarded as an uninhabitable desert, not fit even for grazing flocks, but within a very short time there have sprung up Silverton, Broken Hill, and other mining towns of ten or more thousand inhabitants. The exports for 1886 were valued at £492,029, and for the ten years ending in 1887 there have been exported £1,141,929 from New South Wales alone. Silver is found in each colony of the Australian group, Western Australia excepted. In Queensland there are many silver mines partially worked during the past few years, which will require time and capital to develop fully.

Copper.

About £5,000,000 have been taken from our copper mines. There is said to exist immense areas of this metal. Until this last year the low price of the product had the effect of decreasing the activity in copper mining. A new impetus has been given to the enterprise by the rise in its price, and within a few months of the latter portion of 1887 considerable excitement has been awakened. In 1872 copper sold at £108; in 1886 the best copper sold at £38 7s 6d, making the article scarcely worth the labor of producing it. A rise recently has started up the enterprise. Copper is found in every part of the continent. While the mining and exportation of this metal is remunerative, there are so many other industries so much more so that this one must abide time and greater necessity for its development.

Tin.

Tin was first discovered in Victoria, in the district of the Ovens River, in 1843. The Rev. W. B. Clarke, whose scientific mind led him into many fields of research, found tin in large quantities in New South Wales, near the Murrumbidgee. Afterwards in Inverell, at Tenterfield, and in unlimited quantities at the Barrier Range, in the extreme western portion of the colony of New South Wales. In Queensland large and extensive tracts of this metal have been found at Stanthorpe, Herberton, and North Palmer. In fact Tasmania, New Zealand, and Western Australia are all possessed of large areas in which this metal will become an industry of magnitude. In quality it ranks with the best in the English market, which fact has had the tendency of keeping alive the industry, notwithstanding the depression of the trade. The yield at present is equal in value to the gold product of New South Wales.

Iron.

Next to gold the most desirable metal is iron. This is found in quantities that baffle all estimation. We have seen the iron mountains of Missouri, in the United States of America, and have been amazed at their extent, but it is a problem not yet settled by the scientist of our own continent as to whether we do not possess areas of iron of even greater proportions. It is certain that it exists in many widely separated localities.

It is found in the form of hematite chiefly, and magnetite, which contain in many places fifty per cent. of pure iron. It is associated with coal beds, and from this circumstance smelting works can be carried on at a minimum expense, and thus avoid shipment of dross and slag. At the present time the chief working mines are at Mittagong and Lithgow, in New South Wales, but it is found in Victoria, South and Western Australia, Tasmania, and New Zealand. Its extent and quality in the colonies indicate a future industry that the writer of the present day dare not express.

Shale.

A species of coal called shale, from which is manufactured kerosene, is found in great abundance, and has been actively worked for the past twenty years. The price per ton of this product is about £2 8s 11d, occasionally going lower, and often commanding a better figure. A large number of men are being employed in this industry at the present time, and there is every indication of an increase. The quantity already taken out has been 480,000 tons, and constantly increasing.

Diamonds, etc., etc.

Diamonds and precious stones have become an enterprise of late years of no small proportions. In many parts of the continent are found a great number of most valuable gems. During the year 1885 the Australian Diamond Company obtained from one mine at Bingera 1,134 diamonds, which weighed 209 carats; the Crown Jewel Mine produced 285, weighing 105 carats. Precious stones are found in Queensland and New Zealand in large numbers, and a considerable trade is carried on in this particular, the nature and extent of which is difficult to estimate, from the fact that no very authentic reports are at hand to verify by figures the generally accepted fact.

One stands appalled at the magnitude of Australia's mineral wealth. It is yet in its infancy. Its achievements have been marvellous in the comparatively short time during which the attention of scientists have been directed to her mines. Investigation has seldom failed to bring to light new treasures from the depths of the earth. We cannot wonder that excitement followed discovery, and moved the nations to come and see. Capital came cautiously, and its first ventures were made with a trembling hand, then with a bolder front it sought to grasp the whole, and finally, in a speculative spirit, it plunged in with a reckless daring only equalled by its insatiable greed and tyrannous exactions from the poor laborer. What if frequently it has fallen in the conflict, and thousands have gone down in the wild speculations? It does not impair the wealth of the nation. Her gold and silver are still here. The whitened bones of her fallen victims will yet be shovelled up when succeeding investors come in the true spirit of commercial enterprise and honor, and recognising the rights of the laborer and the interest of trade equally will discover that Australia holds in trust for patient industry and honest toil boundless wealth—that every strata locks within her bosom for her own true sons and daughters the gold, silver, and precious gems that are meant to be the heritage of a future greatness excelling that of the past.

CHAPTER XXVII.

SECONDARY RESOURCES.

WE have briefly enumerated most of the distinctive sources whence the nation expects to derive her future importance. Her wealth in the first instance must be derived from her soil and her mines, but with these there will come to her wealth from abroad in connection with, and by the delopment of, her primal riches.

Commerce.

Nothing has been more remarkable than the development of the trade of these colonies. A person cognizant of the conditions under which the country was first settled, and its enforced dependence upon the Motherland for all, or nearly all, its means of sustenance for many years could not fail to be overwhelmed with the magnitude of its business, and wonder what it is that has given life to, and set all the wheels of industry in motion. While trade cannot be deemed an original source of wealth, without doubt it is an important gauge of a country's prosperity, and a direct source of a people's well-being. It is an incident of wealth, and is a factor in giving value to direct and original labor. The true economist reckons not merely on the depth and areas of gold and silver, flocks and herds, extent of territory and intrinsic wealth, but embraces in his calculations the first and secondary toilers needed to produce the article, and also the long list of workers who, by muscle and brain, are necessary parts of the machinery alike required to pass it on from one to another, until finally it is consumed, which last circumstance gives its real value and worth. Gold would be of very little account in the world in meeting or satisfying any direct necessity of mankind. We cannot eat it; we cannot wear it to advantage independantly of society as constituted. Gold derives its chief value from the circumstance of commerce. It facilitates the exchange of commodities. Through trade it has become the universal medium recognised by all as the standard of values, and hence it is not only the digger of gold that is entitled to the benefits of the metal, it is the entire multitude that is engaged in the trade that enhances its value, and who are equally claimants upon its benefits. The same is true in regard to wool. Wool itself would have no value if it did not stand related to the wants of mankind. The shepherd could have his sheep multiply without limit on the plains, but their wool would be worse than worthless if it were not for the whole machinery of trade that puts it into the hands of those who need warmth of clothing. To give it value the shearer must clip it, the carter must cart it to the mill, the spinner must spin it, the capitalist must buy it, the shipper must ship it to the ends of the earth; and what a multitude of workers are needed to drive and care for the sheep that grow the wool; that feed the horses that carry it to the mill; that spin and weave, and full and dress it; that build the storehouses in which it is kept; that build the ships that plough the sea—the carpenter, the blacksmith, the rope-maker, and the ten thousand toilers that, cooped up in the dingy office, or laboring in the sunshine, work to contribute their share in the grand task. We need say no more to convince the intelligent reader that labor and capital must go hand in hand, and commerce must ever be the bond to unite them.

For nearly forty years after the first colonisation the Australian trade was of the most limited character. A few ships of coal and a few sheep were exported. The first intelligible record we have, sets down the entire commerce of the nation for its first thirty-four years of history at 170,000 pounds of wool, a few shiploads of coal and whale oil—which latter was an active industry in early times—of £34,850 in 1826, and steadily progressing until in 1840, it reached the sum of £224,144, when it began to decline, and wool began to increase rapidly, so that in 1830 the amount of wool exported was 890,750 pounds; in 1840 it was 8,610,775 pounds; in 1850 it was 32,361,820 pounds. Its rapid increase in the two decades above-mentioned showed a degree of prosperity difficult to conceive.

SECONDARY RESOURCES.

Our coal exports began rapidly to increase from the year 1840 to the year 1850, being in this last year 31,008 tons. Tallow became an article of export, and then came gold and the metals since 1851. The country in all her colonies has gone steadily on increasing her trade with all parts of the world. Her imports and exports have shown a growth commensurate with the increase of her population, and equally so with the increase of her internal wealth. The unity of the continent of Australia, and the inseparable character of her interests and commerce, necessitates our considering her as a whole, and not in her separate parts. A comparison of the numbers representing the strength of each colony, either in relation to her inhabitants or her material wealth in regard to mines, manufactories, or other products would be misleading to the outside reader, and unfair to the individual colonies, at the same time serve no purpose historically. The fact that New South Wales may have 1,040,000 inhabitants, and Queensland, with a much larger territory, has not half the number, does not prove anything against the one and in favor of the other. When Queensland shall have been a colony for one hundred years she may, and doubtless will have 3,000,000 souls. We present the statistics of her commercial prosperity for historic reasons, and though we learn from them many things of importance, we think the most important fact they prove is the wonderful progress made, the grand successes achieved, and the equally great advantages the several colonies present, irrespective of any local divisions. The official reports of the year ending 1886 show the value of the imports to be as follows:—New South Wales, £20,973,548; Victoria, £18,530,575; Queensland, £6,103,227; South Australia, £4,852,750; Western Australia, £758,013; Tasmania, £1,756,567; New Zealand, £6,759,013—making a total of £59,733,693.

The value of the exports for the same year is as follows:—New South Wales, £15,556,213; Victoria, £11,795,321; Queensland, £4,933,970; South Australia, £4,489,008; Western Australia, £630,393; Tasmania, £1,331,540; New Zealand, £6,672,791—making a total of £45,409,236.

About thirty-seven per cent. of our import trade is with the respective colonies, and about fifty per cent. with Great Britain, the balance being with foreign countries. The excess of our imports over our exports does not argue any abnormal condition. This could be scarcely otherwise, for it must be remembered that the rapid increase of the population by immigration implies a proportionate number of traders who bring with them large wealth, but who find it to their advantage to purchase in the markets at home. A merchant leaving England or Scotland for Australia brings all he possesses, say £1,000. The fact that he expends £500 in the purchase of English goods, to be sold in Australia, does not argue any disadvantage to this country, nor will it ever do so until it can be shown that there has ceased to be a balance in Australia's favor, when on the one side you place the capital brought to the country, and added to that the result of its investment, together with the product of labor, and on the other side the value of the imports for which his money has been paid abroad. Mr. Brown brings with him his thousand pounds, part of it he invests in mines and flocks, and in the course of the year his flocks have multiplied, and his mines have been developed, and he estimates his sheep and his mining stock to be worth £3,000. The mere fact that Mr. Brown has imported £500 worth of goods from England, and has only exported £400 worth of wool, does not prove that he is not possessed of an abundant increase in his material wealth. There is no evidence of prosperity greater than the rapid increase of both import and export values.

Manufactories

are by no means few. Although we are a young people we have made rapid strides in the manufacturing of the various articles we consume. It could scarcely be expected that a country so young would at once spring into a condition of completeness so advanced as to be able to supply every want from within herself, nor do we conceive that to be a desirable state of things. The fact that our wants reach beyond ourselves, and go to other nations for their products is itself a bond of commercial strength. It would be a limitation that would serve no good purpose to have circumstances spring up that would hedge our people in, and interfere with that prominent principle of expansion—namely, the commingling with other peoples, and the interchanging of commodities; and if our necessities should continue to draw from other nations as imports in the same proportion that we draw their people and effects, we should hail it as an evidence of prosperity. However, as a matter of history, we are pleased to note and record the fact, that our manufactories are keeping pace with our growth. There is no lack of enterprise among our own people in this regard, as attested by the international exhibitions held at Sydney, Melbourne, and Adelaide within the last decade. It is impossible to give the reader definite figures that can be relied upon with absolute confidence, for the reason that during the forming state of an enterprise reports are not always accessible. A man that manufactures tobacco will not always tell the public what he is doing, and how. There are secrets of his business that lead him sometimes to withhold from the public the real facts, and the historian is compelled to accept his exaggerations and want of statements as an incident that the reader will at once take into account. The utmost we can give the reader in safety is the aggregate facts as furnished by the statistician. The number of factories in New South Wales alone in 1884 was 3,327, and hands employed were 37,473, of whom 34,987 were males, and 2,486 were females. The above figures do not give an adequate idea of all engaged in manufacturing, for the reason that the report leaves out all minor establishments, such as bootmakers, tailors, small cabinetmakers, etc. Were all included the number would reach at least 60,000; and in these minor establishments a greater proportion of females would appear. In another chapter, at the close of Volume II, is given a full statistical review as far as officially furnished, but of sufficient fulness to show the great activity of our young nation; and further, that all her interests and wants can be supplied at home.

CHAPTER XXVIII.

COLONIAL GOVERNMENTS.

IN a former chapter we have recited the history of all leading acts of the people tending towards Constitutional Government and their culmination in the granting by the Home authorities a constitution under which each colony should frame its own Parliament. The Act referred to gives to each colony power to modify its terms under certain limitations, and hence, although the several colonies have constitutions very similar, they differ in many matters of minor importance. The Constitution, as given, is the basis of all colonial governments. The reader must understand that each Parliament, after obtaining its independence, can alter and modify some of its provisions in the exercise of their prerogative. The several colonies in the Australasian group have diverged in some minor features. A strong effort has been made of late years to cement the colonies and bring them together and to aid in bringing about a unification. For many years there has been a desire expressed among leading statesmen, not only in this hemisphere but in the mother country, looking towards some Imperial action that would legalise a conference having for its object that result. The intercolonial conferences held in recent years passed resolutions of that import, and basing their action upon these the Imperial Parliament passed an Act in 1885, authorising the holding of an Australian Federal Council, which was by the terms of the Act to be held at least once in every two years, and to be composed of two delegates from each of the self-governing colonies and one from each of the Crown colonies. Those embraced in the provisions of this Bill were the colonies of Fiji, New Zealand, New South Wales, Queensland, Tasmania, Victoria, Western Australia, and South Australia. The objects of the Federal Council were set forth as follows :—

(*a*.) The relations of Australia with the Islands of the Pacific.

(*b*.) Prevention of the influx of criminals.

(*c*.) Fisheries in Australian waters beyond territorial limits.

(*d*.) The service of civil process in any courts of any colony within Her Majesty's possessions in Australasia, out of the jurisdiction of the colony in which it is issued.

(*e*.) The enforcement of judgments of courts of law of any colony beyond the limits of the colony.

(*f*.) The enforcement of any criminal process beyond the limits of the colony in which it is issued, and the extradition of offenders, including the deserters of wives and children, and deserters from the Imperial or Colonial Naval or Military Forces.

(*g*.) The custody of offenders on board ships belonging to Her Majesty's Colonial Governments beyond territorial limits.

(*h*.) Any matter which, at the request of the Legislatures of the colonies, Her Majesty by order in Council shall think fit to refer to the Council.

(*i*.) Such of the following matters as may be referred to the Council by the Legislatures of any two or more colonies; that is to say : General Defences, Quarantine, Patents of Invention and Discovery, Copyright, Bills of Exchange and Promissory Notes, Uniformity of Weights and Measures, Recognition in other colonies of any marriage or divorce duly solemnised or decreed in any Colony, Naturalisation of Aliens, Status of Corporations and Joint Stock Companies in other Colonies than that in which they have been constituted, and any other matter of general Australian interest, with respect to which the Legislatures of the several Colonies can legislate within their own limits, and as to which it is deemed desirable that there should be a law of general application ; provided that in such cases the acts of the Council shall extend only to the colonies by whose legislatures the matter shall have been so referred to, and such other colonies as may afterwards adopt the same. The Governors of each Colony have power to refer questions to the Council for determination. Bills passed by the Federal Council require Royal assent, and when thus received supersede colonial enactments that are inconsistent with them. The Acts of the Federal Council are not binding on any colony unless the legislature of such colony shall have passed an Act declaring that the same shall be enforced therein; nor shall it be enforced unless four colonies at least shall have passed such an Act. Any of the colonies can withdraw from the Federal Council by passing an enabling Act so to do.

The first Federal Council was held in Tasmania, in 1886, at Hobart. Delegates from Victoria, Queensland, Tasmania, Western Australia, and Fiji, attended, while for certain reasons New South Wales, South Australia, and New Zealand, chose to ignore it. The success of this body so far is of doubtful character, as a suspicion very generally prevails among even those colonies who have sent delegates thereto, that there exists a covert anti-democratic tendency, and which is in antagonism to the sentiments of the colonies in this quarter of the globe. That unity of action among the colonies, and a free interchange of her products and a mutual defence of her interests and people are desirable, is conceded by all, and that a universal loyalty to the British Government exists is apparent on all sides; but to be hoodwinked into any Imperial Federation involving an abandonment of their self-governing instincts and democratic principles, would meet with universal condemnation.

While the respective Governments in the colonies are similarly constituted upon the basis of the Constitution given in a previous chapter, they differ in some respects.

New South Wales.

The Government of New South Wales has its seat and capital at Sydney, a city of about 350,000 inhabitants including her suburbs, situated on Port Jackson, one of the most beautiful harbors in the world, and is in direct communication with England, distant therefrom about 14,000 miles by steamship sailing route, 1200 miles from New Zealand, and 8000 miles from San Francisco, connected therewith by steam mail ship service. The Colony has a population of over 1,080,000 inhabitants. Its Parliament consists of two Houses, the Upper House, known as the Legislative Council and having sixty members, and a Lower House, known as the

Legislative Assembly, which, according to the latest amendatory Acts, consists of seventy-four electorate districts, with a representation that increases with the inhabitants thereof, they being entitled at present to 137 members. These Houses correspond in functions to those of the Lords and Commons in England. The members of the Legislative Council are appointed by the Governor on the advice of the Executive Council for life, subject to the following conditions: first, that he does not absent himself from the Council for two succeeding sessions, without the consent of the Government ; and second, that he does not become a citizen of a foreign state, a bankrupt, or defaulter, or is convicted of treason or any infamous crime. The qualifications necessary for holding such a position are, that the member be natural born or naturalised, of full age of twenty-one years. The Governor appoints one of the members of the Council as President thereof—a position he holds at the pleasure of the Governor. The qualifications for membership in the Lower House is as follows :— Every male subject of Her Majesty of the full age of twenty-one years, and absolutely free, being a natural born or naturalised subject, can be elected a member of the Assembly for any electoral district, unless disqualified by becoming a citizen of any foreign state, bankrupt or defaulter, or being convicted of any infamous crime. The duration of Parliament is limited to three years. The qualifications of electors is as follows :—Every male subject of Her Majesty, of the full age of twenty-one years, and absolutely free, being a natural born or naturalised subject, shall, if entered on the roll of electors, and not disqualified or incapacitated for some cause hereinafter specified, be entitled to vote at any election for the electoral district in respect of which he shall be so qualified, that is to say : first, every such subject who, at the time of making out the electoral list in any such district, shall reside, and during the six months then next proceeding, shall have resided in that district ; second, every such subject whether or not so resident as aforesaid who shall have at the time of making out the electoral list and for the six months then next proceeding shall have had within the district a freehold or leasehold estate in possession or have been in the receipt of the rents and profits thereof for his own use of the clear value of one hundred pounds or of the annual value of ten pounds respectively, or who shall then occupy and for the said six months have occupied within the district any house warehouse counting house

W. S. D. TURNER Esq.
IPSWICH.

office shop room or building being either separately or jointly with any land within such district occupied by him therewith of the annual value of ten pounds such occupation being either continuously of the same premises or successively of any two or more respectively of the required value or who shall hold and for the said six months shall have held a Crown lease or license for pastoral purposes within such district provided that no elector possessing more than one qualification within the same electoral district shall be thereby entitled to an additional vote for that district provided also that when any premises are jointly owned or occupied or held on lease by more persons than one each of such joint owners occupiers or leaseholders shall be entitled to vote in respect of such premises in case the value of his interest therein separately taken would under the provisions of the said section entitle him to vote if solely interested.

Ever since 1858 all elections have been by ballot. The Governor is appointed by the Crown and paid a salary of £7,500, and a paid staff is provided. His Executive Council is the Cabinet, and consists of nine members, who are responsible to the Assembly. They are entitled to the designation of Honorable.

The departments of Government are Colonial Secretary, Attorney-General, Secretary for Lands, Treasurer, Public Works, Public Instruction, Justice.

The commercial policy of New South Wales is that of Freetrade. At the two last elections that have taken place since the beginning of 1887 the main issue has been the above policy, and at each was overwhelmingly triumphant. A very limited number of articles are subject to tariff.

Some of the colonies have chosen to make the members of their Upper House elective, not so with New South Wales. At times there have been strong efforts put forward to change the constitution in this respect; whether such a change would be for the best cannot now be discussed as a matter of history, and hence, must be passed by as a question of conjecture. As a rule, the men who have been nominated for membership in the Legislative Councils, in the respective colonies, have been old tried servants of their country, not in the political circles merely, but in the many honorable vocations of life, where they have evinced those qualities that the authorities have recognised as entitling them to a voice in the Council of the nation.

Victoria.

The Government of this colony has for its capital, Melbourne, a city of about 350,000 inhabitants, about the size of Sydney, although there is a brisk rivalry between the two cities which leads their respective friends to contend for the superiority of each according to the friendship of those concerned. It is distant from England and San Francisco about the same as the former city of Sydney, with 600 miles added to the American number and substracted from the English route. Victoria has a population of about 1,050,000—very little, if under, that of New South Wales. In 1854 it received its present constitution. The Governor is appointed by the Crown at a salary of £10,000, together with a paid staff.

The Cabinet, which is the Executive Council, consists of about ten ministers, who are in charge of the following departments:—Treasury, Chief Secretaryship, Attorney-Generalship, Public Works, Railways, Lands and Works, Public Instruction, Trade and Customs, Agriculture, Postal, Defence and Water Supply.

The Parliament consists of two houses, Upper and Lower, which are known as Legislative Council and Legislative Assembly. Membership to both Houses is elective. The Upper House has forty-two members elected by fourteen provinces. The Legislative Assembly consists of eighty-six members elected by fifty-five districts, each of whom is paid a salary of £300 per annum. To be eligible for election to the Upper House a candidate must be an owner of freehold property to the value of not less than £100, while the elector to this branch of the Legislature must be an owner of freehold property to the value of not less than £10 yearly, or or occupier paying rates of not less than £25; (3) Joint owners or occupiers of property sufficient to give each the foregoing qualification; (4) Mortgagors in possession of property rated at not less than £10 per year; (5) graduates, legal and medical practitioners, ministers, certified schoolmasters, military and naval officers, and matriculated students.

For the Lower House or Legislative Assembly the qualification for membership thereto is as follows :—Any natural born subject of the Queen or any alien naturalised by law for five years, and resident in the colony of Victoria for the space of two years, who shall be of the full age of twenty-one years, is qualified to be elected a member of the Legislative Assembly of Victoria. Except (1) a member of the Legislative Council; (2) a Judge of any court of the colony; (3) a minister of any religious denomination whatever may be his title, rank or designation; (4) any person who shall directly or indirectly be concerned or interested in any bargain or contract entered into by or on behalf of Her Majesty; (5) any person holding any office or place of profit under the Crown, or who is employed in the employment of the Public Service of Victoria for salary, wages, fees or emolument except political officers, the Speaker and the Chairman of Committees of the Legislative Assembly; (6) any person attainted of any treason or convicted of any felony or infamous crime in any part of Her Majesty's dominions; (7) any uncertificated bankrupt or insolvent. The duration of Parliament is limited to three years.

The qualifications of electors for the Legislative Assembly are— First: Ratepaying qualifications—Every male person not subject to any legal incapacity, and being a natural born subject of Her Majesty, who is enrolled on the citizen or burgess roll of any city, town, or ward thereof; or the burgess roll of any borough or ward, or the voters' roll of any shire or district, or any riding or subdivision thereof, in respect of rateable property situated in any division of any electoral district. Second: By electors' rights (1) residential qualification—Every male person of the full age of twenty-one years and not subject to any legal incapacity, and who is a naturalised subject of Her Majesty, and has resided in Victoria for twelve months previous to the first day of January or July in any year is qualified to vote for the election of members in the Legislative Assembly for the electoral district in which he resides; (2) non-residential qualification— Every such male person as aforesaid who shall be seized at law or in equity of lands or tenements for his own life or for the life of any other person or for any larger estate of the clear value of £50 or of the clear yearly value of £5 is qualified to vote in the election of members of the Legislative Assembly for the electoral districts in which such lands are situate.

Members of the Council are styled Honorable. The commercial policy of the colony is restrictive—a high customs tariff being imposed upon a large number of articles and an *ad valorem* duty on all with the exception of a very few exemptions.

Queensland.

Queensland Government has its seat at Brisbane, a city of about 90,000 inhabitants, including its suburbs. The Colony itself has a population of about 400,000, besides an estimated population of about 15,000 coolies and natives. The Governor is appointed by the Crown at a salary of £5000 per annum, together with a paid staff. The Executive Council is the Cabinet, who is responsible to the Assembly. Parliament consists of two Houses, the Upper and Lower, known as the Legislative Council and Legislative Assembly. The Legislative Council is composed of thirty-six members, who are nominated and appointed by the Governor for life. Any elector is eligible for membership therein. The president of the Council is appointed by the Governor, and is paid a salary of £1000. The Prime Minister being vice-president thereof. One-third of the above number, exclusive of the President, constitute a quorum. Seats may be vacated by resignation, absence for two years without the permission of the Queen or Governor, allegiance to any foreign state or power, becoming insolvent, being attainted of treason, convicted of felony, or any infamous crime. Qualification for membership therein is being a naturalised or born subject of Her Majesty, of full age of twenty-one years, or having become naturalised by special act of the Imperial Parliament or that of New South Wales before Separation, or by special act of this Colony. Four-fifths of the membership of this Council must consist of persons not holding any office of emolument under the Crown, except offices of Her Majesty's Sea and Land Forces, on full pay, or retired officers on pension.

The Legislative Assembly consists of seventy-two members, elected by sixty districts, and chosen by ballot. The qualifications for which is, any person who shall be qualified and registered as a voter, not being a minister of religion or a member of the Legislative Council, or holding any office of profit under the Crown. The duration of Parliament is limited to five years, subject, however, to dissolution by the Governor. The qualification of electors is as follow :—Every man of the age of twenty-one years, being a natural born or naturalised subject of Her Majesty, or legally made a denizen of Queensland, is entitled to have his name entered on the electoral roll of any district under either of the following qualifications: first, six months residence in electoral district; second, freehold estate of the clear value of £100; third, household occupation six months of clear value of £10 leasehold estate. Members of both Houses are styled Honorable.

The departments of the Government are: Colonial Secretaryship,

Treasury, Public Works and Mines, Public Lands, Attorney-Generalship, Public Instruction, Postmaster-General.

The commercial policy is restrictive. A tariff on about ninety articles being imposed, and an *ad valorem* of 5 per cent. on all articles of import, and an export duty of two shilling on every log of cedar leaving the Colony.

South Australia.

South Australia has its seat at Adelaide, a city of about 100,000 inhabitants, with a population of 600,000 in the entire colony. It obtained its present constitution by Act of Parliament in 1856, but this has been amended several times since in minor points. The Governor is appointed by the Crown at a salary of £5,000 per annum, together with a paid staff. His Executive Council consists of six members and the Chief Justice, and is the Cabinet, responsible to the Assembly with the exception of the Chief Justice.

The Legislative Council consists of twenty-four members, under the operation of an amendatory Act that came into force during the Centennial year, 1888; eight members thereof will retire by seniority every three years, when their places will be filled by the election of two new members in each district—the colony being divided into four electoral districts for this purpose. The qualifications for membership in this House are: Being of full age of thirty years, and a natural born or naturalised subject of Her Majesty, with a residence in the province of three years. Qualifications of electors to this House are the full age of twenty-one years, being a natural born or a naturalised subject of Her Majesty; having a freehold estate in possession, situated within the said province, of the clear value of £50 sterling above all charges and encumbrances; or having a leasehold estate in possession, within the said province, of the clear value of £20—the lease thereof having been registered in the General Registry Office for the Registration of Deeds, and having three years to run at the time of voting, or containing a clause authorising the lessee to become the purchaser of the land thereby devised; or occupying a dwelling-house of the clear annual value of £25 sterling, and the electors having been registered for six months prior to the elections. Elections are taken by ballot.

The Legislative Assembly is elected triennially. Twenty-six constituencies and fifty-two members. The qualifications for admission to this House are simply the qualifications for electors, which are the full age of twenty-one, and enrolment for six months on the roll for some electoral district. Elections to this House are by ballot. Members of both Houses are styled Honorable.

The commercial policy of the colony is restrictive. A customs tariff is imposed on about ninety articles, an *ad valorem* duty levied on above double that number. There is a respectable free list of greater number of articles than is admitted free in most of the restrictive colonies. On all other articles an *ad valorem* duty of ten per cent. is imposed. The Government is carried on in the following departments:—Education, Attorney-Generalship, Crown Lands Administration, Treasury, Public Works, and Chief Secretaryship.

Western Australia.

Western Australia is a Crown colony, having its capital at Perth, a city of about 20,000 inhabitants. The whole population of the colony is a little over 45,000. The colony was founded in 1829, and in its earlier days petitioned the Home Government to be made a penal settlement, which prayer was granted. The benefits sought to be obtained from this arrangement were supposed to be quite equal to the disadvantages thereof, and their expectations were fully realised. Public roads were made, bridges and public institutions were built by this class of labor, which involved the expenditure of large sums of money paid into the colony by the Home Government, and enabled its founders to make a start in material prosperity that was essential, and without which a settlement of free white settlers could not have been secured. The Government at present is representative only in part. The Governor is appointed by the Crown at a salary of £3000 together with a paid staff.

The Council consists of six chief officials and two non-official members. The Parliament consists of but one House, styled the Legislative Council, and includes in its membership the eight members of the Executive Council; four more are nominated by the Governor and sixteen elected by the people, one-third of whom constitutes a quorum. Membership qualification requires a freehold land and property worth £1000 above incumbrance, or of the yearly value of £50. The duration of Parliament is limited to five years. Qualification of electors is full age of twenty-one, £10 household, or property to the extent of £100.

The commercial policy of the colony is restrictive. About fifty articles are subject to special duty, about thirty to an *ad valorem* of 10 per cent, seventy to an *ad valorem* of 5 per cent., about 100 free, and all others subject to 12 per cent. The colony has been just recently granted a Responsible Government, to take effect when certain conditions are complied with, which will probably be the case before many months.

Tasmania.

Tasmania has its capital at Hobart, a town with about 45,000 inhabitants. The island of Tasmania has in all a population of about 175,000 inhabitants, and lies south of Victoria, across the channel called Bass' Straits, about 140 miles from Melbourne. It was a penal settlement from 1803 to 1850, the first white emigrants coming to the island in 1816. There are many smaller islands surrounding the larger one of Tasmania, all under and subject to its Government.

A Responsible Parliament was established in 1854. The Governor is appointed by the Crown at a salary of £5000, together with a paid staff. The Executive Council is the Responsible Cabinet, and consists of four Ministers. There are two Houses of Parliament—the Upper or Legislative Council, and the Lower or Legislative Assembly. The former consists of eighteen members, elected by fifteen districts for six years. Membership qualification—A male subject thirty years of age, natural born or naturalised subject, or having obtained letters of denization of certificate of naturalisation. Electors must be twenty-one years of age, natural born or naturalised subjects having obtained letters of denization or certificate of naturalisation, having freehold estate of £20 per annum clear, or leasehold of £80 per annum under terms of not less than five years; degree of any University in British dominions of Associate of Arts of Tasmania, being legally law or medical practitioner, officiating minister of religion, or retired officer of H.M. Army and Navy not on active service, or a retired officer of the Volunteer Force of Tasmania.

The House of Assembly has thirty-six members, elected from twenty-eight districts for the period of five years. The electors are males of full age, holders or occupiers of land, having letters of denization or certificate of naturalisation, his name included in the Assessment Roll for a period of twelve months next before the first day of November in any year, or is in receipt of income salary or wages at the rate of £60 per annum, and has received an income salary or wages of £30 next or before the first day of November in any year, and is a resident in the district for which the vote given; wages or income to include house per annum £10, rations £20. Elections are held by ballot. The members of the Council are styled Honourable. Municipal institutions exist throughout the island.

New Zealand.

New Zealand, including a group of Islands the chief of which are styled North and South Islands and Stewart Island, has its capital at Wellington, a city of about 12,000 inhabitants. New Zealand was erected into a colony in 1840. The Maori chiefs having ceded the islands to Great Britain. Subsequently they waged bloody wars against the whites and Great Britain with a view of repossessing themselves of the island; notably so in 1850, and again in 1870, but since this latter date there has been universal peace. The Maoris have been assigned to reserves chiefly in the Northern Island. Over a quarter of the Islands have been alienated from the Crown. The population at the present time is about 675,000, the Maoris being set down at about 40,000.

The Government at first was that of a Crown colony. After the first Maori war of 1850, in 1852, a Federal Government was granted by Imperial Act. Under that arrangement the Islands were divided into nine provinces, namely, Auckland, Taranaki, Wellington, Hawkes Bay, Canterbury, Otago, Marlborough, Nelson and Westland, each of which had a Provincial Council elected by the householders in the district. There was a general Parliament of two houses; first sitting at Auckland and afterwards removed to Wellington.

The Upper House consisted of fifty-four members appointed by the Crown for life, three of whom belong to the Maori people.

The Lower House, or House of Representatives was elected every three years on household suffrage, and consists of ninety-five members, four of whom are Maoris. The elector requires to be a holder of freehold estate of the value of £25 or be a resident for six months. Maoris and Europeans are admitted on the same footing, except in the number of electors they represent. Both Houses are styled Honorable. The Provincial Councils were abolished in 1875, and the colony is now divided into seventy-one counties with seventy-three municipalities.

The commercial policy of the country is restrictive, and imposes a

Jas. FROST Esq.
IPSWICH.

tariff duty on 150 articles, an *ad valorem* of fifteen to twenty-five per cent. on a very large number.

Fiji.

The Fijis, embracing over two hundred Islands, are situated about 1,200 miles east from Brisbane, and 1,100 north of New Zealand, and have a population of about 125,000 inhabitants—less than 4,000 being Europeans. The capital is Suva. The Government was established in 1874. The chiefs met in council and offered it to Great Britain in 1859, but it was only formally arranged and the proposition ratified in 1874. The policy of Great Britain was to recognise in part the native Government hence it was divided into fourteen provinces, each of these again into districts. The head men of each district meet in the Provincial Council, and the native chiefs meet the Governor once a year, when their legislation is referred to the Legislative Council, which consists of eleven nominated Europeans, six of whom are officials. The Governor is chosen by the Crown, and paid a salary of £4,000 per annum, together with a paid staff. He has an Executive Council, which is nearly identical with the Legislative Council. The Customs revenues are very heavy.

New Guinea.

New Guinea has just been granted a Government somewhat similar to Fiji, but as yet it is in its formative state and is largely entrusted to the hands of Dr. Macgregor, who has just been recently appointed to undertake the task.

Dr. Macgregor, who was representative of Fiji at the first meeting of the Federal Council, at Hobart, in 1886, took occasion to call special attention to the subject of New Guinea. His own words on the question will best explain his action, and indicate his proposed policy in regard to the formation of an administration for the Island :—

" A sort of drifting policy has prevailed for a considerable time with respect to New Guinea, but in all probability something more definite will be decided upon with regard to it before another session of the Council can take place. Consequently, unless the members of the Council are now to express an opinion on the subject, there might not be another opportunity before some definite action is decided upon. The question is sure to come up in the course of a few months on account of the financial position. The withdrawal of South Australia from the arrangement as to contribution will naturally make it obligatory on the other colonies to reconsider the matter and readjust the contributions that are to be paid. The amount of contribution will, of course, be altogether influenced by the course of policy that is to be adopted with regard to New Guinea. We might, perhaps, rest satisfied with simply proclaiming a protectorate over that territory, and take no further action in the establishment or organisation of an Administration. If that course were decided upon it would be sufficient to leave a flag with some chief on the coast, who would probably keep it for nothing, and no expenditure would be required. But I do not think the people of Australasia or of Great Britain would consider their duty was being carried out unless something much more than that was done. In my opinion, if anything at all is to be done with regard to New Guinea, the first step to take would be the establishment there of a resident staff. I say a resident staff because unless the principal officer charged with the administration of New Guinea is on the spot, I believe he might just as well be in London, or Brisbane, or the moon, for all the good he can possibly do in New Guinea. Experience has shown very clearly that the personal influence that can be exercised by such an officer is invaluable, and that personal influence can only be exercised on the spot. It is necessary, in starting an Administration amongst such a people and in such a place, that very great care should be taken not to make a false start, for if a false start is made it will be exceedingly difficult to retrace the steps and begin anew. The staff must be resident, and must establish itself in friendly relations with the chiefs and the people. Their ways of thinking, their language, their customs and manners, must all be carefully studied before any laws or regulations dealing with their future government can with safety be put in force. This would imply the selection of a suitable spot for the location of the centre of authority, and from this centre civilisation would radiate gradually amongst the people. We can see in the Pacific already the effects that have been produced by Governments started on the lines I have hinted at, and by Governments started on different principles. In the colony of Fiji, for example, where due respect has been paid to native customs and manners in so far as they were not inconsistent with our own European ideas, and where laws have been passed providing for the government of the native race through their own chiefs, we have got an effective administration carried on at no expense to the Mother Country. The same thing could, in all probability, be effected in New Guinea if it was set about in a proper way."

These sentiments were fully endorsed by the Federal Council, and led the Home Government to take immediate action, looking towards the establishment of an administration that would carefully guard the rights of the natives and protect Europeans in the legitimate exploration of the country. Difficulties had been experienced previously by private explorers, who, in their eagerness to discover, failed to make their purposes plain or intelligible to the natives, and this led to conflicts resulting in loss of life and stirring up much enmity. These private parties, who dubbed themselves "explorers," were, as a rule, irresponsible, and more intent upon gain than knowledge, and not always prudent in their treatment of the natives. The selection and appointment of Dr. Macgregor to the important position of Representative of the Crown, to whom is committed the task of carrying out the provisions of the Imperial Act passed in 1888, looking towards the formation of a Government of New Guinea, meets with universal approval. The results thereof will be matter for future history.

The aggregate public debts of the colonies is about £160,000,000 sterling. The revenue raised has a higher average per head than that of any other country.

From the above data the reader will see that the colonies enjoy a freedom almost amounting to an independence. The principle of democracy is rapidly growing and becoming apparent in the management, not only of her politics, but of all her institutions. The people demand the right of governing themselves, and this privilege has been accorded them more and more by the Home Government. In the infancy of its existence, when the continent was utilised for penal purposes largely before free immigration and enterprise were thoroughly established, it was a necessity to govern in an autocratic manner, the great bulk of the people being antagonistic and out of harmony with government of any kind. It required a stern military control to give strength and permanency to the institutions of the young country when first founded, but as free immigration came in, and local enterprises began to assume such shape and magnitude as to identify these early settlers with the country, England showed a disposition to grant to her colonists all the liberty and all the self control it was practicable and prudent to grant. The reader will observe that as this free element became dominant in the colonies, and began to appreciate and value the benefits of a popular education, and to seek for a share in the responsibility of managing their own affairs, England's liberality was commensurate, and she freely bestowed upon the colonies such a constitution as would enable her people to govern for themselves. The only connecting link England reserved for herself between the colonies and the Motherland was the selection and appointment of the Governor who should guard the interests of the Mother Country, but even in this particular there is a growing sentiment in favor of having a voice in the selection of that representative, and the correspondence carried on recently between the Premier of Queensland and the Home Office in reference to the appointment of a Governor to fill the vacancy occasioned by the death of Sir Anthony Musgrave, revealed the extent of this sentiment, for the protest urged by the representatives of the Queensland democracy was very extensively endorsed by the leading statesmen of the several colonies, and borne out by the Press generally. Although existing constitutional difficulties preclude the possibility of recognising this demand, it will no doubt come to be regarded as one of the necessities of the colonies to choose for themselves their rulers.

We observe in the respective Governments above alluded to that manhood suffrage is all but absolute in these colonies. The small monetary qualifications exacted are nominal, and matters of prudence which will, doubtless, disappear with the more general enlightenment of her people. Manhood suffrage can only be beneficial when exercised by a people of intelligence, and, to give effect to this privilege, education must become universal; for an ignorant people will defeat the excellent purposes of any Government where ignorance is accorded all the rights of intelligence. Schools, lectures, and scientific societies must all aim at the dissemination of knowledge and the enlightenment of all her people. The pulpit that was once recognised as the most powerful of all political agencies is relegated to another sphere; its ministers even being barred by special Acts from the privilege of equality in the constitution of some of its Parliaments. This we scarcely can believe to be just or in accordance with the doctrine of a true democracy. Every man and citizen within a democratic country should have accorded to him the right and privilege accorded to any of his fellows. In other words, equality before the law is the recognised intrepretation of all democracy. The only exceptions to this rule are in the case of such as voluntarily accept a position of profit under the administration. The voluntary act in accepting, relieves the body from any suspicion of injustice; but the clergymen deriving no profit from the administration, and being entirely independent of its financial patronage, should not, in our judgment, be deprived of any right as a citizen by virtue of his occupation, which is neither in antagonism to law nor yet subversive of the principles of morality, upon which the force of all law rests.

Our duty as a nation which is fast tending towards absolute independence and freedom is to guard well our institutions of enlightenment without reflecting at all at past efforts in this direction, which, it must be observed, are worthy of all praise both for efficiency and universality ; yet we must, to a much greater extent, unshackle the Press and guard its privileges, extend our common school system, patronise and build up our technological institutions, encourage public lectures, and all other efforts of the kind, so that our people will become fully cognisant of the wants and necessities of their land.

CHAPTER XXIX.

EDUCATION.

GREAT importance was attached to educational institutions from the formation of colonisation in Australia. This doubtless arose from the fact that a large percentage of those who came to the colony in the first instance were people of intelligence and liberal education. Hence, from the beginning we find men of high scholarship, who, appreciating its advantage, sought to secure its benefits for their children. The Church of England, being directly responsible for the moral culture and educational training of the youth, were charged with the duty of creating schools commensurate with the demand. Government provision was made in accordance with this sentiment, and for that reason we find for many years the schools of the settlement were in connection with, and under the control of, the established Church of England. There sprung up a sense of the need of education at an early date. The first school building used was the first church erected by Rev. Mr. Johnson, but which was burnt down in 1795. Governor Phillip, in a communication to the Home authorities, says of the building that "on Sundays it was used for a church, and on week days as a schoolhouse, in which one hundred and fifty to two hundred children were educated under the immediate supervision of the clergymen." The clergy, as a rule, had control of the education of the youth in those days. The schools were all of a private character, open to all who were able to pay the fee required, but under the immediate direction of the clergyman or teacher who had charge, and these were responsible to neither State nor Church, except in a very formal way to the latter, and only when administered by a subordinate officer of the Church. The Church of England, having among them men of advanced learning, gave to these schools from the start teachers capable of imparting instruction of a very advanced type, and for that reason some of the youth in Australia of that day not only availed themselves of the advanced educational facilities, but they acquired a proficiency of no ordinary type. There was scarcely a thought of extending these opportunities to the masses. Their utmost ambition was to have among the people such facilities that the sons of the more wealthy might have advantages suited to their rank and station. It was many years before a move was made by other denominations to establish schools.

The Wesleyan Methodists were among the first to realise the importance of receiving instruction from their own clergyman, and though their primary object was to receive religious instruction for their people, they sought for, and obtained a limited amount of aid from the Crown to pay partly the services of their first minister, who obtained aid as a teacher. From small beginnings began to grow a system of education that was nothing more nor less than private schools under the patronage and support of the Church of England chiefly, and to a small extent under the direction and control of the other Christian bodies, the Roman Catholics manifesting the greatest amount of zeal in organising schools for the instruction of their people The Crown was pleased to offer encouragement to all efforts of this kind, both in money and lands. It does not appear that there was any intention on the part of the authorities at Home to discriminate in favor of even the established Church of England, although the number of English Church people being greatly in excess of all others gave her a decided advantage, which she was not slow to take. There were established in the chief centres of population advanced schools that afforded fair opportunities to the more ambitious, and gave every reasonable facility of acquiring a liberal education, and there were not a few of the first youth of the colony who sought after, and took advantage of every opportunity in this respect. Schools organised and supported in this way could not be expected to go to the sparsely settled districts, but rather to seek the centres of population. Hence the cities and larger towns had a monopoly. The rural districts were comparatively destitute of these advantages. We must not imagine that Australia was peculiar in this respect. This lack was almost universal. There was during the period between 1788 and 1820 a similar laxity all over the world in regard to the instruction of the masses. Even in England, although there were schools in every parish under the control of the clergyman, there was very little done to educate the masses. Prior to the rebellion of 1836-8 the schools in Lower Canada were nearly all under the domination of the Roman Catholics, and in Upper Canada denominational and private schools were the rule. It was at a later date that a national school system was introduced to those provinces. The same is true of the schools of the United States of America. It is not fifty years since the most prominent States of the Union adopted their liberal plan of a free and universal system of instruction to a free people, so that Australia was not so far behind the spirit of the times. She possessed and retained schools of a somewhat crude type, denominational and private, nearly all of a most rudimentary character, and very few of a superior class.

Under such a system the schools were of a very different class. Upon the efficiency of the teacher and favor of the influential depended their success, and hence the character of these first places of learning was diverse. In the larger places the schools were first-class; in other parts they were of the crudest form—sometimes a half-dozen children taught in a half listless manner a few primary subjects by a convict who could take very little interest in the welfare of anybody, or by some unqualified person having no other visible means of support. A few of the better class of schools of that early day have continued through the successive decades that have come and gone. They can point to a splendid record of fifty, sixty, or seventy years' faithful service, and to a brilliant list of scholars who have graced every profession and avocation in the land.

With the rise and progress of the sentiment of responsible government came an earnest thirst for knowledge. An autocratic government, in which one man dictates and an army of trained soldiers enforces his commands, requires very little intelligence on the part of the people ruled; in fact, the less they know the better. "Do this and you shall live, do that and you shall die," is the law of autocracy, and it requires very little intelligence to comprehend its meaning. The nearer the approach to this type of government the less need for schools, all history showing this to be a fact. On the other hand, the closer we come to an absolute democracy the greater the necessity for schools; and the necessity creates the thirst, and the thirst, according to the great law of want, creates the supply.

While there never was a period in the experience of the Australian people when there were not a few schools of a superior character—yet for about thirty or forty years they were few in number, and not easily got at—only the more favored sons of wealth could possibly secure the advantages they offered. There was no uniformity in the course of study pursued at these institutions. That depended entirely upon the ambition of the student, and the ability of the master to teach. The instructors, however, being largely of the clergyman class, were usually well able to teach the classics, and all questions pertaining to the church, both in its historic and dogmatic phases. The catechisms and religious teaching of the respective churches were most conscientiously taught, the denomination having the most schools succeeding best. This fact stimulated the churches to individual effort. An intense rivalry sprung up, the Rev. Dr. Lang leading in the Presbyterian Church; the Wesleyans, under the agency of their conference, extending the work of denominational schools; the Catholics evincing an historic zeal worthy of their past record; and the Church of England, with its prestige and patronage, having the advantage, multiplied schools *ad infinitum*—some of a good quality, and more of a very primary character, and lacking almost all the essentials of a secular school. The catechisms were most rigidly taught, but beyond a very little writing, reading, and rudiments of arithmetic, nothing was ever dreamed of. The assistance these schools received was of a most limited and precarious nature. There was no general sentiment adverse to the principle of State aid; at the same time, there was no organised method of granting the same.

The type of Government obtaining from 1788 (the time of first colonisation) to 1824 was absolutely autocratic; and even afterwards it was practically so, though from that date on there was a nominal Council of advisers for several years. Practically, the administration of affairs, the making of the laws, and the disbursements were in the hands of the Governor, and the aid granted to any enterprise was in accordance with the view he might entertain respecting its merits. Schools, like roads, bridges, court-houses, and churches, were all objects of the Governor's favor and good-will; but as the calls for help were both frequent and large, and the funds at command limited, it was not possible to grant assistance to the extent of the demands. It was no easy task to judge as to the most urgent calls. In a country so new, frequently the question would spring up as to whether it was more important to build a road through to some farming district to enable the poor struggling farmer to get his produce to the market, or to give the money to the schools in some of the more populous centres, where the children needed instruction. It is one of the easiest matters to moralise on the great advantages of education, and its superiority over everything else; but it is not so easy to decide as to which of the two classes should have the first claim under the above conditions. In looking back from this date we might feel disposed to criticise severely the policy of the respective Governors, which failed to give all the encouragement to education, which, at this time appears just. The plan that for many years commended itself to the several authorities was to grant encouragement according to the number on the roll of each school. This, however, led to fraudulent returns, or a system of lending pupils from district to district.

It was not until Sir Richard Bourke's administration that the National School system became a serious question with the people, nor had it, in many other portions of the world, been established. Governor Bourke was a man of liberal and wide views upon all living questions, and had observed the growth of the school question as it presented itself to other nations. Switzerland had already adopted a comprehensive plan, and Germany, too, had embraced in its policy of unification a more liberal plan of school instruction. The United States of America had shown, in many of her more progressive centres, a policy that was beginning to reveal wonderful results, but that which seemed to the Governor to be best adapted to this continent was the Irish National system, that admitted children of every class and age upon the same conditions, excluded sectarian teaching as given in the respective catechisms of the churches, and enjoined in its stead selections from the Scriptures and other good books of a broad, religious, and moral character, without comment, and permitted, as a matter of privilege, the instruction of their several flocks by the ministers of religion on one day of the week.

Governor Bourke's frequent allusion to this subject in his several addresses among the people, and in his communications to the authorities at Home show beyond all doubt that he was not only impressed with its importance, but was zealously interested in its inauguration, and sought in every legitimate way to effect this result. That the Governor was not averse to moral and religious instruction *per se* is evident from the tone of his first address to the Legislative Council in 1831, in which he urges the importance of "moral" provision, as well as what will tend to secure "comfort and convenience" to "all classes of the community." What was done in this respect does not fully appear from the meagre records, except by implication. The schools grew, and a degree of prosperity characterised them during his administration. In 1834 he placed upon the estimates for school purposes £2,806 for the Church of England, and £800 for the Roman Catholics. The failure to recognise the claims of other, though smaller, bodies of Chrsitians doubtless arose from the difficulty of finding a basis of division fair to all concerned. We are justified in this assumption from the general character and bearing of the man. The discrimination that existed in this respect did not escape the severe criticism of some, and a fair distribution imperatively demanded. The Rev. Dr. Lang thundered at the gate of authority with a directness of appeal and plainness of terms that neither failed of being understood, nor was without effect.

Governor Bourke's cherished plan was the introduction of the Irish National system, which he laid before the Parliament in a recommendation to Lord Stanley, Colonial Secretary at the time, and which was favorably entertained as a most appropriate solution of the question for the colonies. Strange as it might seem to us of this age, the strongest opposition was made to the proposition. On all sides the scheme was pronounced inimical to the morals of the country. Churchmen, with a zeal more intense than they had ever shown in teaching the precepts of Christianity, urged that the proposed plan would prove subversive of all moral ideas, and undermine even the stability of government. Governor Bourke was compelled to hold in abeyance his school policy, and to give all encouragement to the denominational efforts in the meantime, which he did with a heartiness and liberality none the less pronounced on account of the opposition he received.

His plan of public instruction met with the endorsement of his successor, Governor Gipps, who committed himself from the commencement of his administration to the principles embodied therein, and sought in every way to impress the colonists with the importance of a system that would extend its benefits to the masses, in the enlightenment of whom is the safety and permanency of a truly democratic type of government. For the same reasons of policy that influenced his predecessor, he did not insist upon forcing this system upon the people. It is not to be wondered at that the few favored ones of a pseudo-aristocracy, feeling the foundations of their ancient privileges giving way before the advancing brotherhood of a modern civilisation, where justice insists upon the recognition of the rights of all, should strike back at the daring spirit of reform that sweeps down all opposition with relentless fury. A change of such proportions as suggested was sure to confront organised power, and to antagonise those who sat in high places; and it was many years before the grandeur of such a system took possession of the thoughts and consciences of the colonists as to make further resistance imprudent and ill-advised. Any principle of justice is sure to win. In this age, and more especially in this land, any question of right is sure to sweep all before it. It only requires the enlightenment of the people to mass them in solid phalanx in support of a principle. Armies may march with measured step, and pride themselves on what they have done in the past, but they are but the gaudy toys of a wooden kingdom compared with the omnipotent manhood of an awakened people who strike in the cause of their own freedom. The struggle was a long one between the churches and the masses. The latter triumphed. Every step taken towards responsible government gave the people an advantage in respect to the education of their sons and daughters. With the enlargement of the Council in 1829, and the granting of a proximate form of responsible government in 1842, and its further unfoldment and completion in the years 1851 and 1856, there came a proper appreciation, on the part of the people, of the need of a radical change in the schools of the nation.

The first to champion the cause of a National system was the Rev. Dr. Lang, who laid upon the table of the Legislative Council in 1843 a scheme of unsectarian schools, even more liberal and extensive than the Irish plan proposed by Governors Bourke and Gipps. His system was met with such a storm of opposition, on the ground of its anti-religious character, that he deemed it wise to withdraw it for a time. Some of Dr. Lang's warmest personal friends were opposed to the measure, and brought powerful influences to bear upon him, and to induce him to abandon the task.

In 1844 Mr. Robert Lowe (now Viscount Sherbrooke), in the Legislative Council, secured the appointment of a committee " to inquire into, and report upon the state of education in this colony, and to devise means of placing the education of youth upon a basis suited to the wants and wishes of the community." The Committee made a thorough examination of leading people in different parts of the country, and became cognisant of the fact that the denominational character of the schools was the chief bar to their success. The rivalry among the religious bodies tended to multiply schools in the centres of population; teachers, of necessity, had to be obtained at a very trifling salary, and hence they were very frequently ignorant and unqualified. The children of the colony were largely without school facilities. The want of system in the course of study, together with the unchristian spirit, that sectarian instruction awakened among the children of the colony was most detrimental even to that intelligent piety that must ever be the strength of a people. The Committee most carefully abstained from any wholesale attack upon the schools indiscriminately. They were pleased to express their approval of many schools under the immediate supervision of the clergy, and others of all denominations that were deserving of highest praise, both for the moral tone and thorough scholarship inculcated; but, at the same time, they most clearly pointed out—first, the great expense of the denominational system; second, the absolute lack of schools in the country districts, and the fact that one-half of the children of the colony, were without instruction, and that nothing but a National system would ever supply the want. The most intense opposition was urged by leading people of all denominations. What the churches most dreaded was to see the religious character of the schools set aside and a secular system introduced. The Roman Catholics, from time immemorial, had controlled the education of their own children in every land under the sun; the Church of England, which formed the majority of the religious element of the country, had been all raised at Home under the Parish School system, and they knew no other; the other bodies of more limited numbers were also divided upon the wisdom of plans proposed, and hence the years of discussion that ensued upon its presentation to the Legislative Council.

There were two systems suggested, the one was that of the British and Foreign School Society, and the other was the Irish National School System. It took years of most earnest examination of this question to fit the people of the colony to approach the subject in a spirit of calm deliberation. Its first announcement was so repugnant to their sentiments and history that it was no easy matter for persons accustomed for generations to regard the Church as paramount in all things to change their views upon so vital a question suddenly.

Several compromises were suggested. The most important was to place the country districts under a National system, and to allow the denominations to carry on their respective schools in the cities and towns, each school drawing aid according to the work done. This, however, did not touch the main evil in the old condition of things—namely, the denominational rivalries and antagonisms that offset all the moral instruction they would receive.

In 1844 Mr. Wentworth succeeded in carrying through the Legislative Council resolutions authorising the introduction and establishment of a school system of a modified character by a majority of only one vote, thus showing how evenly divided were the representatives of the people.

The scope and aims of the plan will be best judged from the resolutions themselves, which were as follows:—" (1) That this Council having taken into consideration the report of the Select Committee appointed to inquire into and report upon the state of education in this colony, and to devise the means of placing the education of youth upon a basis suited to the wants and wishes of the community, resolves : 'That it is advisable to introduce Lord Stanley's system of National Education into this Colony, with this modification, that instead of the clergy and pastors of the several denominations being allowed to impart religious instruction in the schools, the children be allowed to be absent from school one day in every week, exclusive of Sunday, for the purpose of receiving such instruction elsewhere, but that all denominational schools now in existence, having school-houses already built, which have been, or shall be within the next twelve months, conveyed in trust for the purpose of the school, and having now, or which shall have within the next twelve months, an average attendance of fifty scholars, shall be entitled to aid from the Board.' (2) That in order to introduce this system, His Excellency the Governor be requested to appoint a Board of persons favorable to the introduction of Lord Stanley's National System of Education, and belonging to the different religious denominations. This Board to be invested with a very wide discretion as to the arrangements necessary for carrying the system into effect, and all funds to be henceforth applied for the purpose of education to be administered by them. (3) The leading principle by which the Board of Education shall be guided is to afford the same facilities for education to all classes of professing Christians without any attempt to interfere with the peculiar religious opinions of any, or to countenance proselytism. (4) That the Board be incorporated."

In 1847 the sum of £2,000 was appropriated from the public funds by the Legislature towards the expenses of this school system, or at least to accomplish its inauguration, but the appropriation thus made by the Council was vetoed by Governor Fitzroy, who justified his refusal to endorse the action on account of the magnitude and importance of the measure; and secondly, he was in doubt as to whether the great change in school matters, contemplated by the introduction of such a scheme, was the wish of the people. The spirit of autocracy was still dominant in the administration of affairs in New South Wales; though there was a sort of a people's Parliament, it was so only in name. The Governor was unwilling to yield to the will of the people, when they chose to express their wish in a manner and direction that did not harmonise with his own notions of what was proper. This action arrested its progress for a time in the older colony. It did not, however, satisfy its advocates, nor stop their agitation of the paramount importance of a National system of instruction. People were waking from the slumber of ages in all portions of the world, in regard to the need of schools. Its trial elsewhere had been successful, and notably so in Ireland, where Stanley's plan of common education was already bearing good fruit. The colony of South Australia was impressed with the importance of it, and though comparatively young, had felt the need of such a system, and had discussed with intelligence and determination its merits, and carried a measure of a similar kind in this same year. The nature of their scheme was the appointment of a Board of Education by the Governor, with power to grant assistance to schools, which made returns to the Board, and was subject to the inspection of the Justices of the Peace in their respective localities, and an Inspector of the Board.

To us living at this date, such a system of State Schools may appear crude and insufficient. We must, however, remember it was the first triumph of the principle of a Common School system on the continent. It was no easy matter to confront and successfully oppose the powers that were arrayed against its introduction, among which may be mentioned the organised ecclesiastical bodies; the wealthy scions of a waning aristocracy, fearful of the progress being made by a triumphant democracy; and a few schools in the towns and cities which had gained an ascendency over the others by virtue of their locality and an assumption of superiority. Seed of this kind generally grows rapidly. It was not possible to crush out of the heart of the people what was plainly to their interest—they wanted schools, and their felt want was more omnipotent than the *dictum* of any Governor or combination. At all events His Excellency was pleased, in 1848, to grant his consent to the Council's appropriation from the public funds of the foregoing amount, and forthwith appointed a National Board to inspect and supervise all schools of an unsectarian character that might be established under this national system. At the same time another Board was established for the purpose of inspecting all denominational schools to whom aid was granted. One can imagine the spirit of rivalry and antagonism that two Boards of Inspection would occasion, and that would in a short time lead the respective families and friends of each to be in conflict—and yet the very conflict was fruitful of debate and inquiry, and an almost universal interest in the subject that was sure to follow. It was the cry of denominational *versus* non-denominational schools that was raised on all sides, and the people, old and young, were trained to espouse the one and condemn the other; the most bitter prejudices were fostered among the rising generation; the benedictions of Christianity were not frequently bestowed by the one upon the other. Human nature in its uglier temper most frequently showed its supremacy in the discussions on the hustings. Notwithstanding the antagonism engendered, the benefits of an extended education became more apparent, and the friends thereof increased with the years, not without much opposition, but with a growing conviction that the principle in the end would triumph.

When Port Phillip separated from New South Wales and set up as an independent colony, under the title of Victoria, one of the first measures adopted by her Legislature was the establishment of a National School system for the masses, under the inspection of the Government and amenable thereto. Her school policy was identical with that of New South Wales; her two Boards, with the same objects in view, led to the same rivalries. The people in all the colonies were of the same mind in regard to the need of a system of education that would reach the masses and benefit the poor as well as the rich. The progress made by this National system was marked by steady advancement; the drawbacks were many and the discouragements great, but the good to be done from its perpetuation was far greater than the inconveniences, and for this reason no country in the world has ever receded from the plan once it has been adopted.

The gold excitement of 1851 and following years marred its efficiency and checked its development for a time, but so did it effect every other department of labor in the same manner. It was not to be expected that teachers who were receiving only £40 to £80 a year for their services could be restrained from the goldfields where common laborers were offered as much per month. The demoralising effect of such fabulous sums tempted every class from their ordinary vocations, and made them eager to go with the multitude to the mines. Even the clergy in many instances abandoned their flocks, so great was their sense of duty to become missionaries in the mountain wilds, and without any stated salary they were content to labor even on the crumbs that fell from the poor man's table.

With the return of a settled condition of affairs there came a rapid improvement in the schools, until the first principle upon which they were established became almost universally conceded, namely, that its benefits should be extended to all classes.

The second principle of efficiency that was found to be imperative was: "That the State should only assist such schools as imparted a good secular instruction, based upon the Christian religion, but apart from all theological and controversial differences on discipline and doctrine." The teaching of peculiar dogmas and church doctrines in the public schools, under the school system first adopted, gave much offence and wrought up to fever heat in political circles the question: "Was it right to grant State aid to churches?" Those who opposed it maintained that to aid schools in which any church catechism or denominational question was taught, was simply aiding by taxation such a church. This question, presented in such a form, afforded politicians a good opportunity to go to the polls on, and to work up divisions among the different sects, that would serve their purposes in electioneering. A principle of such palpable truth could not fail to impress the people; and, as the leaven influences the entire mass, so the annunciation of this doctrine was quickly followed by a general acceptance of it by the political aspirants, who are always quick to guage the public pulse on all questions of national policy.

It was not long before the colonies, one after another, adopted it as the only plan that would free the country from the bitter feuds into which the antagonistic sectarian teachings were sure to lead.

South Australia was the first to pass an Act to that effect. Its adoption there was regarded by many as a step backwards, and they looked upon the experiment as a dangerous departure from the good old ways of their fathers; the doctrine that fathers may err through sins of omission had not yet been conceded by the nations, and the conservatism that everywhere seemed dominant interposed a bar to reforms in all departments. It took but a few years to demonstrate the wisdom of such a change in South Australia—the other colonies slowly but surely came to see the imperative need of reform in the same direction. Under the Act passed in South Australia one Board was created and had entire charge of the schools—in the other colonies two Boards existed for many years. In the former provision was made for the free admission of orphans and destitute children. The success and growth of the schools was steady and kept pace with the expansion of the country in other respects. The moral effect of its success in other lands had a marked influence on the people of this; even the religious elements were becoming reconciled to the change. We must not blame churches for their conservative adherence to the idea that education apart from church influences is insufficient. That education must be incorporated with the fundamental principles of religion is conceded by all intelligent statesmen, but that these principles can be effectively taught by a thoroughly organised and efficiently supervised secular system is equally apparent; and, perhaps, greater importance is attached to these fundamental truths by a responsible National system than even by churches, who are very apt to emphasise and give chief importance to their distinctive doctrines. Each of the colonies took kindly to the new system, and a growing support was accorded to its advocates by the people, and at each election Parliament was strenghtened by the addition to its members of such as were favorable to its extension.

What chiefly retarded the rapid development of schools in the colonies was the short-sighted policy of limiting the salary of the teachers to £80 as the maximum, and when South Australia, the weakest of the three older colonies, fixed its limited at £100 the Act was deemed to be extravagant and reckless. A school policy that fixes a limit, even at the highest sum above named, cannot command talent of the first order; and, if by any circumstance, ability stumbles into this profession at such prices, it is rarely retained and is usually followed by a much inferior class of instructors, who never fail, first, to disappoint the pupils, and secondly, to induce a want of confidence and disgust—all of which tend to disorganise and impede the progress of the schools.

With the advance of education came a desire on the part of many for a higher grade than was afforded by the ordinary school. In New South Wales an Act was passed in 1851 by the Legislature authorising the establishment of a University in Sydney. This was mainly brought about through the able advocacy of Mr. Wentworth, who is recognised as the founder, and whose statue has been chiselled in marble and graces the halls of the University as a perpetual monument. The religious *versus* the secular idea was the bone of contention here during the years of its incipiency, and the same arguments that had been used in the controversy concerning the secular character of the Primary Schools were now urged by the opponents of a secular University.

The Legislature took hold of the question with a liberality that was princely in those days. Their first provision was an annual grant of £5000, together with an adequate sum for the erection of a building suitable for the purpose. The University for many years had to struggle against a wide-spread prejudice on account of its secular character, which affected the attendance to such an extent that for a time its success was despaired of. Previous to this there had been colleges and schools of a high order, established by the several religious bodies, which, hitherto, had claimed the youth of the land and still continued to keep them. Though the progress of the University has been more satisfactory during the past few years, yet it has not enjoyed a success commensurate with the enormous provision the Legislature has been pleased to make for it. One has not to go far for the cause. No University can be prosperous in a young democratic country that is not as broad as the wants of the people. A spirit of narrow-mindedness in the various departments is sure to cripple its energies and antagonise a large and powerful part of the body politic. While we are aware, it is not the part of the historian to criticise faults or point out errors, yet we will claim the right of suggesting: (1.) No democracy ever existed that did not make ample provision for the higher education of all its different sections, and we do not mean by this that the State should make provision from the public funds, but we do mean that Denominational Colleges and Universities should not only be recognised by the State, by according them equal standing and rank, but they should be encouraged and fostered: (2.) The educational policy should be fraternal in its relation to the nations; the narrow spirit that assumes a superiority upon no foundation is a pitiable exhibition of a superciliousness that is sure to impart to all appliances under its agency, a character like unto itself that is certain to gnaw its own vitals and cause it to die of inanition.

It must be borne in mind that in the general influx of the multitude that come to these shores from all parts of the world there is a very large percentage of educated people—graduates from the several colleges and universities of the world, honorable representatives of all the learned professions—whose influence and co-operation should be, and could be, made a part of the educational development of the colony. A policy that seeks to ignore the scholastic standing of scholars from other lands, is suicidal, and can only result in the wide-spread antagonism which ever tends to disaster and defeat.

No more reprehensible course could be pursued than denying the foreign carpenter or mechanic the right to practice his calling, because, forsooth, he did not learn his business either in Oxford or in Sydney. A democracy like Australia would not tolerate such a spirit of narrow-mindedness in reference to the trades. Her triumphant progress has been achieved by the adoption of a wider and grander policy. It is not the sentiment of the few native-born, whose motto is limited to the selfish theory "Australia for Australians," that has in the past made this grand country what it is, or can be relied upon to mould its future. Some forty years ago a society of a similar character was formed in the United States of America. After having drawn from all other lands some of the best blood and intellect, and having laid the foundations of her future greatness by inviting all mankind to come and find homes, where they might rest in freedom, a few, in the spirit of exclusiveness, conceived the idea of establishing the "No-nothing Society," whose chief principle was "America for Americans." Its movers thought they were strong enough to gather within her fold all native-born citizens, and to deny the foreigner the rights they claimed for themselves. It was a plausible scheme to trap the unthinking. For a time it seemed to captivate the youthful heart, and in consequence grew with a rapidity that gave alarm to the thoughtful; but when the great American mind beheld the vortex into which they were madly rushing they stopped, and recoiling from the terrible calamity, the manly democracy of the country rose grandly to the occasion, and wiped out every vestige of the attempted crime, and bore down its chief advocates into an oblivion from which they have never been able to recover.

We mention the above circumstance to remind ourselves and the more youthful portion of our noble land that there is terrible danger threatened in the several attempts made in many quarters against our liberties—covert, yet none the less real.

The educational policy of the country, no doubt, is intended by the people to be liberal, but there is danger of its intended liberality being defeated by a narrow administration of its affairs.

The repeated attempts made by the Medical Department of the educational system that obtains, to foist upon the country legislation of a narrow and exclusive type, is only one illustration of the want of a broad policy. Under the pretext of guarding the interests of the people, much legislation has been carried through Parliament that amounts to nothing of value so far as the people are concerned, but virtually amounts to the voting of a subsidy of tens of thousands of pounds yearly from the public funds to sustain and keep alive a body of men who, no doubt, feel the absolute need of Government aid, in the shape of salary, to supplement the fees that their own ability would be able to earn if left to their own resources. The medical legislation so far has succeeded in creating a Medical Board. This Board is composed of medical men of the old allopathic type, who are satisfied with their own competency to judge of the qualifications of all physicians and surgeons who may apply. The law of the land does not bar any person from the practice of medicine, but it does make a distinction between a registered and unregistered physician. The people have said through their legislation who shall be admitted to registration, but the above Board are the constituted judges as to whether the applicant is qualified under the law. Only registered physicians are held to be qualified, and only such can be appointed to the several hospitals, associations, insurance societies, etc., so that physicians and surgeons of first rank in scholarship may be rejected by the above Board, and, in the eyes of the law, be unqualified; while, in reality, they may be and are sometimes, the peers of any on the Board. The injustice of this is so glaring that one can scarcely be surprised at the almost universal suspicion that exists in the minds of the intelligent masses that the constant attempts of these representatives of the old system of medical education to legislate in their own interests is not so much from a desire to protect the people as it is from a consciousness that, without additional help from the State, their waning system will leave them stranded and helpless. The collegiate education of a country, guided and carried on in a narrow groove, can scarcely hope for a prosperity equal to the expectations of a free democratic people. All the leading colonies— that is South Australia, Victoria, and New South Wales—adopted the same general policy in regard to their higher education. Each has its own University, with very few minor differences in its administration.

We scarcely need dwell further on the minute details in the development of the system of education in this country. It is sufficient for our purpose to note the earnest desire on the part of the people to do all in their power to secure facilities in this respect equal to that of other countries, and although large sums have been voted from the public funds, the people have never complained, or shown any signs of dissatisfaction in regard to the moneys expended in this direction.

There can be no doubt that the purpose of the respective colonies is to produce in this department a system fair, liberal, and efficient. In theory, the school system of all the Australian colonies is as comprehensive as one will find in most parts of the world, and we think we are correct when we say that in no part of the world are teachers better paid for the number of scholars taught, and the work done. For many years an attempt was made to harmonise the conflicting views by a compromise, partial aid being given to denominational institutions that had complied with certain conditions; but this did not allay irritation, or tend to make the public school work satisfactory.

In New South Wales the Public School system may properly be said to have begun its work on its present plan in 1867, though by no means as comprehensive or efficient as it is at present. What is known in our history as the Public Schools Act was passed in the previous year under the Parkes Government, and became law the 1st of January, 1867. It did not seek to destroy the denominational schools, but rather to perpetuate their existence. The fact that they were the only teaching bodies for many years, and the most important schools for many years more, gave them a claim on the country that no Parliament was disposed to ignore. From this date the schools were to be known as public schools. State aid was continued to denominational schools that came under the regulations imposed, that is such as taught the prescribed course, and refrained from teaching any sectarian religion. This Act created an Educational Council, consisting of five members appointed by the Government, who had supervision of all the schools that derived aid from the State. The Act provided for the creation of half-time schools in thinly-settled localities, and met a want that had never before been supplied. One condition, however, was found to be burdensome, and that was before schools could be established, one-third of the cost thereof had to be subscribed in the locality, which not only was a serious drawback, but was unfair. This clause in the Act was finally removed by Parliament, through the action of Sir Henry Parkes, in 1875. Even the increased amount from the public funds necessary to supplement the former grants was made by the country without a murmur. The half-time schools met a condition that could not be solved in any other manner. First, there were children so circumstanced that their services were needed by their parents for at least half the day, and there were districts so thinly populated that by assembling the few children together, and teaching them during the forenoon, and repairing to a neighboring district in the afternoon, an education could be imparted that would be too expensive if conducted on any other plan. This gave great satisfaction to the country districts, and strengthened Sir Henry Parkes politically, as he was the chief in effecting this reform.

In 1880 a new Act, entitled "The Public Instruction Act," was passed, and which materially changed many of the important parts of the machinery of public instruction. Its important features are:—

(1.) The abolishment of the old Educational Council, and the creation of a Minister of Public Instruction responsible to the people and to Parliament, and who should have supervision of the entire system.

(2.) The teaching is secular, no sectarian instruction being allowed, yet the broad principles of morality are enjoined, and the term, "Secular," is defined to include general religious instruction. Four hours of each day must be devoted to secular instruction, but one hour of each day must be set apart for the religious instruction of the pupils, by the clergyman or authorised teacher of any denomination who may wish to do so, provided children are not compelled to attend religious instruction, unless it is the wish of their parents or guardians; but children excused from their religious teaching must pursue their secular studies during the time.

(3.) All teachers are paid directly from the State funds, and hence teachers are civil servants, entitled to all the emoluments thereof.

(4.) All school fees, except those of the evening schools, are paid into the consolidated revenue, they being the property of the State. The fee is threepence per week. No family, however numerous, shall pay more than one shilling per week. Poor children, upon proof thereof, are admitted free.

(5.) Wherever an average of twenty pupils can be secured a public school may be established.

(6.) Provisional schools, half-time, and house to house schools may be established in the thinly-peopled districts, upon a request being properly presented to the Minister of Education.

(7.) Superior public schools and high schools may be established, the former where there is not less than twenty pupils who are in the fifth grade or class. High schools are established in several of the large towns, and are intended to prepare pupils for matriculation in the University.

(8.) English and Australian history is insisted upon.

(9.) Attendance at school is compulsory between the ages of six and fourteen if the children are within two miles of the school. If they are in attendance elsewhere, or have passed an exemption examination, they are excused.

(10.) All aid to denominational schools has ceased since 1882.

The public schools are arranged in nine classes in respect to the number of pupils in attendance, and the salaries of the teachers classified on the same basis. First-class public schools are such as have an average attendance of six hundred and upwards. The head-master of the class receives a salary of £400, and a house of the yearly value of £100 if he is a married man. This class of school must be in three department—one for boys, one for girls, and one for infants. Mistresses in charge of the girls' department are paid £300, and £40 for rent of house.

Alderman W. JONES.

EDUCATION.   337

A male teacher in charge of a second-class school, which is defined to be a school where the average attendance is not less than four hundred children in three departments, boys, girls, and infants, has a salary of £336, and £100 house rent. The salary of a mistress is £252, and house rent of £40.

A third-class school is one where the average attendance is not less than three hundred, in three departments, with a salary for the master of £252, and house rent of £80; and for a mistress, salary £204, and house rent £30.

A fourth-class school is one whose average attendance is two hundred pupils, in two departments. Salary for master £240, and house £80; mistress, salary, £192, and house £30.

Fifth-class has an average attendance of one hundred, in one department. Master's salary £228, house rent £80; mistress' salary £180, house rent £30

Sixth-class has an average attendance of fifty pupils; one department. Master's salary £216, house rent £80.

Seventh-class schools have an average of forty pupils; one department. Salary of master £180, house rent £50.

Eighth-class schools have an average of thirty pupils; one department. Master's salary £156, rent £50.

Ninth-class schools have an average attendance of twenty pupils; one department. Master's salary £132, and house rent £50.

Tenth-class schools are such as have a less number than twenty pupils, and the master's salary is £108, with £30 house rent.

Both masters and mistresses are appointed to the schools by the Government, paid directly by the Government, all provided with suitable homes, and in no way subject to the local influences that usually arise where the appointing power rests with a local board elected by the people. It will also appear to the reader that the salaries allowed are exceedingly liberal. It is true that in some portions of the United States of America, in the larger centres of population, the salaries of some of its chief instructors are much larger, but such are limited in number. The great bulk of teachers in the sparsely-settled regions do not fare so well. The average here is much greater than in Canada. While the qualified teacher is made to feel his independence of all local influence, there is present the continual stimulus to raise the class of his school, for as soon as it reaches a higher average attendance it carries a higher class salary.

The above salaries are for head-masters, or such as have charge.

Many of the schools require assistants. The salaries of this class are graded also. To a first assistant holding a first-class certificate the salary is £250 to a male, and £168 to a female; to a second assistant with second-class certificate the salary is £150 to a male, and £120 to a female; to a third assistant with third-class certificate the salary is £108 to a male, and £100 to a female.

To a first assistant holding a second-class certificate, salary to male £180, to female £144; to an assistant holding a second-class certificate in a school of the third-class £150 to a male, and £114 to a female. From the above figures it will appear to the reader that the school department values the services of a woman at about three-fourths that of a man.

There is another class of teachers called pupil teachers, whose salary ranges from £66 to £36 for males, and from £48 to £25 for females. About half their time is devoted to instruction, while they are yet themselves receiving their own education. The wisdom of this feature has been frequently called into question, although in some schools it is found to be very satisfactory, while it lessens materially the cost to the State.

The Act authorised the establishment of training schools, where candidates for the profession of teaching are received and prepared for the work of teaching. Three classes of candidates are admitted—first-class, pupil teachers and other teachers who desire special training; second-class, untrained teachers who have been in charge of schools, but need special training; and third-class, such as desire to enter for the first time the profession of teaching. Applicants to the training schools must be twenty years of age (unless they have been pupil teachers), and not more than thirty. They must be free from all bodily infirmities of a nature that would impair their efficiency as teachers. They must be persons of active habits and good reputation and previous history. Before being admitted to the school they must pass an examination in the following subjects:—For the junior class, reading in the fifth class reading book, writing from dictation, grammar, parsing and analysis, arithmetic as far as vulgar fractions, outlines of geography, vocal music, and linear drawing; and to enter the senior class they have to pass an examination in reading from any standard author, writing from dictation, grammar, arithmetic, vulgar and decimal fractions, with square root, geography, vocal music, linear drawing, euclid (books I, and II.), algebra, to simple equations, Latin, and French first book. Females are excused from the senior mathematics and Latin, and take French instead. Before being received the candidate must make a declaration that it is his intention to follow the profession of teaching in the colony, and that he will accept any position to which he may be assigned by the Minister of Education. He has to procure a guarantee from two responsible persons that the whole of the expenses of his training shall be refunded to the State if he ceases, from any cause, before the expiration of the term of service stipulated. The terms of training will be for six or twelve months, as the case may be. An allowance of £8 to married persons, and £6 to single persons per month, may be allowed to worthy candidates during their training. Examinations are held twice a year, and the range of subjects are the usual ordinary subjects of reading, writing, arithmetic, grammar and composition, geography, school management, school books, vocal music, linear drawing, Public Instruction Act and regulations, domestic economy and needlework for female teachers, drill and gymnastics, euclid (four books), algebra to quadratic equations, elementary mechanics, elements of physics, chemistry and physiology, English literature, Latin for males, and French for females (if they should so elect), and history. After having passed the examination the successful candidate is placed in charge of a school, but his certificate of competency is not given until after the public inspector has reported him qualified to manage a school. The design of the training school is to prepare teachers for the primary public school.

The public schools under the Department of Public Instruction are:—

(1.) Primary schools: These are known as public schools, full time, half-time, or house to house schools, and evening schools, as the circumstances of the locality may call for. These schools are classified according to the average attendance, as above stated.

(2.) The superior public school, as before defined, where an average attendance of twenty pupils can be secured, of such as are advanced beyond the fourth grade.

(3.) The high school for boys and the high school for girls, established only in larger towns, and where the sexes are educated separately.

(4.) The Sydney Grammar School, which is being used as a training school.

The growth of the schools since the passing of the Act in 1880 has been rapid, and satisfactory to the great majority of the people. It cannot be expected to meet with universal favor, for it must be remembered that the entire system of secular instruction is in opposition to the settled convictions and conscientious views of a large and respectable portion of the community, who cannot be said to be indifferent to the education of the people. The Roman Catholics have always had a system of instruction that they have regarded as being the best suited to their needs. The many religious bodies have expended time and money in educating the children of the State during the period of its childhood and weakness, and many of them have become wedded to the old ways. While we cannot ignore the splendid work done by these bodies of Christians, and feel that the community owes them a debt of gratitude that cannot be justly paid by an attempt on our part to minify their labors or scorn their claims, yet we must be pardoned if we congratulate ourselves upon what we are pleased to believe is a vast improvement on the schools of the past.

In the case of house to house teaching in the sparsely-settled district the plan adopted is not to pay any stated salary, but instead, to pay the sum of £5 per pupil until the amount reaches the aggregate of £100. This plan stimulates the teacher to a degree of diligence that would scarcely result from any other plan.

When the Act came in force in 1880 there were 705 full time public schools, and 68,823 scholars. In 1887 there were 1,782 schools, and 147,499 scholars, and a corresponding increase in the number of provisional and half-time schools, making a total of 2,390 public schools, and 157,884 scholars. When it is learned that there are about 640 private schools and 40,000 scholars in attendance thereat, in addition, it must be apparent that the colony is not only well supplied with schools, but few countries in the world have as large a relative number. There is about one school for every three hundred persons in the colony. There is vast room yet for progress, both in efficiency and plan, but the rapid changes that have gone on in the management of this department and the very encouraging results are sufficient to induce the belief that the colony has adopted the very best means of accomplishing the result aimed at—namely, the education of the masses, chiefly in the elementary subjects of reading, writing, and arithmetic.

EDUCATION.

While this is the primary purpose of the Public School system, yet the State has gone beyond, and has made provision for the higher instruction of her people, not only in the superior public school and high school as may be required, but in the establishment of grammar schools qualified to impart instruction in all the higher branches, preparatory to the University. The Sydney Grammar School is the chief one of this class in New South Wales sustained by the State at present. There are a great number of institutions of similar rank sustained by church organisations and private individuals, which have no connection with the Public School system, and are wholly sustained by fees from pupils, private endowment or denominational contributions, from year to year. In fact, nearly all the higher tuition of the State is obtained at these schools, many of which have shown an efficiency in the preparation of pupils for the University that reflects great credit upon the organisations which control them. There would be a sad lack of school facilities were these institutions not everywhere to be found. Most people feel greater confidence in committing the education of their children into the hands of religious institutions than they do in sending them to a secular school, especially during the period of their youth, when about to prepare for the real business of life.

The highest school that the State provides under this system is the University of Sydney. This institution was incorporated in 1851, and has power to confer degrees in arts, law, and medicine, and to impart a wide and liberal education to all on equal terms. Since 1884 its powers have been by the Legislature greatly enlarged, so that it can grant certificates and degrees in all branches of learning, except in theology. Since 1884 it admits women on equal terms with the men. The government of the University is vested in a senate of sixteen elective fellows, and not more than six *ex officio* members, being professors of the University. Its range of instruction is as liberal as most colleges or universities of other countries, but by no means more so. The course required for the degree of B.A. is but three years. Four years is the rule in American and Canadian universities, and we have no doubt that in a very few years the course in the Sydney University will be raised to the same rank. Looking at the work of schools from a cosmopolitan standpoint one is perhaps made to feel more keenly the defects of an institution. A defect in the administration of this school, in our judgment, is the enormous fees required. We know of no State institution in the world that fixes its fees at so high a figure—averaging two guineas per term, or six guineas per year, for every branch or subject taught, and taking the average number taught in all universities at eight to ten, there will be required from each pupil from thirty to fifty guineas, which we believe is a serious defect in a State university that is intended to be for the benefit of the masses.

The examinations are yearly, and are held in the chief towns of the colony, and also in Tasmania and Queensland. Not having any University in these last-named colonies this and other facilities are granted to such candidates upon equal terms with those in New South Wales.

There are affiliated to the University St. Paul's, St. John's and St. Andrew's Colleges. St. Paul's, belonging to the Church of England, is governed by a warden and eighteen fellows, six of whom are in priest's orders.

St. John's, belonging to the Roman Catholic Church, is governed by a rector and eighteen fellows, of whom six must be priests.

St. Andrew's, under the Presbyterian Church, is governed by a principal and a council of twelve, four of whom must be ordained ministers of the Presbyterian Church of New South Wales.

It is part of the policy of the University to popularise itself by meeting the wishes of the people as far as practicable. The affiliation of the above colleges is intended to link the denominational schools of the higher class with the University, and blend all efforts into one. This is a worthy aim and a wise plan, and when the spirit of consistency shall prompt its administrators to affiliate in like manner the different sects in its medical department by State encouragement in the establishment and yearly endowment of the homœopathic and eclectic schools of medicine on equal terms with the allopathic school, then will the true democracy of the nation rejoice in another victory for manhood and equality " without the shedding of blood." It would be a peaceful triumph achieved by the omnipotent march of science. Happily the Law Department does not admit of sects. It deals more directly with established principles and forms that admit of no division.

Technical education is a part of the public instruction policy of the State. In 1883 a Board was appointed to promote the technical education of the people by the establishment of classes in the several sciences in their relation to the trades and manufactures of the country. In fact, throughout all the Australian Colonies technical education has received much attention within the last few years, and is made part of the educational policy of the respective Governments. In the larger cities, and in many of the towns, numerous classes have been formed in mathematics, engineering, mining, assaying, analysis, chemistry, farming, dentistry, photography, engraving, printing in all its departments, agriculture, etc. Large sums are voted from year to year to carry on this work. It has been found to be of great advantage to working people who, after pursuing their daily toil, can repair to the lecture-room or workshop and acquire a thorough knowledge of the principles and practice of their trade. Schools of Art are established in almost every important city and town throughout the continent. The Governments encourage the organisation of these schools by the payment of a certain sum for double the amount subscribed locally. In the country districts in mining places there are established reading rooms—the books being carefully selected, and usually of a technical or scientific type— which are found to be of practical utility. The establishment of this method of instruction has awakened among the youthful portion of the community a relish for substantial reading, and serves a moral purpose as well as a scientific one. The indirect benefit derived from this one branch of public instruction cannot be estimated. It will, without doubt, bear abundant fruit in a spirit of ambition and rivalry, which it tends to awaken and foster, and will result in an increased attendance at the higher institutions of learning. The aim of the Public Instruction Acts of the several colonies in Australasia is to meet every educational want, to extend the privileges of a free course to all who desire it, to act fairly to every portion of the community, and to give to the Colony a system that will secure the highest advantages to the greatest number at the smallest possible cost. They are nearly, if not all, identical with that obtaining in New South Wales, compulsory and free, or at most a very small fee is demanded, poor families having the privilege of nearly all grades of education free of charge.

We would scarcely do justice to the cause of education were we to fail in making honorable mention of many of the leading private schools, which are both numerous and efficient. More than one-third of the children of the colonies are educated in this way.

In South Australia the Adelaide University, which was incorporated in 1874, is an institution of higher learning, which aims at giving instruction equal to that of the recognised universities of the world. Among the private institutions of that colony may be mentioned the Wyndham College of North Adelaide, conducted by Wyndham and Sons. This institution has been long established, and has given a wide range of instruction to the youth of South Australia, not only preparing for the University of Adelaide, but caring for the physical as well.

In Tasmania, among the many schools worthy of mention, other than those embraced in the Public School Department, are Christ's College at Hobart; Horton College; Hutchin's School, Hobart; Ladies' Grammar School, Launceston; the Methodists' Ladies' College, Launceston; the Metropolitan College, Hobart; the Presentation Convent, Mt. St. Mary, Hobart; Proprietary Ladies' College, Hobart; all of which aim at a liberal, classical, mathematical, and scientific course—not neglecting, in the ladies' schools mentioned, the ornamental and art branches usually deemed essential to the thorough training of ladies.

Among all the colonies Victoria, perhaps, stands first in the number and efficiency of her private schools. Among the more prominent are the Boarding and Day School for Young Ladies, Fern Vale, East St. Kilda; the Caulfield Grammar School, East St. Kilda; the Church of England Grammar School, on the St. Kilda Road; the College of St. Francis Xavier, at Kew; Educational Institute for Ladies, in Melbourne; the Halstine House Ladies College, South Yarra; the Kew High School, Kew Hill; King's College, Fitzroy; Methodist Ladies' College, at Kew; Presbyterian Ladies' College, Melbourne; St. Kilda Grammar School, and others too numerous to mention. All of the above are efficient schools preparatory to the University. Many of the teachers of these private institutions are scholars of an advanced order. Some of these schools were established in the earlier years before any special move was made towards the establishment of Universities, and hence many of the leading statesmen have received their instruction at these institutions, and look upon their history and work with pride and favor. The Roman Catholics have by far the largest number of private educational institutions of every grade under the efficient management of the numerous brotherhoods and sisterhoods throughout the continent. The prejudice against common public schools is considerable, the wealthier classes preferring to send their children to private schools, and many who are not wealthy also, from the conviction that the moral tone of these institutions is better than that of the public schools.

The educational facilities of the colony are certainly commensurate with the development of every other department of civilisation. It is within the reach of all to acquire an education of the most liberal character, and to receive special preparation for any of the professions or callings in life. In years to come, plans yet untried and methods new will doubtless develop and bring to perfection what is yet only in purpose. The great heart of the people is thoroughly alive to the importance of education in its highest and best form. The liberality with which every demand for money has been met, and the pains taken by the most prominent statesmen in securing the broadest legislation in its behalf, are evidences of the universal sentiment in favor of the highest achievements in this respect.

CHAPTER XXX.

THE RELIGIOUS WORK.

IT is an interesting part of the historian's work to note the religious phase of a country's development. Whatever may be said of individual beliefs and articles of faith, the true observer of human events must acknowledge the work of the Church is an important factor in the advancement and civilisation of any people. All types of government depend upon her people's sense of right and wrong, and this sense can only be cultivated by constant education and enforcement by schools of authority.

The Home Government was not very deeply impressed with the need of religious instruction in planting her first colony in this country. Perhaps her recent failure to keep in submission the colonies in America, and the disastrous defeat she sustained in trying to rule them with a rod of iron, notwithstanding the prayers of the church in her behalf, induced her possibly to distrust the power of prayer. She had not yet learned that it is only the "prayers of the righteous that availeth much," that a people must have a righteous cause before they pray for its success. Smarting under recent defeat, and made to feel that her unholy warfare in America met with favor neither from God or man, she turned towards Australia, with scarcely a thought that the Supreme Ruler of the universe had any interest in the rise or fall of the British Empire, or in the establishment or care of the poor unfortunate convict whom she wished to send into the utmost parts of the sea. It was altogether an afterthought to send out a clergyman to be the spiritual guide of the people. The project of making Australia a penal settlement had been discussed for several years in the

British Parliament, and widely discussed by the Press of the day, and deemed a wise provision. Her rulers, who were largely of the soldier class, and so accustomed to rely upon the rigid discipline of her men and the long range of her guns, gave no heed to the injunction, "Let not the wise man glory in his wisdom; let not the mighty man glory in his might, etc."

When the subject of sending a minister of the gospel out with the first shipment of convicts and their guardians, the proposition was laughed at as a ridiculous waste of public funds, but the urgency of Mr. Wilberforce and other religious persons prevailed with the Government, and reluctantly one was appointed to accompany the young colonists (of nearly one thousand souls) to their new destination at Botany Bay. The Government, however, made no further provision than that of his passage, and the most meagre and parsimonious means of subsistence at the end of his journey. This was happily supplemented by the Society for the Propagation of the Gospel. The Rev. Richard Johnson was the clergyman selected, on the recommendation of Bishop Porteus and Sir Richard Banks. He was no doubt a very worthy clergyman, of excellent Christian spirit, and deeply interested in the spiritual welfare of the classes to whom he was appointed as spiritual guide, but a man possessed of not so much energy and rugged strength as perhaps the nature of his work would naturally call for. While, therefore, he was abundant in his efforts to teach the people of his charge, and did continue his ministrations for many years with a quiet punctuality and perseverance worthy of a clergyman of scholarship and decent severity in some old well-cared for vicarage in the Old Country, he ofttimes labored without sympathy or apparent success, and when he retired from the colony in 1800, twelve years after his first landing, he had little to boast of in regard to the Church's success, and much to complain of. There was a general want of attention on the part of officers and prisoners to the precepts and practices of Christianity. It is not to be wondered at that a very low state of morals should prevail during the infancy of the colony. The indifference to religion that characterised the Home Government in relation to their colonial enterprise, the widespread disregard to all the claims of Christianity on the part of nearly all the officers and soldiers who were appointed to administer the affairs of the colony, and the reckless spirit of most of those committed to their care, tended to make the work of the

Church of little account, and to discourage any laborer in moral reform who was not possessed of an iron will and invincible spirit. A Boanerges, like Peter, would have bearded the lion in his den, would have fearlessly confronted rulers and prisoners alike with the words of rebuke, and make vice at least hide its head. The Rev. Mr. Johnson was a Christian gentleman, of delicate health, benevolent and kindly in his bearing to all, and whose example and life is worthy of all praise, but not fitted to cope with the rough conditions that surrounded this early settlement.

One thing worthy of record here is the fact that to this clergyman is to be credited the honor of having introduced and cultivated successfully the orange enterprise. He was the first to plant the orange seed, and the first to derive profit from this large colonial industry. His farm of six hundred acres of land at Parramatta is still pointed out as the first orange farm of Australia.

The first church was built under the direct leadership and supervision of Mr. Johnson, and consisted merely of wattle branches woven into posts made from the cabbage palm, and then daubed with mud, and covered with bark shingles. It was seventy-three feet in length, thirty feet in breadth, and another part at right angles forty by fifteen feet. It cost in all, when complete, £40, besides labor and material gathered from the surrounding hills. It was used for school purposes as well as divine service. It was opened on the 25th August, 1795, and burnt down on the 1st October, 1799, no doubt by some of the "baser sort" of convicts who were compelled to attend divine service against their will. This, however, did not relieve them from the duty, for the Governor ordered them to attend in future twice upon the Lord's Day as a punishment, but as the punishment came equally upon the officers it soon fell into disuetude. The Rev. Mr. Johnson's success was only partial. In the year 1800 he returned to England.

The Rev. S. Marsden was the second clergyman sent to this field. He came in the year 1794, and was assigned to special duty in Parramatta, where he was successful in building a stone church, St. John's, with a seating capacity for four hundred. It was the first permanent church structure built in the colony; though begun in the year 1794, shortly after the arrival of the Rev. S. Marsden, yet it was only opened for divine service in the year 1803. Parramatta being the seat of Government at that time had residing there many of the most noted people of the colony, and hence the infant church had within her fold, nominally at least, those who could have rendered her great assistance by their sympathy and active co-operation, yet it does not appear from any of the early records that the church received any other than a very formal acknowledgment. The clergy, as a rule, met with very little encouragement from the laity, and for many years had to struggle on against all odds, amid a general disregard of her ordinances, and a widespread spirit of licentiousness that boded little good to the future of the young colony.

The foundation stone of St. Philip's Church, Sydney, was laid by Governor Hunter in 1800. It took four years to complete it. It was a stately edifice for the times, ninety-seven feet in length and thirty-two feet in width, and eight bells in its tower chimed forth in a somewhat crude fashion the hour of service, and bade the people repair to the house of God.

The Rev. W. Cooper and the Rev. Robert Cartwright came to the colony in the year 1809. In 1818 the Rev. Richard Hill was added to the number. In 1825 there were ten clergymen only of the Church of England.

Of all the early clergymen in the Church of England Mr. Marsden seems to have been the most zealous and effective—a man full of earnestness, and a godly desire to establish the Church on a broad and firm basis. He was no time-server. He sternly rebuked sin in all places. He sought neither the smile nor feared the frown of any man, ruler and ruled alike came under his plain condemnation or commendation as he deemed just. Among the officials of his day he had many friends who valued his services beyond estimate, and also many who regarded him harsh and severe without discretion, and more especially towards those once under the condemnation of the law, but now emancipated and honored by the powers that be for their fidelity and general good behaviour. Whatever may be said of the harsher side of his nature, it cannot be said that he ever faltered in his attachment to the doctrines and institutions of his church, but sought everywhere to uphold the dignity thereof, while he exhibited an unvarying kindliness towards all clergymen of other churches who were from time to time sent to labor among the people for their spiritual good.

The conflict in the sentiments of Governor Macquarie and this worthy clergyman was most severe, and will best illustrate the divided sense of the community in relation to those who were at one time convicts. It was the policy of the Governor to encourage the emancipist (as the freed prisoners were called) by every possible means. It was his aim not only to permit them to occupy the lands in common with other people, but to make them feel that where their course of conduct justified the hope of complete reformation he would place them in positions of honor and responsibility, and make them feel the force of their personal manhood as a factor in the good government of the colony. The wisdom of the Governor's policy is not only apparent in the history of this land, but has been in many instances illustrated elsewhere. In contrast with this large-hearted benevolence and broad statesmanship is to be placed the narrowness of the Rev. Mr. Marsden, good man as he was. He could not sit on the same Magisterial Bench with a convict who had been honored with this distinction, but resigned forthwith, under the foolish and unchristian idea that his personal dignity suffered. Well, we must hardly expect perfection from mortal, whether clergyman or laity, at the same time we cannot help feeling how infinitely higher and nobler was the Master than the servant, for he thought it no humility "to receive sinners, and eat with them." Many of the early clergymen were constituted magistrates, and upon them devolved the duty of imposing the penalty of "flogging," a species of punishment that was very much in vogue in the earlier years of the colony. The reader of this day can imagine the effect that familiarity with such punishment would have upon any clergyman's mind, commissioned on the one hand by God to preach the gospel of peace and love to all men, and by the State commissioned to inflict one hundred or one thousand lashes upon the torn and bleeding back of some poor unfortunate convict who might have incurred the displeasure of his greedy task-master, who exacted the "tale of bricks without the measure of straw," and whose only crime possibly was his inability to render the demanded service. The most trivial offences were oftentimes made to appear in the very worst light by the ease with which testimony could be manufactured against a prisoner, and the difficulty every ex-convict experienced in even getting a hearing at all, and when granted that privilege, in having any credence placed upon his testimony. The effect of such a position was disastrous to the clergyman, and ruinous to the convict, for few such could be induced to listen with profit to a man on the Sunday preaching words of peace and righteousness, and on the week day be brought before the same man, and under the forced testimony of the false witness be condemned to the lash and consigned to punishment by the same voice that should have guided him to the cross. One scarcely can see how the Government could have been so blinded and foolish in joining the two offices that were, and always must be, incongruous. The effect of it was to estrange the emancipist from the Church, and to foster a spirit of opposition, infidelity, and hatred to everything ecclesiastical, the harvest of which, no doubt, is to be seen in the widespread want of sympathy with the Church's work that everywhere meets one in these colonies.

We cannot close this chapter without putting on record our conviction that, notwithstanding these defects in a character that had so much to commend it, the Rev. Mr. Marsden was a man of God, instrumental in doing much good, whose labors were abundant, and whose devotion to what he conceived to be his duty was constant, and whose faults were few in the comparison, and who, without doubt, received from his Master that forgiveness that his own harsher nature failed to extend to his fellows.

To the Rev. Mr. Marsden is due the credit of establishing a mission among the Maoris of New Zealand. He early recognised the superiority of that race, and sympathised with them under the cruel treatment they were receiving from the early white visitors to their island homes, who hesitated not to plunder them of all they possessed, and murder them if any resistance was made. In a letter to the Governor how earnestly does he plead their cause against the oppression of his own countrymen—"Europeans have no right to land on their island to destroy their plantations of potatoes and other vegetables, strip them naked of their garments, and ill-treat and murder them if they dare to resist such lawless oppression." He organised "The New South Wales Society for Affording Protection to the Natives of the South Sea Islands, and Promoting their Civilisation."

In 1824 the first Archdeacon was appointed to supervise the church work in Australia. Up to that period the clergy were entirely under the direction and supervision of the Bishops of Canterbury and Calcutta. Communication with these dignitaries was exceedingly slow and impracticable, but under the change effected the Church was enabled to accomplish much more, having the immediate supervision of a man in every way suitable for the arduous work of planting the Church institutions in every new part as soon as there was a nucleus sufficient to justify the hope of permanency and future success. For twelve years, in the relationship of Archdeacon, the Rev. Dr. Broughton was indefatigable in visiting all portions of the colony, and planting the Church on a broad basis, and also evinced a degree of wisdom so marked in dealing with all the political questions that presented themselves for solution in those early times that the authorities at Home made a wise choice in consecrating him first Bishop of Australia, when in 1836 the continent was set apart by itself as a diocese. It no longer had to look to the Bishop of Calcutta for any episcopal acts, having a Bishop of its own. The wisdom of this selection became manifest in every part of Australia. Bishop Broughton was received by the entire Church with a degree of confidence and good-will that enabled him to give to all church work under his direction an impetus which soon became apparent all over the continent.

The all-absorbing question that arose in relation to the Church's work in those years was the question of State aid. The education of the people in the practice of supporting the churches by voluntary contributions, and not by State assistance, has become a part of our convictions of modern time, and for that reason we might be disposed to think it strange that the country would tolerate for so many years a contention on the question at all. It is only another instance of the power of education. The people formerly were taught to rely upon the State; now they are taught to contribute voluntarily, and this we are inclined to believe is "the more excellent way."

The Church grew with such rapid strides that even the work of overseeing her many centres of activity become too much for one man.

In 1841 New Zealand was constituted a separate See, and the Rev. George Augustus Selwyn was consecrated Bishop, with head-quarters at Christchurch.

In 1842 Tasmania was made a separate See, under the jurisdiction of Bishop F. R. Nixon, and in 1847 South Australia and Melbourne were separated from New South Wales, and Bishop Broughton was designated Bishop of Sydney and Metropolitan of Australia and Tasmania. The spread and increase of the Church of England in these colonies have been commensurate with the increase of population, and has from the beginning comprised fifty per cent. of the whole. Every colony of the Australian group has been fortunate in the selection of their bishops. They have been men of great learning, ability and breadth, and have invariably held the confidence and esteem of all classes. The reader is referred to the ecclesiastical statistics for a record of the growth and prosperity of the Church from their own standpoint.

The Wesleyan Methodists have always manifested a lively interest in the spiritual welfare of all classes, and especially in that of the more unfortunate, whether as prisoners or oppressed freemen. The earnest work of the Wesleys and Whitfield among the poor and neglected children of the household of the Church of England, not forgetting those outside her pale, will ever be held as the chief glory of that early band of Christian workers, who in their zeal and godlike self-sacrifice, went everywhere in search of those who were in need of the consolations of a living Christianity. At a very early date they were moved by the earnest appeal of some of the first colonists to inaugurate a mission among the few scattered settlers in New South Wales. The first mention we have in this direction was in a letter in the *Methodist Magazine*, dated July 20, 1812, which describes the moral and religious condition of the colony as one of extraordinary degradation. A few sentences from the letter itself will best present the writer's views, and give the readers of history a glimpse of society as it appeared to one of themselves during the first year of the colony's existence. "Thousands of souls are perishing from lack of knowledge, both in high and low life," says the letter, "Many in respectable situations riot in all the crimes of which their depraved natures are capable, several live in adultery with other men's wives, or with women to whom they were never married; and this example is practised by persons in various ranks in society, and I suppose one-half, at least, is thus circumstanced." There is also an earnest appeal to the Wesleyan Conference to send a "Methodist preacher, one who is attached to the establishment, and who will proceed in the primitive way of Methodism, not in hostility against the Church, but rather in unison with it." It was a fortunate circumstance that the Rev. Mr. Marsden, who was the leading clergyman of the Church of England in Sydney, and who, with great fidelity ministered to the spiritual wants of the colony in several portions thereof, was himself brought up under Methodist influence; and, no doubt, in his heart felt an inward sense of satisfaction when he was made aware that even a small section of the colony were desirous of securing the services of a co-laborer in a field so large and so poorly supplied with moral educators. We are, therefore, not surprised finding a clergyman of the church thus reared, and whose known spirit was one of christian charity and fairness, saying in a letter to the Rev. Mr. Leigh, the first Methodist clergyman : "To give you the right hand of fellowship is no more than my indispensable duty, and were I to throw the smallest difficulty in your way, I shall be highly criminal and unworthy the Christian name." These words were in reply to a letter of thanks sent by the Wesleyans to the Rev. Mr. Marsden for the gift of a piece of land at Windsor for a church. The whole transaction, letter and all, reflects credit from a religious aspect on all concerned.

It was not until frequent appeals were sent by the few who banded together that the conference in England found itself able to respond. The cry from "Port Jackson" became so urgent, and like that from Macedon of old, so importunate, that the great Dr. Adam Clarke personally undertook, under the advice of his brethren, the task of urging the appeal on the attention of those advisers of the Crown who were charged with the management of colonial affairs. As the result of his able advocacy of the cause, he and the Wesleyans had the satisfaction of receiving an official permit for the Rev. Samuel Leigh to proceed to the colony of New South Wales as a teacher, and for which he was to recieve a salary of £50.

On the 15th August, 1815, Mr. Leigh arrived in the colony, and although commissioned simply as a teacher, he felt his primary duty was to minister to the spiritual needs of the people who had so urgently appealed for "help" to the conference at Home, and in answer to which he was sent. Encouraged by the friendly and active assistance of the Rev. Mr. Marsden, of the established Church, Mr. Leigh began earnestly to form into classes such as were to be found of Methodist instruction and sympathy, and in the course of six months had "collected together forty-four members, in six classes, and had held services in fifteen different places. He labored diligently, and without ambition for earthly reward. He was even reminded by Governor Macquarie of the prospect of poverty before him if he did not look after his temporal circumstances, and was offered and urged to take a grant of land for his own temporal needs, but this he declined, choosing to be unencumbered by any worldly affairs. He had many trials to endure, and opposition to confront from those who were jealous of his success, and others who were reminded of the sinfulness of their lives, yet he persevered amid it all, and received, among his rewards for well-doing, the grateful thanks of many who were induced by his godly ministry to forsake sin; and, not least, the constant approbation and help of the Rev. Mr. Marsden, who, though not a Bishop *ex cathedra*, nevertheless maintained and exercised a Bishop's oversight throughout the length and breadth of the land. Among the early associates and Christian helpers we must mention Sergeant Scott, whose piety and noble nature enabled him to render valuable service to the Church in its early struggles against poverty and weakness.

The Wesleyan Society made substantial progress during its first years, though not rapid. In 1820, five years after its inauguration, it numbered eighty-three class members, and several hundred adherents.

The Rev. Mr. Lawry joined Mr. Leigh in the year 1818, and continued for four years to minister to these people, when he relinquished this for a purely missionary field elsewhere.

Failing health compelled Mr. Leigh to take a trip to England, which he did in 1820, but recovering somewhat, his ardent desire to renew his labors in New South Wales led him to return to his former much-beloved field, where for nine years he labored assiduously in preaching and visiting, and had the satisfaction of witnessing the spread and growth of Methodism. He was compelled, on account of enfeebled health, to return to England in 1831, where, after a term of active service in the quieter and more orderly work of the ministry at Home, he died, much respected and beloved by all, at the age of 66, in the year 1851.

The Rev. Mr. Carvosso was the third preacher sent to this colony. He came in 1820, and was everywhere instrumental in building up the Society's interests by his simple, straightforward teachings of his Church.

Sergeant Scott rendered substantial aid to the early Methodist cause by building a chapel for their use, entirely at his own cost of £500.

Governor Macquarie, whose interest in every honest enterprise was constant and practical, gave the body a valuable site in Macquarie-street, upon which was soon erected a stone building of moderate but seemly proportions. From this time forth the Wesleyans grew with quickening vigor, and her helpers became rapidly multiplied. The zeal that characterised their pioneer workman, Mr. Leigh, did not fail to kindle an enthusiasm in the breasts of his co-workers, and also in the entire body at Home, and hence we find new recruits in quick succession coming to this field full of the missionary spirit, and prepared to enter upon a work of hardship and bodily trial, hopeful only to be worthy successors of those who wisely laid the foundations upon which they were expected to build. Mr. Leigh did not fail to impress the parent body of Methodists in England with the importance of this enterprise, and to urge the selection of a superior class of men to be the standard-bearers in the infant Church in this promising land.

Among the worthy successors of this man we have to chronicle the advent of Mr. Schofield in 1827, the Rev. Mr. Horton in 1832, Mr. Orton in 1834, and Messrs. McKenny, Draper, and Lewis in 1836. The extent and success of the Wesleyan mission in this colony necessitated the appointment of a superintendent, and accordingly the Rev. Joseph Waterhouse was entrusted with the oversight of all the work in the Australian settlement, and those in the islands of the Pacific. The polity of the Church is well adapted to a missionary field. A great deal more Christian work can be accomplished by this body in the same period than by any other. Under its modes of procedure every member is constituted an active helper in the work of extending the services. When a person becomes a member of the Methodist Church he is expected to exercise his gifts in some sphere in an active form. The young man is pressed into service as a teacher or leader, exhorter or lay-preacher, and the young woman is employed in the Sunday-school or as a collector or visitor, and as the quality of each one's ability may appear in the actual work of the church they are urged to continue in "labors more abundant," and in this way the smallest effort made by the weakest member is appreciated not only for its own intrinsic value, but more because it forms a part of their complete church life. The value of lay helpers in establishing church services in the sparsely-settled districts is well understood by the Wesleyan Church authorities, not only in Australia, but equally so in every portion of the world. It never could have accomplished the vast results that have marked its history had it not wisely recognised the great value of individual and united labour.

Nearly all the various Church organisations previous to the Wesleys deemed a thorough training and ordination an absolute necessity ere one could perform any church act; but the Wesleys and Whitfield taught their followers that each one was an ordained witness for the Church, and that each had his special work to do. This is the theory that gave effectiveness to their efforts, and which conferred upon each one the power to do that which would build up the several departments of labor. With a much smaller staff of missionaries the Church was enabled to carry forward her work as a pioneer. They were the first to occupy the islands of the seas, and the new continent of Australia, after the Church of England. The growth of this branch of the Christian Church has been characterised by steady progress from the beginning. The State has always dealt with them as an important factor in the moral education of the people, and recognised their work as tending to conduce to the good order of society.

While the Wesleyan Church did not regard a thorough ecclesiastical training as a *sine qua non* to effective ministrations among the less learned, yet none has attached a greater importance to higher education. The efficiency of her schools the world over attests the genuineness of her appreciation of all the advantages they can give. This body has colleges for the special training of her ministry in New South Wales, Victoria, South Australia, and Tasmania, all taking rank among the first institutions of the land. The salary of its clergy is much more liberal than that granted to their ministers in any other portion of the world, so far as we know. The minimum being placed at £200 for a married man, and £150 for a single man—all married men having parsonages provided in addition, and furnished throughout. I think, with the exception of a few Methodist ministers in the leading cities of the United States of America and Canada, those of Australia, both in the rural districts and in the towns, are better paid, and more comfortably provided for than their brethren of other lands.

There are four conferences:—(1) New South Wales and Queensland; (2) Victoria and Tasmania; (3) South and Western Australia; (4) New Zealand. The islands are under the supervision of the conference most directly in communication therewith or contiguous thereto.

There is a general conference held once in four years for the consideration and adjustment of all questions pertaining to the general work of the Church. The President of the general conference is the Rev. J. H. Fletcher, who also sustained the position of President of the Newington College, Stanmore, New South Wales, from its foundation until last year.

The Rev. Joseph H. Fletcher was educated at the Rev. John Wesley's school at Kingswood, England, founded by him for sons of his preachers, and at Wesleyan Theological Institution, Richmond, Surrey; appointed in 1849 to be head-master of Wesley College, Auckland, which post he filled for seven years; engaged in the ministerial work of the Wesleyan Methodist Church in New Zealand and Queensland until the year 1865, when he was appointed President of Newington College, which he left in April, 1887, having been appointed by the conference to be theological tutor for students only accepted and in preparation for the Wesleyan Methodist ministry. He was elected President of the conference of New South Wales and Queensland in 1874 and in 1884, and President of the general conference held at Christchurch, in New Zealand, in 1884. Mr. Fletcher has done a full share of public and literary work amongst his brethren, and has seen colonial life under all its aspects, having witnessed the social dislocations which followed the rush to the goldfields of California and Victoria, and having been present at New Plymouth, in New Zealand, when the town and vicinity were the seat of the last Maori war.

Among the early free settlers drawn to this land were to be found many of Scottish birth, brought up under the Presbyterian faith of Scotland and who were desirous that their children should be instructed in the same way. Some one has sarcastically said that the chief end of a Scotchman is "mountain dew and the shorter catechism." We will regard the first portion of this as a slander, for while, without doubt, they do love good whisky as a rule, the general sobriety that prevails among that race clearly shows that their rugged strength of character and the elevated moral tone that pervades them all is largely due to their high regard for and appreciaton of the religion of their fathers that enjoins honesty among men and faith in God.

It would hardly be consistent for such to remain long in a new land without the kirk and the school-master. These factors, under their new conditions, they at an early date strove to obtain. They comprised most of the settlers on the Hawkesbury, and assembling together they soon subscribed sufficient to build a house suitable for the above purposes, and inaugurated their work among themselves as laymen, hoping in future to secure the services of a minister who would be able to carry on to a successful issue what they had so faithfully begun. Their first church and school building was opened in 1809, and cost £400, but they had to wait fourteen years before a suitable minister could be found who was willing to undertake the mission.

The Rev. John Dunmore Lang was the first Presbyterian clergyman who became actively identified with the colony, and to this eminent divine is due the honor of having established the Presbyterian Church in this country, and also of having given material impulse to the early schools of New South Wales. It was not by any cringing spirit of sycophancy to the powers that were in control that he won, but by a bold, aggressive spirit of energy and independence that demanded recognition and assistance, not as a favor, but as a right. Liberty for his faith and equality before the law were boons bought by Scottish blood, and transmitted to every Scottish son, not as a patronage, but as a heritage under the pledged protection of England's throne. He sought and obtained from the authorities at Home assistance in his work, when his requests for help were rejected by the colonial Governor. He contended for equality only, but he contended like the lion, with tones that all heard, and with a strength that all were afraid to trifle with. Dr. Lang, for many years, stood alone as the clerical representative of the Presbyterianism of Australia. His earnest advocacy of nearly all the important reforms that have been effected during the fifty years of his colonial work gave him an importance in the political and social world that enabled him to accomplish much more for the church of his choice than a man of a purely spiritual temperament. The force of his intellect and the justness of his acts gave him a following in the political world that contributed largely to the Church. On Sunday he was a preacher of the gospel under the forms and requirements of the Westminster Confession of Faith, and on a week day he did not hesitate to roll up his sleeves, and in Parliamentary circles stand to the front and thunder his denunciation against those in high and low places who were abetting wrong, and by most convincing logic, if not by eloquence, moved resolution after resolution in the interest of the masses and of equal rights. Presbyterianism took a firm hold upon a large number of the early pioneers who were of the liberal and reform type, and largely through the influence of Dr. Lang, who never was more happy than when he was in a political contest. From the year 1823, the date at which Dr. Lang first came to the colony the Church grew rapidly, and soon had to increase its staff of clergymen in all the centres of population. There were two distinct parties in the Church for many years that rendered progress less encouraging, the one favorable to State aid to the churches, and the other strongly opposed to it. The Free Church of Scotland, made up of those in the Motherland who were opposed to the principle of State aid, had its following in this country. The old kirk or established Presbyterianism worked side by side with them. Both were one in the promulgation of the doctrines and spiritual methods of the Church, but in temporal matters they were divided. It was not until Parliament abolished all State aid to the churches that very great progress was made by this body of Christians.

They soon afterwards became united, and have ever since grown rapidly, and now rank among Protestant bodies the second in numerical strength, and without doubt second in wealth and social influence. The congregations separately manage the temporalities:—

(1.) There is elected by each congregation a Board from their own number called the Deacons' Court, who manage all the temporal affairs of the congregation.

(2.) There is another body, composed of the minister and elders, who are known as the Session. These have charge of worship and all spiritual matters. They look after the sick, the poor, and all things pertaining to the religious wants of the people.

(3.) The minister and one elder from each Session form the Presbytery, which body has the oversight of the people in that district.

(4.) The members of all the Presbyteries form the General Assembly of the colony.

In 1865 a union of all the different branches of Presbyterianism was effected, a few of the churches not being able to accept the basic principles thereof chose to pursue their work apart from the main body, and are known as the Synod of Eastern Australia. It is believed by most persons that it is only a question of very few years when all will be united as one, in name, as they are now in spirit and church work. In the matter of education, here as elsewhere, they attach great importance to the thorough scholarship and suitable training of their clergy, and for these purposes they have two excellent institutions. The Ormond College, of Melbourne, named after its founder, a man of princely wealth and liberality. The college building cost £22,671, and is affiliated to the Melbourne University. The St. Andrew's

College, of Sydney, was founded in 1867. It is affiliated to the University of Sydney, and is an efficient training school for the clergy. The minimum salary fixed by the General Assembly is £300, with a manse. It is only occasionally that force of circumstances compels a departure from this rule. On the whole, the average salary paid to the clergy of this church is more liberal than they receive in any other country. We refer the reader to the statistics at the end of this chapter for further facts regarding their strength.

Among the eminent clergymen who are truly representative of all that is good and strong in this body may be mentioned the Rev. Dr. Steel. He was one of the chief advocates of a Presbyterian Union, and did much towards bringing about that desirable result.

The Rev. Robert Steel, D.D., Ph.D., minister of St. Stephen's Presbyterian Church, Sydney, is Scotch by parentage, but was born in Pontypool, Monmouthshire, on the borders of Wales, 15th May, 1827. He was taken to Scotland when nine years old, and educated at the parish school of Ochiltree, Ayrshire, and at the Royal Burgh Academy, of Ayr. He then proceeded to King's College and University, Aberdeen, and afterwards for the study of theology to New College, Edinburgh. He labored for a few years as missionary among the non-church-going people in the town of Irvine, and as assistant to the Rev. R. Macdonald (now D.D.), at Blairgowrie. He was settled as minister of the Free Church in the Isle of Cumbrae, in the Firth of Clyde, in 1852; translated to Salford, Manchester, in 1855, and to Cheltenham in 1859. In 1862 he was invited to Sydney, and has continued there for twenty-five years.

In all these places he received substantial tokens of public esteem, and was very useful. He early identified himself with popular religious and social literature, and become a contributor to periodicals. In 1851 he founded *Meliora*, a quarterly review of social science, of which he was joint editor for four years. He was a member of the Executive Council of the United Kingdom Alliance while at Manchester. He has throughout his public life been a public lecturer on many popular subjects, and interested in the improvement of young men. He has for a number of years acted as tutor of church history and pastoral theology to the General Assembly of the Presbyterian Church of New South Wales for the training of young men for the Christian ministry. He has not been a controversialist, but a social reformer, and has been always ready to advocate the temperance cause. He has been one of the clerical counsellors of St. Andrew's College, within the University of Sydney, and for twenty years has acted as agent of the New Hebrides Mission. He paid a visit to these islands in 1874, and published a work upon the mission in 1880. He has issued seven volumes from his pen :—" Doing Good, or the Christian in Walks of Usefulness," 1858; "Samuel the Prophet, and the Lessons of his Life and Times," 1860; "Lives Made Sublime," 1861; "Burning and Shining Lights," 1865; "The Christian Teacher in Sunday Schools," 1867; "The New Hebrides and Christian Missions," 1880; and "The Shorter Catechism," with analyses and illustrations, 1885. He edited the *Presbyterian Magazine* in Sydney from 1863 to 1866, and the weekly paper, the *Australian Witness*, from 1876 to 1880. He took a long tour, by the leave of his congregation, in 1880, and was presented with an address and £630 by his friends and admirers. He visited the United States, Canada, the United Kingdom, Germany, Switzerland, Italy, Palestine, and Egypt. On his return he lectured one hundred times in different places on the scenes of his travels. Exhibiting a charitable spirit, he has secured the respect of the Christian public, as well as that of his own church. Dr. Steel has three sons and three daughters, the former embrace a medical practitioner, a clergyman, and a lawyer, and the latter are married in the colony.

In the larger centres of population the Congregational Church has grown into an important part of the Protestant division of the Christian religion. The peculiar polity of this body vests all authority in the congregation, and for this reason, her growth has of necessity to be confined to the cities, for her administration presupposes the existence of the congregation. Nearly all other bodies of Christians vest the chief power in the clergy, and hence they are more in accord with the missionary idea. The minister of most denominations is sent out to gather the people together, to start even from one as a centre, and thus grow. The government of the church entirely rests with each congregation, who formulates its own articles of faith, makes its own rules for the management of its affairs, and is altogether independent of the dictum of any other body, and is responsible to none but themselves, for which reason they are called "Independents." They usually embrace within their numbers an intelligent class of people who, as a rule, are quite content to take the Scriptures as their rule, interpreted by themselves, with the help of the man they choose to be their minister. They attach no more importance to the interpretations of the Fathers than they do to their own; in fact, believing themselves to be better learned in science and history than the former, they regard their own intelligence as a surer guide to truth than that of those who lived centuries ago. They have always consistently refused State aid, believing churches should be voluntary organisations, responsible only to God and themselves. Thus taught to be self-reliant, they are among the most benevolent examples of self-reliance and liberality. Their clergy are paid more liberally than any other. In Australia they are said to have 57,000 adherents. They have in New South Wales forty-eight churches, costing £153,024, or an average of over £3,000; in Victoria £170,000, or an average of over £3,000; in the other colonies seventy-six churches, at a cost of over £177,000, showing a liberality beyond the average found among other Christian people.

The chief training colleges are the Congregational College of Victoria, Melbourne, and Camden College, Sydney, and a third institution of the kind being created in South Australia, the endowment of which has already reached the sum of £13,450. There is nothing narrow in the spirit of Congregationalism. Her colleges are open to ministers training for other churches on the same terms with those training for her own. In fact, members of other churches can unite with any of her congregations, and become part of her body ecclesiastic without abjuring their own peculiar articles of faith if they simply subscribe to the fundamental principles of the Christian faith.

Almost every other denomination of Protestantism is found in the colonies, Primitive Methodists, Free Church Methodists, Baptists Union and Particular Baptists, New Church Society, German Evangelistical Church, Unitarian Church, Universalist, Protestant Episcopal, Free Church of England, Presbyterian Church in Scotland, Independent, German Lutheran Church, Evangelical Lutheran, Norwegian Evangelical Lutheran, Church of Christ, Bible Christian Church, Welsh Church, Society of Friends, Salvation Army, Catholic Apostolic, and United Methodists. All these phases of the Protestant faith, and many others with some distinctive doctrine, work side by side in the great mission of moral reform, and in fulfilment of the prophetic prayer that "they all may be one." Religion is emphatically free. The age of bitter feuds among religious bodies is past. People do not attach as much importance to shades of belief and customs, old or new, as formerly. The practical rules of an upright, honest life are sufficient to satisfy the people. Doubtless, when these things shall have come to impress the churches as being of much greater importance than their phylacteries, the color of their altar clothes, the size and shape of their robes, and the amount of water they use in baptism, the world will have come nearer the kingdom of Christ, and the churches will have laid again the foundation of its unity.

The Roman Catholic Church is unique in her methods of carrying forward her important enterprises, but, like herself elsewhere, she never falters or fails in her purpose. She began early in the history of the colony to minister to the spiritual wants of the first colonists, and was duly appreciated by the State and the people generally, especially the poorer classes. Some of the early convicts had among their number priests who were convicted of political offences against the Crown, and transported to Australia. Most of these, if not all, were pardoned in a very short time, it having appeared that the evidence taken by the British Courts of that day, and deemed sufficient to convict, was of the flimsiest character, and lacking trustworthiness, but whether guilty or not of an open expression of enmity and opposition to England's rule and methods in dealing with Ireland, the fault or crime alleged was not of such a character as to justify any such severity as was meted out to these offenders. It was a circumstance overruled by the Great Architect of the universe that served to introduce the offices of the Roman Catholic Church long before that body of Christians had permission to officiate under the direct protection and authority of the State. These convict priests were allowed, under restrictions, to minister to their brethren of like faith, and rendered good service to the cause of the Church, and to the good order and discipline of an element in society whose education in every land leads them to reverence ecclesiastical authority.

The early work of the Church of Rome in the colonies was not without much trial and opposition, and its progress at first was slow and interrupted for a time; but discouragements do not deter that organisation from repeated efforts. The one command, "Go ye into all the world and preach the gospel to every creature," is the rule that limits the sphere of its operations, and hence trials, want of sympathy, and co-operation on the part of those who are indifferent or in opposition, only intensify their ardor,

THE RELIGIOUS WORK.

and make their sense of duty more imperious. Her importunity conquered all opposition, and gave her a prestige among the people, second only to the established Church of England. She sought for, and obtained aid from the State from the beginning, as did several of the religious denominations. As an organisation she has never been opposed to State aid, or for that matter, aid from any other source. The supervision of the work in Australia was under the Bishop of Mauritius until 1834, when it was placed in the keeping of Bishop Polding, the first in the See of Sydney having jurisdiction over the entire continent of Australia and Tasmania. This Bishop was a man of great energy and perseverence, and established the Church in all portions of the continent on a firm and liberal policy. He was far-sighted, and took special care of the future wants of the Church. He early saw the importance of obtaining large grants of land for the Church's institutions in the several towns and cities of the country. Much of the wealth of the church to-day is due to the foresight and sagacity of Bishop Polding, who seems to have lost no opportunity of obtaining for his church the most suitable locations in the several centres of population, and in the young towns whose future development was merely indicated by their relation to the growing districts surrounding them.

The success of all the Church's operations has been equal to her expectations. Her wonderful machinery for carrying on her work, and especially that of education, has been her chief source of strength. The unity of her system, and the practical sympathy that her head at Rome gives to every part, insures efficiency in the plans she invariably adopts in gaining a foothold wherever she pleases. She brings to her self-imposed task a wisdom both ecclesiastical and secular that rivals the statesmanship of kings. Bishop Polding was raised in 1842 to the rank of "Archbishop of Sydney and Vicar Apostolic of New Holland," previous to which Tasmania was separated as the diocese of Hobart. The growth of the Church was rapid, and necessitated the division of the jurisdiction for more extended work. In 1884 Adelaide was constituted into a separate See, Perth in 1845, Brisbane and Port Victoria in 1859, Ballarat and Sandhurst in 1874, Maitland and Bathurst in 1865, Goulburn in 1866, and Armidale in 1873. In 1876 the continent was divided into two provinces for the better supervision of the spiritual and temporal interests of the Church. The province of Sydney embraces New South Wales, all the dioceses within the colony, and the whole of Queensland (excepting the northern division), and the Victoria Plains of Western Australia, and having under their influence and instruction about one-sixth of the population. The government of the Church being in the hands of the ecclesiastical authorities, the writer is unable to give the reader more than this brief outline of an organisation that chooses rather to be known by her work than by any specific reports of the methods of accomplishing her mission. The marks of wealth and prosperity that are everywhere apparent in connection with her enterprises are the most satisfactory proofs that demonstrate her general acceptability with the people, and the enthusiastic sincerity with which she applies herself to the realisation of her avowed purpose of conquest and universal victory. Her growth is evidently beyond that of any of the denominations, and in politics she is becoming an important factor. The unceasing energy displayed by the numerous institutions under her control and direction is the one fact that gives effectiveness to her mission. Her voice never ceases to be heard, and when heard is always the same.

We submit the following statistics showing the relative strength of the various religious bodies in the colonies, including New Zealand. These have been carefully compiled from the annual reports of these bodies, so far as we have been able to consult that source of information. When we have been unable to obtain the figures from ecclesiastic sources, we have had to fall back upon the Government reports, which are not always up to date:—

The Church of England has about 1,200,832 adherents, being almost one-third of the population; the Roman Catholics have about 590,210 members, forming nearly one-sixth of the inhabitants; the Presbyterians come next in strength, numbering 324,122; the Methodists of all branches of that Christian body number 256,216, but it is doubtful whether these figures represent their entire strength, as many of their adherents are not embraced in their church reports; the Congregationalists have 60,109; the Baptists, 46,982; other Protestants, about 66,291; the Unitarians, 3000; and the Jews about 10,183.

There is apparent in the comparative reports given for the last ten years a proportionate increase far in excess of the growth of the population, revealing the fact that great activity marks the work of the churches.

These figures reveal only in a superficial way the religious interests of the several churches. The vast amount of self-sacrifice and expenditure of zeal and money in maintaining the several charities that are the immediate result of the Church's work are not matters of public record, and will remain hid from the knowledge of man.

CHAPTER XXXI.

RECREATIONS.

SPORT is one of the characteristics of Australian life. It is impossible for any outsider to form any adequate conception of the meaning of this word in relation to this people. It is a part of their very existence —a necessity of the climate. If the reader entertains the idea that it is simply a pastime, that sport is indulged in for the purpose of killing time, he is very much mistaken. It is a phase of colonial life as difficult of interpretation, and yet as easily understood as the child's rollicking ways and spirit of gleefulness. Australians love sports just as heartily as the child enjoys "see-saw" or "ring around a rosy." The gushing laughter, the rippling smile, and the thousand lullabys of our infant years are nature's voices that proclaim the fact that we are young. They are not the conventional usages of society that have grown up with the ages, and forced upon the youth as the schoolmaster would cram his pupils with the rules of arithmetic. They are not learned any more than laughter is learned, or breathing. These are the involuntary acts of obedience that man delights to pay to the ungrasped intelligence that created life, and put its own signet of love upon every function of our youthful being, and pleasure becomes the pathway of duty.

A universal sentiment of fun pervades the country, and expresses itself in many ways. No country in the world has shown a spirit of joyfulness equal to this. Strangers have been disposed to criticise with severity this characteristic, and many have been led into the belief that the tendency of the people was towards a reckless disregard of the most important duties of life, but in this they have evinced an ignorance, both of the nature of their sports and their results. The fact that childhood is constituted so as to be satisfied only by a proper degree of mirthfulness is evidence that it was the intention of the Creator to make their childlike enjoyments a source of their development and growth. It is impossible to conceive of the young maturing without the influence of recreation. In one respect all youthful moods of gladness are benedictions divine; they are gleams of light intended to paint the cheek with beauty and the life with cheerfulness—both divine fountains of health and happiness. The conditions that give vivacity and jollity to the young are here in profusion, and prolong the characteristics of youth far into the years of manhood. The climate, the sunshine, the bounty, and the beauty of the landscape and sea have not failed to leave their godlike impress upon the child of Australasia, and the result is that the morning of youth extends far into the evening hours of life—paradoxical as the expression may appear.

No people value a holiday as highly as the Australian, and he has many of them. All business closes on Saturday at one o'clock. The afternoon is given up to sports—cricketing, rowing, football, pedestrianism, lawn tennis, bowling, cycling, coursing, horse racing, yachting, excursions, and park and garden promenade constitute the chief outside amusements, while theatres, music, lectures, etc., constitute the inside.

Cricket is the leading national game. The boys, from infancy, are to be found on the cricket field, and their love for it continues right through life. We frequently have seen men of fifty years of age enjoying the sport with a zest equal to that of the youth of sixteen who was playing by his side. It is a gay sight to see on some holiday, or any Saturday afternoon, the cricketers of several teams on the same grounds in their uniforms of white, and distinguishable from one another by a sash or a stripe in their cap only, all in active contest. This game has been popular ever since the early years of the colony. In 1826 the first recorded match took place in the old racecourse, now known as the upper portion of Hyde Park, in the city of Sydney, and continuously from that date to the present it has been prominently brought before the public in the many matches that have been played between the leading teams of England and those of Australia. In every city and town throughout the breadth of the country are to be seen cricketers of all ages, from children of ten up to men of middle age, playing as if their life depended on their success. The stimulus it gives to digestion, breathing, and muscular activity has its effect on the tone and symmetry of their muscular development. The rounded and compact forms one everywhere sees upon the cricket field, and in the sporting circles generally of this country, are the surest proofs of the direct benefit their young men derive from this and other games. Every important paper in the colonies has a column filled with the reports and doings of the various clubs, and they are as numerous as the towns and municipalities of the continent.

Football is a game that the younger men of Australia most thoroughly enjoy. It calls into active exercise the lower extremities, and it is wonderful to witness the agility of some of the players. They acquire such precision, accuracy, and power in the kick, or, more properly speaking, in the application of their pedal extremities to the ball, that one is made to wonder at the astonishing results that can be accomplished. The exercise itself is good, and the mirthfulness of the sport awakens the intensest enthusiasm. The bodily exercise is somewhat severe, and for this reason it is a game most frequently played in cold weather, the winters here being just cool enough to make active sport a luxury to both body and mind. To give the reader who has never been in the colonies an idea of the interest taken by the people in this sport, the mere mention of the fact that at some of their contests as many as fifteen thousand have been present, will be sufficient. Whatever may be thought in some quarters of the evils arising out of the excessive indulgence on the part of the young boys in this sport, nevertheless, from a physical and scientific, and therefore moral standpoint, we are constrained to stand by the boys and their games. Efforts at times have been made to check it. Still it moves on, and grows with the years, and having found it to be a bubbling fountain of merriment the Australian clings to it with a tenacity characteristic. He never gives up a good thing.

Lawn tennis has become exceedingly popular in the few past years. It is a suitable recreation for ladies as well as men. The exercise it gives is not so severe as most other sports, but the pleasurable excitement attendant upon a well-played game is a nerve tonic of great importance. The game being played by both sexes introduces the social element, which, apart from the exercise, is one of nature's undefined fountains of happiness. The union of the sexes is heaven's great law of perfect life. The exclusion of the one or the other from the labor avenues and pleasures of life, we believe, is a crime, and becomes the source of many errors. He was a wise Creator that said "it was not good for man to be alone." The usages of society that would separate them, and then send either the one or the other on a lonely pathway is a perversion and a snare. It is not safe for man to go alone anywhere, or woman either; they should go together. We should join in labor, and go hand in hand up and down the ways of life. The path that is safe for man is safe for woman, and where woman cannot go it is not safe for man. There is nothing that suggests to our minds desolation in all its bare horrors as much as a "bachelor's quarters" with no sound of woman's voice, without the radiance of woman's smile, and the inspiration of her presence. Even her frown occasionally is a gleam of sunshine in contrast to the picture of four bachelors housed together, each one trying to imagine himself happy, because no woman is near to "annoy" him. The very chairs refuse to be soft, or to welcome him, and in his surly, tortuous mood, he seeks the couch. This, too, refuses to give him rest or relief from the wearying lassitude of his grumbling bones, until his senses become dulled, and his spirit finds an imaginary repose in the fumes of his puffed cigar. Lawn tennis is one of the sports that satisfies a natural want. Its popularity here as elsewhere is a matter of congratulation and approval on the part of those who are interested in the social development of the sexes. The fine grass lawns that one meets everywhere have been greatly improved and multiplied since the introduction of this game. Its benefits, therefore, are not confined to the physical and mental tone it imparts, but also to the landscape.

Running is a very popular sport among the more youthful portion of the community. This combines excitement and physical strain to a great extent. We have runners here that have won world-wide fame in this particular. From England and America the very best exponents of this art have been seen upon our grounds, and did much towards giving this sport a stimulus. We have two very superior grounds—the one at Botany Bay called Sir Joseph Banks, and the other the Carrington Grounds, at Surrey Hills, in the city of Sydney. The latter cost £7000, and was only completed in 1886, and named in honor of the present Governor, Lord Carrington. The distances run is always one hundred and fifty yards, and to give the reader some idea of the interest taken in this sport we mention the fact that at the first Carrington Handicap that was run on these last-named grounds in December, 1886, the amount of £525 was paid in prizes to the respective runners who distinguished themselves. On all public occasions the crowds of spectators that find enjoyment in witnessing these sports test the capacity of their largest stands. The game has become national, and its value is appreciated by all classes.

Rowing is a pleasure that stands only second to cricket with the Australian, and one not accustomed to witness much of this sport would be surprised to find the almost universal tendency of the people along the coast and rivers to indulge in this kind of recreation. The inspiration that makes it a pleasure is the facilities that those living in or near the great cities have of indulging in the sport. Nowhere else in the world are to be found such fine bodies of water as the bays connected with the capital cities of Australia —Adelaide, Hobart, Melbourne, Brisbane, and Sydney. This last-named has the unique and beautiful harbor of Port Jackson, celebrated for its beauty and land-locked character, for a full description of which the reader is referred to another chapter. Upon this sheet of water may be seen at all times numerous white sails, and scores of skiffs, and rowers plying their oars in every direction; but on a holiday one witnesses hundreds of these small vessels, row-boats, skiffs, and yachts dotting over the entire expanse, and making a scene unsurpassed in its picturesqueness and beauty. Children develop an enthusiasm in this pastime from their infancy. The nation seems to take kindly to the water. If they are not Baptists in their religious beliefs they certainly are so in their fondness for aquatic sports. Yachting, sailing, and rowing are the chief forms of pastime in this department. The large number of sailors in the first fleet that came to these shores, doubtless, had much to do with the introduction of one or all of these phases of aquatic pleasure, and the fact that this class of people having much time upon their hands favored its development. Some of the best rowers in the world are to be found here. The fact that William Beach, of New South Wales, held the championship of the world for a period of three years has given reputation to this country abroad, and at the same time given an impetus to the sport at Home, but skilled as the above rower has proved himself to be he is by no means the only one distinguished in this department.

The men who have been prominent in this list are: Brennan, Mulhall, R. Green, Punch, H. Green, McGrath, Donnelly, Hickey, Laycock, Rush,

E. Trickett, Messenger, Neil Matterson, Peter Kemp, Tom Clifford, Neilson, and William Beach, who, after beating Hanlan, the Canadian champion, retired from the sporting world, and passed the championship to Kemp, a worthy rival.

Canada, honorably represented by Hanlan, and Australia represented first by Trickett, and afterwards by Beach, were very evenly balanced in the estimation of the sporting world. Trickett had won against Rush, a signal victory in a race rowed on the Parramatta in the year 1877, having previously secured the championship of the world by the defeat of Sadler, England's greatest oarsman of that day. It was estimated that fifty thousand people witnessed this race on the Parramatta, and led to the contest arranged for in 1880, on the Thames, between Hanlan, the Canadian champion, and Trickett, the world-champion. No race ever had awakened such an interest. Hanlan won, and was proclaimed the world-champion. Laycock, another Australian, went to the front to pluck the laurel from the maple leaf, but he, too, quickly joined his comrade at the footstool of Canada's conqueror. Hanlan's triumph seemed complete, and the jewels in his crown seemed to brighten with every contest, until another Australian boy, from out the seclusion of his own immediate circle of friends, challenged the conqueror to come.

William Beach had not the comeliness of form or the skill of method that graced the Canadian, but every line of feature and muscular fibre told the tale that he was a man both brave and strong, and could be trusted by his friends to win back the glory that his country held until dimmed by Canada's excelling lustre. He met the champion on the 16th of August, 1884, and the champion fell, and once more Austalia's supremacy was proclaimed; a second contest on the Thames the following year confirmed the fact that Beach was king; and a third arranged to settle all doubts in regard to the matter was rowed last year, 1887, when on the 26th November, in the presence of a large concourse of people, Beach and Hanlan, both the first among the honorable rowers of the world, worthy exponents of their art, and reflecting equally the honor of their respective lands, met as friends, both kings, and on the Nepean River, one of the most beautiful sheets of water in Australia, there measured strength and skill, and for the third time Beach won by two lengths on a course of three miles.

The interest taken in this sport is general among the younger portion of the community, and is regarded by the authorities as conducive to health and happiness, and is therefore encouraged in every legitimate way.

Bowling is a game popular to a large extent among a class—though not as exhilarating as many of the other sports, it is of sufficient interest to satisfy a large number. The player can retain his interest in this game on through old age. It is well adapted for men of years. The young man who is content with a moderate degree of excitement can find enjoyment in this that proves to be a pleasant source of recreation, and the same sport can hold him in its chains, even when his stiffening joints and quivering muscles tell him that he is growing old, except in spirit. We find on the bowling green men of all ages, the youth of twenty summers, and the man of seventy, equally intent upon his pleasurable task. It is to the aged like going back and drinking from the fountain of youth. The young man of sixty is a pleasant sight more frequently met in this climate than in other parts of the world.

Theatres afford the greatest amount of pleasure to the greatest number of the people in these colonies. The number and variety of public buildings devoted to this amusement is large, and will, in itself, indicate the demand for this class of recreation. In the city of Sydney, of 300,000 inhabitants, there are nine theatres in full swing nightly; in Melbourne, having a population of about 320,000, there are ten; Adelaide, with a population of 120,000, has five; Brisbane, having only 50,000 inhabitants, has three theatres continually running. There is scarcely a town of 4,000 inhabitants anywhere but has its theatre, and occupied pretty much all the time. The buildings occupied in this way are usually paying property, which will show the fact that this amusement is very generally patronised. No people are fonder of the play-house than the Australian. There is very little prejudice, comparatively speaking, against it as an entertainment. In almost all other portions of the world there is a strong settled antagonism between the Church and the theatre. The pulpits thunder away at the theatre, and the latter caricature the former, and so the war goes on between them, and the people divide on the question of theatres in relation to the churches; but in Australia there is very little of that sentiment. Church people go to theatres just as they go to their respective clubs, cricket matches, rowing contests, horse racing, etc., etc.

Clergymen and their people all, with few exceptions, attend, and enjoy a good performance. We have frequently seen the clergyman in his ordinary clerical costume present, and apparently deriving all the benefit that such is expected to impart. Occasionally there is to be found a minister who is of the more pronounced type of an extremist who grows angry with a holy passion when he hears the word mentioned. We knew one such who was extremely opposed to all kinds of amusement. His prejudices were in favor of a demure sanctified visage, and against the ringing laughter that is characteristic of the people here generally. A circus was announced to come off on a certain date in a neighboring town, in connection with which were a few animals of different kinds from foreign lands. On the quiet he went over to the neighboring town on the occasion. One of his young deacons was attracted to the place at the same time, each of them intent upon knowledge. They met at the entrance to the show. After recovering from a slight attack of confusion, which each experienced only for a moment, the clergyman said, "I have often strongly desired to see a *sacred ox*." The deacon replied, "So have I." The world would not have been much the wiser had not the deacon, on his return home, told his wife as a great secret that he had found his clergyman at the circus, and that the poor man got so tired looking at the *sacred ox* that he was compelled to find a seat in the other tent, where the horses were not so sacred. Australians love the playhouse as they love their yachting or regattas, for the tone and healthful excitement they impart. They expend large sums of money in securing the very best talent, and putting plays on the boards in the most elaborate style. The distance of this country from London and New York makes it impossible for the management to rely upon "stars," though even such have found it profitable to visit this country. They rely upon home talent to a great extent, and upon "specialities" brought from other countries under long engagement. The spirit and practice of self-reliance has developed a class of talent not frequently found in stock companies.

Music, both in opera and concert, has not flourished to the same extent. A few good operatic companies have been successful, but as a rule the extraordinary expense connected with its proper presentation is greater than the patronage will justify. Comic opera being properly classed with the general theatrical business is always successful, and very much appreciated for the vein of fun in it that appeals directly to all classes.

While these and many other amusements, such as dancing, socials, tea meetings, etc., are well patronised as means of recreation, the great bulk of the people enjoy out-door sports. Every condition conduces to such a result. The year round the exquisite climate invites the masses to the exhilarating influences of the open air. People love to be out doors, the inside having fewer attractions. The cold nights of other lands compel their people to surround the hearthstone which has a charm that is unknown in this. The people here can appreciate a sky, landscape, river, or field far more than a hearthstone or fireside, whose meaning is only half known. We must not be understood to imply that the Australian cannot enjoy the comforts of home. It is far different. One will meet home attractions here to a greater extent than in most countries. A piano is in almost every house, even in that of the poor mechanic or laborer. Window curtains and furniture of tasty design are everywhere seen, even in the poorest cottages, evincing the taste of the housekeeper and the enjoyment of home that so generally prevails; at the same time, their excelling joy is in the sunshine, in the open air, in the thousand congenial places of resort that a kindly providence and a thoughtful Government have lavishly bestowed.

Pleasure resorts are numerous, and form the chief attraction for the masses. It is not everyone that can avail themselves of the advantages and pleasures of the many games above-mentioned. Few of them are of such a nature that women and children can participate in. The lack is made up in the places of resort that are open to all, and made attractive by the thousand details that find among the multitudes appreciation. Man cannot fail to rejoice in the provision both nature and man has made.

Nature herself has done very much in forming the physical features of the colony in such a manner as to conduce to man's health and pleasure. The great mountain range that runs from north to south serves the purpose of giving every variety of climate that man could wish to meet for every ailment and craving for change.

The dry air of the desert plains, the humid of the coastal region, and the freshness of the mountain elevations give such variety as to suit all classes of invalids or tourists. The country resort has grown within a few years to be a recreation highly valued by that class whose business confines them to the cramped-up conditions of a crowded city.

E. A. BULLMORE Esq.
IPSWICH.

RECREATIONS. 377

Many portions of the Blue Mountains, the Hawkesbury and Hunter rivers have become popular as country resorts, chiefly in the summer months, but not confined to any particular season. There are spots on the Hawkesbury that rival the beauty of any other stream of the world. We have witnessed and sailed through the thousand islands scattered in the river St. Lawrence, below the city of Kingston, in Canada, and have glided down the rapids—Long Seault, Cedar, and Lachine—and have been charmed with their variety. We have sailed down the Hudson, from Albany to New York, and have revelled in the sublimity and picturesqueness of her broken and lofty banks, now in undulations, and now in rugged grandeur, stretching from the water's edge. We have been on the Mississippi, from St. Paul's, in Minnesota, to St. Louis, Missouri, a distance of one thousand miles, and have been amazed at the vastness of that stream, and its beauty in many parts as it widens and narrows in its course through a variety of scenery unique and impressive as one passes along. Trollope expresses our sentiment fully when he says, "In my opinion the Hawkesbury beats the Mississippi."

Besides the scores of pleasure and health resorts afforded by nature, within easy distance of the chief towns, there are many hotels and private sanatoriums of extensive accommodation that meet every want of the traveller, the convalescent, and the pleasure-seeker.

The Government, from the earliest date, set apart large reserves for the use of the public in all towns and cities. These have been beautified as gardens, parks, benches, and walks without number or limit, and all of which are appreciated by the people as common ground, where they are wont to assemble, and in promenade, resting beneath the shade, or in discussion of political or religious questions, they pass hours of profit or amusement, as the exercise may appear to them best.

Having already dwelt upon horse-racing in another place, we have not deemed it proper to speak at length upon this sport in the present chapter. It is a question of debate between cricketers and horsemen as to which has the pre-eminence. Without venturing to give an opinion that would settle the question, we claim the right of saying that, in our judgment, they both have pre-eminence. They are both universal. They are equally popular, and appeal to very different parts of our nature.

The cricketer illustrates the science and art of skill in striking, catching, throwing, all of which brings the excitement and amusement of a self-culture.

Horse-racing lifts into prominence our interest in, and love for, the dumb animal, and hence opens a fountain of pleasure that springs not from personal qualities, but from qualities in the noblest of animals outside ourselves.

The one develops the man, the other develops the horse—both are fountains where the nation loves to drink, and both are for man's healing.

Scores of other means of mirth are constantly engaging the attention of the Australian. Fishing, hunting, camping, lecturing, banqueting, and toddying give additional evidence of the joy that ripples on the surface of society, and sometimes swells its great heart into deepest emotions.

What shall we say of this great fact in Australian life? As a moralist would we condemn? It may be that excesses exist, and tend to mar the poetry of being, but we dare to believe that the fondness for sports that has characterised this country from the commencement is the natural product of the conditions of life here found. As a physicist we cannot fail to see the marked development of a youthful race, buoyant and strong, bounding into a manhood that must command the admiration of the world.

CHAPTER XXXII.

THE ACTING MINISTRY.

THE personality of the reigning Government will awaken much interest in the minds of those of our readers who are curious to know the antecedents of men to whom the people have been pleased to commit for the time being the administration of Government affairs. In a democracy such as we enjoy in this country, we, the people, in the exercise of our franchise, put down one and exalt the other. With every change of public sentiment, which frequently is as fickle as the wind, it is curious to watch the changes we make of leaders to guide our affairs.

In the Centennial year 1888 we transferred the crown from the head of Sir Samuel W. Griffiths as our chieftain, to that of Sir Thos. McIlwraith—both men of herculean strength and mental grasp, both noble spirits, unselfish save in the guardianship of their honor.

The Hon. Sir Samuel Walker Griffith, K.C.M.G., M.A., Q.C., M.L.A., was born at Merthyr Tydvil, Wales, on 21st June, 1845, and arrived in Australia in 1854 with his father, the Rev. T. Griffith, a Congregational minister, whose long residence in this colony and in New South Wales has made his name familiar with the people of Australia. Sir S. W. Griffith was educated at Mr. Robert Horniman's school, Sydney, and at the High School, Maitland, where he took a distinguished rank as a pupil, after which he proceeded to the University at Sydney, graduating there with first-class honors in classics and mathematics, and taking his degree of B.A. in 1863, and the Mort travelling fellowship in 1865, immediately after which he took up the profession of law in Brisbane, studying under and being articled to Mr. A. McAlister. He was called to the Bar in 1867, and immediately thereafter entered upon the practice of his profession, in which he was eminently successful, winning by his perseverance, brilliancy, and plodding industry a first-class position among the barristers of the colony. In 1876 he was appointed Q.C. Having entered Parliament in 1872 as representative for East Moreton, he began his Parliamentary career from that date. In November, 1873, Mr. Griffith was elected for the newly-created seat of Oxley. In August, 1874, he was appointed Attorney-General in the McAlister Ministry. In 1876 he was made Secretary for Public Instruction, when that office was first created under the State Education Act of 1875, he himself being its author, and successfully carrying it through Parliament, and causing it to become the law of the land. In September, 1878, he was appointed Secretary for Public Works, resigning the office on the defeat of the Douglas Ministry. From 1879 to 1883, during the existence of the McIlwraith, or the eleventh Ministry, he led the Opposition in the Assembly. In 1878 he was elected member for North Brisbane, and continued to represent that electorate until the last general election. His popularity from the beginning of his public life was steady and rapid. He espoused the cause of the masses. In politics he was liberal, and opposed to the aggressions and monopolies of the squatting interests, which, from his standpoint, were antagonistic to the interests of the colony. He was especially prominent as leader of those who were opposed to the granting of a large subsidy of the best lands throughout the colony towards a private railway company whose object was to reach the gulf from the eastern side. His leadership of this party was so pronounced and effective that when the scheme of the McIlwraith party failed, and they were compelled to tender their resignation, Mr. Griffith was chosen by the Governor to form a new Ministry in the interests and under the wing of the Liberal party. He took to himself the office of Colonial Secretary and that of Public Instruction, resigning the latter at a later date. In December, 1883, he attended the

Intercolonial Convention held at Sydney, and took a prominent part in the discussions that came before that body. In February, 1886, he represented the Federal Council of Australasia, in company with Mr. Dixon, which Council was held at Hobart, Tasmania. In 1886 he was created a Knight Commander of the most distinguished Order of St. Michael and St. George. In 1887, with Sir James Garrick, Agent-General for the Colony, he was appointed to represent Queensland in the Imperial Conference, which met in London in March of that year under the presidency of Sir Henry Holland, Secretary of State for the Colonies. He was prominent among the many noted representatives in his advocacy of measures tending towards Imperial Federation, and by this act gained for himself great honor, but at the same time much displeasure. Sir Samuel W. Griffith in 1870 married Julia Jennett, daughter of James Thompson, Esq., formerly Commissioner of Crown Lands, East Maitland, New South Wales. He has ever received the endorsement of the church element. He was defeated by what is known in Queensland by the name of the National party, led by Sir Thos. McIlwraith.

The Hon. Sir Thomas McIlwraith, K.C.M.G., M.L.A., is a Scotchman by birth, having been born at Ayr, Scotland, in 1835. His education was liberal, and received at the Glasgow University. At nineteen years of age he came to Australia, landing first in Melbourne, in 1854, and immediately took a position as civil engineer to the Government railways. His ability was soon recognised and his work appreciated by the authorities, and his advancement was rapid, and secured to him some wealth. In 1861 he adopted squatting pursuits in the new colony of Queensland, and followed that line of business for several years with marked success, moving there himself and family in the year 1870. His first constituency immediately upon his arrival in the colony was that of Warrego and Maranoa. This he represented for many years afterwards. He joined the McAllister Ministry as Minister for Works in 1873. In 1878 he was elected member for Mulgrave, and on the defeat of the Douglas Ministry in 1879, he was called upon by the Governor to form a new Government—in which he assumed the office of Premier—that continued in power for more than four years, being defeated in 1883 by the Griffith Opposition. Amongst the prominent acts of Sir Thomas McIlwraith was the annexation of New Guinea. He always advocated the squatting interests of the colony, being among those that deem that interest as being paramount in importance and essential to the growth of the sparsely settled colony. His advocacy of their interest as a class has long been continued and successful at times. After the resignation of his Ministry, in 1883, he paid a visit to the old country, to the scenes of his youth, to his native city of Ayr, the freedom of which was conferred upon him during his visit. Sir Thomas McIlwraith was made an associate of the Institute of Civil Engineers in 1881, and had the degree of LL.D. conferred upon him by the Glasgow University. He was practically out of politics from the year 1883 until 1888, when on the growing dissatisfaction of the colony towards the action of the Imperial Defence Committee and Naval Force Bill, led by Sir Samuel W. Griffith, a strong feeling of antagonism grew up throughout the colony towards the Griffith Administration. Sir Thomas McIlwraith was induced by the party in opposition to head a movement under the leadership of what is known as the National Party of Queensland, and in an appeal to the country was overwhelmingly successful in being returned to the House at the head of the poll, in opposition to Sir Samuel Griffith, and backed by an overwhelming majority from the several electorates throughout the country, and was called upon to form a new Ministry, known as the 13th Ministry in Queensland, and who are still in office although, through declining health, Sir Thomas was compelled to resign his position of Premier, placing the same in the hands of the Hon. D. B. Morehead, he himself assuming the office of Vice-Secretary, and seeking for a few months retirement from the cares of office, and is now enjoying leave of absence from the colony, improving this needed rest by a visit to China and Japan. Sir Thomas McIlwraith is a gentleman of undoubted ability and great perseverance and energy—his influence is felt largely in moulding the institutions of the colony.

The Hon. J. M. Macrossan, the Minister of Mines and Works, who is also junior member for Townsville, is a man of liberal education and sterling business qualities. His first entrance on Parliamentary life was in 1873, when he sat as member of Parliament for the Kennedy. His next constituency was his present one. He has always been identified with the mining industries of the country, and has acquired wide experience and considerable wealth through that enterprise. When Sir Thomas McIlwraith formed the Government in 1879 Mr. Macrossan was made Minister for

Public Works. He resigned, however, in March, 1883, his successor being the Hon. Albert Norton, the present Speaker. He is a native of Ireland, having been born in the County of Donegal, in 1832. He is an exemplary Christian gentleman, and a warm advocate of Irish Home Rule.

The Hon. Hugh Muir Nelson is the Minister of Railways. Mr. Nelson has not previously held office. He was elected for the Northern Downs in 1883, and was returned at the recent election for the Morella District unopposed. During the last Parliament he took a prominent part in financial debates, and showed himself to be possessed of an intelligent grasp of all questions affecting public finance, and won for himself the respect and confidence of the entire Assembly. Mr. Nelson was born at Kilmarnock, Scotland, in 1835, and was educated at Edinburgh at the High School and University, and is a man of wide classical and literary qualifications. He has been a resident in Queensland since 1853.

The Hon. B. D. Morehead, Colonial Secretary and member for the Ballone, was born in Sydney, in 1843. He entered Parliament in 1871, as member for the Mitchell District. In 1880 he was transferred to the Upper House, and became Postmaster-General, and Leader of the Legislative Council, which position he held until the fall of the McIlwraith Government in the year 1883. Mr. Morehead succeeded the late Mr. Low as member for the Ballone, for which constituency he sat till the close of the last Parliament. At the last election he was returned unopposed. Mr. Morehead is engaged in banking and mercantile pursuits, and is a gentleman of extensive experience in business, and great energy, fearless and bold in his attacks upon the Opposition, not easily put down in debate, and has impressed himself upon the members of the House as an opponent not to be overcome.

The Hon. M. H. Black is the Minister for Lands. He is one of the members for Mackay, and first entered Parliament seven years since as representative of his present constituency. He has been chiefly identified as the special advocate of sugar-planting interests. He was born in London in 1833, his father being a member of a well-known publishing firm. He was engaged in pastoral pursuits in the Southern Colony from the time of his arrival in Victoria in 1851, and first went to Mackay in 1871. He is an authority on the subject of tropical agriculture.

The Hon. J. Donaldson, who is Postmaster-General, first entered

THE ACTING MINISTRY.

political life in 1883. In 1884 he represented the Griffith's Government in the Conference between the Houses, to settle differences in relation to the Land Bill. He is a native of Victoria, and is identified with the squatting interests. He has made a special study of the land question in all its aspects.

The Hon. A. J. Thyne, M.L.C., is Minister for Justice, and has been member of the Upper House, since 1882. He is a solicitor by profession, and has always occupied a prominent position in the Legislative Council. He is especially interested in Defence Force matters, and is an enthusiast with regard to the Volunteer branch of the service. He was one of the chief promoters of the Irish Volunteer Corps. He was born at Ballangrave House, County Clare, Ireland, in the year 1847. He arrived in Queensland in August, 1864.

The Hon. W. Pattison, member for Rockhampton, is a minister without portfolio. He was, during last Parliament, the representative of Blackall. His former public career was confined to seats in the Rockhampton Municipal Council, and on the Gogambo Divisional Board. He is chiefly known, however, as one of the early proprietors of the celebrated Mount Morgan Gold Mine, to which extended notice is given elsewhere. He was born in Tasmania and was an alderman of Melbourne. He is an old resident and prominent business man in Rockhampton, where he is deservedly popular and greatly respected. The reason of his inclusion in the Ministry doubtless was a desire on the part of Sir Thomas McIlwraith that the Central Division, as well as the Northern and Southern Districts of the Colony should be directly represented in the Cabinet.

The Hon. A. Norton fills the arduous post of Speaker. He is the member for Port Curtis. He possesses in an eminent degree the qualities of gentlemanliness and good temper. In 1867 he was summoned to the Legislative Council, but a year later he resigned. In 1878 he was elected by Port Curtis without opposition, and became Minister for Works in the McIlwraith Government in 1883. After being twice returned for Port Curtis he has now been elected Speaker. Mr. Norton enjoys the honor of being Speaker in the largest Assembly ever elected in Queensland, viz., seventy-two members as against fifty-nine—the greatest number in any previous Assembly. Mr. Norton was born at Elswick, near Sydney, in 1836, and arrived in Queensland in 1860.

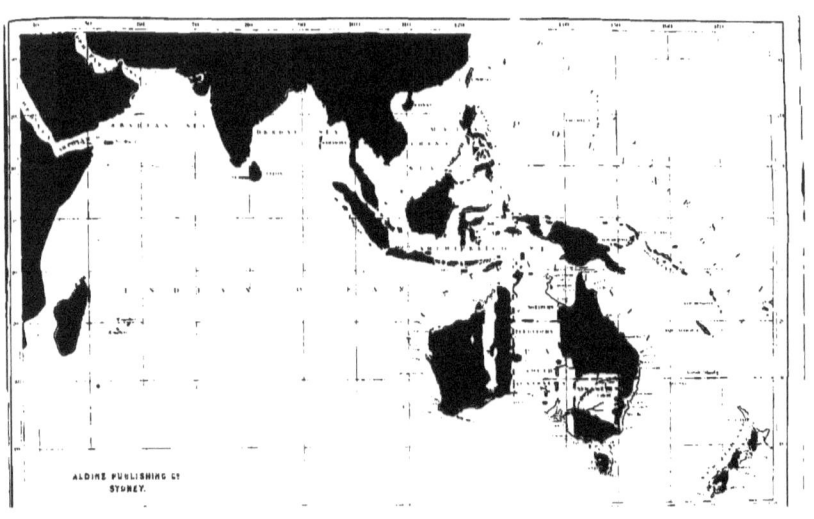

www.ingramcontent.com/pod-product-compliance
Lightning Source LLC
Chambersburg PA
CBHW051726300426
44115CB00007B/475